George Washington
on Coins and Currency

Also by Heinz Tschachler and from McFarland

George Washington and Political Fatherhood: The Endurance of a National Myth (2020)

The Monetary Imagination of Edgar Allan Poe: Banking, Currency and Politics in the Writings (2013)

The Greenback: Paper Money and American Culture (2010)

George Washington on Coins and Currency

Heinz Tschachler

McFarland & Company, Inc., Publishers
Jefferson, North Carolina

Library of Congress Cataloguing-in-Publication Data

Names: Tschachler, Heinz, author.
Title: George Washington on coins and currency / Heinz Tschachler.
Description: Jefferson : McFarland & Company, Inc., Publishers, 2020. |
Includes bibliographical references and index.
Identifiers: LCCN 2020027737 | ISBN 9781476681108 (paperback : acid free paper) ∞
ISBN 9781476640341 (ebook)
Subjects: LCSH: Money—United States—History. | Numismatics—United
States—History. | Washington, George, 1732–1799—Numismatics.
Classification: LCC HG501 .T73 2020 | DDC 737.4973—dc23
LC record available at https://lccn.loc.gov/2020027737

British Library cataloguing data are available

ISBN (print) 978-1-4766-8110-8
ISBN (ebook) 978-1-4766-4034-1

Printed in the United States of America

McFarland & Company, Inc., Publishers
Box 611, Jefferson, North Carolina 28640
www.mcfarlandpub.com

For Gerhild,
who leaves no one behind

Table of Contents

Acknowledgments

Pictures serve important functions in a book. They exemplify what is being said in the text, they draw attention to what is not or is no longer present in readers' minds, and they allow readers to participate in or even contradict the argumentation wrought in the text. A cultural history of George Washington on coins and currency, like any cultural history, must give pictures their due. This is easier said than done, though. One first needs to identify and track down the pictures; the next step is to secure the rights to use them in a publication. None of this would have been possible without the generous help of a great many people and institutions.

I particularly thank Jennifer Johns and Alex Till (Pennsylvania Academy of the Fine Arts, Philadelphia), Robert Kelley and Douglas Mudd (American Numismatic Association Money Museum, Colorado Springs, Colorado), Hillery L. York and Kay Peterson (Division of Work and Industry, National Museum of American History, Smithsonian Institution), Sara B. Weber and Natasha Lyandres (University of Notre Dame Special Collections), Chris Murray (Rhode Island Currency, New York), Q. David Bowers (Heritage Auctions), and Carina Rasse (University of Klagenfurt). I also want to gratefully cite the Eric P. Newman Education Society (St. Louis, Missouri), Heritage Auction Galleries, the Library of Congress, the Yale University Art Gallery, the Dallas Museum of Art, as well as the Philadelphia Museum of Art.

Among the many people who shared their thoughts and opinions with me as I developed my plans for this book were Anthony Hall, René Schallegger, Shauna Bennis, as well as students from my graduate seminars on political iconography. A particular thank-you goes to Stefan "Steve" Rabitsch (Graz, Austria) for reading portions of the manuscript, offering valuable comments, providing a plethora of leads and useful hints and, beyond that, for remaining a steadfast friend, an inspiring colleague, and an intellectual companion. Appreciation also goes to Hubert Emmerig and Martin Baer (Institut für Numismatik und Geldgeschichte, Universität Wien), Gottfried Gabriel (Friedrich-Schiller-Universität Jena), Christian Thiel (Universität der Bundeswehr, München), Stefan Hartmann (Universität Augsburg), Nadja Gernalzick (University of Vienna), Cindi Roden (Washington, D.C.), and Mark Thistlethwaite (Texas Christian University, Fort Worth). Thank-yous are also owed to Martin Stermitz and Ute Brinckmann (Landesmuseum für Kärnten, Klagenfurt, Austria) as well as to the friendly and efficient staff of the library and interlibrary loan desks at the University of Klagenfurt. A leave of absence award from the university in support of this project made it possible for me to give my undivided attention to the manuscript. For this, I am indebted to the good faith of Vice Rector Martin Hitz.

Last but not least, gratitude goes to the editors at McFarland, in particular to David Alff, who has been exceptionally helpful and gracious in shepherding yet another book of mine into print.

Prologue: "Americans for George"

Ever since the thirteen colonies decided to separate from England, the guardians of the currency have had to contend with or try to contain possible losses and other "freaks of fortune." By the same token, success and good fortune have had its talismans throughout America's monetary history. Alexander Hamilton knew this all along. For the young nation's first Secretary of the Treasury and chief architect of the U.S. Mint, monetary tokens were "vehicles of useful impressions."[1] Almost two hundred years later, Michel Foucault noted that accepted currency had "peculiar properties of representation."[2] Both Hamilton's remark of 1791 and Foucault's comment of 1971 call to mind that coins and, by extension, pieces of paper money are more than mere commercial conveniences, representing a specific value. They also carry symbolic value, which provides external backing and stabilization to the monetary system. While coins and currency perform their proper function by encouraging trade and investment, facilitating the paying back of debts, and serving as a measure as well as a store of value, they are at the same time documents of culture, cultural products that speak to the identity of a group of people, a place, and a time. Accepted currency thus can also serve as a proxy for a nation's power and its citizens' social identities.

The current one-dollar bill, for instance, performs its cultural work principally through the characteristic portrait of George Washington, based on Gilbert Stuart's "Athenaeum" version of 1796. The portrait secures the bill's credibility. It assures those who handle and use the bills every day that they are trustworthy, as trustworthy as the country's first president, whose printed presence legitimates the notes. Portraits are iconic. According to the French philospoher Marie-José Mondzain, the icon's properties—"likeness, manifestiveness, moral stimulus, and sacredness"—have made portraits ideal vehicles of political iconography, endowing them with significance, and enabling them to perform important social functions. Through the medium of portraiture, authority becomes a sensate thing. In this sense, George Washington's portrait is truly iconic, not merely in the semiotic sense of a likeness, but in the more profound sense of symbolizing something else. "The icon acts," Mondzain wrote. It makes visible something absent—not least what a commentator called the "innermost essence" of the person portrayed—which it preserves for posterity.

George Washington's portrait affects people not only cognitively but also emotionally, providing a model for and stimulus to moral behavior. It refers people back to their origins, and it enables them to form a sense of identity and to acknowledge the legitimacy of the existing social order. Altogether, the portrait is a sacred image deserving of veneration.[3] When the rites have been performed in the name of the Father of His Country, therefore, Americans are really, and not just symbolically or imaginatively, in the presence of the metaphorical father (spelled with an implicit capital "*f*"). Today, Washington's face on the one-dollar bill serves to unite a nation stymied by congressional gridlock and a perpetual adolescent in the White House, and deeply divided along the rift lines of class, ethnicity, age, and gender. The bills may be worn out, but to discard them and to replace them with another form of currency means to discard the talismanic face of the nation, and with it, to undermine the tendency, among Americans, to understand the nation metaphorically in family terms.

The late John McCain—military hero, maverick Republican Senator from Arizona, and Republican presidential nominee in 2008—likely was not aware of the iconic properties of Americans' beloved "Georges" when, in July 2015, he (together with Mike Enzi, Senator from Wyoming and Senate Budget Committee Chairman) proposed a law to eliminate one-dollar bills from circulation. Called the *USA Act* (for Unified Savings and Accountability), the legislation would implement recommendations included in the Government Accountability Office's annual report to reduce waste and create efficiencies throughout the federal government. One of the key savings in this legislation would be the replacement of the one-dollar bill with the more sustainable and efficient dollar coin. The switch was estimated to generate at least $4.4 billion and up to $13.8 billion in taxpayer savings over thirty years. These are impressive figures, and two organizations, the CAGW (Council for Citizens Against Government Waste) and the Dollar Coin Alliance, have endorsed the proposed legislation. The Act has been read twice and referred to the Committee on Environment and Public Works. To date, no further action is tracked. The Act has passed neither the Senate nor the House; it has not reached the President, let alone become law. In fact, the proposed law has met the fate of previous efforts to eliminate the one-dollar bill, which also never made it past committee review.[4]

It is not unusual for proposed laws to falter at committee review. Yet attempts to replace the one-dollar bill with a coin have always met with noisy protests also from the American public. The media, in particular, have a feast day whenever news is released that the one-dollar bill is to be replaced by a coin. For instance, *The Examiner*, a daily tabloid-sized paper published in Washington, D.C., had the following headline on the title page of its weekend edition for April 27–28, 2012: "DOLLAR BILL UNDER THREAT: CONGRESS CONSIDERING ELIMINATION OF DOLLAR BILL." The headline suggests a narrative in which the one-dollar bill figures as an endangered species, while Congress is the evil power bent on destroying what the American public deems worth preserving. Perhaps there would have been a different story if the coin that was to replace the dollar bill had been gold or silver, that is, *specie*. This not being the case, the lowly bill was justly seen as an endangered *species*.[5] As with any endangered species, there is a surplus value invested in the one-dollar bill that goes way beyond the monetary value printed on it. That value, I will argue throughout, cannot be separated from the cultural meanings invested in the Father of His Country.

The story of the contest between eliminating the one-dollar bill and keeping it is a long one, and it is worth recording in some detail. In the early 1960s, the United

States government commissioned the consulting firm Arthur D. Little and Company to review the entire supply of the nation's currency. In 1965, the Treasury Department published its report on the currency situation. The report went to a congressional committee. Nothing was heard of it thereafter. In 1974, the Treasury Department had another needs analysis done, and once again by a private consulting firm. At the same time, both the United States Mint and the Treasury Department started assessing the nation's monetary situation. In 1976, in time for the Bicentennial of the Revolution, concrete measures were put on the table, including the introduction of a one-dollar coin in lieu of the one-dollar bill.[6] The new coin came in 1979, a year after Jimmy Carter's election to the Presidency. It was issued to honor the noted feminist leader Susan B. Anthony. Ms. Anthony's portrait was put in place of General Dwight D. Eisenhower's, which had been chosen by the incoming Nixon administration in 1971. Minting of the "Susies" began with tremendous enthusiasm, but despite heroic efforts on the part of the United States Mint, the coin was never widely accepted by the public. I have never seen one.[7] Alternatively, if I have, like most Americans I might have mistaken it for a quarter because of its size. The quarter at least fits the slots of vending machines, in contrast to the Anthony dollar, which does not even look like it was *worth* a dollar and so ended up in storage.[8]

The introduction of the Anthonys may have flopped but plans to phase out the one-dollar bill went down even less well with the American public. Gene Hessler, a renowned numismatist, even warned against the negative consequences a mere redesign of the one-dollar bill might have on the global economy: "A change in the design of our familiar greenback could send the world's economy into a tailspin."[9] Frank Annunzio, a Democratic representative from Chicago's 11th District, in July 1978 solemnly promised that he would do everything within his power "to resist the discontinuance and even the decreased production of the one-dollar bill."[10] Thereafter, the authorities contented themselves with thoroughly revising and redesigning dollar bills from $2 denomination and above. The purpose of the exercise was to adjust the nation's currency to international standards, in particular to standards of currency security. One question was kept simmering, however—the question whether the United States should follow the example of other western nations such as Canada, Britain, or France, all of which had eliminated their bills with the lowest denomination and replaced them with coins.

As if to prove that the United States was not behind the international community, the U.S. Congress in 1999 authorized a new mini dollar. Gold in color and with a smooth edge, there would be no more mistaking it for a quarter. Thanks to Treasury Secretary Robert Rubin, who by virtue of his office had the final say in the coin's design, the obverse shows a portrait of Sacagawea, the Shoshone Indian woman who, with her infant son, allegedly guided Meriwether Lewis and William Clark on the first national expedition across the North American continent. The introduction of the Sacagawea dollar coin coincided with the bicentennial of the expedition. The reverse of the new coin is graced by an American eagle, with an obvious effect. As in the case of the Indian-head cent or the buffalo nickel—or else of the 1929 half eagle, a five-dollar coin with the head of an Indian brave on one side and the American eagle on the other, not to mention paper notes featuring Ta-to-ka-in-yan-ka and other Native Americans—it reflects the subjugation of Native Americans as a colonized people. But there is more.

Per the Native American $1 Coin Act of September 20, 2007, new reverses have been introduced. The first coin in the series displays a veritable down-to-earth theme, as the Citizens Coinage Advisory Committee in June 2008 put in first place a design featuring a Native American woman planting maize. As of 2009, the Sacagawea reverses have honored Native American tribes through design themes such as the creation of the Cherokee written language, the Iroquois Confederacy, the Olympian Jim Thorpe, even the Pueblo Revolt.[11]

The Sacagawea Dollar did not fare much better than its predecessor, despite a massive marketing campaign. The campaign, which cost taxpayers some $67.1 million, did nothing to lift coin usage above about one percent of dollar transactions. People "just aren't buying the idea," a 2002 article in the *Sacramento Bee* was headlined.[12] Disappointing news of this kind must have reached the upper echelons in the Clinton administration, prompting a General Accounting Office recommendation that no more money be spent on marketing the coin, even though the Office also said that the government could potentially save up to $500 million annually, mostly on production, shipping and on account of the greater durability of coins.[13] The recommendation did not deter from lobbying work a special interest group called "The Coin Coalition." The group, which was founded in the early 1990s, lobbied to have all one-dollar Federal Reserve notes replaced with one-dollar coins, purportedly to cope with the rising prices of transit fares. While the group claimed that the unwillingness of the government to phase out the one-dollar bill prevented the Sacagawea dollar from becoming popular, it rather seems that they confronted powerful adversaries—the Mount Vernon Ladies' Association and, more importantly, "Save the Greenback," an organization of Bureau of Engraving and Printing employees and paper and ink suppliers opposed to phasing out the paper dollar.

"Save the Greenback" successfully prevented a dollar bill phase-out with the help of legislators such as Virginia Representative Thomas M. Davis, who introduced the Save the Greenback Act, Mississippi Senator Trent Lott, and Massachusetts Senator Ted Kennedy. It would be a mistake, however, to assume that the controversy was merely another "battle" in a "culture war." None of the players ever acted entirely disinterestedly. For instance, Senator Lott's constituency included the powerful cotton industry, which produces fabrics used in the paper dollar, and Senator Kennedy's constituency included the Crane Paper Company, which produces American banknote paper. Conversely, the Coin Coalition was funded by vending machine companies, video arcade owners, and the soft drink industry, who all had an interest in eliminating maintenance costs associated with dollar bill validators. The National Bulk Vendors Association likewise supported the Coalition, as did copper miners and other interest groups.[14]

The alleged intention of Congress to appease mining interests continued to be a popular suspicion. "Are we going to let [Arizona] mining interests and a South Korean metal company win?" a posting asked in early 2012. "Help America help itself!" The posting appeared on the Facebook page of a group called "Americans for George." The name indicates the group's purpose—to prevent a one-dollar bill phase-out. The Americans for George Coalition, the official website announced, "is an ad hoc group of like-minded individuals, businesses, and organizations seeking to ensure that the citizens of the United States maintain the ability to choose their preferred currency. The members of the coalition oppose efforts to eliminate the dollar bill and replace it with a dollar coin. Our coalition is now 140 organizations strong." The coalition's first publicity stunt was a big show at the Metro Center Station in Washington, D.C., in March 2012. Under the motto "Tell Congress to stop wasting time trying to eliminate the $1 bill," supporters were asked to sign a petition, and they were told that some 83 percent of Americans opposed replacing the one-dollar note with a one-dollar coin. Thus prompted, a large number of people left postings on the coalition's website. In some of these postings, pleas were made to resist "changing people's habits and traditions." Others pointed to the "real history" behind the one-dollar bill. "How," one posting asked ominously, "do we replace all that national symbolism, much of which dates to the founding of the nation, with a mere scrap of metal alloy?" Similarly idealistic valuations underwrote postings like "You can't replace a uniquely American icon with a nondescript piece of spare change" and "the dollar bill is more American than the #coin." Perhaps the most felicitous and apposite posting dates from February 20, 2012: "Happy Birthday #GeorgeWashington, may your memory live on via the #dollarbill!"[15]

"Americans for George" did not emerge out of the blue but was formed in response to legislation proposed by Arizona House Republican David Schweikert and two other House Republicans in September 2011. Called the COINS Act (the acronym stands for "Currency Optimization, Innovation, and National Savings Act"), its purpose was getting rid of one-dollar bills for one-dollar coins to save money.[16] The proposed law was referred to the House Financial Services subcommittee, which held a hearing to explore phasing out the dollar. Schweikert's proposed bill was co-sponsored by some fifteen or so House Republicans; among the House Democrats present at the hearing, several lawmakers sounded like they were not about to consign all those "Georges" to history. One lawmaker said that men didn't like carrying coins in their pockets or their suits; another is on record for saying that existing coins have proved too hard to distinguish from quarters. "If the people don't want it and they don't want to use it, why in the world are we even talking about changing it?"[17]

Why indeed? One reason might be the General Accounting Office's report of huge annual savings. Yet the same report estimates that the "cost of producing coins for a full replacement is never fully recovered," foreseeing a net loss over the first four years due to minting costs.[18] At the hearing held by the House Financial Services subcommittee an official at the U.S. Mint testified that most of the 2.4 billion $1 coins made in the past five years were languishing in Federal Reserve vaults. The coins were so unloved that production was halted in 2011, thus saving the government some $50 million. Nonetheless, the COINS Act was introduced to the House on September 20, 2011. Three days later, Massachusetts Senators Scott Brown (Republican) and John Kerry (Democrat) introduced a competing bill to the Senate. Called the Currency Efficiency Act, the bill was aimed at protecting the paper dollar from what the senators called a "massive overproduction" of the "unpopular $1 coin." "The $1 coin is misleading because it costs taxpayers so much more," Brown said. "In fact, we have over $1 billion worth of extra $1 coins sitting idle in vaults, and that's set to double over the next several years." The Brown-Kerry bill would prevent the minting of $1 coins when a surplus of them exists. The two senators argued that $1.2 billion worth of $1 coins are sitting in the Federal

Reserve's vaults, not in circulation, which was adding considerably to the Federal Reserve's storage costs.[19]

The Currency Efficiency Act was read twice and referred to the Senate Committee on Banking, Housing, and Urban Affairs on the day it was introduced.[20] The COINS Act did not fare any better. Following its introduction, it was immediately referred to the House Committee on Financial Services. On October 4, 2011, it was referred to the Subcommittee on Domestic Monetary Policy and Technology.[21] This marks the latest action to date in Congress, though it is not the end of the story. It was none other than Senator John McCain who took upon himself the task of keeping the matter alive. Thus, in July 2013 he addressed a meeting hosted by the CAGW (Council for Citizens Against Government Waste) and the Dollar Coin Alliance; two years later, he (together with Wyoming Senator Mike Enzi) proposed the *USA Act*, which, as we have seen, is yet another—and in all likelihood the last—proposal to eliminate one-dollar bills from circulation.[22]

These sometimes bizarre debates and practices were first brought to my attention by a dear colleague. As an Englishman, this colleague remembered only too well the heated debates in his own country about the possible end of the British pound following the introduction of the euro. The idea of tinkering with the pound was not well received in 1990s Britain. Margaret Thatcher, one of the leading figures in the neo-liberal counterrevolution against Keynesian orthodoxy, presented herself as a staunch nationalist when she defended her desire to maintain an independent currency. Similarly, Mr. David Heathcot-Amory, a conservative member of Parliament who was vehemently opposed to the European Union's common currency project, in May 1994 expressed his concern that the introduction of the euro would "dilute" national identity. (Mr. Heathcot-Amory lost his seat in 2010, though it's easy to imagine where he would have stood in the Brexit debate.) The archbishop of Canterbury too has been quoted as saying "I want the Queen's head on the bank notes," thus joining the chorus of those who choose to understand the nation metaphorically in family terms.[23]

There have been many other "badges of national identity," especially during the "Keep the Pound" campaign, in which imperial or even martial images were evoked as Britain was seen "under attack" from the Continent per the evil euro. On a 1999 campaign postcard, for example, Britannia is depicted on the white cliffs of Dover, with her back to the wall, ready to take on the enemy from Continental Europe. In 2003, a photograph made the rounds in European news media that showed an Englishman in traditional clothes carrying an elaborate placard inscribed with "Keep the Pound / No surrender / Stuff the Euro / Rule Britannia."[24] That rule became a reality on Friday, January 31, 2020. At 11 p.m. UK time on that day, the United Kingdom left the European Union, relegating its citizens to a form of splendid isolation. To some Britons, the prospect had been frightening. As the historian Sir Michael Howard said, "difficult problems and challenges are best addressed with partners and allies." This seems a wisdom that the modern Brexiters seek to trample, cheerfully convinced that everything will work out well in the end because it always had for Britain.[25]

In the 1990s, the French too had risen to the challenge the euro posed to the idea that every nation-state must have its own territorially homogeneous and exclusive currency. In a book titled *La Monnaie Souveraine*, economists and social scientists attempted to find answers to the question why abandoning the franc and replacing it with the euro so dramatically stirred up people's emotions. The general hypothesis is telling. What allegedly caused so much restiveness was not the transfer of economic power so much as it was the question of national identity. For, the euro as a form of supra-national currency was about to circulate in a space of markets that is completely detached from the idea of a community of common social values.[26] (In 1995, even the European Commission felt "for some people, the change [to the new euro notes] will feel almost like a change of identity."[27])

One of the most vociferous critics of the euro was the economist and social scientist Bruno Théret, who charged the euro's designers with grossly neglecting the lived experience and social fantasies of a dominant majority within Europe's societies, coming up instead with "sad symbols" on a currency "without soul or culture." For modern currencies to be accepted and considered legitimate, Théret argued, they must be able to both symbolize a community based on a political territory and transcend social contradictions.[28]

Théret offers two explanations for the "symbolic deficit" in the postmodern aesthetics of the euro notes. The first is that symbolic, psychological, or political dimensions were entirely outside the horizon of the social scientists responsible for the design of the euro. The second is that the economists on the project were exclusively interested in the exchange value of the euro, and thus profoundly distrusted political or symbolic dimensions, which for them were only archaisms or expressions of special interests. Yet does the euro really contribute nothing towards a culturally constructed sense of inclusion? To most people, the bridges and arches, windows and gateways that appear on the various denominations of euro notes seem to suggest little more than a kind of coming together, which would make the euro a bank draft drawn on a remote future. Maybe that was the intention of the designers.

Upon closer inspection, however, the monuments on the euro notes—Romanesque gateways, Roman aqueducts, Victorian iron and glass windows, or modern bridges—are not timeless so much as they are rooted in a time *before* the modern nation-state. They may also be rooted *after* it, which would make them post-national as it were.[29] From the beginning, the euro notes had to say "Europe," all of them, and there could not be anything too particular, or anything that might offend the nationalistic feelings of any participating country. Thus all the Eurocrats could agree on as being quintessentially European—without offending anyone—were generic architectural details. Equally inoffensive was the decision, in 2013, that the second series of Euro notes was to carry a portrait of Europa, the figure from Greek mythology that lent her name to the continent. Hence the series is titled the "Europa series."[30]

The controversies over and the—often fierce—resistance against the euro in countries like Britain or France are proof of the fact that the coins and bills that people carry around in their wallets cannot be separated from questions of national identity. It is no coincidence, therefore, that in debates about the euro, American dollar bills were often held up as models. Dollar bills are replete with symbolic representations of the community within which they are universally valid—the United States of America. On dollar bills the legal authority of the state is conflated with the nation's history and nationalistic imagery, from the Great Seal to the presentation of the Declaration of

Independence, from the Lincoln Memorial to the White House or Independence Hall and, not to forget, portraits of the nation's presidents (as well as of some eminent Americans who were not presidents). For an American Studies analyst, therefore, it was only fitting to take a closer look at dollar bills (and, to an extent, coins).

I began this project with a look at the one-dollar bill, the most widespread and most familiar of all dollar bills, and the one that to Americans is the dearest by far. More than 60 percent of all dollar bills in circulation are one-dollar bills, altogether some 13.2 billion that had soaked up some four thousand tons of ink. It is also the most widely produced note: Forty-five percent of all notes printed each year are one-dollar notes. The look and color of the one-dollar bill have a degree of recognition that is truly fabulous: "In the most remote place the appearance and color of a U.S. $1 bill, like the shape of a Coca Cola bottle, is a recognized icon," Gene Hessler noted.[31] Yet recognition does not mean that the verbal and visual symbols on the "singles" are read. Coins and paper bills are not distributed primarily for their *meanings*. They are expected to *function*. What counts are numbers, not words or images. Coins and currency do not tell stories; they will be counted. In the context of monetary communication, the methodological principle underlying the *Anti-Oedipus* makes perfect sense—not to ask, "What does this mean?" but, instead, "How does this work?"[32] Yet for those people who do not want to merely possess pieces of currency, that is, for people whose interest is not distracted by monetary value, it is certainly worthwhile paying attention to the verbal and visual symbols surrounding the magical numbers. The very reluctance of people to part with their beloved "Georges" demonstrates that the currency provides an often-neglected surplus value.

By the time this book goes into print I will have spent close to two decades exploring the symbolic values that provide external backing and stabilization to monetary systems. The intellectual capital I have been accumulating forms the basis of the present analysis of the political iconography of America's money, using the metaphorical Father of His Country as its focal point. The present book is not therefore interested in "the real man" who, as Marcus Cunliffe wrote, "has become entombed in his own myth—a metaphorical Washington Monument that hides from us the lineaments of the real man."[33] The "real man" is of relevance rather to biographers and historians, whose legitimate business is to constantly "rediscover" or at least to "reconsider" the nation's founder and its first president.[34] But to deny that the Washington legend exists, stressing instead the "human" qualities of the man, is pushing things too far. However suspect it may be in the eyes of history, the legend does exist, as essential to acting and knowing as history itself, except that it evokes emotions, not dispassionate analysis, and so my own interest is in renderings of the Father of His Country, the metaphorical figure Americans need to believe was and would continue to be there for them.

The Father of His Country, Marcus Cunliffe demonstrated, is one of the four guises of the "metaphorical Washington Monument," the "hero figure."[35] This figure has been given expression in all kinds of media—in artworks, in poetry, fiction, and drama, in political and religious discourses, in eulogies and biographies—and has been duly discussed and analyzed. But "metaphorical Washington Monuments" have also appeared on coins and currency. While they have received not nearly as much attention as other media, coins and currency certainly are worth a closer look. Inscribing currency or stamping coins with likenesses of George Washington is neither contingent nor accidental; rather, it reveals carefully calculated design choices. Coins and currency after all are documents of culture that speak to the identity of a group of people, a place, and a time. They reveal patterns of consumption and regulation and, consequently, allow us to draw conclusions about political convictions, gender roles, and other social relations. If I will be keeping an eye on money, I will be doing this in a quite literal sense. Therefore, I will not be offering a master plan for the frugal use of money, but rather one for "reading the notes" (to borrow from David Blaazer) and, by extension, coins. This agenda necessarily entails paying attention to the visual and verbal signs and symbols printed on paper bills or stamped on coins so that they will be accepted *as* money.

A note on terminology (which is truly confusing) seems in order. For Richard G. Doty, a former curator at the Smithsonian's National Numismatic Collection, "'currency' is any and all money actually in circulation at any given time." "Coins" are officially used currency made from pieces of metal; officially used currency manufactured from paper is called "paper money" or "paper currency." "Money" is the most comprehensive term, denoting anything that measures value and circulates, "as long as it does so by agreement of the people it serves." The explanation offered by Arthur Nussbaum, an economic and legal historian, is somewhat different: "In the technical terminology of American legislation, bank notes as well as other paper money, such as the later U.S. Notes, National Bank Notes, and Federal Reserve Notes, are called 'currency' (a term meaning simply circulation in early legislation), whereas the term 'money' is generally reserved for coins. This is a residue of the common-law tradition, which considered bank notes simply as commercial instruments. The old terminology, however, has not been sustained in more recent legislation and, in conformity with the economic and legal literature of our day, we shall speak of 'paper money' and, on the other hand, include coins in the term 'currency.'" Different again is the distinction made by the Federal Reserve Board, between "currency" (meaning paper money) and "coins."[36]

Today's monetary tokens—and paper bills in particular—lack intrinsic value. They have neither use value nor exchange value. A modern coin may be useful to change a standard mignon battery; a high-denomination paper bill may be useful to light a cigar and thus to give to gaping spectators a demonstration of one's wealth and power, as well as of one's ability to misuse money so blatantly. (There are other forms of misuse, such as tax evasion, reason enough for economist Kenneth Rogoff's plea for the all-out elimination of larger-denomination bills.[37]) As for exchange value, today's currency is "legal tender for all debts public and private," yet neither coins nor paper bills can be exchanged for gold or silver. But money cannot do without the conviction that it is backed by more than itself. Thus, modern money's sheer lack of value is made up through all kinds of aesthetic-ideological compensations. The visual and verbal signs and symbols printed on paper bills or stamped on coins are, then, "functional encroachments" that provide the necessary backing for money's appearance of value as well as for the value of the appearance. We might even say that money is *re-financed* from realms outside the economy, such as religion, politics, and the arts. The ensuing designs—the "rhetoric" of coins and currency—are justly called "accompanying measures for building trust." Money's rhetoric, therefore, is persuasion, for money needs to appear credible *as* money and, through its "imagined" value, encourage recognition of one's membership in a well-bounded community. As the late Hans Tietmeyer, a former president of the German Bundesbank, once said, "credibility is the name of the game."[38]

Mr. Tietmeyer's statement perfectly illustrates how fraught money is with religious associations—and has been since ancient times, as is evident from words like *credit* (from Latin *credere*, to believe), *creditor*, *debtor*, *bankruptcy*, *obolus*, *pecunia*, or *money* (from *Moneta*, the Roman goddess). Indeed, key concepts of finance are religious terms converted into monetary ones: Thus, "mass" became "emission," and "praise" became "price." Writers and poets have made creative use of the convertibility between religion and theology, and the world of money, not least among them Shakespeare, whose *The Merchant of Venice* (c. 1596–1598) may well be "the most prominent foundational poetical document" of the encroachments into language by the world of money.[39] And in Goethe's *Faust*, money even provides an answer to the nagging question "what holds the world together in its core."[40] Contemporaries might want to answer the question with a popular adage from the musical *Cabaret*, "Money makes the world go 'round."

If, as Liza Minelli famously sang, money makes the world go 'round, it does so in an utterly unpathetic way, defined as it is in purely quantitative terms. In contrast, the empirical form of monetary tokens has always displayed aesthetic features, which constitute their rhetoric. This rhetoric turns monetary tokens into objects of contemplation, in opposition to what is generally understood as money talk—the monetary discourses of economists, politicians, bankers, and others. And it is by virtue of their rhetoric that coins and currency have been seen as "history we hold in our hands," to paraphrase numismatist James Earl Jones. This should not be taken to mean that coins and currency are "sources." The metaphor, the British historian Peter Burke maintains, "is a vivid one but it is also misleading, in the sense of implying the possibility of an account of the past which is uncontaminated by intermediaries." Monetary history too knows a whole chain of intermediaries, including earlier historians, collectors who arranged the pieces, mint employees who struck them, etc. Coins and currency are, then, not so much "sources" as "traces" of the past in the present, of a past in which specific materials connected to specific phases in economic development—precious metals to mercantile capitalism, paper to industrial capitalism and mass production.[41]

Coins and currency may also be understood as documents of *culture*. Among numismatists, however, a cultural perspective still is the exception rather than the rule. The meticulous descriptions of coins and currency in guidebooks or auction catalogs are proof that numismatists largely follow the classificatory paradigm of what once was called "natural history."[42] And if they see value in coins and currency, it is customarily defined in terms of rarity and age. Thus, one needs to turn to historians for alternatives to the collector's view. A prime example is the German economic historian Hans Gebhardt. Gebhardt's pioneering study not only complemented Georg Simmel's philosophical theory of money; published as *Numismatik und Geldgeschichte* (*Numismatics and the History of Money*), it was a passionate plea for a turn from coin-heavy numismatics to the (cultural) history of money. Gebhardt's study was published in 1949, but it took another generation for his plea to be heeded, most notably by the historian Bernhard Löffler, the political scientist Birger P. Priddat, the media psychologist and economist Stefan Hampl, and by the philosopher Gottfried Gabriel, whose *Ästhetik und Rhetorik des Geldes* as well as "Aesthetics and the Political Iconography of Money" set the agenda for a new era. As for English-language research, cultural history perspectives have been adopted by Richard Doty in *America's Money—America's Story*, Heinz Tschachler in *The Greenback*, as well as by scholars as diverse as David Blaazer, Robert Garson, Emily Gilbert, Virginia Hewitt, John R. Katsion, and Douglas Mudd.[43]

Part I

Vehicles of Useful Impressions

When the Rev. Samuel Davies in 1760 reminded the British, "George was our father, too," he was referring to George II, the English King, who had died in October of that year. In 1774, Nathaniel Niles still valued that veneration, this time reserved for George III: "[L]et the world see that their king is dearer to the Americans than their blood."[1] At the time of the first Continental Congress, several delegates clung to the pleasing fiction that a benevolent George III was under the evil spell of a tyrannical ministry, and they implored the king as their "loving father" to employ his royal prerogative to rescue his colonial subjects. Two years later, the hope that "the horrors of civil discord [could be] prevented" had given way to a furious disillusionment. George III no longer figured as the "Father of His Country" but had become a "tyrant" neglecting his "children." This was the rage of unfulfilled expectations, a willful denial and suppression of a much-valued family connection. The "expected father of his people" had looked on "the violation of American rights [...] with a most unfatherly calmness."[2] The charge was a severe one. First raised in this form during a meeting of the Congress, it found its way into one of America's most "sacred" documents. "A Prince whose character is thus marked by every act which may define a Tyrant," the Declaration of Independence concludes, "is unfit to be the ruler of a free people."[3]

As a piece of secular Scripture, the Declaration of Independence holds a special place in the political and cultural history of the United States. Yet what many colonists felt about the sovereign in far-away London was also articulated through more "profane" documents—pamphlets, newspaper articles, editorials, broadsides, songs and poems, prints, cartoons, and speeches, sermons, letters, plays, fiction, and, not to forget, pieces of paper money and coins.[4] For instance, a Maryland bank note produced by the woodcutter Thomas Sparrow and the printer Frederick Green, displays a veritable revolutionary tableau, advertising the identity and merits of the colonial fraternity. An allegory of Britannia is shown receiving a congressional petition (abbreviated as "CONG PETI") from a female figure representing America. America is shown trampling on a scroll marked "SLAVERY" and holding a liberty cap in front of American troops gathered under a flag inscribed with "LIB" (for "LIBERTY"). As for the metaphorical father, George III is depicted trampling on a scroll marked "M.[AGNA] CHARTA" as he is about to set fire to a city (Annapolis or Baltimore) under attack by a British fleet. Even the frame of the bill is trimmed with patriotic propaganda. At left is a Latin motto, "PRO ARIS ET FOCIS" ("FOR ALTARS AND HEARTHS"), at left a few words in English that reveal the urgency of the cause, "AN APPEAL TO HEAVEN." The notes were issued in denominations of $⅔, $1, $ 1⅓, $ 1⅔ (12s 6d), $ 2⅔ (20s), $ 4 (30s), $ 8 (£ 3), and $ 16 (£ 6), to a total of $ 266,000 (£ 100,000).[5]

The purpose of the issue, which was done without the British government's approval—that is, illegally—was to finance the acquisition of gunpowder (hence the colloquialism "gunpowder notes"). The bills were redeemable against Spanish silver dollars until January 1, 1786, to the generous rate of 4s and 6d to the dollar. The liberty cap (also known as Phrygian cap or *pileus*) recalls the Roman tradition. It was worn by former slaves on the day of their manumission. The tradition was revived in eighteenth-century France, when the cap became to symbolize liberation from tyrannical rule. Unsurprisingly, it became tremendously popular with the Jacobins. In the aftermath of the battles of Lexington and Concord in April 1775 American "patriots" too adopted the cap as a symbol of liberation from tyrannical rule and, as well, of republican government.

The Maryland notes communicate a visible decline in the colonists' faith in their sovereign and a preparedness for rebellion, together with liberty and republican rule as the only form of government that is fit for America. Yet the back of the notes is much more low-key, even conciliatory, as if the inflammatory pictorial rhetoric of the front had to be somehow controlled. We see Britannia and America joining hands; the olive branch between them suggests peace. The symbolic message is reinforced through another Latin motto suggesting that peace was still more desirable than war—"PAX TRIUMPHIS POTIOR."[6] The Maryland notes are from July 1775. A little over a year later, the iconography on some Virginia notes is much more drastic, the mood openly furious, furious enough to act against England. An allegorical figure—Virtue, with spear in hand—is seen standing with her foot on the prostrate form of Tyranny, whose crown lies nearby. The motto too could not have been more direct: "*SIC SEMPER TYRANNUS.*" "Tyrannus" is, of course, grammatically incorrect. It was set right in the 1778 issue. Henceforth it read, "SIC SEMPER TYRANNIS" ("Thus always to Tyrants") and can be read on the flag of the state of Virginia to this very day.[7]

1

The Father of His Country and America's Money

The outcome of the conflict between the English mother country and the United Colonies is well known. Less well known is that the revolutionaries faced a deeply divided people. Thus, their assumed task was "to extract consensus at all costs," to appeal to what Thomas Jefferson in 1825 called "harmonizing sentiments."[1] These sentiments were imaginatively recast in the trope of "a more perfect union" (in the Preamble to the Federal Constitution) as well as in the national motto, "E Pluribus Unum" (adopted for the Continental Congress in 1782). The two phrases suggest that the newly forming national identity had no place for apocalyptic conflict. Even controversy was to be avoided as much as possible. Many Americans, for instance, were hostile to the notion of a national federal republic in 1787, so the Federal Constitution, in creating one, never mentions the words "national," "federal," or "republic." The "limits and forms of the sayable," to borrow from Foucault,[2] were transcended by other means, chiefly by the personification of public virtue. Construed thus, the separation from England was seen as a natural movement towards control of one's own destiny. Often, however, the separation implied a deeply traumatic experience, the irreparable loss of the orphan. The distinction, Robert Ferguson suggests, depends at least in part on assumptions about the maturation process in America. "Only children can be orphans." And, one might add, only children can be expected to cast together their completed or at least stilled angers in the role of founding fathers.[3]

In the end, the austere and commanding figure of Washington became the undisputed symbol of authority, and, since George III was destroyed as a symbolic entity, the exalted title of "Father of His Country" was transferred onto him.[4] The identification of George Washington with the newly forming nation constituted an act of communal incorporation, much as it constituted an act of mutual recognition between leaders and led. In these acts, leaders—the "gods of the clan," in Durkheim's words—are deemed superior in dignity and power, that is to say, "sacred," not because of any inherent qualities so much as because they symbolize something greater than themselves—the moral authority of society or nation.[5]

George Washington became the moral authority of the American nation when the Continental Congress appointed the Virginian Commander-in-Chief of the Continental Army, then gathered in Cambridge, Massachusetts. At this point Washington may not have been ready for America, but America was ready for him. As of June 19, 1775, he was America's "living 'tribal' totem."[6] His name became the signal for unlimited panegyric in prose and verse. He was the pride and glory of America. In his hands was put "the sword of liberty ... by the unanimous voice of his country."[7] In January 1776, Levi Allen, younger brother of Ethan Allen, hailed Washington as "Our political Father and head of a Great People."[8] And just over a year later, Brigadier General Henry Knox, possibly drawing from his vast reading in the writers of classical Rome, wrote, "the People of America look up to you as their Father, and into your hands they entrust their *all*."[9]

The image of George Washington as a metaphorical father was first spelled out in print and brought to people's attention through countless sermons and orations roughly between 1775 and 1779. But it was the production and dissemination of pictorial representations that provided the new nation with a face. Great artworks bear this out, Gilbert Stuart's "Lansdowne Portrait" for example, but so does down-home folk art, such as the crude figure identified by the initials "GW" that a John Hough, Jr., had engraved in 1777 on his privately emitted fractional notes.[10]

The iconic face of the nation helped constitute national identity, provided a model for and stimulus to moral behavior, much as it worked to affirm the credibility of banks by aligning with patriotic feelings and deep historicity. If this act was crucial at the

Private fractional note, 9d (⅛ Dollar), John Hough, Jr., Waterford, Loudoun County, Virginia, c. 1777 (Eric P. Newman Numismatic Education Society).

beginning of the republic, Washington's pictorial presence is perpetuating national memory also in the late twentieth and early twenty-first centuries. Representations of him are ubiquitous in the visual culture. Bank notes as well as coins, tokens, medals and countless other objects likewise feature him as a central figure of consensus, a national symbol much like the Stars and Stripes. As the face on the dollar bill, Washington's iconic portrait (based on Gilbert Stuart's painting) has appeared in its present form since 1929. Selection of the Father of His Country then was justified in terms of the first president's "more permanent familiarity in the minds of the public than any others."[11] In addition, Washington's head (after Jean-Antoine Houdon's bust) resurfaced in 1932, when it was stamped on the new quarter, to celebrate the two-hundredth anniversary of his birth. And it has seen a new incarnation in the $1 Presidential Coins program, which began with the Washington dollar in 2007.

The bicentennial celebration of Washington's birth ushered in a new era in America's numismatic history. Before, United States coinage had been under the spell of the Mint Act of 1792. Although the U.S. Senate had included in a bill to establish a mint a provision to put on coins "an impression or representation of the head of the President of the United States for the time being," the House of Representatives after much debate struck the provision from the bill, refused to recede from the change when the Senate returned the bill, and prevailed in the final passage of the act, which mandated instead the use of an emblem of liberty, inscription of the word Liberty, and the year of the coinage. The decision had far-reaching consequences for America's coinage. Although any number of medals and tokens bearing Washington's portrait are known from 1783 onwards, and although in 1863 a 2-cent pattern was made with his portrait, the face of the nation did not appear on circulating coins for another century and a half.[12] In the present book, therefore, coins are not treated as extensively as paper money. Bank notes and similar papers have been the monetary vehicles to disseminate the face of the nation the most frequently and, arguably, the most effectively, bringing Washington's likeness quite literally into the hands of viewers. As Q. David Bowers noted, "George Washington is the most widely featured American historical figure to be found on paper money. He is shown in many ways, including his portrait within an ellipse or rectangle, his bust in the classic style, standing with a horse, standing alone, and in other poses."[13]

In view of Bowers' finding, it should be asked why Washington coins, medals, and stamps have been extensively researched (and collected with equal enthusiasm), while there is hardly any literature on illustrations of Washington on paper money and, as well, only a very limited interest among collectors.[14] One explanation may be found in the "hierarchy of materials," which traditionally has ranked paper last, even behind aluminum. Paper money was suspicious from its inception. How could its low material value be representative of real value? Paper money, therefore, came to be called "soft money," as opposed to "hard cash." The two terms do not constitute a neutral pair, but a value-laden one in which they are differentially weighted so that one element in the dichotomy is more valued or powerful than the other. Gifts, for instance, may be given in "hard cash," but not in the form of a bundle of crumpled notes. And only coins made from precious metals were "natural" money, as Karl Marx postulated.

Marx had only endorsed a view developed in Ferdinando Galiani's mid-eighteenth-century tract *Della Moneta*: "Although gold and silver are not by Nature money, money is by Nature gold and silver." The view was common enough among contemporary economists. It is reflected, for instance, in a piece of advice published in *Hunt's Merchants' Magazine* in 1842: "[T]he only true regulator of the currency is, *never to receive or pay bank bills except at their specie value*."[15] Such advice, together with the underlying assumption that only precious coins constitute "natural" money, relies upon a conception of nature and money that paper began to unsettle (and that new forms of plastic and electronic money altogether erase).[16]

Next to the "aesthetics of materials" we should look to the "aesthetics of symbols" to make sense of the somewhat reluctant interest in paper money.[17] On bank notes and similar financial instruments, the only direct reference to an objective reality is the number, which indicates the value. This is the reason why numbers are so numerous on paper bills. Yet the significance of bank notes does not exclusively lie in these purely functional elements. Verbal and visual symbols surrounding the numbers are important in themselves. Since the material value of paper is low, bank notes are not supposed to look like paper, nor feel like paper to the touch, and they should appear more valuable than paper. Hence, we find increasingly elaborate trappings and visual designs, which more often than not are unrelated to economic parameters like function and intended use, conferring, instead, a surplus value to the notes that goes well beyond their material value.

There is another aspect to the "aesthetics of symbols": Bank notes are generally considered mass products that constitute the lowest common denominator for a public. However artistically convincing bank notes may be, they usually are considered as "not quite art," and thus not worthy of serious scholarly debate on that ground alone.[18] While a point can be made that on bank notes "the representational subject-matter is suggested by the chance shape and appearance and purpose of the material to be decorated,"[19] this is true of coins as well. And coins *have* been subject to serious scholarly debate all the same. Bank notes, for their part, have large, rectangular spaces that make them an ideal rhetorical medium for advertisement and propaganda, for consciously chosen ideas as well as for unconscious assumptions, and thus for serving functions beyond the mere economic.

In the United States, numismatic composition often has been stimulated by national pride, sometimes to the extent that every feature on paper bills constituted a patriotic design. This is especially true of post–Civil War federal paper money. Notes from this era have even been considered as "the only true American contribution to the arts."[20] The compliment—and it *was* meant as a compliment—obviously does not apply to notes from the colonial and revolutionary eras. Yet even these notes—the Massachusetts bills of credit, the Maryland notes of 1775, the Virginia issue of 1776, to name just a few—were issued not merely to serve as a medium of trade but quite intentionally as objects of meaningful connotations, metaphorically exemplifying social ideals and understandings. In short, they served as "vehicles of useful impressions," in Alexander Hamilton's memorable words of 1792.[21] These latter, non-economic functions, warrant a closer look at the currency and, by extension, coins.

Americans are exposed to coins and currency at every moment. More importantly, coins and currency are the only forms of art of which this can be said. They are a form of official, historical art specifically designed to reach citizens in every epoch of United

States affairs. It is no exaggeration to say, therefore, that "money talks." The expression tells us that money is a medium that functions like language. Language facilitates the exchange of ideas; money facilitates the exchange of goods and services.[22] Yet money's ability to communicate value and symbolism is not tied to money's use. In other words, money's functionality is independent of a specific material. Since almost anything can serve as money, the beauty of monetary tokens likewise is independent of their use as a medium of exchange or means of payment.[23] This is not to say that signs and symbols get onto monetary tokens by chance or in a natural way. For cultural studies analysts, the issue is crucial. Cultural studies analysts explore the diverse relations between visuality, culture, and society. They are interested in the cultural, social, and historical premises and conditions of the visual, much as they are interested in the impact of the visual on culture and society.

Politics cannot do without visual representations for the staging of power. And viewers often find it difficult to distance themselves from the hegemonic force of pictures. Hence image criticism needs to find answers to the question how pictures are employed in the production, questioning, and changing of meanings and understandings. Image criticism also needs to explain how and in what contexts pictures are produced, and how they are consumed and received. Pictures, most cultural studies analysts will agree, suffuse our daily life, and they largely determine who we think we are and with whom we belong. A thorough analysis therefore must go beyond looking at pictures in isolation; just as important is to consider their reception and their impact within different cultural and social contexts.

Cultural studies analysts distinguish between two areas of visual analysis, respectively called "iconology" and "iconography." Although the two terms are often used as synonyms for any visual studies practice, the distinction is important. "Iconology" and "iconography" denote two distinct methodological levels. Etymology helps us clarify the distinction. The two roots respectively are *graphein* (to write or describe) and *logos* (knowledge). Iconography thus is a descriptive practice, whereas iconology is an interpretative practice that goes beyond description.[24] Iconology is interested in sources, which it relates to one another and brings together in a conclusive interpretative act. Iconology also attends to what images are and how they convey meaning, as well as to the art historical, historical, social, and political contexts of image production and consumption. Through its own hermeneutics, iconology also focuses on images' inner tensions and structures, as well as on their interplays of time and affect, of showing and concealing.

Iconology cannot do without its twin and prerequisite—iconography. Iconography focuses on specific images, pictures, and likenesses, such as photographs, advertisements, computer games, television, religious icons, and images on coins and currency. Its goal is the systematic documentation, categorization, and identification of pictorial motifs. The iconography of coins and currency seeks to describe the material and formal manifestations of coins and currency in all their concrete visualizations. It analyzes the forms of images, their contents, and, not to forget, concrete monetary practices. In other words, it asks what is being represented and how, as well as what kind of ideological work coins and currency do in the everyday lives of users and consumers. This sounds easy enough, though in reality it is highly complex. It is never entirely clear, for instance, what kind of message is received by the people who handle coins and currency, how engraved or stamped messages are received, whether they are received at all, or whether meanings are decoded in the way they were intended by their producers (who might, for instance, intend the visual design for the purpose of legitimating the state, or a bank, or capitalism).[25]

Coins and currency are not discrete signs so much as a combination of multiple elements of signification and security, a complex of materials, forms and shapes, colors, numbers, letters, elements that are obvious and hidden, overt and covert. It is no surprise, therefore, that the iconography of coins and currency has its own language, together with its own grammar, which includes syntax, semantics, and pragmatics. We talk about a note's face and back, its rectangular space, its types of design features, much as we talk about a coin's obverse and reverse, that which faces you and that which is turned away from you, hence its head or tail. We also talk about different denominations and types of notes and coins.[26] When bank notes and similar papers were introduced in the North American colonies, their chief purpose was to provide local economies with the capital necessary for their development. This meant that the "bills" had to be accepted by people in their everyday lives. Today this is still so. Bank notes and similar papers may be different one from the other, yet there are common features that allow users to identify them *as* money. Even never-seen-before foreign notes are usually identified as money.

Paper bills now are printed on both sides, front and back, or recto and verso, and they are usually multi-colored; they are rectangular in shape, and their sheer size when compared to coins leaves ample space for all kinds of visual arrangements or engraved work. Illustrations or ornaments on bills are called "vignettes," to distinguish them from the frame and the lettering. Portraits, allegorical scenes, or motifs from history are used as vignettes. The dictionary defines vignettes as "any small, pleasing picture or view," and so vignettes range from ornate ones, such as the faces of the "Educational series" Silver Certificates from the 1890s, to simple portraits or buildings. Collectors usually go for lavish embellishments, though the Treasury Department has consistently stated that to deter counterfeiting, bills should have ample open or plain space on both sides. Either way, the visual order on bills is never random. There always are certain "planimetric compositions," such as the use of "margins," blank areas at the border of a note beyond the design or printed information, and the arrangement of design elements in the form of a collage—the central "portrait" may be slightly offset, individual elements may display a kind of choreography, color and style may be used to achieve an overall context. Often, several vignettes by different engravers (whose names are not always known) are used to create the face and back of a given note.

"Portraits" are pictorial representations of humans, particularly of heads. The source of the artwork is usually a photograph, or a photograph of a painting or print, though at first portraits were done from paintings or prints. Portraits may be framed in ellipses or rectangles, they may be executed in classical style or in down-to-earth folk art, though ideally, they are "made emblematic or allegorical through pose, accessories or background."[27] Most portraits concentrate on either a head or a bust (the head, shoulders, and a portion of the chest). Full-figure portraits are possible, but have not been widely used for living people, as the style means the subject's head must be very small, and most "princes" having themselves portrayed insist that their faces be identifiable. Hence, full-length portraits are more often used for allegorical representation. The most popular portrait style has been the "profile," whereas the facing or "full-face" portrait is less common. Still other portrait styles are "three-quarter," "jugate," and "vis-à-vis." Verbal symbolism ("lettering" or "script") is traditionally divided into two categories, "inscriptions" (slogans, mottoes, etc.) and "subscriptions" (decrees, etc.). The graphic integration of script and the design of individual letters impacts on users' moods and feelings. Thus, certain notes are known by their nicknames, like "Lazy Deuce," "Sawhorse Reverse," "Technicolor Note," "Indian Chief Note," "Bison Note," or "Battleship Note."

Banknote design is highly artistic, though it is not art for art's sake—function, too, is important.[28] Different designs are used to distinguish different "denominations," the face or stated value printed on a bill, even different "classes" or "types" of notes—United States Notes, Silver Certificates, Federal Reserve Notes, and so on. "Series" designations indicate a change in design or some other aspect of a note. Collectors tend to be interested in the "printage," the printing quantity, which often but not always is a guide to availability. "Security features" are likewise purely functional, as they comprise aspects of the design or printing of a note intended to deter copying or counterfeiting. On early notes, security features consisted of wavy lines cut between a numbered note and its stub kept in a book at the place of issuance; on later notes, minute design elements were expertly engraved, there was an increasingly complex lathe work, and there was printing on special paper (often with silk fibers embedded). In recent years, security features included watermarks, color-shifting ink, micro-printing, and embedded polymer strips.

A distinction is also made between "bank notes" and "paper money." Originally, "bank notes" were receipts made out to the owner for coins deposited in a bank. In contrast, "paper money" refers to a circulating medium crated by a *public* institution. (Thus, a "counterfeit" is a bill in imitation of an original design, but printed from false plates, by someone *not* authorized to issue paper money.) There are two forms of "genuine" paper money: that which may be redeemed in coins (hence with an "obligation" printed on the bills, that is, a promise to pay or "will pay") and that which is simply declared to be "legal tender for all debts public and private," without the possibility of redeeming the notes for precious coins.[29]

The emblematic eloquence of bank notes—the result of color, formal arrangements, figures, and other characteristics—adds legitimacy to notes so that they are accepted as currency. Yet the achieved harmony secures the notes' credibility from outside the monetary realm. We find historic information concerning the issuing institution, as well as the decree authorizing a note's production, and its location. Functional information includes the denomination, the institution guaranteeing a note's value, and a note's form, which tells us whether it is purely symbolic or redeemable in gold or silver. Identificatory information indicates a note's class or type (for instance, United States Notes), its serial number, or its position relative to comparable objects. This is the standard classification provided by, *inter alia*, Mugnaini or O'Donnell.[30]

By another classification, documentary or rationalizing elements are distinguished from aesthetic or mystifying one. The first category comprises decorative elements (pure ornamentation, like frames, guilloches, or hatch patterns, as well as security features and identificatory and functional information); the second category comprises all kinds of symbolic or idealistic elements (state seals, pictures of important buildings, reproductions of paintings, portraits of distinguished persons, allegories, and abstractions). Symbolic or idealistic elements are more complex as well as more time-bound and dependent on context. Importantly, these elements do not just mirror an external reality; they are constitutive of reality, putting in concrete terms a simulation of closeness that allows noteholders to partake of the centering effect of the communal.

Regarding coins, the most obvious physical attribute is the material from which a coin is produced—gold, silver, copper or one of its alloys, aluminum, and plastic. Also important is the method to produce coins, casting or striking. Casting is simpler; molten metal is poured into a pair of joined molds which are then separated or broken. Striking, in contrast, involves impressing an image on a "planchet," the disk of metal of which a coin is made. Striking is done with the help of "dies," pieces of hard metal bearing images that are incised into their surfaces in reverse. Collectors will look for differences between "strike doubling" and "doubled dies." The differences are noticeable from the effect of the "secondary images," which in the first instance are flat and shelf-like but raised and rounded in the second instance. Over time, dies may become "worn," leading to what is known as an "orange peel effect," as well as to a lack of detail especially on the low-relief areas of the "field," that is, the area around the "type" or "dominant design," or the area that provides its background. "Weak strikes," the result of not exerting enough pressure, are also unwelcome among collectors, who bemoan the lack of detail all over the fields and the generally dull, lack-luster look of such coins.

Numismatists also pay attention to a coin's "module," that is, its diameter, much as they are careful about a coin's weight. In antiquity, weight was the only way of regulating a definite exchange value. Many coin denominations derive their names from weights, for instance the pound, from the L. in *libra*. In earlier times, weight was a grave security concern. Hence, we still find coins on which the "edge" is marked with a series of tiny ridges and grooves. Corrugating or "reeding" the edges through a milling procedure was a measure adopted in order to curtail the "clipping" of coins by cutting or boring into their edges, filling the holes with cheaper material. Milling was first applied in France during the seventeenth century, and later adopted by Britain, Spain, and the American colonies. The invention of coining machinery also allowed for more prominent "rims," which put an end to "filing," an easy way to cheat when coins varied in diameter.[31] Today, rims may be rounded, with tapering edges, or with reverse (incuse) lines. "Reeding" also helps to distinguish "proof coins" from "business strikes." On the former, the reeding does not bevel downward, whereas on the latter, it does not go down all the way to the edges.

In colonial America, among the first coins were patent farthings of James I and Charles I, together with pennies and sixpence of Elizabeth I—all found at archeological sites at Fort James, Virginia. Also important for the early colonial economy were Dutch *daalders* ("lion dollars"), which were first used to purchase Manhattan from Native Americans. When the first coins were struck in New England in the mid-seventeenth century, they were denominated in the money of England, such as the Lord Baltimore sixpence. This Maryland coin helped facilitate commercial transactions that were usually accompanied by barter and by trading tobacco. Other colonies, too, were in need of coinage. Best known are the Massachusetts Pine Tree shillings, large silver coins that were struck from 1652 to about 1680. The silver had come from silverware and Spanish coins. Pine Tree shillings likely did not circulate outside Massachusetts. Once these coins reached New York or Philadelphia, they usually were cut down to the weight of a Spanish *real*, worth one eighth of a dollar. The image remained, though. A symbol of the lush forests of the New World, the pine tree may well have suggested a separate identity from Britain. A three-penny piece struck in Connecticut some eighty years later displayed another denizen of the North American forests, a deer, as well as proudly proclaiming the American origin of the metal used to create the token. These modest first efforts established an idea that would soon be acted on in a bolder, more consistent way.[32]

The colonial and Revolutionary economies saw very little coinage in circulation,[33] so an American identity promoted through money had to rely on paper for the purpose. It was only after the end of the War of Independence that a distinctive coinage helped inculcate the American idea. Within the legal framework of the Articles of Confederation, states enjoyed the right to coin money during the years after the battle of Yorktown. Not all states took advantage of this right, but those that did added to the growing store of national images, with renditions of American eagles, the national shield with the motto *E Pluribus Unum* ("FROM MANY, ONE"), seated personifications of Liberty, as well as a number of images—chiefly of Justice (*Justitia*)—that were disseminated also by means of paper notes. With the adoption of the federal Constitution in 1787, the national government took over from the states the obligation of producing and providing money. Given the constitutional prohibition against a federal paper currency, it was the coinage that became a veritable reservoir of all the symbols of a young nation striving to find its iconographic and artistic identity. While the purpose of the new federal coinage clearly was "to provide democracy with instruments of visual beauty," the iconographic and aesthetic problems involved were overwhelming. As a result, the new coinage came into being through reformulations of and adaptations to European courtly traditions, from sculpture and painting to decorative engravings. Benjamin West's canvas *Omnia Vincit Amor*, "Love Conquers All," was inspired by the Italian Renaissance, though his Venus figure entered America's numismatic repertory as Liberty, dominating a major segment of the coinage.[34]

The distinctive symbolism on the new coinage was the proud and self-confident expression of the newly achieved political sovereignty. In other respects, though, the coinage remained subordinate, even derivative, the plaything of forces operating outside the nation's boundaries. The Coinage Act of 1792 specified a "dollar" to be based on the Spanish dollar and of 371 grains and four 16ths part of a grain of pure silver and an "eagle" to be 247 and four 8ths of a grain of pure gold. The choice of the value of grains goes back to Alexander Hamilton's decision to base the new monetary unit on the average weight of a selection of worn Spanish dollars. Hamilton instructed the Treasury to weigh a sample of these coins and the average weight came out to be 371 grains. A new Spanish dollar was usually about 377 grains in weight, and so the new American dollar was of slightly less value than the Spanish dollar.[35]

The United States dollar, then, originally was defined by weight at the same time as it was hitched to the money of another powerful empire. For America's coinage as we know it today, weight is no longer an issue, and neither is the monetary system of another empire. Instead, what we look for is the "mark" certifying a piece of metal to be of a definite exchange value and issued by a public authority to be used as money. "Type" or "dominant design" refers to the central device or motif of either face of the coin. On one face of the United States silver dollar of 1795, for example, the type is the bust of Liberty facing right; on the other, the American eagle. On the obverse, the "field" is taken up by a circle of stars, with the word "LIBERTY" spelled out at the top, and the year, "1795," at the bottom; the "field" on the reverse is filled with a wreath and the inscription "UNITED STATES OF AMERICA." The "legend" describes the verbal content or script, in our case "LIBERTY," "1795," and, indicating the issuing authority, "UNITED STATES OF AMERICA."

The silver dollar's design was continued until 1798, when new reverses were prepared; the obverse, engraved after Gilbert Stuart's 1795 sketch, now lost, lasted until 1836. New reverse designs appeared at various intervals through 1836, manifesting all the symptoms of a fledgling nation trying to create a coinage that was to be as dignified as that of the world's leading powers, England and France. The impact of the Flowing Hair silver dollar, which was struck from bullion deposited by Mint Director David Rittenhouse, is best described by the words from the New Hampshire *Gazette* of December 1794: "The *tout ensemble* has a pleasing effect to a connoisseur; but the touches of the graver are too delicate, and there is a want of boldness of execution which is necessary to durability and currency."[36] While the coin lacked artistry, there is a crude vitality, and its role in the creation of an American sense of identity cannot be denied. Still, this role was out of proportion to the coin's commercial success.

The silver dollar, like other early United States coins, was outnumbered by other coins, especially the ubiquitous golden *onzas* (Spanish coins, approximately one ounce

Silver Dollar, Flowing Hair type, 1795, obverse and reverse, diameter 39–40 mm (American Numismatic Association Money Museum).

of gold each) and silver pieces of eight of Spanish America. The silver pieces (the legendary *ocho reales*) of 423.7 grains each were struck at half a dozen mints in Spain, and in any of the two dozen or so mints in Spanish America. In what was to become the United States, they were commonly known as "Mexican Dollars." And there were many of them. The mint in Mexico City alone produced more than 20 million silver dollars annually. Although most of them were shipped to the Spanish main, large quantities entered the North American colonies. "Mexican Dollars" not only became the basis for the American dollar. They were so important—by 1830, approximately one in every four coins in circulation came from one of the Spanish colonial mints—that they remained legal tender in the United States until they were demonetized in 1857.[37]

The Spanish "pieces of eight" and *onzas* were not the only foreign coins circulating in America. There were also Brazilian *reis*, French *francs*, as well as Portuguese, Dutch, and English coins. A 1793 law demonetized a few, while it officially permitted the circulation of the gold coins of Great Britain, Portugal, France, Spain, and Spanish America, and the silver coins of France and Spain.[38] Allowing foreign coins to circulate was, simply, a stop-gap measure, to make up for the near-complete absence of precious metal in North America. Until the discovery of gold in California in 1848, the American $5 half eagle was the highest denomination of federal gold seen in circulation with any degree of frequency, but it was encountered not nearly as often as the Spanish doubloon or *ocho escudo* piece. To make matters worse, from the outset American gold coins were worth more than their stamped value. Although large quantities of $5 coins were minted and a smaller number of $2.50 quarter eagle gold coins were also struck, federal gold coins were not seen in general circulation after 1820. The overvalued coins kept disappearing from circulation into bank vaults or private coffers, or else were being exported and melted for a profit at their destination, which in most cases was London. The practice has become enshrined in the colloquialism about the American eagle taking wings and flying away.[39]

A flying eagle appeared on the new silver dollar of 1836. The dies for this coin were made by Christian Gobrecht, who had already made himself a name with banknote plates before he was hired by the United States Mint. The new coin was short-lived, though. Congressional representatives found the design too daring, or perhaps they were too painfully aware of the colloquialism attached to the flying eagle. Still, the coin is noteworthy because its flying eagle is the first bird on U.S. coinage that was derived from nature rather than from heraldry. The bird was designed by Titian Peale, of the gifted Peale family, who also created illustrations for John James Audobon. In contrast, Thomas Sully's seated Liberty on the coin's obverse was modeled after a figure from the Parthenon temple in Athens. Sully's design ushered in an era of neoclassicism in America's numismatic art, with designs that gave the coins both dignity and originality—as when a new three-dollar piece featured an Indian princess with her head crowned with a circle of feathers, the band of which was inscribed LIBERTY, or when in 1856 the flying eagle made a reappearance on the new cent, in James B. Longacre's design.[40]

The Civil War constituted an interruption in coin design, though the war's emotional climate brought forth an urge to acknowledge God on the currency, from DEO EST GLORIA to GOD OUR TRUST to, finally, IN GOD WE TRUST. In this form, the motto was first used on the two-cent piece in 1864, at the same time "most Gothic and most expressive of the Civil War." And, Cornelius Vermeule adds, if the designers had added flanking cannons to the shield, arrows, and wreath of the obverse, the coin would have been "the consummate expression of Civil War heraldry."[41] As the centennial of the republic approached, America's coinage more and more came under the spell of academic revivalism. William Barber's "Liberty Seated," for instance, looks as if it had been modeled after some Greco-Roman sculpture. George T. Morgan, another designer at the Mint, created the "defiant eagle" class of pattern coins, though his eagles, supposedly created in imitation of real life, actually seemed more heraldic than ever before. Small wonder that there was increasing public dissatisfaction with America's coins. The sentiment reached a peak in a long and vehement attack on the silver coinage in the June 1876 issue of *Galaxy* magazine, which demanded that portraits of the founders—Washington's or Franklin's—be incorporated on the regular coinage. If the die-pressed wooden medals and plaques that had been issued for the Centennial Exposition of 1876 were graced by such portraits, why should the nation's official currency not follow suit?[42]

Altogether, the coins created during and after the Civil War were always in step with the art of patriotic festivals—the centennial in 1876—and major expositions—the World's Columbian Exposition, held in Chicago in 1893 to commemorate the 400 years of modern America's existence. The year before, a half-dollar was struck to honor the quatercentenary. The coin is generally considered the first United States commemorative coin, though artistically it was "a great disappointment."[43] The official medal, in contrast, was a numismatic masterpiece. The creation of Augustus Saint-Gaudens, it is said to mark the beginning of a great artistic upheaval, though it did not become effective until the decade 1906 to 1916 when, under the auspices of Theodore Roosevelt, Saint-Gaudens together with his students gave the United States "one brilliant set of coins that from cent to $50 gold piece had no artistic peers on the face of the earth."[44]

The numismatic creations of Saint-Gaudens were exceptional, but more often than not, the art of U.S. coinage was sacrificed to economic and political pressures unrelated to efforts at creating a worthy monetary series. For years, the silver lobby and its opponents turned on or off the flow of coins, particularly silver dollars. The elimination of the gold standard meant that no gold coins were produced between 1933 and 1984. In 1971, the Kennedy half dollar, which from 1965 was the only *circulating* coin with any silver content, was removed and replaced with a copper-nickel alloy. (Silver dollars were last minted in 1935.) Low-value alloys do not strike well, yet modern commerce has been unappreciative of coinage in high-relief. Striking in high relief requires enormous force, usually generated by machinery invented before 1800. In contrast, die- and coin-making machines of today place a premium on shallow relief and "safe" designs.[45] Another complaint raised by Vermeule concerns the century-old law that mandates the appearance of an eagle on all reverses, which has all but "cramped the autonomy of our designers." Moreover, the law also limits changes in circulating coin designs to every 25 years (though the law is cast aside whenever a crisis such as a presidential assassination dictates). Another persistent obstacle to original design is the insistence on formulaic mottoes such as "Liberty," "E Pluribus Unum," and "in God We Trust."[46]

At least some opportunity for creativity was restored by the appearance, *inter alia*, of the Eisenhower dollar, the creation of Bicentennial coinage, the emergence of the

American Arts gold medallions, and "the startling and wholly unexpected rebirth of commemorative coinage."[47] On commemorative coinage, many persons, places, and events, all with an inherently American content, have received their due. An equally exciting trend has been the series of celebratory quarter dollars paying honor to each state in the order in which it entered the Union. Unlike earlier commemoratives, the State quarters, which were introduced in 1999, were released directly into circulation, inspiring discussion and collecting among a wide segment of the public. Yet as Gary Marks, a former chairman of CCAC, the Citizens Coinage Advisory Committee, argues, true reform requires a revamping of the overall design process, so that art becomes a higher priority than it currently is.[48]

The very existence of the CCAC or, for that matter, the Fine Arts Commission, shows how complex the process of making coins has become. When minting of U.S. coins began in 1794, the chief engraver of the U.S. Mint created the design he felt was the most appropriate. Today, a sketch must go through an approval process involving various committees before a design is approved for minting. Once a sketch is approved, it is transformed by a sculptor-engraver into a model twelve times larger than the actual coin. A negative is cast from this model, which is then "touched up." Legends and letterings are also added at this point. As a last step, a positive model (called a "galvano") is made from the negative, and this finished model is then approved for minting by the Mint director and the Secretary of the Treasury.[49] Yet no matter how simple or complex the process of achieving an "approved sketch" is in coinage design, the products always reveal certain codes. These codes extend to the choice of subject matter, ways of representation (from literal depiction to more abstract and arbitrary symbols and metaphors), point of view, composition, the rendering of details (from a figure's hair to the kind of lettering), use of borders, and so on—whatever affects the general appearance and, by extension, the generation of meaning.

The pictorial language of coins is never arbitrary or random. Termed "style" in numismatics, it usually follows historic contingency and, importantly, the context of production. In every era of American history, the "style" of coins has been influenced also by paintings, drawings, engravings, sculptures, monuments, or photographs.[50] The grand allegories of Benjamin West at one extreme and a photograph of a bear in a California zoo at the other end of the spectrum have worked their messages into design. In between are full-face portraits of actual, eminent Americans, which gradually replaced the ubiquitous renderings of Liberty. Among these eminent Americans have been George Washington, Abraham Lincoln, Thomas Jefferson, Franklin Delano Roosevelt, Benjamin Franklin, and John Fitzgerald Kennedy. Occasionally females were represented, such as Susan B. Anthony and later Sacagawea, both of whom came to grace a one-dollar coin.[51]

The resurgence of full-face portraits on United States coinage reflects the tendency, in numismatic art, towards anthropocentrism. But space is limited on coins (much more so than on bank notes), which necessitates the suggestive synecdochal simplification inherent to all visual media, leaving out elements that are not essential for an understanding. Thus, we often see types rather than individuals, their complexities reduced to features that are quick and easy to grasp and understand, if not outright stereotypes. So why use human figures at all? Would not abstract symbols be just as good?

Human figures (and, of course, heads) are privileged means of representing and legitimizing fundamental norms and values. On America's coins and currency, the image of the metaphorical father is one of the most important elements in the manufacturing of consent. George Washington's hallowed face (or else, his full body) strengthens and reinforces social cohesion so that the currency becomes a bond of union—like a common language. Washington's image thus is both a personal quality mark that promises value and an artistic representation of the giver of the promise, the one who helps maintain trust in the currency.

Political emblems and, on bank notes, signatures (until the arrival of federal paper money, they were usually those of the cashier and bank president) also serve to uphold trust. In the past were added so-called obligations, which sound familiar even today—such as "The Central Bank of Tennessee will pay ONE DOLLAR to the bearer on demand." The wording suggests that bank notes were not considered as real money but only as surrogate money, a substitute for cash that stands for a certain sum in coin. During the age of hard money (for most of human history, that is), only coins were considered a means of payment, cash.[52] Thus, the holder of a bank note had a right to have the note exchanged for specie, usually gold or silver coins, by the note-issuing bank. Now that money has become purely symbolic or token money, the strength of a currency no longer rests on money's material value but on the trust and confidence that people have in it. Money that must be accepted solely upon trust is called "fiduciary" money. The term comes from the Latin word *fidere*, to trust or to have faith in, though some commentators have said that such money is acceptable as money simply because the government or a central bank says that it has value (hence the related term "fiat" money).

America's federal currency from the Reconstruction period onwards has been a "legal tender for all debts public and private." Public Law 89–91 (Act of July 23, 1965) extends this definition to read: "All coins and currencies of the United States (including Federal Reserve Notes and circulating notes of Federal Reserve banks and national banking associations), regardless of when coined or issued, shall be legal tender for all debts, public and private, public charges, taxes, duties, and dues." This means that U.S. paper dollars and coins are good not only for their exchange value in the circulation of commodities but, first and foremost, for the paying back of two kinds of debts. The former debt is incurred in commercial transactions, the latter in transactions between the government and the citizens, that is, in transactions involving taxes and interest incurred on government bonds.[53]

Legal tender clauses are not particularly enlightening. David Standish's summary thus is apt: People are expected "merely to use [coins and currency], not ask questions, and keep the faith."[54] The phrase "keep the faith" refers to the precarious value of a paper money that depends entirely on the government's will and can be annulled by the very law that created it. The loss of legal value then is the loss of all value, since the paper notes are not convertible. Since the law guarantees value only as "empty value," government agencies can only decree a "forced currency," whose face value is only a "fiction of value."[55] Credibility cannot therefore be understood on a rational level alone. It is a fiction that, in the absence of alternatives, we habitually believe in, even must believe in, much as in religious life we must believe in God. In a monetary economy, therefore, trust in God is transferred onto coins and currency. God is, of course, represented merely as a verbal image, whereas his representative on earth, the secular Lord, comes to us through visual images. The symbolic arrangement, of which the current one-dollar bill is the premier example, at one and the same time highlights the theological character of the monetary system and points to the accession of the father to the rank of privileged subject, the "general equivalent of subjects." Both the reference to God and the portrait of the Father of His Country, at once singular and reflecting God's face, confer value to money—the common equivalent that makes possible the exchange of goods—by maintaining the illusion of money, that is, the belief that money belongs to the members of a community, that it is *their* money and that they can have trust in it.[56]

This contract usually works, though at times people's trust seems in need of some more active support. Whenever there is a crisis, therefore, confidence in the currency is ensured by what in modern parlance is called a marketing offensive. One such crisis occurred during the revolutionary period and the early republic, when George Washington was cast as a figure of stability, a moral leader, a bulwark against fragile and quarrelsome states as well as against rebellious locals, economic depression and hyperinflation, and a guarantee against a reversion to monarchy; another crisis came in the years before and during the Civil War, when George Washington was seen at the same time as the guarantor of national unity (in the North) and the leader of the first American revolution, now to be followed by a second one (in the South); then in the late nineteenth century, when the specter of mass immigration led authorities to use Washington's likeness on the currency to bring "doubtful members" of the community into the national fold; during the nativist climate of the post–World War I era, when the prevailing sense of white supremacy was reinforced and male fears assuaged by "the more permanent familiarity" of presidential portraits on the currency; and in the present crisis, when a country divided along the rift lines of class, ethnicity, age, and gender, and stymied by congressional gridlock and a perpetual adolescent in the White House is seeing an increased investment in patriotic symbols also on the currency, at the same time as the actual use of currency is increasingly confined to the "cash ghetto." During each of these crises George Washington served as a symbol of national consensus, continuity, and stability to which citizens are called upon to defer. Nor is this constellation a matter of coins and currency alone. During all these times demand for pictures of Washington generally peaked, together with the demand for moral inspiration emanating from them.[57] Altogether, therefore, the hallowed face of the Father of His Country provides and always has provided at least a semblance of stability in periods of domestic turmoil, and of continuity and comfort in times of international crisis and decline.

2

The Mark of the Prince

As a mere slip of paper, the current one-dollar bill has very little material value. What makes it valuable is, for one thing, its denomination, one dollar. But value also accrues from its distinguishing feature, the hallowed face of the Father of His Country. As Michel Foucault argued, money "does not draw its value from the material of which it is composed, but rather from its form." The form, that is "the mark or image of the prince." Foucault quotes here from Scipion de Gramont's treatise on the *Denier royal* (1620), though he might as well have drawn on Thomas Hobbes' *Leviathan* (1651): "Mony (of what matter soever coyned by the Soveraign of a Common-wealth,) is a sufficient measure of all things else, between the Subjects of that Common-wealth." And further, "Coyne [...] is not considerable for the Matter, but for the Stamp of the place." Thus, any object can be used as money, as long as it possesses certain "peculiar properties of representation."[1]

The "money form" (de Gramont's "mark or image of the prince" as well as Hobbes' "Stamp of the place") serves to make acceptable as money both coins and paper bills. Coin and paper are nevertheless different as means of storing and transferring value. The difference accrues from their dominance in their own historic phase of economic development. As Sergio Rizzo explains, "precious metals are to mercantile capitalism what paper is to industrial capitalism and what plastic and electronics are to post-industrial capitalism."[2] The situation is different in America, however, where bank notes have been omnipresent in everyday life from early on. This is not to assert any innate quality—neither in the material itself nor by way of ascribing certain character traits to all Americans—so much as it is to acknowledge that in America paper money has been bound up with questions of sovereignty to a degree unmatched by coins.

The beginnings of paper money's ubiquity must be sought in historic contingency. Although from the start of European settlement in North America metal was the undisputed basis for most of the colonies' money, not enough coins of any kind were available ever, and there was an almost complete absence of precious metals in what is now the United States of America—gold was not discovered in any usable quantity until 1848 and silver even later.[3] These facts left the colonists little choice. Like it or not, they had to make do with paper money, which developed early and increased rapidly. Massachusetts led the way in 1691, and by 1750, every single one of the thirteen colonies was using paper money. On the eve of the Revolution, "the money supply in America consisted of one-fourth specie and three-fourths paper money."[4]

Paper money undoubtedly gave the United States the "capital elasticity" it required for its development as a nation. Paper money financed its revolution, making it the first nation in world history to do so, it financed westward expansion, the North's victory in the Civil War, and it unleashed the productive capacities for an industrial revolution that soon eclipsed its European rivals.[5] But paper money was problematic from its inception. The uncertain relation between a bill's denominational value and its material value caused a great deal of anxiety and, often, resistance.[6] Additionally, from about 1727 the British government kept suppressing the circulation of paper money. Many acts, declarations, and bills touching on money reached the colonies, furnishing "the first distinctive provocation to the American Revolution."[7] Even as cautious a person as George Washington predicted, in 1766, that the ban on colonial money might "set the whole country in flames."[8] These were prophetic words indeed. For the patriots, paper bills became the preferred vehicle of political propaganda. The images on them both reflected and reinforced the ideals about and identities relating to political sovereignty that were then prevalent. Notes issued by the provincial assemblies respectively of Maryland and Virginia became veritable calling cards of revolutionary thought, contributing to the consolidation of a genuinely "American," that is, republican identity. A delegate to the Continental Congress even claimed that a paper currency backed by all the colonies together would form "a new bond of union to the associated colonies."[9] The use of paper bills as vehicles for discrete moral and political lessons that would eventually form "a new bond of union" testifies to the need, in complex societies, for common values and beliefs, together with their ability to produce them. For the "associated colonies" the manufacturing of consent was a matter of life and death.

At the dawn of the American republic, national identity was not a given. The Revolution created a break with the past. New identities had to be forged. Attempts were made at the creation of a distinctly American position in a wide range of areas. The shaping of people into American citizens involved experiments in fine arts, architecture, literature, science and philosophy, coins and currency, and linguistics. "Every engine should be employed to render the people of the country national," wrote Noah Webster shortly after the Revolution, "to call their attachment home to their country; and to inspire them with the pride of national character." Some of the experiments are better known than others and their legacy continue. Webster himself published an *American Spelling Book* in 1783 and established distinctly American forms of spelling (such as using an "s" instead of a "c," as in defense, dropping the "u" from "harbour" or "labour," and reversing the "re" in "theatre" and "centre") and introduced such words as "tomahawk" and "prairies," words not used by English lexicographers.[10]

The new paper currency that was to "render the people of the country national," to use Noah Webster's words, became known as "Continental Currency." The designs came from Benjamin Franklin, who began by rejecting British numismatic conventions, which, by representing the nation in the person of the king, the royal coat of arms, and a female allegory, Britannia, only perpetuated "the dull story that everybody knows, and what it would have been no Loss to mankind if nobody had ever known." Far more useful, Franklin wrote, would be to include on the currency "Some important proverb [...] some pious moral, prudential or œconomical Precept, the frequent inculcation of which by seeing it every time one receives a Piece of Money, might make an Impression upon the Mind especially of young Persons, and tend to regulate the

Conduct."[11] For motifs, Franklin turned to books in his own library—Joachim Camerarius' *Symbolorum ac Emblematum Ethico-Politicorum*, Diego Saavedra's *Idea principis Christiano-Politici Symbolis*, Weigels' *Emblematum Repositorium*. From these venerable tomes, Franklin selected several emblems that visually expressed discrete moral and political lessons.[12]

George Washington passed away on December 14, 1799. In the Senate, Samuel Dexter promptly called upon Americans to "consecrate the memory of the heroic General, the patriotic Statesman and the virtuous Sage; let them teach these children never to forget that the fruit of his labors and his example are their inheritance."[13] Yet how do people commemorate? How can commemoration become a stimulus to moral behavior? And should it? As word of Washington's death spread from Mount Vernon, selectmen or councilmen ordered bells to be tolled and guns to be fired, requested churches to drape their pulpits and altars in black cloth, and called town meetings to draw up plans for appropriate funeral ceremonies. Eventually, funeral rites and commemorative observances were held in various forms all over the nation, so that the Father of His Country almost literally had "a tomb on every hill and in every valley of his bewailing country."[14] Funeral processions were attended by thousands of people, some 6,000 in Boston alone, with more at the state funeral held in Washington City on December 26, 1799.

Popular feelings were also articulated through all kinds of pictures, from mourning pictures to true apotheoses, as well as through verse, odes, hymns, sonnets, even prose poems, some brief, some running over hundreds of lines. At least one of these works was written in German, by a Pennsylvania farmer named Christian Jacob Hütter, in whose *Washingtons Ankunft in Elisium* the departed hero strolls around heaven chatting with Brutus, Columbus, Franklin, and William Penn. Another oddity was a fictitious "Lady Washington's Lamentation for the Death of her Husband." All of these products were not only circulated in a variety of print media—pamphlets, broadsides, and periodicals—but also spoken or sung at civic procession, religious services, and commercial theatricals all across the nation.[15] Fellow feeling was fueled by words and expressions like "general grief," "general sorrow," "the People's grief," or "the country's woe," as well as from generalized titles like "Columbia's Distress" or "America in Mourning."

Such figures were common to the poetry of public mourning, which, for the most part, showed all the characteristics of neoclassical poetry—extravagance of figure and gesture, authorial anonymity, and depersonalized sentiments as the condition of establishing grief as a national affect. Neoclassicist conventions already shaped the elegies American colonists had written a generation earlier for King George II.[16] But grief in a republic ought to be different. Americans "seemed to realize intuitively that there could be no liberty without union," Barry Schwartz explains, "and when they expressed praise of Washington, the benefits of union were often affirmed in their next breath." "When WASHINGTON lived," one of his mourning countrymen recalled, "we had one common mind—one common head—one common heart—we were united—we were safe."[17]

In death, the nation once again rallied around Washington. Putting aside party and other animosities, Federalists and Democratic-Republicans, northerners and southerners, men and women mourned the passing of their first president. Veneration of the nation's hero brought unity to a diversified society. No longer reviled as the first Federalist, Washington assumed his place as the Father of His Country.[18] Congressional representatives too united in a synchronized corps when they were debating about a proper memorial for the deceased president. Tellingly in this debate, which took place in December 1800, Representative Clairborne stated his preference for "a statue to mausoleum, because the former, from representing the form and features [of George Washington] would inspire the beholder with more lively emotions than a mass of stones formed into a pyramid."[19]

As an additional tribute to the Father of His Country, the proposed statue might have been paid for by dollar notes from the Washington Bank of Westerly, Rhode Island, which had received a State charter only a few months after Washington's death. The bank, which at the time served a community with expanding agricultural, fishing, and shipbuilding activities, still exists today, known as Washington Trust. In 1800, the bank's officers commissioned Amos Doolittle of New Haven, Connecticut, to engrave bank note plates with a vignette of George Washington on each denomination note. Doolittle, who left his name as a vertical imprint on the note's left edge, was an excellent line engraver but he had no talent for vignettes. Not only is Washington's profile bust crowned with a laurel wreath tiny in size. As he also was unable to duplicate repeatedly, each note on the copper plates renders Washington's image slightly differently.

The bills from Westerly's Washington Bank, which opened for business on August 22, 1800, were the very first official paper notes bearing an image of Washington.[20] Others soon followed, as images of the Father of His Country were found to affirm the credibility of banks by aligning with patriotic feelings and deep historicity. When the Washington Bank opened for business, it also issued notes that still reflect the influence of Britain's monetary system, notes that were, for instance, good for 11 cents or 8 pence.[21] But it was the dollar notes that mark how the commodification of Washington's memory coopted sympathy's nationalizing power.

To modern eyes, the notes from the Washington Bank do not even remotely look

A $1 note, Washington Bank, Westerly, Rhode Island, 1800 (Division of Work and Industry, National Museum of American History, Smithsonian Institution).

like classic bank notes, though strictly speaking, this is irrelevant. Any object can be used as money, as long as it possesses certain "peculiar properties of representation," not the least of which is the "mark or image of the prince."[22] Thus, Washington's down-home portrait on the notes from the bank in Westerly was not inappropriate. And Americans had become accustomed to seeing Washington's image on all kinds of cheap merchandise with which British manufacturers flooded the marketplace in the wake of his death—commemorative dishes, pitchers, linens, and prints, advertised as suitable "to enrich the labours of the needle upon white satin [...] an agreeable pastime for the ladies."[23] Washington himself might have been amused about all this attention, though he would have been much less tolerant about the bank notes. Washington throughout his life had resisted the idea of having his name or image on official documents, including on coins or bank notes. For this committed republican, such practices were simply "monarchical."

When on April 30, 1789, New York chancellor Robert R. Livingstone administered the oath of office to Washington, he followed it up by intoning "Long live George Washington, President of the United States." The spectators under the balcony of Federal Hall responded with huzzas and chants of "God bless our Washington! Long live our beloved President!" This may sound odd, but they celebrated in the only way they knew, as if welcoming a new monarch with the customary cry of "Long Live the King!"[24] Washington was visibly moved by the ceremony, though in his inaugural address, delivered in the Senate chamber, he gave expression to altogether different convictions: "[T]he preservation of the sacred fire of liberty, and the destiny of the Republican model of Government, are justly considered as *deeply*, perhaps as *finally* staked, on the experiment entrusted to the hands of the American people."[25] Less visibly, Washington also had refused coat buttons engraved with his portrait or his name. Instead, he chose metal buttons that had the heraldic eagle of the republic chased upon them.[26] Other buttons and memorabilia came with simple inscriptions such as "Long Live the President," "Memorable Era," or "Remember March Fourth, 1789." Of course, medals with Washington's portrait did circulate, though they were privately produced, as were, later, cent trials struck by a Robert Birch, which carried a brief reverse legend, "G*W Pt" (for "George Washington President"), the final gasp of the movement to honor the nation's first chief executive on its coinage.[27]

Alexander Hamilton, revolutionary hero and longtime companion of George Washington, might not have objected to using the president's portrait on the currency. Like most Americans, he would have felt obliged to render gratitude to Washington for his services. Yet Americans also felt that the show of gratitude should not be too elaborate, and not take inappropriate forms. These conflicting duties required a delicate balancing act. As Hamilton wrote in May 1792, "The devices of the coins are far from being a matter of indifference, as they may be made the *vehicles of useful impressions*." This being so, the then Secretary of the Treasury who also oversaw establishing the first Mint, continued, with due diplomatic restraint, "They ought [...] to be emblematical, but without losing sight of simplicity."[28]

Congress, in contrast, was deeply divided over the designs of the new coins. The Senate had approved of a draft version of the Mint Act that stipulated that all coins bear a portrait of the current president. This, the proponents of the Act said, would mean little more than to honor General Washington, President Washington, and the man Washington. The house of Representatives, however, rejected the draft after a long and thorough debate, not because it applied to Washington but because it might create a precedent for future presidents. Representative John Page from Virginia, for instance, told his colleagues in the House that the American people needed no added ways to honor Washington. "They have his busts, his pictures everywhere." To put Washington's likeness on the coinage "would be viewed by the world as a stamp of Royalty on our coins." Convinced that all impressions or images of presidents would only imitate "the flattery and almost idolatrous practice of Monarchies with respect to the honor paid to their Kings," Representative Page's conclusion was, "I am certain that it will be more agreeable to the citizens of the United States, to see the head of Liberty on their coin, than the heads of Presidents."[29]

Representative Page also opposed impressions of an eagle on the coinage because the "King of Birds" was too regal for the coinage of a nation emerging from colonies that had cast aside their king and his royal governors. The Representative's honest republican convictions did not go down well with other members of the House. An episode published in *The American Apollo* in 1792 accounts for the ridicule the representative's proposal met:

> In the late debate in Congress on the Mint Bill, the motion for striking the President's head upon the coin was warmly opposed by a certain gentleman, in a very lengthy speech, as favoring monarchical principles. A gentleman from this State [of Massachusetts] rose, and said, he perceived the same objection might be made to the Eagle on the reverse of the coin, and he thought it would be best to substitute a more harmless and less monarchical bird, and begged leave to recommend a GOOSE.[30]

Underlying the mirth and hilariousness of this comment are more serious questions: How should a republican form of government be represented? And, can it be represented? There were models, certainly, mostly in the form of female allegories. But even these models often came with monarchical insignia—scepter and sword, a throne with lions on the side, etc. Moreover, none of these figures could be called iconic, that is, was recognizably republican at first sight. At best, they suggested classical antiquity, such as triumphant Victoria, dignified Justitia, Caritas in her motherly care, or Libertas in all her pathos.[31] Libertas had been emblematic already at the beginning of the Roman republic. On coins from the third century BCE she is depicted with the *pileus*, the liberty cap, and a staff that is reminiscent of a scepter, even though Libertas was to represent the rights of free citizens.[32]

America's founders were aware of the many ambiguities surrounding allegorical figures of classical antiquity and they were wise enough to desist from personalizing their republic too flagrantly. Still, everyone knew that numerous Washington-head coins and medals were already in circulation, just as no one had complained when in 1783 Congress had commissioned an equestrian statue of Washington. But to stamp Washington's head on coins that were issued by the very institution that he presided over was a different matter. By refusing to let this happen, Congress made sure that veneration of the person was separated from the prestige and authority of the office of President. At the end of the day the lawmakers agreed on two visual symbols—an allegorical representation of liberty and an eagle.

Selecting an eagle for the nation's iconography indeed was somewhat outlandish, as the noble bird was customarily associated with military and imperial might rather than with the ideals of independence and republicanism. To establish that fit, the eagle was said to be "the symbol of supreme power and authority and signifies the Congress."[33] Liberty and the eagle thus epitomized what had been obtained so dearly—political sovereignty, based on a free people and embodied in a glorified individual.

That individual was, of course, George Washington. Glorified he may have been, yet he was not to be represented on circulating coins until 1932, when his head was stamped on the new quarter, to celebrate the two-hundredth anniversary of his birth.[34] The bald eagle, in contrast, had first appeared as an American symbol on a Massachusetts copper cent coined in 1776. In 1782, it was placed with outspread wings on the new nation's seal. It was first used on a document of September 16, 1782, issued from Nassau Hall, Princeton, which was then the nation's capital. Since then it has appeared on the reverse of many United States coins, most notably the silver dollar, half-dollar and quarter, as well as the gold coins appropriately named eagle, half eagle, quarter eagle, and double eagle.[35] The design of the heraldic or emblematic eagle shows many parallels to Augustin Dupré's medal commemorating the American Declaration of Independence.

Dupré's medal, which was commissioned by Thomas Jefferson and struck in Paris in 1790 to 1792, has become known as the "Diplomatic medal," since it was to be presented to foreign statesmen who had aided the American colonies in their struggle for independence. The medal is of considerable numismatic importance for its contribution to the vocabulary of America's coinage. This goes way beyond the eagle motif on the reverse. The obverse features a figure of Mercury, the god of commerce, and, importantly, a seated "Indian Queen," personifying America, in grass skirt and with feathered headgear, holding a horn containing fruits and grains. The "Indian Queen," Cornelius Vermeule found, is that "curious mixture of noble savage and seated Artemis which the French Rococo could concoct out of a nymph by François Boucher (1703–1770) and a vague understanding of what went on among the native inhabitants of the New World." Its importance for America's numismatic iconography began in 1854, when James B. Longacre adopted the "Indian Queen's" headdress for his head of Liberty on the gold dollar and the gold $3 coin, both better known as "Indian Princess Head" dollars; to these, Longacre's "Indian Head" cent was added in 1859.[36]

Over time, Liberty also came in other guises on the currency. On the $50 Legal Tender Note of the 1874 and later series, she is dressed as Columbia. On still other notes, she is shown wearing a feathered headdress, thus with the Native American attributes she had had before Independence. Often, she appears together with the American eagle, wings spread. Altogether, these allegorical representations reveal both the historic (ab-) uses of the woman's body to image an American national identity and the symbolic appropriation for the national symbolic of an indigenous population that in reality was colonized. It is not that these meanings were in any way planned. On the contrary, they came into view only much later, with the emergence of gender-based scholarship.[37] If anything was planned from early on, it was the function of the nation's currency as a vehicle of political messages. These messages, Representative Williamson was happy to see, were "consistent with Republican principles." Indeed, the choice of symbols and mottoes established a clear dividing line between the new national identity based on the Constitution and the old system based on monarchical-aristocratic traditions. The daily usage of the new coins helped disseminate patriotic messages proclaiming the ideals of the fledgling nation. The coins thus became material signs documenting the close links between the world of finance, economic stability, and political sovereignty.[38]

George Washington seems to have seen these links as well. "[A] Coinage of Gold, Silver, & Copper," he wrote to William Grayson on August 22, 1785, "is become indispensably necessary...."[39] As America's first president, Washington explicitly referred to the beginning of the national coinage in his fourth annual address, November 6, 1792. The first coins produced at the United States Mint probably were struck in December 1792. On December 18, 1792, Thomas Jefferson wrote to Washington that he had "the honor to send the President 2 cents made on Voigt's plan, by putting a silver plug worth ¾ of a cent into a copper worth ¼ of a cent."[40] Three months later, the first coins, altogether 11,178 cents, were delivered to the Treasurer. On October 15, 1794, the first silver coins were sent by the chief coiner. The shipment consisted of 1,758 silver dollars. George Washington took notice, writing to Congress on November 19, 1794: "The Mint of the United States has entered upon the coinage of the precious metals.... There is a pleasing prospect that the institution will, at no remote day, realize the expectation which was originally formed of its utility." Further realization of the Mint's utility came on December 1, 1794, with a shipment of 5,300 half dollars, on July 31, 1795, with a shipment of 744 half eagles, and on September 22, 1795, with a shipment of 400 eagles.[41]

Washington's letter to Congress was prompted, not by the gold coins, but by his receiving one of the first silver dollars struck by the Mint. In October 1794, Mint Director David Rittenhouse presented to Secretary of State Edmund Randolph one of these dollars, which was to be given to President Washington. A letter Randolph wrote to Washington on October 16, 1794, confirms this. The letter included the following line: "The silver coin of the U.S. bears upon its face so much neatness and simplicity, that I cannot restrain myself from transmitting a dollar for your inspection."[42] Washington was not in Philadelphia on October 16. He was at Fort Cumberland, Maryland, commandeering some 13,000 militiamen in an attempt to suppress the "Whiskey Rebellion," and did not return to what was then the nation's capital until October 28, 1794. It is uncertain when he received Randolph's letter and the silver dollar, then the largest silver denomination and a crown-size coin of the nation. What is certain is that the coin was passed along to George Washington to demonstrate the mint's success in striking the nation's first silver coinage.

More than a hundred years later, John Ward Dunsmore imagined the demonstration of the mint's success as a ceremonial act of state. Dunsmore's painting is typical of the Colonial Revival period of the late nineteenth and early twentieth centuries.[43] Its protagonists—Dunsmore as well as his contemporaries Henry A. Ogden, Jean Leon Gerome Ferris, and Howard Pyle, together with a later generation around Walter Haskell Hinton and John Henry Hintermeister—considered themselves as guardians of historical culture. All of them were intrigued by the Father of His Country and devoted significant portions of their careers to portraying public and private events from his life, producing, between them, more than three hundred pictures. Some of these were sold to private collectors, but for the most part they were used as illustrations in books and magazines such as *Harper's*, as jigsaw puzzles, as artwork for advertising, and as material for the art-calendar industry, begun to flourish with the invention of the three-

John Ward Dunsmore, *Washington inspecting the first money coined by the United States*, c. 1915 (Library of Congress, Prints and Photographs Division).

color printing process. Two works by Hintermeister, for instance, *Founding the First National Bank* (1923) and *Signing of the Constitution* (1925), were used on calendars produced by the Osborne Company.[44] Hintermeister's use, for *Signing of the Constitution*, of a painting from the Fraunces Tavern Museum collection was typical. All of these painters made a living from the romantic appeal of colonial America and thus drew heavily upon both previous artworks and published biographies. And all their works oozed orderliness, inoffensiveness, and Anglophilia, anything but revolutionary fervor.

As regards the original revolutionaries, they saw themselves as defending the same liberties that their own fathers had struggled for. It was the Revolution that enabled them to become fathers themselves, the fathers of all Americans.[45] In this capacity, they were called upon to secure and protect the rights of citizens—primarily, the rights to "Life, Liberty and the pursuit of Happiness." The Declaration of Independence spelled out governmental responsibilities in the following way: "That to secure these rights, Governments are instituted among Men, deriving their just powers from the consent of the governed." But that was not all. The piece of secular scripture also stipulated that it was "the Right of the People to alter or to abolish" the government whenever it "becomes destructive of these ends [...] and to institute new Government, laying its foundation on such principles and organizing its powers in such form, as to them shall seem most likely to effect their Safety and Happiness."[46]

America's new coinage was to be as impressive as the new nation and the new government. It was at once to provide democracy with instruments of visual beauty and to allow the fledgling nation to meet the world's leading powers, England and France, on an equal footing. Additionally, gold and silver coins—"real" money—were to disabuse citizens from the inflationary "Continental Dollars." The "Continentals" were paper bills emitted by the Continental Congress from 1775; originally redeemable in Spanish silver dollars at a ratio of 1:1, they—like the paper bills emitted by the several colonies—were to help finance the War of Independence. The bills' rhetorical function was unequivocal, to generate and maintain loyalty and allegiance to the Revolution. At first the bills were imprinted "The United Colonies," from May 1777 onwards they bore the imprint "The United States." The power of conviction emanating from the visual design must have been overwhelming, otherwise people would not have put up with the bills' depreciation, which by 1785 had reached a ratio of 75:1.[47]

The downfall of the Continentals affected the vast majority of the people. There were ruinous losses, for rich and poor alike, as debts contracted for good money were paid off with almost valueless currency. Speculators of course profited by the situation. In patriot-controlled territories, prominent political leaders were sometimes suspected of profiteering and of fraudulent dealings in handling the monies or supplies. Sometimes riots resulted, as in Philadelphia in 1779, while the second Continental Congress was in session. A year later, George Washington wrote to Congress that, contrary to his wishes, Continentals were to be made "uncurrent" in army camps, leaving him to petition the legislature to "offer liberal encouragement for loans of gold and silver, to pay their quote of men for military service."[48] British loyalists were only too happy to undermine faith in the Continentals. After their legal tender status had been stopped, an article in *Rivington's Gazette* on May 12, 1781, gleefully noted:

> The Congress is finally bankrupt! Last Saturday a large body of the inhabitants with paper dollars in their hats by way of cockades, paraded the streets of Philadelphia ... with a DOG TARRED, and instead of the usual appendage and ornament of feathers, his back was covered with Congress' paper dollars. This example of disaffection ... was directly followed by the jailer, who refused accepting the bills in purchase of a glass of rum, and afterwards by the traders of the city, who shut up their shops, declining to sell any more goods but for gold and silver.[49]

Continental issues were stopped in the fall and winter of 1779, when the bills hit bottom. Then, a pound of coffee in Philadelphia cost 97.5 pence, up from 15.5 pence in 1770.[50] After 1779, the several states began to print paper money of their own, also in large amounts and also depreciating rapidly, sometimes more badly than the Continentals did. Some states even manipulated exchange rates to encourage specie inflows from other states. Small wonder that versifiers acclaimed George Washington as the only one capable of stemming the threat of anarchy:

> At his approach vile Faction stands aghast,
> And civil Discord breathes, in pangs, her last;
> Paper emissions, too, at his command,
> With legal tenders, fly this happy land.[51]

Washington himself was more than a little skeptical about the usefulness of paper money. He had experienced the wartime financial crisis, when farmers refused to sell supplies to the Continental Army, and personally had lost "very considerably" because of continental paper. In a letter to Thomas Jefferson he expressed strong feelings about the diverse states "falling into very foolish & wicked plans of emitting paper money."

Such a currency, he wrote in 1787, only led to "ruin" rather than facilitate commerce, it would "oppress the honest, and open a door to every species of fraud and injustice."[52] Two years later, the Constitution of the United States was adopted, the balance of authority shifted from the states to the national government, and state bills were finally prohibited.[53]

3

Constitutional Prohibitions and the Era of Private Banking

Under the Constitution, the states could make "silver and gold a legal tender in the payments of debts," but only the national government would have the authority to "coin Money, regulate the Value thereof, and of foreign Coin" (Art. I, Sec. 8, §5). The Constitution's wording clearly reflects the framers' idea of making the United States a hard-money country, that is, a country whose currency consisted mainly of gold and silver. Even Thomas Jefferson and the Republicans, though accused by the Federalists of speaking "all French," thought that the money of a free republic should be gold and silver. For Jefferson, only land and precious metal constituted "real" property. As for paper money, to most of the delegates it implied a promise that might be broken. While there was initially a clause in the Constitution that permitted the federal government to issue paper money, it was quickly eliminated. As a delegate from Delaware said, granting the government the right to issue paper money would be "as alarming as the mark of the Beast in Revelations." It would be better, another delegate urged, to "reject the whole plan than retain the three words 'and emit bills.'"[1]

Overall, records of the Constitutional Convention rather bear testimony to thoroughly pragmatic reasons, in particular to the delegates' fears that if the government held power to issue paper money, it simply could not be trusted to avoid inflation. When the delegates had finally thrashed out their Constitution, the document implicitly denied the federal government the right to issue paper money, at the same time as it explicitly denied the individual states the same prerogative. Art. I, sec. 10, § 1 of the U.S. Constitution says, "No State shall [...] make any Thing but gold and silver Coin a Tender in Payment of Debts." Therefore, the question is, if the States cannot issue paper money, this must mean that the federal government can. This is not the case, as the Tenth Amendment—which James Madison had drafted, along with the rest of the Bill of Rights—says, "The powers not delegated to the United States by the Constitution, nor prohibited by it to the States, are reserved to the States respectively, or to the people." This means that the Constitution does not "delegate" the power to "make any Thing but gold and silver Coin a Tender in Payment of Debts" to the federal government. Therefore, government at *no level* has the power to make anything but gold and silver coin tender in payment of debts. Effective of 1789, therefore, neither the states nor the federal government were authorized to issue paper money.[2]

In practice, ways were found to circumvent both the constitutional prohibition of paper money and the ban on making graven images. Let's begin with the graven images.

Bronze Medal of George Washington ("Manly Medal"), 1790, diameter 48 mm (Yale University Art Gallery).

Originally, God's commandment to Moses, "Thou shalt not make thee a graven image" (Deut. 5:8), had two distinct functions: One was to separate the two realms of the divine and the human; the other was to prevent the idolatrous worship of a representation. In that sense, both Washington's rejection of the English numismatic tradition, which made use of the ruler's image as a matter of course, and his penchant for a republican ethos were politically correct. Political correctness did not, however, dispel the quasi-monarchical veneration and idolatrous worship of his person. Already during his lifetime, Washington's numismatic presence was only too obvious. At least eleven medals (sixteen by another counting mode) show representations of him as commander in chief, including one offered to the public by James Manly of Philadelphia early in 1790.[3]

The "Washington Manly" medal was offered in tin ("white metal"), bronze, silver, and gold, the latter selling according to weight. It has the distinction of being the first commemorative medal struck in the United States. A notice in New York's *Gazette of the United States*, soliciting subscribers to the "Manly," praised medals in general as "the best method of transmitting to posterity the memory of the heroes and patriots of the age, and one of the most honorary compliments a grateful people could confer on their favourites"—in this instance, of George Washington, whose likeness had been taken by Joseph Wright.[4] Another famous medal was the "Washington Before Boston" piece, which had been commissioned for the "Comitia Americana" series as early as 1776 in recognition of Washington's victory over the British General Howe, but was not released until about 1790. The medal's obverse shows a profile bust of George Washington; its reverse features the General, three officers on horseback, and the city of Boston in the background. Most likely the medal (#47 in Baker's nomenclatura and commonly seen as the Holy Grail of Washingtoniana) was struck in Paris the year before, as Congress had subcontracted the production to France because the United States then had no minting facility and private manufacturers lacked the capability to strike quality pieces.[5]

As for the first Washington coin struck during the Confederation period, the prize goes to the "Georgius Triumpho" tokens from 1783. Struck in copper, the tokens were produced through the 1820s. The "Georgius Triumpho"[6] is also the most famous token by far, because the head shown on its obverse bears a strong resemblance to that on some coins of George III. Among numismatists, no one seems certain exactly who is depicted on the token. Its reverse motif seems to be purely American. It shows the goddess of Liberty behind a framework of thirteen bars, which nicely represents the thirteen colonies. On the corners of the framework are fleurs-de-lis, the national emblem of France, and thus a credit to the country for helping the patriots win the Revolutionary War. Liberty is holding an olive branch and a liberty pole, and she is partly encircled by the motto "VOCE POPULI." The legend, which translates as "By the Voice of the People," likewise seems to be American, as in England "the people" then had no voice that meant anything.[7] The date 1783 also seems clear enough. It was the date of the Treaty of Paris, which officially ended the Revolutionary War. It is safe to say, therefore, that the coin depicts America's triumph over George III.

The question whose head is depicted on the obverse—George Washington's or the English King's—is a matter of debate. It is known that the portrait was copied from a British-Irish halfpenny of 1781. These pennies probably were made in Birmingham, England, for export to America, as many tokens were. In an 1857 publication of the American Antiquarian Society the Georgius Triumpho copper still is referred to by the name "Tory copper." Two years later, the *American Numismatical Manual* cites it as the "Tory penny." The manual's author, Montroville W. Dickeson, also mentions that the coin's origin, England, had prejudiced many patriotic Americans against this "harmless copper." As Dr. Dickeson concludes, "either carelessness, ignorance, or the want of something more appropriate has given us a facsimile of the head of George III, as represented upon British coins." Yet there is no clear identification, on the coin, with "the then living original," as there are no numerals following the "Georgius." Thus, the portrait is

Georgius Triumpho Copper, 1783, obverse and reverse, diameter 28.5 mm (reproduced from the original held by the Department of Special Collections of the Hesburgh Libraries of Notre Dame).

as applicable to George Washington as to any other George. The "Georgius Triumpho" copper, Q. David Bowers concludes, is "a thoroughly American coin depicting George Washington, but the wrong George was used, as nothing better was available."[8]

A year after the "Georgius Triumpho," coins appeared with a crude profile head of George Washington, and WASHINGTON THE GREAT, D.G. around. The reverse showed thirteen rings with the initials of the states, an early imprimatur of the identification of Washington with the newly independent nation.[9] As of 1785, copper coins were struck in New Jersey, showing a uniformed bust and the inscription GEN. WASHINGTON on the obverse; the reverse showed a shield with E PLURIBUS UNUM around.[10] A 1786 copper cent from New York state also shows a profile bust on its obverse, with the fitting inscription "Non Vi Virtute Vici" ("I conquered by virtue, not by force"); the reverse shows an allegorical composition with insignia of Liberty and Justice.[11]

Following Washington's death in December 1799, two funeral processions were held in Boston, respectively on February 11 and 22, 1800. The Newburyport diemaker Jacob Perkins produced medals for both events. Many varieties of the so-called "Perkins Funeral Medal" are known; probably the best-known variety shows, on the obverse, a bust of Washington facing left surrounded in a wreath and the inscription "HE IS IN GLORY, THE WORLD IN TEARS"; the reverse displays a funeral urn and two semicircular lines of text that render Washington's life story. (Another, less common type has skull and crossbones on its reverse and was probably struck for a funeral procession held by the Masons.) The medals were originally made with a small hole at the top; a small loop of wire would be put through the hole so that the medal could be pinned onto clothing or suspended from a string. Most medals were worn in the funeral parades of 1800, in Boston, Philadelphia, and other places, but they were also sought after as souvenirs and were worn annually in later years on February 22, Washington's birthday.[12]

Among other pieces issued around 1800 is the "Hero of Freedom" medal, which extols Washington as "THE PRIDE OF HIS COUNTRY AND ORNAMENT OF HUMAN NATURE." The centennial of Washington's birth in 1832 provided opportunity to the production of even more medals; Washington medals also were created for the United States' centennial celebration in 1876 and the centennial anniversary of Washington's inauguration in 1889. A generation earlier, around 1860, the United States Mint produced a medal that not only honors the first president but also highlights other Washington specimens in its possession. Known as the Cabinet Medal, the piece's reverse depicts the upright case (the "cabinet") that contained the Mint's holdings of other Washington pieces, surmounted by a bust of the Father of His Country. The obverse shows a Washington profile similar to the Houdonesque one on the "Washington Before Boston" medal.

Altogether, some 340 Washington medals, coins, patterns, and tokens have been counted.[13] In 1778, Voltaire commissioned a Washington medal in Paris; its wording said that Washington was a general of the Continental Army. The very first Washington medal was a peace medal; struck in 1776, it was distributed among the tribes of the Abenaki (Wabenaki) Confederation in Massachusetts. The medals became a popular medium of exchange when the British began to produce their own medals, asking the Indians to exchange them for the American medals. Another peace medal was engraved by the silversmith Joseph Richardson and struck in 1795. Its obverse shows Washington greeting a pipe-smoking Indian in a setting of rural industry. The reverse is graced by a somewhat primitive version of the new nation's heraldic eagle.[14]

The Washington coins and tokens struck from 1783 to 1795 bear likenesses that in most instances were faithfully reproduced. They were all designed to honor the first president. Many of these pieces were of English origin. English collectors craved Washington memorabilia; and the producers expected orders from the United States government. After all, the original draft of the Mint Act submitted by the U.S. Senate explicitly required an "impression or representation of the head of the President of the United States for the time being." One example of a coin minted in England is the "Ship Halfpenny" of 1793. Its obverse shows an entirely successful portrait of General Washington in military dress, with the legend "WASHINGTON PRESIDENT." The reverse depicts a three-masted ship on sea, with the legend "HALFPENNY" and the date "1793" below.[15]

Another example of a foreign-produced coin is the Confederatio Copper of 1785—one of the most image-heavy coins ever. Its dies were from the same engraver who made the 1773 Virginia halfpenny that served as model for the Georgius Triumpho copper. The Confederatio Copper's obverse shows the goddess Diana leaning on an altar and trampling on a crown. Her helmet, on the altar, strongly resembles the Phrygian cap, the *pileus*. A legend, "AMERICA INIMICA TYRANNIS," winds itself around the goddess. Finally, there was at least one pattern coin carrying Washington's portrait. The pattern, the so-called "Getz Half Dollar" of 1792, shows Washington's portrait and the inscription "G. WASHINGTON PRESIDENT I" on its obverse; on the reverse is the inscription "UNITED STATES OF AMERICA."

The dies for the "Getz" were engraved by Peter Getz of Lancaster, Pennsylvania, on behalf of Robert Morris, the former financier of the Revolution and now responsible for establishing the United States Mint. The design for the new coin was based on

Getz Half Dollar, pattern, 1792, obverse and reverse, diameter 33.9 mm (reproduced from the original held by the Department of Special Collections of the Hesburgh Libraries of Notre Dame).

an English model, the "Washington Cent" minted by John Gregory Hancock of Birmingham in 1791. George Washington had rejected Hancock's designs, the "General of the Army" pieces. A casual remark by Washington's spokesman, that presidential portraits merely reflected the practices of a Nero and a Caligula, provoked Hancock's ire. In 1792, Hancock responded by creating new designs that portrayed Washington as a degenerate, effeminate Roman emperor.[16] The Pennsylvanian Peter Getz was less vengeful. He had trial pieces struck both in copper and in silver. Robert Morris had the trial pieces, which were probably intended for the half dollar and cent, distributed to senators, representatives, and other dignitaries. Both designs were rejected by President Washington, however, who did not want his portrait on the first United States coinage. No "Getz's Revenge" coins were to follow, though.[17]

None of the Washington coins and tokens from the Confederation period had any official status. The idea of portraying the Father of His Country on the nation's official coinage would have pleased Benjamin Franklin, though, whose views had considerably softened since the successful termination of the War of Independence. In a letter to John Jay of 1785 the sage wrote that America should place images of her honored great on the money, as the ancients had done: "[By] this means the honour was extended through their own and neighboring nations, every man who received or paid a piece of such money was reminded of the virtuous action, the person who performed it, and the reward attending it … and the numbers struck gave such security to this kind of monument against perishing and being forgotten, that some of them exist to this day." No longer considering the use of portraits as exclusively a monarchical practice, Franklin now thought "images of praiseworthy persons, printed on the nation's coins, could also inspire the citizenry, while at the same time glorifying the United States."[18]

Washington's portrait would have been entirely fitting for the proposed coinage, which was to have been struck in precious metal. Gold is the transcendental vehicle of meanings, the "Lord of Commodities," hence the economic equivalent of the Lord God, whose worship develops into an end in itself. His representative on earth is George Washington, the Father (founder), whose worship likewise developed into an end in itself and whose portrait would have served as the image or mark of the "prince," the familiar portrait of the ruler in the European tradition.[19] Franklin's vision of "enriching virtues" was not universally shared, though. There were heated debates in Congress. Many representatives feared that a new monarchy would arise and that placing a portrait of the nation's first president on the coins would only advance this course of events. The debates also affected a wider public. For instance, on April 14, 1792, the *Columbian Centinel* published a letter to the printer dismissive of such fears: "The choice of a First Magistrate of the U.S. originates in THE PEOPLE—and the man whom they chuse [sic] is deserving every honour that a free people can confer."[20]

The worthy New Englander's words may well have been prompted by a pattern for a gold eagle, a $10 piece weighing 16.12g, that was expressly struck for, presented to, and carried by George Washington. Its obverse features a bust of Washington surrounded by the lettering "WASHINGTON PRESIDENT" and the date, 1792. The reverse features a heraldic eagle based on the seal of the United States. The edge bears the lettering "UNITED STATES OF AMERICA." Most likely the pattern (a proposed coin), which is the earliest gold pattern prepared for the U.S. coinage, was produced by Jacob Perkins of Newburyport, Massachusetts. Only one example of the coin was made.[21] Congress was not swayed, though, and the passage concerning "an impression or representation of the head of the President of the United States for the time being," which had been outlined by Robert Morris, did not become a part of the final text of the Mint Act. Instead, the Act mandates the use of "an impression emblematic of liberty, with an inscription of the word Liberty, and the year of the coinage."[22]

Despite all these noble efforts at the new nation's coinage, the hard-currency paradise that the founders envisaged was not to be. The United States Mint, proposed by George Washington and established in 1792, was unable to provide a steady and reliable supply of coins, so that all kinds of foreign coins continued to be in circulation. In particularly short supply were coins of smaller denominations, which were partly needed to pay the increasing number of laborers. Importing these coins in bulk was hardly a practicable solution and, for Americans with a nationalistic turn of mind, it was not a desirable one.[23] What had been done during the Revolution was also being done now: Public and private groups and merchants taking up the slack on the local level and issuing tokens as well as small change notes, called fractional currency or scrip.[24]

As for "real" money, that is, gold or silver coins, there simply was not enough precious metal around. Gold was not discovered in any usable quantity until 1848 and silver even later. During the Napoleonic Wars, the British confiscated large amounts of silver dollars, which they overstamped with a portrait of George III (as if in belated revenge for the loss of the king's status as the Father of His Country) and declared to be legal tender in England.[25] In the United States, not even the massive quasi-imports of foreign coins, especially of Mexican silver dollars, met the growing demand for circulating currency. This fact eventually became of considerable concern to American lawmakers. In December 1830, a United States Senate committee report stated, "The fact that we have no gold coins in circulation, is not the intended effect of our institutions."[26]

The effect may have been not intended, but the situation was not to be remedied any time soon. In 1832, President Andrew Jackson vetoed the re-chartering of the Bank of the United States, a national institution that would have issued paper money for all the states. The veto, the beginning of Jackson's "bank war," culminated in the Panic of 1837, the result of Jackson's "Specie Circular," and lingered on well through the 1840s, leading to bankruptcies and influencing the daily lives of the people. "The land stinks with suicide," Ralph Waldo Emerson noted in his journal in May 1837. And, the sage of Concord added, "It is easy for the philosophic class to be poor."[27] Was this an allusion to Brook Farm, that experiment in community, the founding of which should not be separated from the grim historical circumstances surrounding it on all sides?[28]

While romantic reformers turned to "man's better angels," the grim historical circumstances also provoked quite different responses, in the form of an outpouring of imaginative literature, most notably by Hawthorne, Melville, and Poe. These three writers—later known as the "triumvirate of darkness," in Harry Levin's apt term—imaginatively explored the general experience of alienation and deception: Poe in a heroically sinister fashion, Hawthorne in a tragically romantic one in *The House of the Seven Gables*, and Melville in a nihilistically comic one in *The Confidence-Man*, which is appropriately is set on a Mississippi riverboat called *Fidèle*.[29] Another unintended consequence of Jackson's "bank war" was the continued absence of precious coins, which only added further fuel to the vastly expanded use of paper money. Even the constitutional prohibition of paper money was circumvented by licenses to print and issue paper currency, which the federal government or individual states granted to private banks, insurance companies, canal companies, or railroads. The era of the private note lasted until the Civil War. By then, portraits of George Washington had been printed on hundreds, if not thousands, of different notes, beginning with the notes issued by the Washington Bank of Westerly, Rhode Island.[30]

George Washington himself had serious misgivings about the paper money he saw, though he was not opposed to paper money on principle, as long as it was federal money. Once elected president, he was quick to support—against Madison's and Jefferson's opposition—chartering the Bank of the United States, the B.U.S.[31] Washington also had good memories of the success of the Bank of North America, the continent's first commercial bank. Formed by Robert Morris when he became Superintendent of Finance for the Confederation Congress in 1781, the bank, which was located in Philadelphia, brought order into government finances at the same time as it engineered a stable medium of exchange. Bank of North America notes—popularly called "Morris notes"—served as a stable currency in Pennsylvania and enabled the Continental government to purchase supplies and pay wages during a critical year of the war of independence.[32] Thus there was reason to believe that a "well conducted bank" like the B.U.S. could establish a stable currency regime.

The notes issued by the Bank of the United States, it is important to point out, were not issued by the government. They therefore constituted a medium of exchange that could expand and contract in response to economic contingencies rather than the whim of politicians. Moreover, the notes were limited by the "boundary" of its assets, promoting economic growth without the risk of runaway inflation.[33] In another regard, the Bank of the United States was exceptional, as the government owned a fifth of its shares. Other banks too could and did issue private notes, debt obligations that—at least theoretically—were redeemable in specie on demand at the issuing bank. These notes also circulated as paper money and provided valuable liquidity in a growing economy in which specie money remained scarce. So important was a reliable money supply that George Washington in his "Farewell Address" of 1796 admonished Americans to "cherish public credit," as he considered it "a very important source of strength and security."[34]

In 1790, there were only four banks chartered and in operation between New Hampshire and South Carolina. The number was up to twenty-nine by 1800, and ninety by 1811. Only five years later, in 1816, there were 260 of them; in 1835, banks numbered 704 as compared to 330 in 1830; by 1859, there were 1,365 of them, and most of them were issuing paper notes. By 1861, the number of banks totaled 1,601 throughout the United States, with $207 million in circulating notes, up from $62 million in 1813 and $120 million in 1836.[35] These figures roughly correspond to the growth of the nation's population, which by 1850 was nearing 25 million, and to the extension of the national boundaries from coast to coast.[36] All of the new territories were shortly seeing settlement and, as well, a proportionate number of note-issuing banks and similar institutions—usually about a decade before the territory became a state.

Altogether, some eight thousand fiscal entities issued paper notes in the United

States between 1790 and 1865. Most of them were banks, though insurance companies, railroads, turnpikes, factories, hotels, churches, and other institutions also were in the paper money business. These entities, which operated under State charters, free banking laws, and in a few instances without any authorization whatsoever, put into circulation notes in a wide range of—often quite unusual—denominations. Since the average bank issued currency in half a dozen different values and in many more different designs, the total number of notes is estimated to run into the tens of thousands, not counting denominations and designs for which none are known to survive at all, and not counting those which are still waiting to be found, such as notes from the Cass County Bank in La Grange, Michigan, from the 1830s. La Grange then consisted of a few buildings on a small lake. No record has been found of any such bank being chartered or doing business until about three hundred sheets of notes were found in the late twentieth century, including $3 notes with a central vignette of an Indian after a successful hunt and a crude portrait of George Washington at left. Even without additional finds, the total number of notes and styles far exceeds the number of dated and mintmarked varieties of federal coins, from 1792 down to the present.[37]

Many of the notes from the era of private banking were of great beauty of design and color and are therefore widely collected today.[38] Also widely collected are notes from the colonial area, though not for any great beauty of design and color. There was a noticeable restraint to the visual rhetoric on early paper money. True, on occasion, there are frames or a few ornaments, decorative letters or fields around the denomination, perhaps even watermarks. Yet text was excessive, and so the first bills resembled documents and contracts rather than classic bank notes. For one thing, neither the technology available to producers nor their limited financial resources would have allowed anything more "artistic." Yet the documentary style also was deliberate. Images were considered dubious or untrustworthy, thus unnecessary. Moreover, the notes were not seen as money but only as representative of money—which came in the form of precious coins. Thus, the signatures, seals, and similar official insignia that were printed on early notes did not serve any aesthetic purpose so much as they had to secure the notes' credibility. These "official" signs were at the same representative of an authority guaranteeing the notes' value and indicative of the convergence of late medieval documentary culture and an even older numismatic tradition.

Perhaps the best examples of early bank notes are the "bills of credit" issued by the colony of Massachusetts Bay in 1691. The notes not only constitute the first authorized paper money issued by any government in the western world. They are also the earliest engraved examples from copper plates, serving as a standard for later emissions, in Massachusetts as well as in other colonies.[39] None of these notes were aesthetically convincing, but neither were notes from the Revolutionary period and the early republic. The former, I have shown, were instruments of political propaganda, serving the cause of American patriots. The latter were nondescript, continuing the documentary style of colonial currency and, as in the case of notes from the Bank of North America, often expressed their value according to the old English system of shillings and pence, even as their issuers were moving toward a new system—hence the notes proclaimed that they were worth one-ninetieth or three-ninetieths of a dollar. Notes from the Washington Bank, Westerly, Rhode Island, were part of the Washington hagiography.

Predictably, notes from the Bank of the United States engaged in promoting republican symbolism.

The Bank of the United States, which received its first charter in 1791, soon became the largest money-printing operation in the country, providing something like a uniform currency. Its notes enjoyed a high reputation both at home and abroad, buying the entire Louisiana Territory from Napoleon in 1803. By 1830, the B.U.S., in its second charter since 1816, had issued over $100 million of notes, or about 20 to 25 percent of paper money in circulation. By contrast, a typical state bank would have issued $100,000 to $200,000 of notes.[40] Several notes from the Second Bank of the United States bore portraits of George Washington and other luminaries, though in general notes from the private banks were much richer in imagery: There were allegorical figures as well as archetypal images of prosperity, from smokestacks to bank buildings. Real people also made it onto the notes, yet the portraits of bearded gentlemen and grizzled war generals are indicative rather of a downward spiral of currency design. So are depictions of George Washington as a semi-nude Roman consul, which in the late 1820s graced notes from the National Bank of New York.

The notes from the Second Bank of the United States may not have been as rich in pictorial features as notes from private commercial banks, yet they display entirely new forms of ornamental art, patterns created by machines rather than images incised by an engraver. Mechanical engraving was done by geometric lathes—resulting in, for instance, "rosettes," that is, a concentric accumulation of sinusoidal waves ("petals") in an elliptic arrangement, epicycloidal "loops," "straight line rulings," "ovals," or other forms described in a general sense as "guilloches." The word "guilloche," Andrew Hurle explains, "is a borrowed term that properly refers to the interlacing of bands found on Greek and Roman architecture, rather than to any configuration of printed line." The terminological ambiguity indicates that machine-engraved patterns had little or no connection to tangible objects in the natural or social world. Before they appeared on paper money, they were virtually unknown in both the fine and the decorative arts. Developed specifically for securing the credibility of bank notes, machine-engraved abstractions certified printed money by establishing new conventions for its appearance. Moreover, the ornamental designs coming from machines encouraged paper money circulation with no need for personal endorsement, a true godsend in an increasingly anonymous mass society.[41]

Coins, especially precious coins, were different. Coins, Sergio Rizzo explains, reflect an altogether different stage in the "ideological evolution" of monetary forms.[42] As products of the age of mercantile capitalism, the ornaments on coins—oak leaves, acanthus leaves, lilies, pine trees, etc.—typically show a real connection to tangible objects in the natural or social world. Take, for instance, that mighty and ubiquitous Renaissance coin, the Florentine florin: A circle of pure gold stamped on its reverse with an image of St. John the Baptist, the city's patron saint. The florin takes its name, like Florence itself, from the word for flower, *flore* in Tuscan vernacular. Officially, the flower of Florence is called a lily, *giglio*, and so an image of a lily is stamped on the obverse of the florin—even though it is so stylized that it looks more like a flag iris, and it bears two long, decorative stamens that sometimes end themselves in tiny *gigli* to create a play of infinite regression.[43]

The floral tradition persisted well into the present. For example, in Austria before the introduction of the euro, an edelweiss flower was stamped on the reverse of the ubiquitous one-schilling coin. The flower constituted a truly synecdochal relation: The edelweiss (*Leontopodium alpinum*, "lion's paw") is a small white flower that grows in the high Alps, and the Austrian schilling was colloquially referred to as the "Alpendollar" (or the "Alpine dollar").[44] Not flowers, but pine trees graced the first coins struck in New England in the mid-seventeenth century. Another tangible object in the natural world, a deer, was stamped on three-penny pieces struck in Connecticut in the early eighteenth century. The images not only represented any natural world, but the new world, the origin also of the metal used to create the tokens. As modest as these first efforts were, they established an idea that would soon be acted on in a bolder, more consistent way—political sovereignty.

It is not that bank notes were entirely devoid of illustrations that represented tangible objects in the natural world. Perhaps the best example are notes using Benjamin Franklin's nature print technique. The technique, which Franklin invented in 1739, was originally intended as an anti-counterfeiting device. It involved using real leaves, making a thin, positive lead cast from them, and then nailing the cast into a printer's chase along with normal type. The result looked like an engraving, yet it was not. Astonishingly, no counterfeiter ever caught on to Franklin's method, which was not discovered until the 1960s.[45] Nature prints were used until the Revolutionary period. On bank notes from the era of private banking, however, use of tangible objects from the natural world was largely abandoned. The notes instead displayed almost innumerable notables and dignitaries, usually in the form of portraits within elliptic frames, but also on horseback, leaning against desks, or in other poses reminiscent of aristocratic models. The illustrations range from the well-known to the obscure.

George Washington was, of course, a favorite subject on notes issued by the private banks. John Muscalus indexed altogether 1,700 notes that featured the Father of His Country. The notes came from 969 banking institutions in 34 states, the District of Columbia included, though as Muscalus notes in his preface, the list is *not* "absolutely all inclusive." Most of the banking institutions that issued notes featuring Washington were located in New York State (145), closely followed by Massachusetts (117), with Pennsylvania trailing in third place (84). The largest number of notes came from Massachusetts (221), followed by New York State (210) and Pennsylvania (177). The fewest banks issuing such notes (1–2 banks, with 1–4 notes each) were located in Arkansas, Kansas, Minnesota, Texas, and Nebraska. Denominations typically ran the gamut from $1 to $1000, with occasional oddities such as $1.50, $3, $4, $11, and $12. Fractional amounts—in denominations of 10¢, 12½¢, 25¢, and 50¢—also were issued by several banks. And there were real curios, such as notes in denominations of 6¼¢, issued by the Farmers Bank of the State of Delaware, Dover, the Baltimore Savings Institution, Baltimore, Maryland, the Washington County Savings Institution, Hagerstown, Maryland, and the Taylorsville Delaware Bridge Co., Taylorsville, Pennsylvania.[46]

The average banking institution issued two to four Washington-related notes, though there were exceptions. The Bank of Commerce, Georgetown, DC, issued five such notes, each with the identical central vignette, two female allegories with cornucopia and anchor flanking a portrait of Washington, in denominations of $5, $10,

$20, $50, and $100. The Washington County Bank, Richmond, Rhode Island (with later locations in Carolina Mills and Charlestown) issued eleven such notes, in denominations of $1, $2, and $5, all in the 1850s through 1860s. Eleven Washington-related notes are known also from the Mississippi & Alabama Railroad Company's Bank, Brandon, Mississippi, in denominations of $10, $20, and $25, issued in the late 1830s through the 1840s. In the 1850s–1860s, the National Bank, Providence, Rhode Island, issued twelve Washington-related notes, in denominations of $1, $2, $3, $5, $10, $100, and $1000. Two banks issued altogether eighteen such notes, the Exchange Bank of Virginia, with the parent bank at Norfolk, and the Washington Bank, Boston, Massachusetts. While the former issued notes in denominations of $5, $10, $15, $20, $50, and $100, notes from the latter bank were in denominations of $1, $2, $3, $5, $5, $20, $50, and $100, with illustrations showing Washington on horseback, standing by his horse, and as portrait.[47]

Multiple issues of Washington-related notes are also known from the Bank of Augusta, Augusta, Georgia; the Lynn Mechanics Bank, Lynn, Massachusetts; the Highland Bank, Newburgh, New York; the Farmers Bank of Bucks County, Bristol, Pennsylvania (relocated from Hulm Ville); the Northern Bank of Kentucky, Lexington; the Bank of Penn Township, Philadelphia, Pennsylvania; and the Washington Bank, Westerly, Rhode Island. All these issues not only testify to Q. David Bowers' finding that George Washington is the most widely featured American historical figure to be found on paper money.[48] They are also proof that Washington's pictorial presence resulted from a carefully calculated design choice. While Washington was acknowledged as the founder, the universal and transcendental symbol of national unity, images of him also worked to affirm the credibility of the banks by aligning with patriotic feelings and deep historicity and to bolster the note holders' commitment to the transactions facilitated by these financial instruments. Since all that note holders had was a distant bank's promise to pay, Washington's pictorial presence helped model an attitude of trust and confidence in a climate of uncertainty that accompanied the purchase of goods or the speculation in land without hard currency.[49]

Between 1824 and the early 1830s, the Peoples Bank of Paterson, New Jersey, issued $1 notes that showed Washington on a rearing horse, possibly modeled after one of the numerous equestrian portraits of the general that had been circulating from the mid–1770s. (One of these portraits, a mezzotint, purportedly was executed from a drawing, from life, by Alexander Campbell of Williamsburgh, Virginia.) The identical vignette was used on $100 notes from the Bank of Virginia, Richmond, Virginia, from the 1810s to the 1850s, on $20 notes from the Derby Bank, Derby, Connecticut, in the 1820s, as well as on 50¢ notes from the Potomac Savings Bank, Washington, D.C., in the early 1850s, and on $3 notes issued by the Mechanics and Traders Bank, Portsmouth, New Hampshire, in 1859.[50] In the 1830s, the Bank of New Brunswick, New Brunswick, New Jersey, issued $5 notes featuring a Lansdownesque vignette of Washington at right; in 1838, the short-lived Bank of Madison County, Madisonville, Mississippi, used the identical vignette on its $50 and $100 notes.[51] Perhaps the least successful notes in terms of design were $100 notes issued in the 1850s by the Farmers and Mechanics Bank, Camden, New Jersey: a huge "C" (for 100) is centrally placed in oval die, with "ONE HUNDRED" written in the borders; a tiny, left-leaning Gilbert-Stuart-inspired portrait of Washington is in the upper-left corner, resembling a tear-off coupon stub.[52]

Because Washington was so closely identified with the new nation, he often appears together with allegorical representations of liberty. On $10 notes issued by the State Bank in Trenton, New Jersey, in the 1820s, Liberty, complete with staff and cap, and Ceres, with her cornucopia, flank a shield showing three plows; above the shield is a horse head. The state seal is centered at the top, while Washington's portrait is placed at right.[53] There is considerably more patriotism in $20 notes issued by a bank in Saline, Michigan, also in the 1820s: A vignette at right shows Lady Liberty, her left arm around a medallion with Washington's portrait, as if protecting the father of his country; the national eagle looks down from a wall behind which is a shield with the inscription "E Pluribus Unum."[54]

Patriotic feelings and deep historicity also emanate from $3 notes issued by the Morris Canal & Banking Company, Jersey City, New Jersey, in the 1820s and 1830s, a vignette, engraved by Asher B. Durand, showing Washington seated with a tablet, writing his Farewell Address. Somewhat later, the motif is also featured on $5 notes from the Mechanics Bank of Baltimore, Baltimore, Maryland, as well as on some half dozen banks from the states of Mississippi.[55] Patriotism also oozes from $5 notes issued by the Pejepscot Bank, Brunswick, Maine, in the late 1850s, and from $10 notes from the Battenkill Bank, Manchester, Vermont, in the late 1840s, on which an oval portrait of George Washington is paired with a central vignette showing the presentation of the Declaration of Independence in Congress. The $1 notes from the Metropolitan Bank, New York, New York, feature Washington standing, in

A $20 note, Bank of Saline, Michigan, 1838, detail (Eric P. Newman Numismatic Education Society).

his general's uniform, the presentation of the Declaration of Independence, and Liberty with shield. A view of the United States Capitol is the central vignette on $10 notes issued by the Belknap County Bank, Meredith, New Hampshire, in the 1850s.[56] There is a touch of sentimentalism and nostalgia on $3 notes issued by the New Market Bank, New Market, New Hampshire, in September 1860. Below a large 3, an old man is seen showing a Houdonesque bust to a child on his lap.[57]

The $3 notes from the Detroit City Bank from the late 1830s bore a vignette, designed by Freeman Rawdon, of a goddess and an especially patriotic American eagle wearing a cameo with a picture of George Washington on its breast; in addition, a portrait of Washington is at left; at right is a portrait of Thomas Jefferson.[58] From the mid–1830s to the 1840s, the Bank of Illinois, Shawneetown, Illinois, issued $2 notes bearing a framed portrait of Washington flanked by two scrawny-looking birds, presumed to represent the national eagle. A huge eagle on a shield, wings spread, forms the central feature of $10 notes from the Mutual Bank of Castleton, Castleton, Vermont, late 1850s to 1865; a portrait Washington in an oval frame is at left. The Washington-with-eagle motif could be found on notes already in the 1820s, as issued in the denomination of $100 by the Bank of Chester County, West Chester, Pennsylvania (medallion-head portraits of Lafayette appear at left and right). From 1859–1861 the Columbian Bank, Elizabethtown, Illinois, issued $5 notes with Washington's portrait slightly off-center and a huge eagle about to fly off at left. A similar eagle forms the central vignette on $3 notes from the Farmers Bank of Illinois, Metropolis, Illinois, early 1860s; Washington's portrait on these notes is pushed to the upper left corner.[59]

The $20 notes from the Bank of Gettysburg, Gettysburg, Pennsylvania, in the 1850s showed Washington's portrait flanked by Liberty standing (at left) and Liberty kneeling (at right) and surmounted by an eagle. The design was also used on notes of various denominations issued by the Bank of Commerce, Washington, D.C.[60] A medallion portrait of Washington flanked by two cherubs is the dominant feature on $1 notes from the Union Bank, Swanton Falls, Vermont, 1850s. The West River Bank, Jamaica, Vermont, in the 1850s issued $10 notes on which a medallion portrait of Washington is flanked by an angel (at left) and a cherub (at right).[61] On a $20 note, issued by the Farmers & Mechanics Bank in Camden, New Jersey, in the 1850s, Liberty is resting her right arm on a shield bearing an oval portrait of America's first president.[62] On $3 notes issued in the mid–1850s by the Tiverton Bank, Tiverton, Rhode Island, Liberty and Justice are flanking a shield-like portrait of Washington surmounted by a large eagle.[63]

At the start of the Civil War, two muses placing a laurel wreath on a bust of Washington, placed behind the U.S. coat of arms, dominate $3 notes issued by the Bank of North America, Boston, Massachusetts, and $10 notes issued by the short-lived Bullion Bank, Washington, D.C.[64] A vignette characteristic of Washington's apotheosis is the centerpiece on $5 notes from the Lynn Mechanics Bank, Lynn, Massachusetts, on $10 notes from the Windham County Bank, Brattleboro, Vermont (both from the 1850s), and on $100 notes issued in the 1860s by the Citizens' Bank of Louisiana, New Orleans; the vignette features Washington's bust surrounded by three muses of arts in classical attire.[65] Finally, $10 notes issued by the Bank of Poughkeepsie, Poughkeepsie, New York, 1840s, the Wabash River Bank, Jasper, Indiana, the Orono Bank, Orono, Maine, and the Lafayette Bank of Cincinnati, Cincinnati, Ohio, 1850s, show medallion portraits of Washington and Franklin, and four cherubs flanking a central X.[66]

The nation's first president is also shown in the company of presidents following him. If no one could deny that Washington was known as the Father of His Country, to all presidents since, and to all Americans, the presidency has been the office of national fatherhood. For instance, $5 notes issued in the 1840s and 1850s by the Mechanics Bank, New Haven, Connecticut, show the first five presidents in an ornate arrangement along a huge "V" (the Roman numeral for five).[67] The identical design is used on $5 notes from the Lafayette Bank of Cincinnati, Cincinnati, Ohio, 1850s, as well as on spurious $5 notes of the Union Bank of South Carolina, from 1859.[68] $10 notes, issued at mid-century by the Frederick County Bank, Frederick, Maryland, as well as by the Piscataqua Exchange Bank, Portsmouth, New Hampshire, show the first ten presidents, arranged on a huge "X," the Roman numeral for ten.[69] A somewhat odd composition graced the $5 notes that the International Bank, Washington, D.C., issued in the late 1850s: George Washington's portrait at center, flanked by portraits of Andrew Jackson and James Buchanan (from left), and Henry Clay and Thomas Jefferson (from right); the oddity of the composition is matched by the fact that the International Bank was non-existent, represented only by fictitious notes.[70]

In the 1850s, the engraver, inventor, and founder of the Continental Bank Note Company, W.L. Ormsby came forth with $5 notes bearing a remarkable design on their backs: On a backdrop of bright orange he printed five circular spaces, representing the denomination, with the 5 repeated hundreds of times in each of the circles. At the center of each circle was a portrait of George Washington. Also unusual was the circles' spatial arrangement. Modern habits of seeing would expect a circle in each of the four corners, with an additional one at center, completing the quintessence. Ormsby's choice, however, was a linear arrangement in two rows, two circles above and three below. The arrangement evokes the "Hand of Fatima," after the daughter of the Prophet Muhammad. The "Hand of Fatima" or "Hamsa," after "khamsa," an Arabic word meaning five, relates to warding off the evil eye.[71]

The era of private banking ended in the 1860s, when the federal government taxed private notes out of existence. Thus, when the Farmers and Mechanics Bank in Milford, Delaware, was chartered in the fall of 1861, it became one of only a few banks in the North organized after the Civil War began. The $3 notes of the bank, ink-dated October 21, 1861, featured a Gilbert Stuart-inspired portrait of George Washington at left. A portrait of George Washington at bottom left graced the $1 notes issued by the Strafford Bank in Dover, New Hampshire, in 1862, a last sigh from private banking.[72]

Part II

The Antebellum Period and the Civil War

The onset of private banking coincided with the aftermath of the American Revolution. No longer able to ransack British history for heroes, many patriots then turned to classical history for inspiration. Ancient Rome in its republican phase provided uplifting examples also for banknote designers. In the late 1820s, for instance, Asher Durand designed a vignette that depicts George Washington as a Roman consul, donning a toga and carrying the fasces, a bundle of rods enfolding an ax. Washington's powdered wig was, of course, a gross stylistic incongruity that raised quite a few eyebrows. In Richard Doty's irreverent comment, for instance, Washington is making his escape from a village bathhouse.[1] But would a laurel wreath have been more desirable? Laurel wreaths were the prerogatives of the caesars; a Washington adorned with such a wreath surely would have been even less fitting. The bundle of twelve rods enfolding an ax posed less of a problem. A symbol of sovereign virtues from early on, it was first born by kings, later by office holders in the republic and, finally, by victorious military commanders. The bundle (*fasces*) was usually carried by minor officials (*lictores*) marching up front and clearing the way for the consuls, magistrates, and other authorities. Washington himself had identified with the stern code of honor and duty in ancient Rome so fully that a visitor from England felt compelled to comment on his "Roman face,"

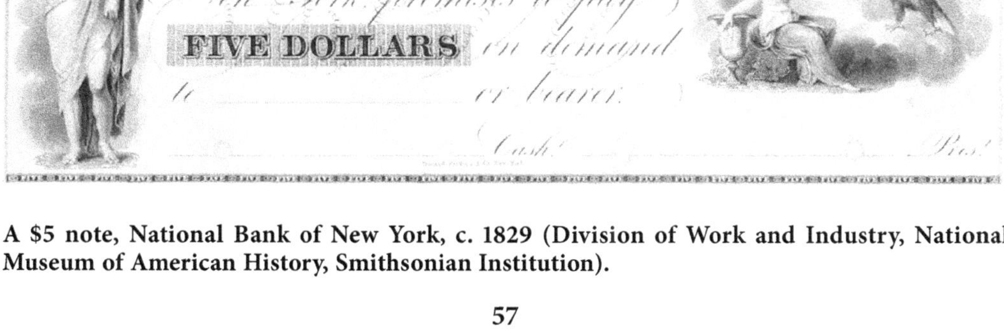

A $5 note, National Bank of New York, c. 1829 (Division of Work and Industry, National Museum of American History, Smithsonian Institution).

expressive "of Sagacity, of Prudence, and of Moderation."[2] The dignified nobleness attributed to Washington was the product of life-long self-cultivation, taking as inspiration two popular works by or about Romans, filtered through English sensibility: *Seneca's Morals*, which he acquired in his teens in a translation by the English pamphleteer Roger L'Estrange, and Joseph Addison's *Cato*. The tragedy, written in 1712 and first performed in 1713, was Washington's favorite play and, the Bible excepting, there is no literary text that he quoted from more frequently.[3]

4

The Cult of Antiquity

George Washington's America, Marcus Cunliffe wrote, was "in a way more truly 'Roman' than the mother country."[1] If it had not been, men like Washington would not have been able to create a new nation on the republican model. The lessons of the classical past suggested that an extensive republic was a working possibility. America, it has been said repeatedly, became a nation legally long before it was one culturally. When it did, antiquish iconography prevailed. On the obverse of the "Washington and Independence" tokens of 1783, for instance, was stamped a left-facing, laureate bust of Washington dressed in a toga that is held in place at the left shoulder by a button. Around is the inscription WASHINGTON & INDEPENDENCE / 1783. On the reverse, Liberty is seated on a rock, surrounded by water. The lady holds a sprig of olive in her outstretched right hand and supports a liberty cap on a pole with her left. The legend UNITED STATES arcs across the top.[2] Closely related to the "Washington and Independence" tokens are the "Unity States" cent tokens. While the obverse is identical to the "Washington and Independence" token, the reverse is inscribed with ONE CENT, surrounded by the legend UNITY STATES OF AMERICA.[3]

Antiquish iconography also was a favorite choice for currency designers. Asher Durand's "bathhouse" vignette has been mentioned.[4] Another example of a "Roman" Washington can be found on a $2 note from the Farmers & Mechanics' Bank of Michigan, c.1829–1830s, which shows a standing Washington in a toga. The identical vignette was used on $10 and $50 notes issued in the 1830s through the 1850s by the Mount Vernon Bank, Foster, Rhode Island; on $500 notes from the Commercial Bank, Providence, Rhode Island; and on $50 stock certificates from the Ulster County Bank, Kingston, New York.[5] Also antiquish is a 50¢ note from the Bank of the State of South Carolina, Charleston, with a portrait of Washington at center, flanked on each side by three cherubs.[6] On other notes, Washington appears together with other historic personalities, most likely for the purpose of building trust and confidence. On $20 notes issued by the Franklin Bank in Boston in the later 1830s, for instance, the antiquish-looking statue of George Washington standing (from the Massachusetts State House) shares the stage with a portrait of Benjamin Franklin and a vignette of Daniel Webster, the hypnotic orator and senator from Massachusetts who at the time—when Andrew Jackson's war against the Bank of the United States was raging—often cited the first president's stand on monetary matters.[7]

The identical Washington vignette was used, *inter alia*, on $1 notes from the Merchants and Planters Bank of Magnolia, Florida, on $2 notes from the Farmers and Me-

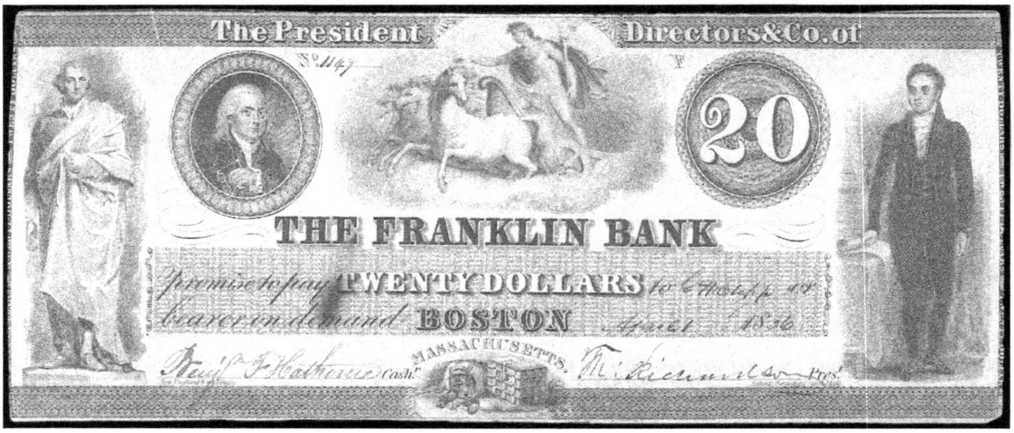

A $20 note, Franklin Bank, Boston, 1836, front (Division of Work and Industry, National Museum of American History, Smithsonian Institution).

chanics Bank of Michigan, Detroit, Michigan, from the Bank of Singapore, Singapore, Michigan, and from the Mechanics Bank, Newark, New Jersey; on $3 notes from the Bank of Hawkinsville, Georgia; on $5 notes from the Farmers Bank, Orwell, Vermont; on $6 notes from the Bank of Potomac, Alexandria, DC; and on $100 notes from the Bank of Mississippi, Princeton, Mississippi, also in the 1830s; on $5 notes from the North River Bank, New York, New York, and on $10 notes from the Merchants and Planters Bank of Florida, in the 1830s and 1840s; on $50 notes from the Mount Vernon Bank, Providence, Rhode Island, in the 1850s; and on $100 notes from the Bank of Selma, Selma, Alabama, in the 1860s.[8] The antiquish style remained popular through the outbreak of the Civil War. On a $10 note issued by the Windham County Bank, Brattleboro, Vermont, in the late 1850s, Washington's decidedly "Roman" bust is surrounded by three scantily clad female allegories. The same vignette was used for $100 notes from the Citizens' Bank of Louisiana, New Orleans, issued in the early 1860s. It is tempting to relate the somewhat pained expression on the first president's face to the ladies' sparse clothing.[9]

The design on the Citizens' Bank of Louisiana notes may have been a concession to contemporary taste, but representations of semi-nude female figures on bank notes also served as anti-counterfeiting measures. It was widely believed that people's attention was directly proportionate to the amount of bare skin visible on the notes.[10] Banknote companies were, however, also guided by other considerations. In 1855, the Pawtuckaway Bank in Epping, New Hampshire, emitted $2 notes that bore a medallion with a version of the Stuart portrait surrounded by rather chastely clad female figures. The figures are allegorical representations of agricultural pursuits. While they transform Washington into a kind of king of the hill, their appearance also suggests innocence, youth, and purity. The bank people likely were attracted to these virtues because what good were they in the hard-battling arena of capitalist expansion? The notes' producers, the Boston firm of Danforth, Wright & Co., may well have been reasoning along these lines.[11]

A version of Stuart's Athenaeum portrait is the premier eye-catcher on $1 notes from the Elm City Bank, New Haven, Connecticut, 1850s.[12] The same is true of $1 notes issued by the Presidents Bank in Washington, D.C., in 1852. In this instance, the portrait is flanked on each side by a large "1" set in a rectangular field. Thus, the "1" not only marks the denomination but also serves as a reminder that Washington was the first president and, to borrow from Henry Lee's eulogy, "first in war, first in peace, and first in the hearts of his countrymen."[13] Additionally, in our western number system the one represents beginning and origin. The one also suggests unity and wholeness; it contains everything that may come about. And, not to forget, traditionally the one has been related to a person's upright position. This is all very well, but the Presidents Bank was a fraudulent, possibly non-existent bank, and so to use Washington as the bank's crown jewel made perfect sense.[14]

Valid $1 notes with Washington's portrait did exist, though, as for instance from the Boylston Bank, Boston, Massachusetts, 1845 to 1860s, and from the Franklin County Bank, Greenfield, Massachusetts, late 1840s and 1850s (Benjamin Franklin appeared on the bank's $2 notes).[15] In a wider context, use of Washington as a brand had become common practice by mid-century. His image was universally recognizable and who would dare to *not* accept a paper bill graced by the face of the nation? Would not such a person be immediately exposed as unpatriotic? Moreover, Washington's image on currency notes subliminally promoted the idea that these bills as well as the financial institutions issuing them were trustworthy, as trustworthy as the country's first president. (This was a weighty argument, considering that at mid-century about half of the bank notes in circulation were counterfeits, fake, spurious, bogus, altered, or raised.[16])

The Washington brand is tone-setting also on $10 notes emitted by the Mechanics Bank of Pittsburgh circa 1855; in this instance, the Father of His Country nobilitates craft and industry—at left, a carpenter is seen sawing a board; at right, a mechanic is resting, with factories in the background.[17] Also in the 1850s, the Union Bank of Weymouth and Braintree, Weymouth, Massachusetts, emitted $1 notes with a slightly off-center Washington portrait and a large vignette showing a railroad train emerging from under a viaduct—the Father of His Country endorsing progress.[18] Around the same time, the Rhode Island Central Bank, East Greenwich, Rhode Island, issued $5 notes on which Washington's portrait looks benignly at a central vignette depicting a couple with their infant child, an evocation of domestic bliss that had found a visual expression in sentimental paintings of the time.[19] Beginning in 1854, the Cherokee Insurance and Banking Company in Dalton, Georgia, issued $5 notes with a portrait of Washington at center; at left are three Indians looking in awe at factories—built, presumably, on land that once was theirs.[20] In 1861, the Bank of Penn Township, Philadelphia, emitted $1 notes with two Washington vignettes—respectively his portrait and his tomb at Mount Vernon; $5 notes from the Bullion Bank in Washington, D.C., also from 1861, displayed the identical design.[21] Also in the 1860s, the Fairhaven Bank, Fairhaven, Massachusetts, put into circulation $50 notes with a modest Washington bust at top left.[22]

Branding also included the judicious use of the place name Washington, D.C. (or Washington City, as the nation's capital had been called following the name giver's death). Unsurprisingly, there was a Bank of Washington (which opened in 1809, was chartered in 1811, and converted to a National Bank in 1885), whose combination of a Washington bank name, a Washington city name, and George Washington on notes has made it one of the most desirable names in DC. In addition, there have been a short-lived Central Bank of Georgetown and Washington (1815–1820), a Patriotic Bank of Washington (which opened in 1815 and became the National Bank of the Republic in 1865), a Farmers Bank of Washington, D.C. (a non-existent Bank represented by fictitious notes), an equally non-existent Washington Bank, a Washington City Bank (likewise a fictitious enterprise), a Western Bank of Washington (also non-existent), and a Virginia Bank of Washington City, which also may never have operated.[23]

Outside of the nation's capital, the roster of names chosen to inspire trust begins with the Washington Bank in Westerly, Rhode Island (established in 1800, it was the first bank to have a portrait of Washington on its notes). Washington County Banks existed in Calais, Maine, Williamsport, Maryland (became the Washington County National Bank in 1865), at Union Village, New York, and in Richmond, Rhode Island (with later locations in Carolina Mills and Charlestown). Banks of Washington could be found in Lebanon, Kentucky (one of forty banks chartered in 1818, though it operated only for a short time in the summer of 1819, when it stopped redeeming its notes), in Washington, North Carolina, and in Washington, Pennsylvania, which in 1836 became home to a Franklin Bank of Washington. The George Washington Bank, Salem, Massachusetts, was a non-existent bank represented only by notes altered from other banks. Washington Banks opened in Boston, Massachusetts (established in 1825, it became the Washington National Bank of Boston in 1865), the City of New York, and Miamisburg, Ohio (this "bank" belonged to the Washington Social Library Company and had assumed banking privileges illegally; it was in business ca. 1839–41).[24]

Additionally, a Bank of Washington and Warren operated in Sandy Hill, New York (the bank possibly never existed; its notes, including $1 notes showing Washington on horseback, in his general's uniform, may have been intended to pass as notes from the Washington and Warren Bank, also in Sandy Hill, on record 1817–1825); a Lake Washington and Deer Creek Rail Road and Banking Company operated in Princeton, Mississippi; a Washington Banking Company in Hackensack, New Jersey; a George Washington Bank in Corning, New York (later the George Washington Banking Company); a Farmers Bank of Washington County in Fort Edward, New York; a Freemen's Bank of Washington County in Hebron, New York; a Franklin's Bank of Washington in Washington, Pennsylvania; and the Bank of Ohio had a Guernsey branch in Washington County, the oldest county in the state of Ohio.

Mount Vernon was another Washington-related name chosen to inspire trust. John Muscalus' index lists three such banking institutions, each of which featured the Father of His Country on its notes. One is the Bank of Mount Vernon, Mount Vernon, Indiana, which issued $5 and $10 notes in the 1850s; another the Mount Vernon Bank of the City of Boston, which had a medallion bust of Washington on its $2 and $10 notes from the 1860s; the third is the Mount Vernon Bank, Foster, Rhode Island, which issued $10 and $50 notes featuring a Roman-looking, standing Washington in the 1830s through 1850s.[25]

For us of the twenty-first century, it has become customary to link Washington's iconic portrait with the $1 bill, that is, with the lowest denomination. There is, however, nothing natural in this arrangement. For instance, in April 1854 the Rockingham Bank in Portsmouth, New Hampshire, issued a new series of notes, in denominations from

$1 to $100. The $1 note showed a portrait of John Jay, one of the signers of the Treaty of Paris. The $100 note had an oval portrait of George Washington at the center and a vignette with the American eagle on a shield at left—apparently, only the nation's most sacred symbols were deemed fitting for the bank's highest denomination.[26] A similar arrangement was used for notes from the Bank of Cape Cod, Harwich, Massachusetts, on whose $100 notes appeared a portrait of George Washington and a vignette showing a standing Justice draped in the United States flag.[27] $100 notes issued by the Farmers & Merchants Bank, Memphis, Tennessee, from the 1830s to the mid–1850s, were graced by a medallion portrait of Washington flanked by two female allegories, with a heraldic eagle perched atop.[28] The Bank of Augusta had used a good portrait of Washington for its highest denomination, the $100 note, from as early as the late 1810s through the 1820s.[29]

About twenty or so banking institutions had illustrations of Washington on their $500 notes. Most of these notes were issued in the 1850s, though there are earlier examples, most notably the notes from the Commercial Bank of Providence, Rhode Island, which featured a standing Washington dressed in a toga. Also notable are the $500 notes from the State Bank of New Brunswick, New Jersey, on which was printed an ornate vignette featuring Stuart's portrait of Washington, the patriotic notes issued by the Chatham Bank in New York City in the 1850s, on which Washington's portrait is flanked by flags and a drum, with a naval vessel in the background, the $500 notes from the Brighton Market Bank, Brighton, Massachusetts, on which Washington's portrait is flanked by a female allegory and a cherub, and the $500 notes from the Lechmere Bank, South Cambridge, Massachusetts, which paired Washington's portrait with a view of the United States Capitol, a highly symbolic design choice, as Washington had been deeply committed to the development of the nation's new capital, then known as the Federal City.[30]

The highest denomination with images of George Washington was of $1000. These notes were issued by some sixteen banks, almost all them located in the Northeastern United States—exceptions being the New Orleans Canal and Banking Company (also referred to as Canal Bank) and the Union Bank of Tennessee. The $1000 notes of the latter bank, issued during the 1830–40s and payable both at the parent bank in Nashville and at a number of branch banks, uniformly bore a portrait of Franklin at left and an image of Houdon's Washington bust at right.[31] To reserve a nation's most highly regarded symbols for the highest denomination of the currency can have quite unforeseen consequences, though. In the former GDR, the German Democratic Republic, the highest denomination used to be the 100 Mark note (later abbreviated as MDM), which showed a portrait of Karl Marx on its face. A portrait of Friedrich Engels was put on the second-highest denomination, the 50 Mark note. The notes were issued, with variations, from the late 1950s until the 1980s, when increased currency circulation made higher denominations an economic necessity. Plans were made for denominations of 200 and 500 Marks, confronting the authorities with an uncomfortable question: Who was to be put above Marx? The authorities (state and party officials) finally settled on motifs representing the public housing program for the 200; the state seal and a vignette of the State Council Building (Staatsratsgebäude) was chosen for the 500. Neither denomination was ever emitted, though, as the German Democratic Republic imploded in 1989.[32]

Mishaps occurred not only in the former German Democratic Republic. Dollar notes in denominations of 10 and 50 are known from Astor, Green Bay, dating to the mid–1830s. The notes show a vignette of Shawnee chief Tecumseh at left and a portrait of George Washington at right. Tecumseh is depicted as a warrior, complete with bow and arrow, and so the arrangement suggests that he is taking aim at the nation's first president.[33] George Washington is not the only target of Tecumseh's marksmanship. Other hapless victims of the warrior's rage include Hebe (on notes from the Union Bank of Florida in Tallahassee and from the Mechanics Bank in Augusta, Georgia), and a railroad train (on notes from the Bank of Darien in Savannah, Georgia, and the Monroe Rail Road and Banking Company in Macon, Georgia).[34] Railroad trains were emblematic of the relentless onslaught of western civilization, so it does make sense for Tecumseh to direct his bow and arrow at them. But Hebe? Hebe was the cupbearer for the gods and goddesses of Mount Olympus until she was later married to Heracles. While one might argue that Hebe stands for the entire western tradition, and thus a possible abomination to the Shawnee chief, there is a story that is closer to home. The Roman equivalent of Heracles is Hercules. This mythological figure played an important role in the iconography of the Revolutionary War. It was no lesser man than Benjamin Franklin who in 1782 suggested to use Hercules for the Libertas Americana medal. The medal, which like the "Washington Before Boston" piece of about 1790 was commissioned for the "Comitia Americana" series, on the obverse shows a bust of Liberty, with flowing hair and the Phrygian cap on a pole behind her; the reverse shows the infant Hercules, symbolic of the fledgling United States, strangling two serpents representing the British armies at the battles of Saratoga and Yorktown.[35]

It is impossible to determine whether any of the banknote arrangements intentionally had Tecumseh take aim at his hapless victims. All we know is that Tecumseh had organized Indian resistance against the Americans and that he was killed in the War of 1812 on the side of the British. All other exemplifications are merely symptomatic, based on a "hermeneutics of suspicion." Notes from the Marble Manufacturing Company of New York are beyond insinuation, though. The notes, which date from the 1820s, are true beauties (a rendering of an equestrian statue of George Washington is an especially high example of engraving art), yet they became worthless almost instantly, as the bank failed after only a year in business. The Eagle Bank of New Haven, Connecticut, which also issued notes bearing images of George Washington, shared the same fate in 1825. A solitary $5 proof note is the only surviving example of the Bank of Hawkinsville, Georgia. The note shows a version of General Washington that is reminiscent of John Trumbull's painting *Washington at Verplanck's Point*. The Bank of Hawkinsville opened for business in 1831. In 1839, notes from the bank were rejected by other banks. In 1842, the bank's charter was amended to rename it the Merchants Bank.[36]

Notes from failed banks illustrate the dark side of private banking. Private banks and similar note-issuing institutions (railroads, navigation companies, insurance companies, even private merchants) were formed because of the constitutional ban on federal and state-issued paper money. Private banking made available the cash necessary for the rapidly expanding economy of the young nation. And private banking also accounts for the impressive variety of visual designs. Exact figures are not available, though it is estimated that there must have been tens of thousands of different designs.

In the words of Richard Doty, a late curator at the National Numismatic Collection, there was "a pictorial richness never approached, let alone exceeded, before or after."[37] Yet private banking had its seamy side, too, thanks largely to insufficient controls by state and federal authorities. It is hardly unfair to talk about a completely corrupt system of mysterious credit, debt certificates, stock, and deliberate depreciation, not to mention rampant counterfeiting. The following story likely is one of the most memorable examples of practices and procedures that were customary at the time.

In 1839, a group of investors from Buffalo, New York, arrived in the little town of Gallipolis, Ohio. There, they started a bank with a capital of $200,000. The bank's directors authorized an issue of $175,000 of circulation. The notes quite unabashedly invited confidence in them and in the economic opportunities that they would underwrite. Especially noteworthy are the messages that the visual images on the bank's $100 bills were sending out: In the central vignette, there is a strongbox and a cornucopia overflowing with precious coins; at right, there is a canal and river pulsating with trade and commerce. The scenes quite literally radiate with optimism and strength. So too does the appearance of Hermes, the ancient god of commerce and trade, and one of the most popular male allegories in vignette art from the early nineteenth through the mid-twentieth century. Designed and engraved by George W. Hatch, Hermes appeared, *inter alia*, on $20 notes from the Merchants' Bank, New York, ca. 1830s to 1840s. Yet Hermes (also named Mercury) was also the patron god of thieves and tricksters. It appears that the choice of image was appropriate for the Bank of Gallipolis. The bank's gentlemanly managers printed over a million dollars' worth of notes above what their charter allowed them to do, and then scattered the money as far away as possible from their bank, without any intention whatsoever to redeem it. The bank collapsed two years later, as did most banks founded in the western states at the time, even if they did not engage in fraudulent business. Many banks simply found themselves unable to redeem even modest emissions of notes, and after suspending specie payments, simply failed.[38]

"The evil of the time," the editor, writer, politician, and diplomat Charles Francis Adams remarked in *Hunt's Merchants' Magazine* for December 1839, "is a great want of confidence."[39] The ominous remark by President John Quincy Adams' son and President John Adams' grandson was prompted by the various paper bills from private banks, such as the bills from the Bank of Gallipolis. Americans in the antebellum period indeed had every reason to closely watch the currency. The absence of paper money issued and controlled by a powerful authority in particular contributed to a situation in which whoever was wealthy yesterday could be poor today, and vice versa. Under such circumstances, it became everyone's vital interest to make monetary transactions as quickly as possible, to avoid long-term transactions, and to learn to take up economic opportunities instantly. "Never Keep a Paper Dollar in Your Pocket Till Tomorrow," read the inscription on a satirical token issued in Connecticut in 1857 by an observer of the difficulties with paper money.[40] A stranger could also spell trouble, especially if he was arriving at a bank's door with a bulging carpetbag in hand, demanding specie to the full value of the many different notes he presented for payment. "It was the redemption problem that bedeviled the antebellum dollar bill," a modern commentator remarked. "A sound bank would redeem its notes at par in gold. But how could you be sure it was sound, unless you tried redeeming its notes? And if everyone tried to redeem its notes, what started as an inquiry would turn into an autopsy when the bank ran out of reserves. If only people could have more confidence."[41]

The problem of confidence was, at least in part, also a matter of the dissemination of information, of publicity. Only "bad" (as well as truly wayward) banks were written about in the newspapers and financial journals like *Niles' Weekly Register*, *Hunt's Merchants' Magazine*, William M. Gouge's *Journal of Banking*, or *The Mercantile Advertiser*. Properly conducted institutions, in contrast, attracted little notice. Nor did activities that were considered normal practice. Nevertheless, citizens did have enough reasons not to trust people and paper dollars. People trying to create a new town tried to drive up real estate values on land they owned. Often enough they sold sections of land they knew were worthless. Others paid for purchases in counterfeit bills. Still others sold useless patent medicine, watered-down whiskey, phony lottery tickets, stolen horses and cattle and, at least in fiction, forged letters and delivered them to rich people, asking them to pay postage themselves.

The scheme of the "sham-post" forms an episode in the revised version of Edgar Allan Poe's story "The Business Man," which appeared in the *Broadway Journal* of August 2, 1845. The central character, tellingly named Peter Proffit, discloses without compunction, "Nobody hesitates at paying for a letter—especially for a double one—people are *such* fools—and it was no trouble to get round a corner before there was time to open the epistles."[42] Peter Proffit undoubtedly answers to the contemporary ideal of the self-made man, an ideal that Poe set out to deconstruct, emptying out its meaningfulness as a mere social construct. Proffit's operations to defraud other people, however, are all on a small scale—like the diddler's, who might, for instance, accept a genuine fifty-dollar bill as a reward for handing over a pocket book he had allegedly found, though the "large amount" of money in the purse is later seen to be merely "'a counterfeit presentment,' and the whole thing a capital diddle." Activities of this kind, and there are many more in the satirical sketch Poe published in the *Broadway Journal* of September 13, 1845, are said to be different only in scale from what true "financiers" then were doing by way of "magnificent speculation." Accordingly, a diddler (the verb "diddle" means "defraud") may be regarded as "a banker *in petto*—a financial 'operation,' as a diddle in Brobdingnag. The one is to the other, as Homer to 'Flaccus'—as a Mastodon to a mouse—as the tail of a comet to that of a pig."[43]

What conclusions can we draw from Poe's irreverent language? "Diddling," like "The Business Man," does not require much explication; straightforward accounts of frauds are simply entertaining. And they were extremely popular at the time, both in the form of fictitious magazine items fleshed out by narrative illustrations and of life stories peddled about by impostors—of Poe's fictitious diddler as much as of that celebrated Connecticut Yankee showman, P.T. Barnum, whose chief personal aim was "to put money in his coffers."[44] Barnum first tried to achieve his goal in Bridgeport, Connecticut, but when lotteries were banned there in 1834, cutting off his main income, he moved to New York City. It took him less than a year to begin as a showman, with his purchase (from another showman by the name of R.W. Lindsay) and exhibition of a blind and almost completely paralyzed slave woman, Joice Heth. Heth, Barnum claimed, was now 161 years old and thus the nation's sole living connection to the Father of His Country. She had been George Washington's nurse, raising him from infancy, suckling him at her breast, fitting him out in his first clothes, and swatting him on the behind if he misbehaved. People swarmed into her chamber for fourteen hours a day, caressing her hand and inspecting every inch of her body. Barnum was not even done with her when after months of labor, "the Greatest Natural and National Curiosity in the World" died in February 1836. He staged a public autopsy, for which 1500 people paid 50 cents each—adding another $700 to the thousands of dollars that he had already made.[45]

The doctor who performed the autopsy, David Rogers, one of New York's most prominent physicians, swore at the end that Joice Heth could not have been more than seventy-five or eighty years old. Barnum was unperturbed. He anonymously fed stories to the press that emphasized his "Yankee ingenuity" by earning a small fortune in the course of playing a rich practical joke on the American people.[46] In putting over his joke, if only for a little while, Barnum had made the Father of His Country come alive. Washington in the flesh had gone, but thanks to Barnum the entire nation could cling to his memory and identify with his image.[47] This is also what the painter Rembrandt Peale wanted to achieve with a lecture tour he undertook in 1857 to 1858, albeit with a different purpose. Peale's intention was to establish George Washington as a powerful example and stimulus to moral reform. "There is a Virtue in the looks of a Great Man," Peale said at the end of his lecture, titled "Washington and His Portraits."[48] Peale's tour coincided with a tour by Massachusetts orator Edward Everett. His "Oration on the Character of Washington" became spectacularly successful; he gave it no fewer than 137 times from March 1856 until the spring of 1861, most spectacularly in 1856, when seven thousand people waited inside New York City's Academy of Music to listen, eventually filling the aisles and part of the stage so as to share in the great event.

In Everett's lecture, Washington is presented as a hero for *all* Americans, "the beacon of light which guided the country through that broken and stormy sea" of the Revolutionary War. This had been "an age of great men and great events," but "the star of Washington shines the brightest and in the highest sphere," full of "a latent power we have not measured, a mysterious beauty of character [and] a moral fascination." Altogether, memory of Washington, that "model of a patriot President," is "founded upon a life of services to his country and mankind, without a parallel in history." To show respect to his memory is, therefore, a sacred duty of all "citizens of America." The oration ends with a timely plea that North and South cling together in memory of Washington and his principles, especially the exhortations he had included in his Farewell Address, to not let the Union break down. The disintegration of the Union, Everett warns, is a "great woe to our beloved country, [a] catastrophe for the cause of national freedom." Should it happen, the bells of the ships passing Mount Vernon "will strike the requiem of constitutional liberty for us," though at the time, 1856, Everett was still hopeful that "that sorrow and shame shall never be."[49]

5

George Washington, Gallant Revolutionary

If Everett hoped that memory of George Washington might help stave off the impending sectional conflict, he was wrong. Nor did he see that in the naming of the Father of His Country also was the strength and beauty of a successful revolution, a revolution that was led by an equally strong and beautiful revolutionary. As Thomas Jefferson wrote to Dr. Walter Jones on January 2, 1814, Washington's "person, you know, was fine, his stature exactly what one would wish, his deportment easy, erect and noble; the best horseman of his age, and the most graceful figure that could be seen on horseback."[1] In *Seventy-Six*, a revolutionary romance published in 1823, John Neal vividly describes Washington as the gallant General on horseback, a favorite subject with writers of Revolutionary romance and, much more recently, with Stephen Brumwell, the author of *Gentleman Warrior*. Here is John Neal:

> Washington passed us now, at a slow, warlike movement, his tall martial person habited in a uniform which I will try to describe:—the waistcoat was buff, plain buff, without an atom of gold upon it, very long and opening at the bottom, with flaps; the coat, what we call a French blue, rather worn and dusty, exceedingly tight in the arms and open always;—breeches buff, and boots in the clumsy fashion of the day, reaching to the knees—but without any expression: the whole costume wearing the look of what is meant for service, rather than parade. As he passed us, he uncovered to our general salutation, with a dignity and plainness that I never saw equalled. But do what he would—he was always George Washington—full of beautiful simplicity and power.[2]

Already the poetry of the Revolutionary period readily depicted Washington as a warrior. As early as June or July 1775, Philip Freneau (who eventually came to fiercely criticize the President in the *National Gazette*) hailed Washington as one who is "Bold in the fight, whose actions have aw'd / A Roman hero, or a Grecian God." Unsurprisingly, revolutionary ballads struck a similar tone, summoning, in Jonathan Mitchell Sewall's "War and Washington," Americans to "shout, and shout America! And conquering Washington."[3] In 1780, David Humphreys, one of Washington's aides and later his authorized biographer, wrote, "I go where'er the battle bleeds: / To-morrow—(brief then be my story)—I go to Washington and glory." In 1795, Richard Snowden's poem on the American war saw Washington's "courage rise as the flowing tide." Epic poetry, too, came to celebrate Washington as a warlike hero, the country's "greatest son, in that young martial frame, / From yon lost field begins the life of fame."[4]

In the antebellum period, Washington Irving explained the "*beau ideal*" of the Father of His Country's existence as the direct outcome of "the aristocratical days of Virginia."[5] Of course, Irving also injected a goodly dose of republicanism into the Virginia gentleman, though the British tradition is unmistakably there—a timely concession to Southern sentiments at a time when regional tensions were heating up fast. Irving not only offered a common heritage to both sides. His image of Washington as a Cincinnatus who, "gladly, when he had won the cause, hung up his sword never again to take it down," likewise would not have been offensive to anyone.[6]

Pictorial representations of Washington also popularized the dramatic flair of Washington as a gallant revolutionary. Painting the Father of His Country as a soldier began with John Trumbull in the 1790s, to include such well-known artworks as *Washington at Verplanck's Point*, *General Washington at Trenton*, and *The Death of General Mercer at the Battle of Princeton*, which depicts him as an impetuous man of action. The general on horseback also dominates numerous renderings of Washington's epic crossing of the Delaware River on Christmas night, 1776, en route to the Americans' victory over the British forces at Trenton. The daring crossing helped boost American morale at the start of the Revolutionary War, and as numerous versions of the subject indicate, the theme became a particularly popular one for nineteenth-century American painters and engravers. A lithograph by Nathaniel Currier appeared almost contemporaneously with Washington's Irving's description of the Virginia gentleman in *Life of Washington*.[7]

Somewhat earlier is an engraving of the crossing by George S. Lang, taken from Thomas Sully's well-known painting of 1819, *Washington at the Passage of the Delaware*, now at the Museum of Fine Arts, Boston.[8] The engraving probably would be forgotten today, had it not been for Edward Hicks, who, like many folk painters, often took inspiration from the prints or paintings of other artists. *Washington at the Delaware*, painted around 1849, the year of Hicks' death, was based on Lang's engraving. It depicts Washington at the Delaware River. In the background, troops row across icy waters; Washington sits on a white horse in the foreground on the right side of the canvas. As a devout member of the Society of Friends, Hicks was well aware of the Quaker proscription against the "vanity" and "temptation" of "ornamental painting," and throughout his career he struggled to reconcile his artistic and religious convictions. The military subject of Washington at the Delaware might be deemed especially curious in view of Hicks' pacifism, but he managed to justify his choice by describing Washington as an instrument of God. For Hicks, Washington was

> that distinguished instrument in the hand of the infinitely wise Jehovah ... [who established] the American Republic, a system of government the most healthy and happy, the most successful and generous, now under heaven ... and while virtue, liberty and independence continue to be esteemed among the children of men, the name of Washington will be pronounced with veneration and respect by millions of intelligent beings.[9]

Though Washington did not take part in the signing of the Declaration of Independence, Hicks recognized that the general's military victories had secured the freedoms proclaimed in that historic document in Philadelphia on July 4, 1776. Indeed, Hicks directly linked the two subjects in 1836, when he painted versions of *Washington at the Delaware* and *The Declaration of Independence* on opposite sides of a wooden tavern sign. The Chrysler's *Washington at the Delaware* is almost certainly the last of at least nine versions of this subject that Hicks produced over a twenty-five-year period (now at the John A. Harney Collection, Trenton; the Abby Aldrich Rockefeller Folk Art Center,

Williamsburg; and other collections). Two of these works (one in private collection, the other at the Mercer Museum, Doylestown, Pennsylvania) appear on commemorative wooden signboards that Hicks painted in 1833. Interestingly, they were hung at either side of the bridge spanning the Delaware River at the very spot crossed by Washington and his troops on Christmas night, 1776.[10]

Paper money iconography of the time likewise indulged in images of Washington as a "gallant revolutionary."[11] In 1841, for instance, the Monmouth Bank of Freehold, New Jersey, issued $5 notes with a vignette of a uniformed General Washington on horseback, leading his troops into the battle of Monmouth. The notes' design, the result of a happy merger of machined ornamentation, visual imagery, and script, stressed the importance of the historic event—on June 28, 1778, the Continental Army led by Washington defeated British troops under Sir Henry Clinton.[12] According to George Wait, who wrote the authoritative book on New Jersey currency, the person on the right is the Marquis de Lafayette, one of Washington's surrogate sons in his extended military family. Wait didn't know who the man in the left-hand vignette was, nor, apparently, does anyone else. Initially, the bills were issued in denominations of $1, $2, and $5 in the 1820s, though with different portraits at left and right, and without the overprint of the denomination, which was intended to discourage counterfeiting. (The 1841 note likely was the first to use the color red as a deterrent to forgers.)[13]

Promoting a common history and a collective identity was the message on numerous currency notes of the antebellum period. Circulation of the bills also bolstered regional or local pride and encouraged their public acceptance at a time when paper money often—and for good reason—was derided as "filthy rags."[14] Historic memory clearly dominates the $1 notes issued by the Old Colony Bank, Plymouth, Massachusetts, from the 1830s to the 1860s; the notes depict the landing of the pilgrims, with a portrait of George Washington at right.[15] Also from the 1830s, $5 notes from the American Bank, Providence, Rhode Island, depict Washington crossing the Delaware River (seen in the background) after the Battle of Trenton in 1776. The Washington vignette was engraved by Asher Durand after Thomas Sully via George S. Lang. It was also used,

A $5 note, Monmouth Bank, Freehold, New Jersey, 1841 (Division of Work and Industry, National Museum of American History, Smithsonian Institution).

A $5 note, American Bank, Providence, Rhode Island, 1830s (courtesy of RICurrency.com).

inter alia, on $1 notes from the Washington Bank, Miamisburg, Ohio, on $2 notes from the Falmouth Bank, Falmouth, Massachusetts, on $5 and $10 notes from the Merchants Bank, Newburyport, Massachusetts, on $20 notes from the Washington County Bank, Williamsport, Maryland, and on $100 notes from the New Hope and Delaware Bridge Company, Lambertville, New Jersey.[16]

In 1839, the short-lived Hernando Rail Road and Banking Company, Hernando, Mississippi, issued $5 post notes with a standing Washington in his general's uniform at left. In the 1830s and 1840s, $5 notes from the Catskill Bank, Catskill, New York, $20 notes from the Rhode Island Agricultural Bank, Johnston, Rhode Island, as well as $50 notes from the Bank of Sandusky, Sandusky, Ohio, showed another standing Washington in his general's uniform. Similar designs could be found on $2 notes from the Washington Bank (Washington Society Library Company), Miamisburg, Ohio, 1840s, and on $10 notes from the Greene County Bank, Bloomfield, Indiana, 1854. The Bank of Kentucky, Louisville, issued $100 notes depicting a standing Washington in his general's uniform, with the Marquis de Lafayette at right. Ten years later, the Chemical Bank, Washington, D.C., issued notes in the denomination of $1 25/100 with the identical Washington vignette. Another standing Washington in his general's uniform, sword drawn, his left leg on a tree trunk and arm outstretched, came to grace $5 notes from the Grocers Bank, Bangor, Maine, in the 1850s, as well as $1 notes from the Mount Joy Bank, Mount Joy, Pennsylvania, in the 1860s.[17] Banks in New Hampshire and Vermont from the late 1830s to the early 1860s issued notes showing General Washington leaning to his white charger.[18] From the 1840s, several banking institutions issued notes featuring a version of Gilbert Stuart's painting *Washington at Dorchester Heights*—$1 notes from the Frederick County Bank, Frederick, Maryland, $3 notes from the Commercial Bank, Bristol, Rhode Island, $3 and $5 notes from the Mechanics Bank in Boston, Massachusetts, and $5 notes from the Berks County Bank, Reading, Pennsylvania.[19] In the late 1850s, the short-lived Northwestern Bank of Georgia, Ringgold, came forth with $5 notes bearing a portrait of Washington at right and a rendering of the Battle of Lexington at upper left.[20]

The surrender of British General Charles Cornwallis at Yorktown in 1781, needless to say, also came to grace America's currency during the antebellum era. One example are the $5 notes issued by the Continental Bank, Providence, Rhode Island, in the early 1860s. The Continental Bank in Boston, Massachusetts, printed the Cornwallis vignette on its $20 notes, the Continental Bank in New York on its $1000 notes. The $3 notes from the Oxford Bank, Oxford, Massachusetts, $5 notes from the Bank of Chester, Chester, South Carolina, $10 notes from the Merchants Bank, Newburyport, Massachusetts, $50 notes from the Monument Bank, Charlestown, Massachusetts, and $100 notes from the Liberty Bank, Providence, Rhode Island, likewise bore the Cornwallis vignette.[21]

In the late 1850s, the short-lived Stock Security Bank in Hackensack, New Jersey, issued $5 notes that showed Liberty and a Minute Man flanking a medallion or plaque of America's first president; an eagle surmounts Washington's bust.[22] In the early 1860s, $100 notes from the Bank of Rhode Island, Newport, Rhode Island, bore the Battle of Bunker Hill as their central vignette. The death of General Joseph Warren at the Battle of Bunker Hill is featured on a number of notes from the Monument Bank, Charlestown, Massachusetts, together with the Bunker Hill Monument; in the 1850s, $10 notes from the bank bore a portrait of George Washington, with the Bunker Hill Monument at right.[23] On $5 notes issued by the Washington County Bank, Richmond, Rhode Island, late 1840s through 1863, the central vignette features a cameo bust of Washington protected by Liberty; at right, two Native Americans regard the portrait with awe; at left, an officer from the Continental Army (possibly Washington) looks at the glorified image. The vignette probably was engraved by Toppan, Carpenter & Company and adapted from a drawing by F.O.C. Darley.[24] Another Rhode Island bank, the National Bank, Providence, from the 1850s through 1865 issued $2 notes bearing a central vignette showing Washington on horseback and his staff, one reading a dispatch. In the early 1860s, the design was also used for $1 notes from the Union Bank, Philadelphia, Pennsylvania. Washington reading dispatches in the field, an officer writing on a drum, and other staff appeared on $5 notes from the Bank of Phoenixville, Phoenixville, Pennsylvania, from 1858, and on $50 notes from the Bank of Rhode Island, Newport, in the

A $5 note, Continental Bank, Providence, Rhode Island, 1861, vignette, surrender of Cornwallis at Yorktown, 1781 (courtesy RICurrency.com).

1860s. As late as 1866, the Diamond State Bank, Seaford, Delaware, issued $5 notes with a central vignette showing Washington on horseback and officers in camp.[25]

All these issues, and there are many more, show that the image of Washington as a gallant warrior, uniformed, with sword drawn or on horseback, was never completely replaced by later, decidedly unmilitary images of him, such as Stuart's "Athenaeum" or "Lansdowne" portraits, even though the latter were embraced as iconic as soon as they appeared. Nor did the sentimental image of George Washington the man completely overwhelm the warrior image. While republican virtues, civil moderation, as well as Christian piety no doubt became part of the collective consciousness, so did military zeal and political passion. The currency notes of the antebellum era are ample proof that memory of the Revolution, of common suffering and privation, together with the victorious outcome that gave pride to patriotic Americans, also captured the world of business.

A large number of notes even depicted the first first couple, George and Martha. A particularly striking example are $1 notes issued by the George Washington Bank in Corning, New York, from the 1850s through the beginning of the Civil War. On the front, a medallion portrait of Martha Washington is held by two angels at top center, while her husband's image (engraved by Alfred Jones, one of the best banknote engravers of the nineteenth century) is at bottom right. On the back, George Washington takes center stage, with the numeral "1" on either side. Equally eye-catching are the $1 notes the Southport Bank, Southport, Connecticut, issued during the same period. Red panels outline both large white 1s and the medallion portraits of the first first couple (George at left, Martha at right).[26] Somewhat earlier, the Smithfield Exchange Bank, Greenville, Rhode Island, also issued $1 notes with medallion portraits of George Washington and Martha Washington; the notes are similar to notes from the Bank of Black River, Proctorsville, Vermont, 1845–1860s, and from the Battenkill Bank, Manchester, Vermont. Notes from the Cuyler's Bank of Palmyra, Palmyra, New York, issued in the 1840s to 1850s bore a portrait of Martha Washington on the $5 and a portrait of George Washington on the $10 denomination, a marvelous articulation of the gender-based hierarchy of the time.

Medallion portraits of George Washington and Martha Washington were also printed on $10 notes from the Bank of Albion, Albion, New York, late 1840s to 1850s; a rendering of the presentation of the Declaration of Independence, placed slightly off-center, complemented the arrangement. In the 1850s, the Bank of Rutland, Rutland, Vermont, issued $2 notes with medallion portraits of George Washington and Martha Washington, while The City Bank of Columbus, Columbus, Ohio, used the arrangement for its $50 notes, and the Haverhill Bank, Haverhill, Massachusetts, as well as the Lynn Mechanics Bank, Lynn, Massachusetts, put the two portraits on their $500 notes. Somewhat later, a vignette depicting the national eagle with shield, with medallion portraits of George Washington and Martha Washington at left and right appeared on $10 notes from the Bank of Lansingburgh, Lansingburgh, New York. On the eve of the Civil War, the Bank of the Republic, Boston, Massachusetts, issued $20 notes with medallion portraits of George Washington and Martha Washington flanking a female allegory with sword, eagle, and shield.[27]

In the antebellum South, pictorial renderings of George Washington are rather rare, especially when compared to the many references to him in political discourse and public speeches. One such reference concerns the naming of the westernmost territory of the United States. The territory's preferred name had been "Columbia," though it was eventually named "Washington Territory," later the state of Washington. There was vociferous protest, during the debate in Congress, about possible confusion and the monotonous repetition of the unvarying name, though at the end of the day, Representative Stanton from Kentucky prevailed: "I desire to see, if I should live so long," Stanton is quoted as saying, "at some future day, a sovereign State bearing the name of the Father of his country."[28] As for images, one can fruitfully turn to the currency. The $4 notes from the Bank of the State of North Carolina, for instance, prominently bore a medallion head of George Washington at left.[29] Another set of $4 notes, this from the Bank of Washington, Washington, North Carolina, displayed portraits both of George and Martha, with a central vignette showing the national coat of arms flanked by five allegorical figures.[30]

In the 1850s, the Bank of Middle Georgia, Macon, Georgia, released $5 notes with an oval portrait of Washington flanked by two female allegories, "Navigation" (with an anchor) and "Agriculture" (with a cornucopia). The vignette was also adopted for $3 notes from the Mississippi Mutual Insurance Company, Aberdeen, Mississippi.[31] $10 notes issued by the Bank of Louisiana, New Orleans, in the 1850s to 1860s likewise feature an oval portrait of Washington, behind the national coat of arms and flanked by two allegorical figures, possibly Liberty and a Native American–lookalike Columbia crowning him with a laurel wreath.[32] An oval portrait of Washington, surmounted by an eagle and flanked by Liberty (at right) and another allegorical female, graced the $100 noted issued by the Louisiana State Bank, New Orleans, from the late 1850s through the 1860s. Starting in 1857, the Commercial Bank of Brunswick, Georgia, issued $2 notes with a central vignette of President Washington surmounted by a heraldic eagle and regarded by Liberty at left and two allegorical females at right. Below, at left, is an oval portrait of Thomas Jefferson.[33] As for higher-denomination notes, in 1860 the Central Rail Road and Banking Company, Savannah, Georgia, emitted $500 notes with a dominant central vignette: a "Houdonesque" bust of George Washington behind the national coat of arms is flanked by three allegorical figures, one of whom is crowning the bust with a laurel wreath.[34]

Perhaps the most remarkable pieces of paper currency from the antebellum South are $5 notes issued by the Central Bank of Tennessee in the late 1850s. In the lower right corner, General Washington appears on horseback; in the opposite corner a veteran is shown returning home to his farm, presumably from the war against Mexico. That war, it should be pointed out, gave rise to a new wave of adulation of soldier-farmers and, concomitantly, of the Cincinnatus legend. Washington had commonly been seen as a Cincinnatus incarnation; in the 1840s, appeals to the American Revolution were thus used to stimulate the war spirit in the country.[35] On the banknote vignette, Washington's outstretched arm points to the home-coming scene, as if blessing the event. (Ten years later, the scene would have been an apt pictorialization of a popular song, "When Johnny Comes Marching Home Again."[36])

Washington's benediction constitutes a truly fatherly gesture, reinforcing memory of a man who considered the entire nation as his "family." But what kind of family was it

A $5 note, Central Bank of Tennessee, Nashville, TN, 1856 [?] (Division of Work and Industry, National Museum of American History, Smithsonian Institution).

going to be? In the North, the Mexican War was widely viewed as a proslavery swindle, with an eye toward expanding slave lands to the west. Texas, which had become a state in 1845, was a key arena in the battle. In Congress, a majority of representatives, Abraham Lincoln included, repeatedly voted to ban slavery in any territory snatched from Mexico. And Texas, as Matthew Karp argues in a recent book, "was above all a slaveholding republic" which, Southerners were convinced, "required US support—and, if necessary, US protection."[37] Seen in this way, the picture of Washington on the Tennessee notes must have worked like a magic charm, bolstering the Southern view—like the cheap Revolutionary thrillers and paperbacked lives of Washington and his generals that were mass-produced at the time.[38]

On the Tennessee notes, Washington is accompanied by a framed, slightly off-center portrait of Charles Carroll, Maryland's delegate at the Continental Congress and one of the signers of the Declaration of Independence. The only catholic present at the convention, Carroll (1737–1832) was also a political outsider. He despised the Whiggish doctrines of parliamentarianism and majority rule. Instead, Carroll adhered to notions of checks and balances, as well as rules of moral behavior based on natural law (unchanging principles based on nature and God that define reality and humankind). Conservative ideas of this kind had come to eighteenth-century America through the writings of Bolingbroke and Sir Robert Filmer. They reached a new height of popularity in the antebellum South, due in part because the South increasingly felt discriminated against by the majoritarian rule in Congress.[39] The Washington vignette was used on a number of notes from other banks ($5 notes from the Atlanta Bank and the Bank of Penn Township, $10 notes from the Village Bank, Danvers, Massachusetts, $20 notes from the Planters Bank of Fairfield, South Carolina, $50 notes from the Bank of Savannah, Georgia, $25 notes from the Central Bank, Middletown, Connecticut, and $2 notes from the Bank of Chicago),[40] but never as effectively as on the Tennessee notes.

Except for the notes from the Central Bank of Tennessee (the bank lasted until 1858, when it failed), none bears the homecoming scene or Carroll's portrait. The impact of the two images should not be underestimated. They are indicative of the dramatic changes in visual representations of the nation—from *E PLURIBUS UNUM* ("Out of Many, One") to the sectionalist presence of "the South." While portraits of Charles Carroll were popular on notes from Southern banks,[41] other "native sons" also made it onto various notes then. Several bills carried portraits of George M. Troup, a former governor of Georgia and a leading advocate of states' rights. Southern sectionalism became even more pronounced when former South Carolina Congressman and United States Vice President John C. Calhoun appeared on paper currency. Calhoun had died in 1850, but his pronouncement, from a Senate speech of 1837, that "Abolition and the Union cannot co-exist" had entered the collective memory. His portrait, which was featured on dozens of notes issued throughout the entire South, sent a clear message across the Mason-Dixon Line. The same can be said of $50 notes from the Bank of the Empire State, Rome, Georgia. The notes showed, at upper left, a seated woman with a scythe and a portrait of Washington. The central vignette, however, pictures Liberty seated with cap and pole, and a vigilant soldier standing with a rifle beside a shield surmounted by a bust and bearing the state arms.[42]

Several Southern banks altogether dispensed with portraits of George Washington, replacing him with "native sons." This is especially true of Kentucky banks, which often replaced the first president with Henry Clay, Kentucky's most famous politician for much of the antebellum period. The Northern Bank of Kentucky, for instance, had Washington's portrait on its $100 notes in the 1840s to 1850s. From the 1850s, a portrait of Henry Clay took his place.[43] Even more powerful is the representation of "Southernness" on $10 notes issued by the Bank of the State of South Carolina, Charleston, in 1861. The notes depict the dramatic rescue from the British of American prisoners that took place in South Carolina towards the end of the War of Independence, with portraits of two South Carolina generals—Daniel Morgan (at left) and Andrew Pickens (at right)—added for good measure. Ironically, the notes were produced by a Northern company, the New York–based American Banknote Company, though the designs conveyed more than local patriotism. They portended the impending collapse of the Union and the coming of the Civil War.[44]

The general preparedness for a military confrontation can be seen from the visual design also of Northern currency. Although war-related violence was not generally deemed an appropriate subject for banknote design, there were a few battle scenes. One can be found on $10 notes issued by the Salem Bank, Salem, Massachusetts, in 1862. The vignette (one of the latest-created vignettes in the obsolete series) shows Union soldiers in a Civil War battle scene.[45] A furious finale came in January 1865, with $1 notes issued by the Bank of Montgomery County in Norristown, Pennsylvania. A central vignette placed above the bank's name shows the bank building; at bottom center is a small bust of Washington, reminiscent of Houdon's. The composition is framed by the portraits of no fewer than four Union generals: clockwise from upper left, they are General Adam J. Slemmer, General Winfield Scott Hancock, General John F. Hartranft, and Colonel John W. Schall (all of whom had connections to Norristown).[46]

Again in 1865, the year the $1 notes were issued, the Bank of Montgomery County became the Montgomery National Bank. The name change does not mean that the bank was now owned by the federal government. Still, it indicates the dramatic change in the relation between region and center that came about with the Civil War. When it was over, Northern victory indeed had redefined America—the "Union" of individual states was now an indivisible "nation."[47] (Thus, people stopped saying "the U.S. *are*" and learned to say, "the U.S. *is*.") Regarding America's money, no longer did private, state-chartered banks issue their own notes; instead, note-issuing became the exclusive privilege of the federal government. As Senator John Sherman declared, "if anything should be national, it should be bank notes." Sherman, who was a Senator from Ohio, had been instrumental also in establishing the "National Currency Bureau," which later became the "Bureau of Engraving and Printing." The notes issued by the Bureau provided the government with an unparalleled opportunity for officially sanctioned propaganda. Senator Sherman's hopeful words that the images emblazoned on the new notes would promote "a sentiment of nationality" fully illustrate the degree to which authorities saw them as effective carriers of symbolic messages. With the help of these messages, they could at the same educate citizens about their country and endear them to the authorities responsible for issuing the notes.[48]

The legal basis for a national banking system was established by various acts passed respectively in 1863 and 1864. These acts were primarily intended as "a money-raising scheme for the Union war effort."[49] As a side effect, private notes soon passed out of America's monetary history. If they were not redeemed for coins, they became worthless. A remark by Treasury Secretary Salmon P. Chase, that private notes constituted merely an "unnational circulation,"[50] indicates that they had also lost whatever ideal value they might have possessed. The policy of securing note issuing for the federal government worked chiefly by attrition. A "death tax" imposed on notes from state-chartered banks made sure that these banks converted to "National" banks. Another measure was to make the United States notes (the "greenbacks") a legal tender for public and private debts, which effectively made the acceptance of federal paper money mandatory. The policies were extremely successful. By 1867, over ninety percent of the total currency held by the public and the banks was of Civil War origin, that is, of types of money that had not existed only six or seven years earlier—United States notes (the "greenbacks"), National Bank notes, Gold and Silver Certificates, other United States currency (such as interest-bearing Legal Tender notes), and fractional currency.[51]

The national banking system that came into being as a corollary to the Civil War had been a long time in the making. Alexander Hamilton already during the War of Independence had articulated his firm conviction that finance was critical and that therefore Congress must have control of "coining money; establishing banks on such terms and with such privileges as they think proper; appropriating funds and doing whatever else relates to the operations of finance."[52] Hamilton's plans to create a national bank of issue were fiercely opposed by James Madison during the constitutional debates. In the *Federalist Papers* of 1787, for instance, Madison called the current "rage for paper money" an "improper or wicked project," whose effects on the "necessary confidence between man and man, on the necessary confidence in public councils, on the industry and morals of the people, and on the character of republican government" was, simply, "pestilential."[53]

All reservations about and objections against notwithstanding, on December 12, 1791, the Bank of the United States, chartered by Congress and later known as the

First Bank of the United States opened for business at Carpenter's Hall in Philadelphia, which was then the seat of the federal government. Madison's congressional speech on the Bank Bill, delivered on February 2, 1791, had not had the desired effect.[54] The combined forces of Hamilton and the Federalists legitimized the Bank of the United States by the "general welfare" clause in the federal Constitution. Modeled after the Bank of England, the Bank of the United States became a depository for federal funds, a fiscal agent for the government, a facilitator of major commercial transactions, and the largest source of paper money operating in the country, providing something like a uniform currency. Its notes enjoyed a high reputation both at home and abroad, buying the entire Louisiana Territory from Napoleon in 1803.

The Bank of the United States was never as successful as its proponents wished, though. For one thing, it was not a truly "national" institution, despite the fact that the federal government owned a fifth of the shares, and also despite the fact that its notes were receivable in payments to the federal government. For another thing, fierce opposition instantly beset the bank. Opposition came from two principal sources, from Southern agrarians like Jefferson, who never understood banks but nevertheless claimed that the Bank of the United States was unconstitutional, and from the state banks. Congress' refusal in 1810 to renew the bank's charter thus was a clear give-in to the national mood of financial free enterprise and state power. The republicanization of the banking system marked not only a return to a horse-and-buggy view of economic development, but also a victory to hard-money advocates who regarded the Bank of the United States as merely another "paper mill" that, rather than hold other banks in check, actively encouraged them in their "pernicious activity of issuing a paper currency" that would inevitably depreciate.[55] Once the Bank of the United States had lost its charter, almost all of its notes were redeemed. This move makes them excessively rare today; at the time, it whisked more than $7 million in hard cash out of the country to refund foreign stockholders. The result was a national shortage of gold and silver, which led many banks in the country to stop redeeming their notes.

The War against England made the situation even worse. The Democratic Republicans had killed not just any bank but the premier instrument for borrowing money and financing the war effort. Commercial banks, which were grossly undercapitalized, were in no position to take the BUS's place as lenders to the government. Starting with the banks in Baltimore, which had become alarmed by a battle between British and American troops that had taken place a few days before, there was soon a general suspension of specie payment. The situation was of increasing concern to the federal government, which expected and depended on prompt payment of debts, taxes, and tariffs. Only a national bank, Secretary of the Treasury James Alexander Dallas wrote in December 1815, could "relieve the country and the Government from the present embarrassments."[56]

In 1816 Congress did charter another central bank, the Second Bank of the United States. The bank lasted until 1836, when it became a victim of the financial and economic crisis following Andrew Jackson's populist war against the BUS. Jackson had won a political war over the Second Bank, though his victory had done nothing to alleviate people's sufferings from the uncertainties of paper money. On the contrary, the destruction of the Bank of the United States removed all restraints from the commercial banks, enabling them to behave more waywardly than ever. Eliminating the Bank of the United States, whose notes had constituted the most reliable form of paper money in the antebellum period, thus only made worse the difficulties that continued to plague America's money until the Civil War.

From a modern point of view, the introduction of federal paper money shows, above all, that Andrew Jackson may have won the battles of the day against Henry Clay and his fellow Whigs, though the Whigs would win the larger contest. "America's future," the historian Daniel Walker Howe concludes, "lay predominantly within the Whig vision of economic development and a stronger central government."[57] Among the first and certainly the best-known politician to wave the banner of the Whig vision was Abraham Lincoln. As a Whig state legislator in Illinois, Lincoln, though he was an admirer of Henry Clay, backed William Henry Harrison before the party convention. Tellingly, Lincoln tied his support to the question of a national bank of issue. Lincoln had demanded such a bank already in a speech he made in 1832 while campaigning for office himself. Now, he made a number of campaign speeches in behalf of Harrison, in which he explained that the former Bank of the United States had "established and maintained" a sound and uniform circulating medium and that it "can do so again, by the *aid* of [the national] government," whose most "imperative" duty to the people is that of "furnishing them a sound and uniform currency."[58] Lincoln's defense of the Bank of the United States notwithstanding, Illinois went to Martin Van Buren, though in Lincoln's hometown of Springfield, voters delivered a majority to the Whigs.

Lincoln continued to battle for a central bank of issue, arguing that the agrarian state of Illinois needed more not less government. Illinois, Lincoln saw clearly, depended on safe and easy credit. With a *national* bank of issue out of reach, he defended the Illinois state bank against the Democrats.[59] The bank also was an important element in Lincoln's program of modernization and internal improvement paid for by public money—the "Illinois System," in analogy to the "American System" of John Adams and Henry Clay, called into existence since federal money was not forthcoming. Lincoln remained an active and loyal Whig until the newly organized Republican Party absorbed most northern Whigs in the 1850s. The "Illinois System" may have failed, yet it initiated a nationalizing trend that bore fruit in 1861, when the economy became a central element in Lincoln's patriotic nationalism. As regards a new Bank of the United States, Lincoln's private notes of March 1848 indicate that, were he president, he would "*not* urge it's [sic!] reagitation upon Congress," though should Congress see fit to establish such an institution, he certainly would "*not* arrest it by veto."[60]

As President, Lincoln *was* in a position to exert "the power of regulation." Furnishing a "sound and uniform currency," he saved the Union not just militarily but also economically.[61] Under Lincoln, the United States government turned worthless paper into legal tender, simply by putting its stamp on it. Yet it did so, not in an illogical or unnatural way, as critics of paper money had feared, but in a thoroughly *political* way. When the transition was completed, the promise of specie money or specie-backed money had been superseded by one that rested on a far more abstract and transcendent notion—the credit of the nation. At first, this meant little more than a confidence that the federal government would be able to pay its bills. However, with the war effort being represented as a struggle for the preservation of the union, these obligations assumed a deeper significance. That significance can be summarized as the "standardization" or "territorialization" of money.

To define a currency as "territorial" is much broader than to simply refer to it as a "national" currency, the term that monetary historians use the most widely. As the political scientist Eric Helleiner explains, a "national" currency is not "territorial" unless and until (1) there are no other currencies—whether foreign or privately issued domestic—in the land, and (2) the currency is homogeneous in quality—not varying, for instance, in value in different regions.[62] Territorial currencies are always tied not just to nation building but first and foremost to the development of state monopolies. This development impacts on the visual design of the currency, much as the new currency reshapes people's social relations. Additionally, the development of state monopolies goes hand in hand with the reformulation of the relations between state and citizens. Citizens must get used to administrative centralization that, for instance, enables the state's total control over the currency within a given territory. For this purpose, the United States in 1865 established a "National Detective Police Force," whose task was to control counterfeiting, to generally protect the currency, and to guarantee the free and unimpeded circulation of United States Notes (which had been made a "legal tender for all debts public and private").

If the "National Detective Police Force" (it later became the Secret Service) was a symptom of the city of Washington's—the center's—rising influence in all walks of American life, so was the establishment of a national postal service, the federal regulation of banks, and the consolidation of the tax system.[63] All these measures involve the work of cultural elites, and so does establishing a territorial currency. For the new notes to be accepted, the manufacturing of consent was essential. Paper money lacks intrinsic value, and so citizens must trust the promise of value given by the state. All kinds of images and symbols were therefore used to communicate ideological and political messages to the American people. Visual symbols proved particularly useful, as their meanings could be understood also by people who were unable to read and write. The symbols and images effected a multiple transfer of meanings. The notes' visual aesthetics was transferred onto the economic value of the currency, which in turn was transferred onto the political value of the state. Importantly, the notes were deliberately inscribed with the qualities they were supposed to exemplify. In this sense, they served to reinforce what Michael Billig has termed "banal nationalism," that is, the hotchpotch of ideological practices and habits that reproduce the nation on an everyday level.[64]

The primary motive for the creation of a uniform currency—the bolstering of the territoriality of the nation-state—is reflected in a statement made in 1861 by John Sherman, a staunch supporter of National Bank notes. Such notes, Senator Sherman said, would help foster a sense of national unity not just by producing economic benefits to individuals but also by encouraging communication between citizens:

> Every citizen [...] who is supplied with such a currency—a currency which will be equal to gold through every foot of our territory, and everywhere of the same value, with which he can travel from Oregon to Florida and from Maine to New Mexico, would feel and realize, every time he handled or looked at such a bill bearing the national mark, that the union of these states is verily a personal benefit and blessing to all.[65]

All federal notes emitted after the Civil War bore a common impression, as all were issued by the federal government. The common impression—what Senator Sherman called "the national mark"—read either "United States" or "United States of America." All notes also came, in continuation of early documentary traditions, with the seal of the Treasury Department and the signatures of its chief representatives, the Secretary and the Treasurer. Signatures still are crucial features of a paper currency. Signatures constitute a semblance of personal obligation, which softens the anonymity and impersonality of the notes. But when in 1861 the New York banknote companies printed the first greenbacks, the Treasurer and the Registrar of the Treasury personally signed them.

Signing bills was a purgatorial task, according to a contemporary, whose "self-imposed limit was a thousand sheets (four thousand signatures) a day. For a single day … this would not be a hard task; but to follow it for weeks and months, as I did … would, if it were a punishment, be too inhuman to be inflicted upon the most guilty of criminals."[66] Congress had enough consideration in this matter, and authorized signing by proxy. It did not take long until, as we learn from an account published in 1883, "70 clerks at $1,200 a year were kept busy in writing their own in lieu of these officers' names." The problem was not public expense so much as the fact that "so many different hands destroyed all the value of signatures." The signatures, which were to guarantee the trustworthiness of the notes, being those of clerks, were no protection against fraud, and the Secretary was "in sore perplexity."[67]

At this point a Mr. Spencer M. Clark, who was then Superintendent of Constructing the Public Buildings, proposed facsimiles of the signatures and of the Treasury seal, to be engraved and printed on the notes in special ink, and by a special process. The proposal was accepted by Secretary Chase and was given official sanction by Congress. This considerably speeded up production, though it did not entirely alleviate concern about the value of signatures, which was appropriate in an era when handwriting was an index to a person's character. Additionally, signatures and seals point to the origin of paper money in late medieval documentary culture, thus preserving the memory of the personal touch, and with it the primacy of embodying authority. The persistent adherence to signatures and seals confirms and maintains belief in their quasi-magical qualities.[68]

The look of the new notes issued by the federal government in the postbellum era was different from anything that people had seen before. Gone were the colorful notes of the era of free banking, when banks would personalize their notes with elaborate designs of individuals, scenes, or other details meaningful for their locality. Gone also were plans for making the currency system more secure by mandating local or regional designs that would indicate "the locality of the bank, or of the town, or state, at least, the section of country, to which they belong."[69] Instead, there were notes "bearing a common impression," as they were all issued and controlled by the federal government. The creation of a single homogeneous currency also involved the removal of foreign coins from domestic circulation and the elimination of old and worn money, as well as of "thalers" and other "foreign inscriptions" on currency. Just as important were attempts to stamp out counterfeiting, which during mid-century had been so rampant that, some writers estimate, at times roughly forty percent of the money in circulation was counterfeit.[70] Altogether, the rise of a homogeneous currency in the postbellum years greatly facilitated economic relations across the—still rapidly expanding—territory of the United States. On the level of culture, the new, homogeneous currency provided citizens with a common "monetary language" within a common fiscal order.

The nation that emerged from the crucible of the Civil War had less need for an awesome, remote, and largely unreal gallant revolutionary as its symbol of nationality or national unity. Instead, images of Abraham Lincoln began to occupy a larger space in the American psyche. This is evident, for instance, in the number of books and articles published. Baker's *Bibliotheca Washingtoniana* lists ninety-eight for the 1850s, thirty-nine for the 1860s, and just over thirty for the 1870s and 1880s. Reverence of Lincoln already set in during the presidential campaign, when he was hailed as "our Prairie King." The title "King" would have been impossible for Washington, the icon of republicanism, but for Lincoln it spelt natural nobility and leadership. Lincoln was seen as a man of the people, "No gentleman, like Washington," as the poet Richard Henry Stoddard would later write. Nor did Lincoln's contemporaries detect any similarities to the Roman heroes that had served as models for the founders already during their lifetimes: "No hero this of Roman mould, / Nor like our stately sires of old." In fact, Lincoln's heroic status was so new and so quintessentially American that it could only have come from Nature: "For him her Old World moulds aside she threw, / And, choosing sweet clay from the breast / Of the unexhausted West, / With stuff untainted shaped a hero new."[71]

Following Lincoln's assassination in 1865, however, there was a resurgence of tradition, with the martyred president explicitly represented as a "A second Washington! / So great in every virtuous plan."[72] Elevated to the role of Savior of His Country, Lincoln was expected to "affirm and reassert the principles of Washington." Praise of the Father of His Country was somewhat disingenuous, as it effectively broke Washington's unique hold on the nation's affections. "Mt. Vernon and Springfield will henceforth be kindred shrines," one eulogist declared.[73] Much more frequently, however, we hear religious overtones in the eulogies. A Christian martyr, a Moses, even a Jesus Christ were used as sources for Lincoln imagery. In one instance, Lincoln is shown in heaven, embraced by Washington, who is about to crown the martyred president's head with a laurel wreath.[74] If Lincoln was established as the North's new heroic martyr, he was also, more generally, seen as a figure of pathos and humanity. (For white southerners, Robert E. Lee became the parallel icon, visible for instance in a statue dedicated in Charlottesville, Virginia, in 1924; the planned removal of the Lee statue was the pretext for the "Unite the Right" rally there in August 2017.) George Washington, in contrast, became rather more an object of nostalgia. When the Ohio representative Rutherford B. Hayes visited Mount Vernon in 1866, the Father of His Country appeared to him as "formal, statue-like, a figure for exhibition."[75]

Representative Hayes' words are from a visit to Mount Vernon in 1866. Hayes might have paid for his fare with new federal currency notes. On these, portraits of Lincoln soon outnumbered representations of Washington. (In 1866, crude portraits of Washington and Lincoln were considered for the nickel five-cent piece.) Less than a year after Lincoln's election to the presidency, his portrait was printed on $10 notes—on 14 million of them. The first of these notes were "Demand Notes," which still were redeemable in coin. In 1862, they were followed by "United States Notes," which were made a legal tender for all debts public and private, thus effectively unredeemable. Both types of notes were typical for war times—they demonstrated the North's sovereignty, internally as well as externally. The message these notes conveyed was unambiguous—the master in the house is Abraham Lincoln.[76]

The Confederacy responded by printing on the currency a portrait of its president, Jefferson Davis. They did not forget the nation's founder, though. George Washington was eminently present at the swearing-in of the Confederate administration in 1862. Not only did the ceremony take place in Richmond, Virginia, on Washington's birthday, February 22. It also took place on Capitol Square, under the Washington Monument of which Thomas Crawford's colossal equestrian statue is the centerpiece. This may seem odd, as does the fact that elements of Crawford's statue were incorporated into the Seal of the Confederate States—after all, Washington had come to symbolize America's national *unity*. For the statue's inauguration, Alfred Mitchell had written an epic poem in couplets, concluding in these words: "Princeton was thy jewel—Monmouth was thy crown; / But what completes thy glory, is thy battle at Yorktown!"[77]

Verse written by James Barron Hope and John R. Thompson was also written for the occasion in Richmond, Virginia. Thompson, editor of the *Southern Literary Messenger*, made a plea for national unity. Asking what the purpose of the ceremony was, he answered: "'T is that we here in gratitude renew / The patriot-vows to country ever due, / And on this holy altar firmly swear / The blessed compact never to impair."[78] And Virginia Governor John Wise, speaking the name of Washington, exclaimed at the ceremony: "Magic name! If none other under Heaven can draw us to each other, that talisman can touch the chords of unison, and clasp us hand to hand, and bind us heart to heart, in the kindred heirship of one Patriot Father … for, in the very naming of that name, there is … the strength and beauty of *National Union*."[79]

Many Southerners, John C. Calhoun included, had a different view. They saw the Revolution of 1776 as the first step towards the second American revolution, the secession from the Union. The view that the South must rebel against Northern oppression even as Washington had done against the British was to lend legitimacy to this momentous event—both morally and under international law. John Richter Jones, author of *Slavery Sanctioned by the Bible*, produced in 1858 a Revolutionary romance in which Washington is called "rebel" at least on four occasions. An anonymous piece of newspaper verse, titled "Rebels" and published shortly after hostilities had begun, presents the conviction that Washington belonged to the South particularly well: "Rebels! 'tis our family name—/ Our father, Washington, / Was the arch-rebel in the fight / And gave the name to us—a right / Of father unto son."[80] On the South's state papers, pictures of George Washington as a son of the South also prevailed, on the 20¢ stamps and on the currency—for instance, on $5 notes issued by the Bank of the Commonwealth, Richmond, on a $5 warrant of the Confederate State of Texas, on $10 notes from the Traders Bank of Richmond, on $5 and $50 Confederate States notes, and on various notes from the Bank of Pittsylvania, Chatham, Virginia.[81]

The notes from the Bank of Pittsylvania are especially noteworthy. For one thing, there was a notable change in design once the Civil War had started. On the bank's $20 notes, Alfred Jones' engraving of Washington was replaced by a vignette featuring

A $50 Revenue Bond Scrip, State of South Carolina, 1872 (Division of Work and Industry, National Museum of American History, Smithsonian Institution).

a woman riding on a deer; by contrast, on the $5 notes the portrait of a woman was replaced by a portrait of George Washington. The printing technique, too, had changed. Before the war, the bank's notes were produced by the American Bank Note Company in New York, using the customary siderographic method. This method was too costly for Southern banks during wartime, and so notes were produced using lithographic printing. Lithographic printing was much cheaper and simpler, yet the results left much to be desired. The method does not yield precise and bold lines, and so the new notes—Civil War Emergency Issues—appear somewhat "blurred." The Confederate Department of the Treasury at first made use of the steel-plate engraving machinery at the New Orleans office of the American Bank Note Company, but this small facility in no time was completely overwhelmed with work. It also did not help much that some Southern banks began contributing old (and in many cases worn out) printing plates to the Treasury. In the end, most bills from the Confederate States of America were produced through lithography, as for example the $50 notes from 1861, with Washington's portrait at lower right and an allegory of Justice at left.[82]

Though one would expect an increase in "Southern" imagery once the war was under way, this was not the case. The image, on an 1862 note from the Commercial Bank of Richmond, Virginia, of a Confederate soldier with battle flag, defending Southern womanhood from Yankee depredations, was an exception rather than the rule. One reason, Richard Doty explains, is that it "took *time* to create new images, and time was precisely what Southern bankers and their customers did not have."[83] Some patriotic images were indeed created in the South, but scenes of Southern heroism were to be found rather on notes from Southern states or from the Confederate government. Yet even among these notes, a great many were designed not so much to celebrate the South's white heroes as to validate a system that held blacks in perpetual slavery. "Bond after bond, bill after bill," Harold Holzer found, "suggests a preoccupation with reminding note-holders, investors, debtors, and ordinary citizens alike, that slavery, one of the most important elements of Southern economy, would continue to exist in perpetuity, protected by law and sanctioned by tradition, and all but divinely ordained in iconography."[84]

Even more telling is the inclusion, on a $10 note produced for the Central Bank of Alabama, Montgomery, by a group of Northern printmakers hired by the Confederacy, of the iconic Gilbert Stuart portrait of George Washington. Clearly, the portrait served as "a reminder that the greatest of all American presidents to date had been a Southern slaveholder, and, by implication, a supporter of the Confederacy and the perpetuation of the slave system."[85] The co-presence, on Southern notes, of George Washington with scenes that were typical of a slave-holding society is hardly surprising. What is noteworthy is that such scenes were still used during the Reconstruction era, as on scrip notes issued by the State of South Carolina in 1872. Was this done in order to emphasize the South's moral and cultural superiority over the North?[86] Hard as it is to imagine, as late as fifteen years after the Civil War had ended Jefferson Davis, the former president of the Confederacy, wrote that "African servitude" in the South had been "the mildest and most humane of all institutions to which the name 'slavery' has ever been applied."[87]

6

Ornamenting the Façade of Hell

On the Revenue Bond Scrip, two properties of money come to the fore. First, that money, represented by the various currency notes, really is the great equalizer. Second, that the mass production of bank notes and similar papers was an epiphenomenon of capitalist expansion. Capitalist expansion meant the accumulation of more and more money, yet the money form increasingly was without backing. In other words, instead of the real possibility of redeeming paper for precious metal there were mere promises, of growth and of the regaining of value. Thus, the ornaments printed on the various notes had to provide legitimacy to capitalist expansion. Additionally, they served as ways and means to cope with or even conceal economic and social instability. And they would help appease white males' racial anxieties, their fears for their traditional prerogatives as well as their unease over Eastern and Southern European immigration. Unsurprisingly, the guardian spirits printed on bank notes represented happiness, prosperity, economic health, fertility, and so on. The pastoral charge was to deflect from the strict and punitive deity, who saw the accumulation of riches as sinful, an instance of avarice. The guardian spirits gave their blessing to and protect monetary dealings, lending a measure of dignity to financial institutions and instruments.

Banknote designers were only too happy to employ representations of George Washington to lend dignity to their notes. In the early 1830s, the Bank of North America, Philadelphia, issued $50 Demand notes on which Washington is depicted on his white stallion accepting a purse of banknotes from a goddess dressed in classical garb. The goddess is standing in front of the pillars of the bank; at her feet is the inscription "CHARTERED 1781." With the Patriot army seen camped in the background, the vignette, which was engraved by Asher B. Durand and produced by Carpenter Toppan, is an allusion to how the Bank of North America helped finance the war effort. The goddess herself could be an allegorical symbol of France, which supplied most of the cash used by Robert Morris to fund the majority of the Bank's initial offering. (In 1791, the Bank of North America was succeeded in its role as a central bank of sorts by the first Bank of the United States.) There is also a more topical allusion. The design can be seen also as a memento to George Washington's stand on monetary matters, which during the 1830s—the time of Andrew Jackson's bank war—was often referred to by Daniel Webster. Perhaps for that reason the design was also used on $20 notes from the Citizens Bank, Scituate, Rhode Island.[1]

Accompanying measures for the purpose of building trust also came in the guise of allegorical figures, mostly female ones. These guardian spirits are a good reminder

A $20 note, Citizens Union Bank, Scituate, Rhode Island, 1830s (courtesy RICurrency.com).

that from its beginning, money had been under the spell of ethics. Roman coins, for instance, frequently were stamped with a female figure, identified by the inscription "Moneta" as the goddess of coins (L. *moneta*, coin). "Moneta" was one of the aspects of the goddess Juno, and originally meant "advisor," from *monere*, to warn or admonish. A temple built to Juno Moneta in Rome became the site of the first Roman mint, in the third century BCE. Juno Moneta usually was depicted with a cornucopia and a pair of scales, symbolizing (distributive) justice. On $500 and $1000 notes issued in the 1830s by the Tombigby Rail Road Company, Columbus, Mississippi, a standing Moneta is receiving a bag of coins from Mercury in clouds at right.[2]

On $5 notes from the Bank of East Tennessee, an angel extends a hand to Ceres at left and hands an apple to a woman with a sextant at right; however, the three females are placed under the authority and supervision of Liberty and the national eagle, who eye them critically, perhaps in order to lend a less risqué appearance to the composition.[3] The ensemble of allegorical figures on the notes from the Bank of East Tennessee conjures up an era *before* the mass-scale dissemination of paper money. In that era, personality was grounded in real values, such as land, and the communal work of the land was considered as a necessary precondition of virtue and, concomitantly, of the foundation of the nation. Working the land took for granted chattel slavery and other forms of exploitation, which shows, in unflattering directness, that morality and decency never were part of the harsh reality of money-making. "Nowhere more naively than in these [nineteenth-century notes] does capitalism display itself in such solemn earnest," the German critic Walter Benjamin wrote in an essay from the late 1920s. "The innocent cupids frolicking about numbers, the goddesses holding tablets of the law, the stalwart heroes sheathing their swords before monetary units, are a world of their own: ornamenting the façade of hell."[4] Clearly for Benjamin, money was more than a medium of exchange or a means for the preservation of value. Its very materiality, he was convinced, makes it an ideal medium for the communication of social and cultural values. Benjamin even suggested that there is also a religious or at least a quasi-religious dimension. Words such as "solemn," "cupids" and "goddesses," and "hell" clearly point in this direction.

Benjamin's essay was originally published in German as "Einbahnstrasse" in 1928. Seven years earlier he composed a fragment titled "Kapitalismus als Religion" ["Capitalism as Religion"], which remained unpublished in his lifetime. In it, Benjamin suggested that a comparison be made between religious paintings ("the images of the saints of the various religions") and the ornaments on bank notes ("the banknotes of different states. The spirit that speaks from the ornamental design of banknotes"). Such a comparison, Benjamin argued, would reveal the religious structure of capitalism, as well as the fact that capitalism, by colonizing religion, had itself become a religion, or at least a cult, thus a religion without dogma.[5] Benjamin, who had studied with the philosopher Georg Simmel in Berlin, was convinced that capitalism had emerged as religion's parasite, drawing on its resources until it became identical with it. Capitalism thus appears as a religion without dogma, a religion that placed the cultic over the doctrinal. Hence, the images on bank and government notes bear a structural similarity to the images of the saints of the various religions. However, under capitalism the originally religious emblems return as commodities: the ornamental design of banknotes serves to technically normalize capitalist exchange. That exchange, while it produces consumption, is based on credit, the receiving of which creates indebtedness, or guilt, though under capitalism, there is no release from either debt or guilt. The cult has only one goal—getting into debt. Hence there is no atonement that binds it to the reform of the present; instead, it is merely bound to its demolition.[6]

The American Civil War also was a form of "demolition." And it was an expensive one. Once the first shots had been fired at Fort Sumter on April 12, 1861, each side was in desperate need for money for the war effort.[7] The Confederacy at first left the money business to the private banks, though the exigencies of the war proved disastrous to them, so that they took to typesetting notes, sometimes overprinting older paper. State banks also took to issuing paper money, sometimes doing a little touch-up work on antebellum vignettes to "defederalize" the imagery.[8] Finally, the Confederate government took over the note-issuing business itself. While State governments and the Confederacy were accustoming the people to public rather than private notes, both were issuing only paper *promises*. The problem arose in part because of a constitutional clause that allowed both the southern states and the Confederate government to issue paper, while neither could make them legal tender. The combined result was a flood of worthless paper, made worse by counterfeiting. The situation became so bad that the Confederate government even decided to honor counterfeits as genuine. Most of these counterfeits came, not from counterfeiters in the South but from legitimate printers and engravers in the North who sought to undermine the Southern currency while turning a profit. The strategy seems to have worked, as the greenbacks, the enemy's money, were much sought after; they were exchanged, at first clandestinely, then quite openly, at a ruinous discount on Confederate notes. At General Lee's surrender at Appomattox, the Confederate currency was worthless; its use value, if it had any, was in serving as wall insulation in homes. John Kenneth Galbraith's observation is quite to the point: "The miracle of the Confederacy, like the miracle of Rome, was not that it fell but that it survived so long."[9]

The Union, which was bound by the Independent Treasury Act of 1846 to pay all expenditures in gold or silver, at first experimented with bond sales, then with a variety of taxes, at first on the states, then on income. A year later came taxes on alcohol and tobacco, playing cards and billiard tables, carriages and yachts, medicines and advertisements, manufactured goods and farm produce, licenses and stamps, dividends and inheritances. Tariffs were also raised, and the conversion of paper notes into gold or silver was suspended. Whoever was in possession of coins hoarded them. To make commercial transactions possible, postage stamps were used as substitutes for low-denomination coins. In August 1862, the Union began to distribute "fractional notes." Notes of the first issue—in denominations of 5¢, 10¢, 25¢, and 50¢—still were called "postage currency" because the tiny notes looked like contemporary postage stamps, had their same color-to-denomination relationship, and were even perforated along their edges, though they bore no glue and could only be used for money, not for mailing letters. This proved to be unworkable as the stamps soon became dirty, sticky, and unfit for use.

Other solutions included small envelopes printed with stated values of postage enclosed. Postage stamps inserted in a round encasement with a transparent mica window were also offered, though they were soon discontinued as being too expensive to produce. Finally, pictures of stamps were printed on paper, creating different denominations. As of 1863, the year of the second issue, the notes were regularized, and the designation changed to "fractional notes." Yet whatever name these representatives of value came by, they were a veritable boon for counterfeiters. Consequently, the government kept changing their visual appearance through the fifth and final issuance, in February 1874. This is the only issue on which Washington's portrait did not appear. On all other issues, his portrait had been pictured, the fifteen-cent issues excepting. This does not detract from the high honor and respect in which the Father of His Country was held then. The nation was still young, and patriotism or national pride was an important motif in its culture. Today fractional notes carrying Washington's portrait are collected as "patriotic" types.[10]

Postage stamps were invented in England; they were introduced in the United States in 1847 during the Mexican War. Gilbert Stuart's "Athenaeum" portrait of George Washington appeared on the first ten-cent stamp. (The second subject to adorn postage stamps was the first postmaster, Benjamin Franklin.) Postage currency and fractional notes varied in size, from 65 × 45 mm to 96 × 55 mm, proportionate to their denominational value. Most of the portraits are said to be by Joseph Ourdan, one of the first engravers to come to the National Currency Bureau and eventually Chief of the Engraving Division. The 25¢ note Postage Currency was produced by the American Bank Note Company. It carried, appropriately enough, a row of five Washington portraits—one for each of the overlapping 5¢ stamps. Altogether, there were few exceptions to the Washington-mania. One was the 5¢ fractional note from the third issue of 1864. This note was to have been graced by a portrait of Meriwether Lewis, the explorer; as it happened, Spencer M. Clark, the first head of the National Currency Bureau (as the Bureau of Engraving and Printing was originally called) had his own portrait printed on the note. This rare act of institutional narcissism caused a scandal and prompted Congress to pass a law that prohibits the use of portraits of living persons on all state papers: "No portrait shall be placed upon any of the bonds, securities, notes, fractional or postal currency of the United States while the original of such portrait is living."[11]

The rhetorical purpose of adorning the currency with a portrait of the Father of His Country was fully understood at the time. Washington was a cherished tradition, and the people were generally more interested in that tradition than in the biographical person. While they would welcome books that were morally instructive, they would expect the same from pictorial renderings. The critic and writer Henry Tuckerman even observed, only partly in jest, that seeing the first president's portrait on the new postage stamp currency would help reform the nation's morals: "...that dear and hallowed countenance now appropriately forming the postage stamp of the nation, which thus coming hourly before the American vision, ought to reform, by its silent monition, political varlets and degenerate citizens."[12]

Tuckerman had a good point here. How could people avoid seeing Washington's portrait when tens of millions of fractional notes were distributed from 1862 to 1876? It is doubtful, however, whether Tuckerman would have said the same about the $500 notes the Union had been issuing since 1861. The notes' front was graced by the Fairman portrait, in a modest frame and—unlike in Gilbert Stuart's original—looking to the viewer's right, into the nation's glorious future as it were. Washington is flanked by two allegorical figures, respectively called Justice (at left) and Transportation (at right). Only a little later, $100 notes were issued, featuring a Lansdowne-type George Washington standing between two female allegories, Guardian (at left) and Liberty (at right). Yet considering the high denomination of these types of notes, their awareness level likely was rather limited; moreover, the notes were in circulation only from one to three years—as interest bearing notes, they were usually redeemed by their maturity date. Two types of these notes circulated, the Compound Interest Treasury Notes and the Interest-Bearing Treasury Notes. Both were at the same time Legal Tender (United States) Notes and interest-bearing, the former maturing after three years at 6 percent interest, the latter maturing after one, two, or three years, at 7.3 percent interest.[13]

The opulent symbolism and highly manipulative constructions of image and text on printed money of the time was cotemporaneous with two overlapping trends—first, the emerging state monopoly of banknote production and emission and, second, a new interpretation of bank notes, from representing money to money in its own right, that is, token money. When the Treasury Department around 1863 acquired a sophisticated geometric lathe, the designs on the new federal notes began to follow artistic conventions such as perspective, composition, symmetry, line ruling, or spatial distribution. Notes also displayed a co-presence of image and text, and background images often were overlaid with script. All these features come together on the $1 United States (Legal Tender) Note from 1869. Known among collectors as "Rainbow" note because of its colorful front, it carries a portrait of George Washington and a vignette showing Christopher Columbus in sight of land. The ideological message the note conveys may be rendered, in shorthand, as the "Columbus-Washington-Connection" and will be treated at some length in the following chapter.

The "Rainbow" note placed the Father of His Country on the dollar bill, and there he has remained, the moral exemplar for all Americans. The 1869 note also was an artistic and technical success. Through the end of the Civil War, portraits and other representations printed on currency notes were too awkward and clumsy to claim a true likeness, let alone to be aesthetically pleasing. Washington's iconicity was, therefore, owed to the great portraits by Gilbert Stuart or Rembrandt Peale, to Jean-Antoine Houdon's sculptures, to the many prints, engravings, and copies made from these and, not to forget, to objects of folk art. Regarding banknotes and other types of paper currency, from the colonial era printing was usually done from copper plates. Because of the softness of the material, engravings wore easily and had to be re-engraved every so often—an open invitation to counterfeiters. Moreover, there also was a dearth of original artworks suitable for transfer onto printing plates. A colony's seal (usually a woodcut), the sign of the institution guaranteeing a note's value, was all that could be expected by way of visual aesthetics.

Good examples are the bills of credit issued by the Province of Massachusetts Bay in 1691. The colony had attempted to establish a mint from the 1650s. All attempts failed, however, prohibited by royal commissions claiming that it was the king's exclusive prerogative "to be stampt upon the coyne of New England."[14] From December 10, 1690, therefore, the Province of Massachusetts Bay began issuing £7,000 worth of Bills of Credit. The bills were printed from set type plus illustrations. They were issued in denominations of 5s, 10s, 20s, and £5, passing current in all payments equivalent to money. Although their express purpose was to pay for soldiers and supplies for Sir William Phipps' disastrous military expedition to Quebec during King William's War, the preamble to the law justified the venture by referring to "the present poverty and calamities of the country, and through a scarcity of money, the want of an adequate measure of commerce." Neither poverty, nor calamities, let alone the scarcity of money went away with the first issue. On February 3, 1691, and May 21, 1691, a further £400,000 in bills was authorized by the provincial government.[15]

Certain of these bills bear the date as "February the third 1690," but this is the old or Julian calendar, and the actual date of issue was 1691 by today's system.[16] Economic historians refer to the Massachusetts venture as "not only the origin of paper money in America, but also in the British Empire, and almost in the Christian world."[17] Arthur Nussbaum, too, claims that the Massachusetts issue "constitutes one of the most important events in monetary history."[18] Eric Newman writes that issuance of these bills earned for early paper money of America the distinction of being the first authorized paper money issued by any government in the western world.[19] Richard Doty makes a similar point, calling Americans "the first people in the western world to circulate state-issued and state-supported currency."[20] Last but not least, John Kenneth Galbraith observes, "[i]f the history of commercial banking belongs to the Italians and of central banking to the British, that of paper money issued by a government belongs indubitably to the Americans."[21] What is mentioned less often is that the Massachusetts Bay bills traded up to a third below par. Still, they constituted the norm for subsequent emissions, in Massachusetts as well as in other colonies.[22] Aesthetic demands remained simple, though the notes from the Revolutionary era proved useful as vehicles of political propaganda. They also are of considerable historical interest.

Notes from the early republic likewise had little similarity to classic bank notes. Historical interest thus is the most that can be said about them. All this changed from about 1820, when improvements in printing technology began to take effect. One of the most important innovations was Jacob Degen's "geometric lathe," an engine turning machine that, from 1816, opened a way of mechanically engraving very precise, intricate, and repetitive patterns—generally described as "guilloches"—that were difficult to counterfeit. In 1809, Jacob Perkins bought the "stereotype" technology from Asa Spencer, a way of mass-producing an intricate, virtually random arrangement of letters and words on bank notes. In the process, a group of different elements made in steel were locked into a frame. Individual frames had spaces into which small slugs with lettering could be inserted—for the names of the state, town, and bank. Aesthetically, the finished notes were not much to write home about, but the success of the "Patent Stereotype Steel Plate" (PSSP) was secured by Perkins' invention of the process of siderography. Siderography is a way of transferring impressions from a steel plate to a steel cylinder in a rolling press, which made possible the almost unlimited and, above all, identical reproduction of steel printing plates. Steel plates almost instantly replaced the soft copper plates, and in lieu of the crude woodcuts that had served as originals, more elaborate engravings and decorations were employed. In due course, backprinting was introduced as a measure to make bank notes safer. Further innovations made possible the use of multiple plates, another important contribution to banknote security.[23]

Part III

From the End of the Civil War through the 1920s

During the first half of the nineteenth century, many gifted engravers came to the United States from Europe. While they made important contributions to the development of banknote aesthetics, production costs at first put a limit to the application of their skills. Even so, much labor went into the production of printing plates or dies, especially for intaglio printing. The material on which notes were printed—paper—was cheap, so the production process itself had to create at least the semblance of value. A true revolution came with the mechanical production of precise, curving lines, which made it possible to engrave finest details in steel, much as the invention of the geometric lathe allowed for the most sweeping designs, useful for rosettes, borders, and for the "medallions" upon which could be added the denomination of a note or the name of the issuing bank. If the Industrial Revolution had been ignited by John Wilkinson's precision boring machine that enabled James Watt's steam engine to power pumps and mills and factories all over England, so did "precision engineers" (the phrase is Simon Winchester's) like Jacob Degen, Asa Spencer, and Jacob Perkins, to name but a few, enable a technological complexity that eventually transformed banknote production from craftsmanship to industrial mass production.[1]

Small artisanal shops (one such was owned by Benjamin Franklin) at first formed partnerships, then amalgamated into ever-larger companies (like the American Bank Note Company, the ABNCo.), which had the financial power to employ the most sophisticated machinery. Still, the plates mostly were slapped together from available originals, and there was a flourishing trade in archival material among individual banks.[2] When banknote production and emission became a state monopoly, around mid-century, cost no longer was such a decisive factor. Thus began what is known as "the Golden Age" of banknote aesthetics. Many great names relate to that period—Asher Durand, Charles Burt, Louis Delnoce, Alfred Jones, or the Smillies, all of whom left a heritage of remarkably detailed engravings. Their works are fraught with symbols, graced by patterns of gorgeous colors, and often displaying highly manipulative constructions of image and text—all in the interest of nobilitating money that had become purely symbolic.[3]

Following the Civil War, improvements in printing technology made printing cheap, fast, and flexible, and they permitted strikingly detailed imagery to be placed on notes. National Bank notes especially of the first charter period (1863 to 1881) today are greatly appreciated by collectors for their beauty and the superb quality of the picture engraving. Contemporaries too became aware that banknote engraving as well as the artwork behind it had reached new and unprecedented heights. In February 1862, an article in *Harper's New Monthly Magazine* assured its readers "bank notes executed in America [are] superior to any others in the world."[4] Lest this be written off as so much jingoism, here is what a writer, addressing the merits of F.O.C. Darley's banknote designs, remarked in the *London Art Journal* in October 1860: "This is the first time that we have ever heard of bank-note engraving being considered applicable, and pre-eminently so, to illustrations professing to have a high Art character."[5] One visitor to the United States even called banknote-engraving "the only true American contribution to the arts."[6] Given the prejudices of the European educated bourgeoisie, this may have been faint praise. In the world of paper currency, however, it should be seen as a true compliment, like the words of the critic James Harvey, for whom these notes constituted "the money of civilization."[7]

7

The Only True American Contribution to the Arts

American banknote engraving of the second half of the nineteenth century is justly appreciated for its contribution to beauty. Witness William S. Baker's comment, in his 1875 book *American Engravers and their Works*:

> In the department of Bank Note engraving ... this country stands unrivalled. No such work has been produced elsewhere, and its gradual development from the rude essays of the early practitioners, to the almost perfect productions of the present day, forms not only a most interesting feature in the art, but furnishes also an instructive teaching of the wholesome influences of our form of government.[1]

Such recognition deserves acknowledgment even today, though a closer look is in order. Bank notes are at the same time similar to and different from artworks like paintings. The value of paintings, especially of oil paintings, stems from their desire to educate as much as to lend allure or authority to their own messages. This suggests a cultural authority, a form of dignity that is vastly superior to vulgar material interests. Bank notes, in contrast, suggest both wealth and spirituality or culturedness. "Quoting" art, they also propagate a society's belief in itself. But they do so in a deeply nostalgic, conservative way. Following the art critic John Berger, bank notes sell the past to the future. That past was original portraits and history paintings, art forms that already were beyond their peak by the time banknote-engraving established itself as "the only true American contribution to the arts."[2]

There is, as well, another form of lagging behind in banknote engraving. We might even say that that lag is a necessary condition for banknote engraving. Banknote "art" comes into play only once an original painting or portrait has been interpreted regarding the printing of banknotes. It usually takes one to two years until a print-ready engraving is completed. From a large oil painting, that is, whereas engravings from portraits or individual vignettes take much less time.[3] The first result of a banknote engraver's work is a drawing. From it, a design model is produced, usually ten times the size of the final bank note. Banknote engravers do not work in color. Light and shadow are produced through lines—straight, wavy, bold, fine, with wide or narrow spaces; even small dots are engraved. Once the design model is finished, it is mechanically or photographically reduced to its final size before it is transferred onto steel, the printing plate or a die. There is another important difference between banknote engraving and the fine arts. Banknote production is never the work of a single (and solitary) genius. It is a collaborative, highly complex process, thus the perfect paradigm of the highly specialized mass production in the age of industrialization. Small wonder, then, that for many designers—in particular James Smillie and Asher Durand—involvement with bank notes was only a preliminary step towards their future careers as portraitists, genre or landscape painters.

Modern banknote production not only required the work of "precision engineers," but also developed hand in hand with the emergence of state monopolies over money. In 1864, Spencer M. Clark, who was then head of the National Currency Bureau, filed the following report:

> An inventory showed 2 steam engines, one four horsepower and one thirty horsepower; 7 engine lathes; 2 planing machines; 15 transfer presses; 72 hydraulic presses; 4 hydraulic receivers; 25 hydraulic pumps; 96 roller presses; 6 Hoe & Company cylinder presses; one Washington press; one Ready Proof press; 22 numbering machines; 9 trimming machines; 7 separating machiens; 14 sealing presses; 4 double-acting separators for Fractional Currency; and other equipment, for a total of 324 devices. Operating this machinery were 237 males and 288 females, but the number varies. The production included other federal imprints besides paper money.[4]

Today, almost all bank notes are produced in state printing offices, such as the Bureau of Engraving and Printing (BEP), the printing office of the Banque de France, the German Bundesdruckerei, or the Österreichische Staatsdruckerei, the Austrian State Printing House. Also involved in banknote printing are the producers of printing presses, the suppliers of banknote paper, metal foils, security threads, holograms, paints and inks, printers, engravers of portraits and pictures, of letters, numbers, and lines, and not to forget the specialists operating geometric lathes and other mechanical devices that are capable of producing the most intricate patterns—including the famous "spider webs" on current $1 bills, "[G]reen spiderwebs designed by T-Men / to prevent foul counterfeit," in Allen Ginsberg's poetic rendering.[5]

"Spider webs" as well as other intricate line patterns are purely ornamental; they serve to identify a particular type of notes and/or contribute to banknote security. Such patterns originated in the late eighteenth-century, when all kinds of repetitive processes began to be mechanized. The persons that operated machines like the geometric lathe, however, remain largely anonymous. Only the names of the designers and engravers of historically or idealistically relevant features of a banknote are being remembered.[6] Phrased differently, design elements that are of historic or idealistic relevance—seals, pictures of important buildings or monuments, history paintings, portraits of outstanding personalities—comprise the "art" printed on nineteenth-century bank notes. Hence on U.S. currency we find reproductions of artworks such as *The Baptism of Pocahontas*, *The Landing of the Pilgrims*, *Washington Crossing the Delaware*, *Jefferson presenting the Declaration of Independence to John Hancock at the Continental Congress*, and *The Embarkation of the Pilgrims*—all on National Bank notes of the first series and all from the famous Americana paintings in the Capitol Rotunda.

Reproductions of artworks on bank notes repeat and amplify the epistemological confusions that plagued people concerned with the notes' security. The visible resemblance to other notes had to provide the grounds for assuring both a note's power to circulate and its authenticity. For notes that carry art, the disappearance of the original is particularly disturbing, as "art" is customarily connected with originality. Thus, there are originals as well as copies and, of course, forgeries of artworks. But what is a banknote original? The printing plate? The dies? The designer's model? The first design sketch? Perhaps each individual note is an original. After all, each note can be distinguished by its serial number. Whichever way one decides to see it, it will be difficult to base a bank note's artistic ambition on originality and uniqueness, or else on some enduring quality that is unrepeatable and that gives it its claim to the status as a work of art, that is, its aura.

Walter Benjamin's classic essay on the work of art in the age of mechanical reproduction can help us in distinguishing paper money art from other art forms. Benjamin keys in on the impact of the new technologies of cultural production on modern culture, arguing that infinite repeatability is one of the essential characteristics of the modern means of cultural production. Mechanical reproduction, he said, affects the uniqueness and authenticity of the work of art, destroying as it were its "aura" and, worse, shattering the tradition in which works of art had been embedded. Instead of "uniqueness and permanence" we have "transitoriness and repeatability."[7] Benjamin's rhetoric has a parallel in the different connotations of the terms "culture" and "industry," also (but not exclusively) popular with members of the Frankfurt School. Whereas "culture" bears connotations of refinement, learning, taste, and aesthetic contemplation, the term "industry" carries those of the evils of capitalism, of standardization, homogenization, the "masses," and, as well, the quasi-religious guise in which cultural objects appear. Interestingly, Theodor Adorno, although he too upheld the culture/industry dichotomy, sharply criticized Benjamin's rejection of modern society. There is, Adorno argues, no absolute difference between an "auratic" and a "mechanically reproducible" work of art. Nor is there an absolute difference between "traditional" and "modern" societies. Instead they are, always and forever, implicated one in the other.[8]

Still, Benjamin's insistence on an artwork's aura is important. Historically, the artwork's aura (which corresponds to the aureole or halo in Christian iconology) developed into the gilt frame corresponding to and defining the artwork and, from there, into the frames on paper bills, which hold portraits of "great men" as well as images of signal moments in a nation's history.[9] Frames define a picture, insofar as the frame's function as a border allows us to see an object *as* a picture and not merely as something *in* a picture. Yet in the case of an artwork the framing is a unique occasion; in the case of bank notes, the framing can be repeated ad infinitum. The process is similar in photography. One can make any number of prints from a photographic negative. To ask for an "original" is pointless.[10]

Benjamin mentions money only once in his essay relating artistic reproduction to economic production. Nevertheless, money—paper as well as coin—serves better than photography to highlight the relation between production and reproduction. As in photography, one can make any number of prints from a currency plate or any number of strikes from a die. Yet unlike a photograph, a piece of currency is at the same time a copy and unique, both artful reproduction and active participant in the relations of production. The "original" plays no role, except as something that is kept from the public by the authorizing institution. This may be intentional. We rarely get to know anything about how an "original" comes into being, what designs had been suggested, etc. Thus, the social constructedness of money as an instrument of control remains invisible; instead, money appears as "natural," as something "organic."[11]

In the world of money, the artwork's aura, together with the tradition in which it is embedded, is of no concern. Instead, we look at money's status as a means of payment, which is not even obliterated when it is devalued as such. Phrased differently, money's function as a means of payment precludes the status of coins and currency as artworks. In contrast, the status of coins and currency as means of payment demands trust. And it is the very reproducibility of coins and currency that strengthens trust.[12] Indeed, visual appearance largely decides how users assess and evaluate coins and currency. Technical progress, after all, does not only mean mass production, but also means standardization. Both the mechanically produced look and the reproducibility of the artworks printed on bank notes contribute to their ineffable uniformity, a decisive factor in their broad acceptance. To the extent that bank notes are accepted as "authentic," an entirely new and most complex notion of the presence of the original must come into play.

From the beginning of the republic, elites could count on people's familiarity with George Washington. Portraits and other representations of Washington were, however, employed not only in efforts to reform morals and propriety but also to increase patriotic feelings. When Washington sat for Gilbert Stuart in 1796, the nation's future was still in doubt. Washington was the one man around whom all could rally, and what, Chief Justice Marshall pontificated, would more effectively spark the noble emotions of emulation and patriotism than a portrait of the Father of His Country and its first President? Stuart's serene Washington provided just the right icon. His Washington, the writer and art critic John Neal wrote in an 1823 novel, "was less what Washington was, than what he ought to have been." Neal's sentiment became a commonly accepted position throughout the century. As late as 1880, the *Magazine of American History* printed a passionate plea to establish a "national standard" for Washington's likeness, on the grounds that "the authentication and erection of a standard image to represent the Nation's Father, is an act of sacred dedication to the claims of eternal posterity."[13]

Claims of eternal posterity may well have influenced the decision to have Alfred Sealey engrave Gideon Fairman's version of the Gilbert Stuart portrait for the $1 United States Note of 1869, for an honorarium of $500. Not only was the $1 denomination printed in large numbers. Low-denomination notes also circulate more widely, as they are more likely to be spent than higher-denomination notes, which are often hoarded, serving as a means of the preservation of value rather than a means of exchange. The United States (Legal Tender) notes of 1869 were originally issued in lieu of Series 1862, which bore a portrait of Salmon P. Chase, the Secretary of the Treasury at the time. The 1869 notes were non-redeemable, though their description is somewhat confusing. Technically, the notes are United States Notes, thus "legal tender for all debts public and private"; yet at the bottom they carry the description "Treasury Notes." Because of their colorful front, they have become known as "Rainbow" notes.[14]

Washington's framed portrait is at center front. Two laurel leaves are modestly placed under it, thus downplaying the association with caesarism, which would have been rather ominous. The lettering above the portrait, in contrast, is loud and bold—"THE UNITED STATES," large and conspicuous enough to emphasize the identification of George Washington with the American nation. Washington's face is—as in Stuart's original and as on most currency notes until 1923—looking towards the viewer's left, into the past. What Washington sees by turning to the past is, however, not the arrival of

A $1 United States (Legal Tender) note, 1869, front, 7.42 × 3.125 in. (American Numismatic Association Money Museum).

the Pilgrims (which might have been the obvious choice) but Christopher Columbus in sight of land. The Columbus vignette was done by Joseph P. Ourdan after a painting by Christian (sometimes called Charles) Schussele, *Columbus, Discovery of Land.* It shows a bearded captain among his crew. Columbus is wearing a tunic, knee breeches, and a mantle. A few of the sailors are jubilant, if not ecstatic, pointing toward the land in the background. Others are on their knees, praying, their eyes on the captain. Columbus is depicted in an upright position, looking dignified and self-confident, his right hand over the heart. The emphasis in the representation clearly is on Columbus' heroic character as well as on the epochal moment of discovery.

The note's composition—Washington's portrait in the center, looking at Columbus at left—suggests both a chronological and a causal relation between the "face of the nation" and the momentous event of October 12, 1492. Claudia Bushman has termed the relation, which collapses mimesis and diegesis, showing and narrating, the "Columbus-Washington-Connection." The "connection" is the basis of a larger cultural narrative, with Columbus and Washington as the main protagonists. Put simply, the narrative suggests that Washington became the Father of His Country *because* Columbus had discovered the New World *for* Americans.[15] The narrative continued to be an important element in the American popular imagination, as the design was kept for subsequent series, in 1874, as well as for several series from 1875 to 1917 (all with the "sawhorse reverse," so called because the inscription "United States of America" was set in a flattened "X" reminiscent of a sawhorse).[16] The design's longevity is somewhat surprising. The prevailing taste in a time of perceived nationhood usually demanded more "realistic" representations—scenes from everyday life, family idylls, or, by way of reminders of bygone times, scenes from pioneer life or Indian battles. Portraits, in contrast, usually convey a sense of greatness, suggesting a worthiness of emulation that rather went with the neo-classicist ideals of the early republic or the "Colonial Revival" of the late nineteenth century.[17]

Neither bank notes and similar papers nor coins depict realities outside of themselves. Their visual designs therefore are constructions (what W.J.T. Mitchell called "image-texts") that are shaped by, and help shape, history. Moreover, the relations between sign and referent are highly ambiguous. As Mitchell aptly remarked, "image-texts" are permeable, allowing history to as it were "slip through the cracks."[18] The arrangement, in 1869, of Founding Father of the new nation (an American of the present) and discoverer of the continent (a man of the European past) provided ideological stability and comfort for a nation that had been ravaged by the Civil War. The beginning of the "Columbus-Washington-Connection" must be sought in the War of Independence, though. Then Columbus was used to legitimize the rebellion against England, the mother country. Although the navigator himself had been convinced that he had reached India, not America, he was nonetheless found serviceable as the protagonist of a counter-narrative against prevailing myths—of pious puritans as well as of noble cavaliers. Thus, the discoverer in the service of the Spanish kings transmogrified into an "American" hero, if not a messiah. His voyages along the coasts of the Americas came to both reflect and anticipate the settlement, putatively ordained by God, by the English colonists—as, for instance, in Joel Barlow's epic poem *The Vision of Columbus* (1787), which in 1807 became the much more expansive *Columbiad*, or else in William Dunlap's play *The Glory of Columbia* (1803).[19]

In the rhetoric of the early nationalist poets and writers (next to Dunlap and Barlow, one should mention Philip Freneau and Timothy Dwight), the United States of America was the culminating point of a historical trajectory reaching back to antiquity. Casting the notion of the westward course of empire (*translatio imperii*) into epic form, these writers reinforced and secularized the "providential" readings of Puritan historians, who had emphasized their mission of establishing in America the groundwork for a protestant model state (the "errand into the wilderness," in Perry Miller's apt phrase). During the Revolution and the early national period, historical determinism was fused with the argument of "nature"—a philosophical principle on which the building of the new nation was legitimized against the "unnatural" tyranny of England. It is no coincidence, therefore, that Noah Webster's *American Spelling Book* ended with two pages of important dates in American history, beginning with Columbus' discovery of America in 1492 and ending with the battle of Yorktown in 1781.

There is no mention in Webster's of God, the Bible, or sacred events. "Let sacred things be appropriated for sacred purposes," he wrote. As Joseph J. Ellis explains, "Webster began to construct a secular catechism to the nation-state. Here was the first appearance of 'civics' in American schoolbooks. In this sense, the speller became what was to be the secular successor to *The New England Primer* with its explicitly biblical injunctions."[20] The spelling book first appeared in 1783, then titled *The First Part of the Grammatical Institute of the English Language*; it was changed to *The American Spelling Book* in 1786, and again in 1829 to *The Elementary Spelling Book*. It was the most popular American book of its time; by 1837, it had sold 15 million copies, and some 60 million by 1890. By that time, three major biographies and histories of Columbus had been published, attesting to the discoverer's prestige. The books' authors—Washington Irving (1828), George Bancroft (1834), and William Hickling Prescott (1837)—did not see Columbus as man of a remote past, but rather as a romantic hero and pioneer, one to help legitimate westward expansion, a harbinger of civilization, of modern times.

Of the three biographies, Irving's stands out as an effort to establish a genuinely American literature. As Irving wrote in the Preface, the subject of Columbus "was of so interesting and national a kind, that I could not willingly abandon it."[21] That goal had its price, though, in that historical reality became a wish-fulfilling myth. Irving believed that history was shaped by truly heroic characters. Thus, "the re-creation of national history was, to a large extent, a necessary extension of the individual's identity and history."[22] But Irving also wanted to use history writing to teach—"furnishing examples of what human genius and laudable enterprise may accomplish."[23] The phraseology—"human genius and laudable enterprise"—suggests Columbus' nobility, in contrast to his companions and, especially, his followers, "the dissolute rabble which it was his misfortune to command."[24] By elevating Columbus, Irving redirects blame from the Spanish empire (and, by implication, from western civilization) to later generations. The moral is quick to follow: If only Columbus' successors had followed the explorer's "sound policy and liberal views," not only would Spain look different today; altogether, the Americas "would have been settled by pacific colonists, and civilized by enlightened legislators; instead of being overrun by desperate adventurers, and desolated by avaricious conquerors."[25]

Columbus' soul, Irving quotes from a Spanish commentator, "'was superior to the age in which he lived.'"[26] Ultimately, imagined superiority—a model masculinity as it were—was sufficient for Irving to integrate a Catholic-Spanish *conquistador* into the family lineage of Anglo-Protestant America. Irving's Columbus is, then, not only a model for Spain but more so a kind of Founding Father for the Americans and their errand into the wilderness.[27] But by placing the responsibility for the consequences of civilization's destructive power not on the projector and policy-maker of the voyages of discovery but on his followers, Irving had to employ what John D. Hazlett called "a very awkward double standard," blame for evil deeds on the followers, and ignoring "the obvious connection between Columbus' policies and the eventual destruction of the island paradise."[28] Clearly, Washington Irving was no Cooper, who in his Leatherstocking cycle tirelessly explored the dilemma of Natty Bumppo as the unwitting vanguard of the eventual destruction of the American wilderness. Nevertheless, Irving's *History of the Life and Voyages of Christopher Columbus* became spectacularly successful, especially among the general public.[29] New editions were published almost every year until 1850, then about every two or three years. Altogether, there were about one hundred and seventy-five editions from 1828 until 1900, some of them expressly for the use as schoolbooks.[30] And that is not counting the many translation—into Spanish, French, German, Dutch, Greek, Italian, Polish, Swedish, and Russian, all before Irving's death in 1859.

By the time *Columbus* was being prepared for Irving's Complete Works edition in 1980, the biography had seen almost 200 editions. "Few books in modern times," Andrew Burstein wrote, "have had such a reach, or such an impact."[31] The work, especially the one-volume abridgment of it that Irving first published in 1829, was the most popular biography of Columbus in the English language until the publication of Samuel Eliot Morison's *Admiral of the Ocean Sea* in 1942.[32] If Morison's biography won the Pulitzer Prize in 1943, Irving's own attempt also gained official recognition. In 1829 Irving was made a member of the Spanish Royal Academy of History, at the proposal of the eminent historian Martín Fernández de Navarrete. In 1830, he was awarded a gold medal by the Royal Society of Literature in London, followed by an honorary doctorate of civil law from Oxford in 1831.[33]

Thanks largely to Irving's *History of the Life and Voyages of Christopher Columbus*, the explorer's place in narratives of westward expansion was secure. In later attempts towards justifying westward expansion, both the secular story and the notion of divine providence often were linked to racial doctrines of the superiority of the white race. For Thomas Hart Benton, senator from Missouri and a loyal follower of Andrew Jackson, it was self-evident that whites form "the superior race."[34] Thus, arrival on and settlement of America's west coast constitutes a "change" in the course of human history that is "greater, and more beneficent" than any previous events in history. As the whites bring "civilization," it can only be beneficial that "the White race will take the ascendant, elevating what is susceptible of improvement—wearing out what is not."[35] Indians for Senator Benton fell into the latter category. In the East, they already had largely disappeared—having "resisted civilization," they deservedly "met extinction." This, the worthy senator continues, "is a cause of lamentation with many. *For my part, I cannot murmur at what seems to be the effect of divine law.* I cannot repine that this Capitol has replaced the wigwam—this Christian people, replaced the savages—white matrons, the red squaws—and that such men as Washington, Franklin, and Jefferson, have taken the place of Powhattan, Opechonecanough, and other red men, howsoever respectable they may have been as savages."[36]

The glorification of Columbus as an *American* symbol of the discoverer who discovered what he had not even sought is also a good example of an "invented tradition."[37] So is the poetical denomination "Columbia" for the North American colonies. Or else, the renaming of New York's venerable King's College—in 1781, during the revolutionary era—into Columbia College and, in 1896, into Columbia University. In 1786, South Carolina's new capital city was named Columbia. In the same year, the official seal of the United States was first presented to the public in the *Columbian Magazine*. In 1791, a year before the tercentenary of Columbus' discovery, a congressional committee under Thomas Jefferson and George Washington settled on "Territory of Columbia" for the new federal district (at the same time, the name of the new capital city was decided upon—"City of Washington").[38] Little more than ten years later, explorers Meriwether Lewis and William Clark accomplished their final leg to the Pacific Ocean along the Columbia River. In 1892, the World's Columbian Exposition was dedicated in Chicago. (It opened only in 1893, because of delays.)

Again in 1892, New York City got its Columbia Avenue, in celebration of the quadricentennial of the discovery of America. President Benjamin Harrison called upon the American people to celebrate the event. The President meant it to be a holiday to recognize both Native Americans, who had been here before Columbus, and the many immigrants—including Italians—who were just then coming to the United States in astounding numbers. It was to be a national holiday that was *not* about the Founding Fathers or the Civil War, but about the *rest* of American history. And it was to be a holiday to get beyond the prejudices that, soon before the first Columbus Day holiday, had led to two tragic events—the massacre perpetrated on the Lakota Sioux by United States troops at Wounded Knee on December 29, 1890, and, in 1891, the mass lynching in the parish prison at New Orleans of eleven Italians by a mob led by prominent Louisiana politicians and businessmen.[39]

President Harrison did not allude to either of these tragedies in his proclamation of the holiday, and so teachers, preachers, poets, and politicians used Columbus Day rituals to teach their ideals of patriotism, westward expansion, the destruction of the American wilderness, and the elimination of the indigenous population included. That kind of patriotism remained tone-setting for later Columbus Day rituals, focusing not just on the importance of loyalty to the nation but, increasingly, on themes such as citizenship boundaries. Unsurprisingly, therefore, Columbus' reputation suffered considerably in the years to follow. Caught up in the swirl of anti-immigration sentiments, the discoverer was identified as an "Italian," that is, as someone of genetic inferiority, and thus became persona non grata.[40]

Columbus' descent begun in 1892, the year of the Columbian celebrations, which is customarily regarded as the apex of the explorer's popularity. Upon closer inspection, however, Columbus was at best the eminence grise of Chicago. The hero of choice was George Washington. Columbus of course was commemorated, through a replica of the *Santa Maria* anchored in the lake, a copy of the convent of La Rabida, a half-dollar commemorative coin, and the Exposition's official medal, created by no less an artist than Augustus Saint-Gaudens. Other than that, every major state of the Union displayed relics of the nation's first president, whose virtues were expounded also through foreign-language addresses, implemented as a means of attempting to educate newcomers to American citizenship.[41] Historians like Justin Winsor, Eugene Lawrence, and Charles Francis Adams began to question the significance of Columbus and his discovery for the progress of the American nation. In their wake, the discovery itself was credited to any number of individual explorers or groups—from the Portuguese to the Chinese to the Basques to Leif Ericson.[42] In themselves, these questionings were only symptoms of a deeper social conflict: the growing ethnic and cultural diversity of American society during the era of the New Immigration, 1880–1924. Then, strong nativist sentiments emerged against newcomers from Southern and Eastern Europe; concomitantly, Columbus' status as an important figure of social cohesiveness was challenged. While immigrant groups continued to claim him as their hero, his significance for the symbolic constitution of the nation was in steady decline, at the same time as emphasis on a distinctly *American* past was given more and more weight.

In terms of national identity, the United States after the Civil War was facing a paradox. Although the country was then the most democratic and, both territorially and constitutionally, one of the most clearly defined nations, the basic political problem, once secession had been averted, was how to assimilate a heterogeneous mass of people who were Americans not by birth but by immigration. Americans, the British historian Eric Hobsbawm found, "had to be made. The invented traditions of the U.S.A. in this period were primarily designed to achieve this object."[43] And they were to achieve that object in the context of intense racism. American historians became the first to propose the Teutonic-origins theory of American civilization. The theory resulted in the ideologies of Anglo-Saxonism and Anglophilia, which made a Dr. Henry Fairfield Osborn reclaim Columbus for the "Nordic race," the "conservation" of which "has given us the true spirit of Americanism." Osborn, a conservationist at the American Museum of Natural History (AMNH) and a former professor at Columbia University, wrote this in his preface to Madison Grant's 1916 book *The Passing of the Great Race*. Grant's pseudo-scientific work of white supremacism was widely praised at the time, including by

Theodore Roosevelt and, later, Adolf Hitler. Grant's infamous book also influenced the Immigration Act of 1924, the Johnson-Reed Act, which restricted immigration from Eastern and Southern Europe and Africa and banned migrants from the Middle East and Asia.[44]

Prior to the passing of the Johnson-Reed Act, American elites still engaged in efforts to Americanize immigrants. These efforts included encouraging immigrants to accept rituals commemorating the history of the nation—the Revolution and its Founding Fathers (July 4), and the Protestant Anglo-Saxon tradition (Forefathers Day, Thanksgiving Day)—as indeed they did, since these now became holidays and occasions for public and private festivity.[45] Former President Theodore Roosevelt used one such day—October 12, 1915, *el día de la hispanidad*, and hardly an American holiday—to refute the idea of a "hyphenated Americanism." "Americanism," Roosevelt, who at the time had begun to envision another campaign for president, famously declared, "is a matter of the spirit and the soul. Our allegiance must be purely to the United States."[46] Three years later, Roosevelt used the occasion of the State Republican Convention in Saratoga, New York, to proclaim, "There is room here only for 100 percent Americanism, only for those who are Americans and nothing else."[47]

While Trump advisor Stephen Miller may have used the quote to lend weight to his white rage, it must be said, in fairness, that the "Bull Moose's" rhetoric was neither exclusionary nor racist, and anything but one-dimensional. Theodore Roosevelt, Leroy Dorsey has demonstrated, "struck a rhetorical balance among the competing impulses of racism, nativism, assimilation, ethnic diversity, and group hopelessness by reworking a myth foundational to the nation's origin."[48] Roosevelt's rhetoric may sound harsh, yet it sought to provide a way for "others" to achieve equality as Americans. The prerequisites were strength and character. For Theodore Roosevelt, everyone could join "Americans, pure and simple" if they embraced this notion of "Americanism." "Americanism" of course was grounded in myth, particularly the frontier myth in the form of a heroic combination of individual strength and character. Anyone who demonstrated these traits could, regardless of origin, become a true American, earning an exalted status that he or she had heretofore been denied. Conversely, native-born whites could prove themselves unworthy to be "American." The nativists' prevailing rhetoric in particular Roosevelt saw as the opposite of his brand of Americanism. Their "'boasting and vainglorious ignorance of everything good and bad in this country,'" he said, made them "unfit," regardless of race or place of birth.[49]

Theodore Roosevelt died in January 1919. The nativists' "boasting and vainglorious ignorance of everything good and bad in this country" persisted, however. During the 1920s, anti–Catholicism contributed to Columbus' decline in the nation's collective consciousness. The sentiment was a specialty (albeit not an exclusive one) of evangelical Protestants, who charged Catholics with undermining the American nation. No Catholic could be truly American, many anti–Catholics foamed.[50] Anti-Catholicism also provided ideological ammunition to the Ku Klux Klan. A 1923 KKK tract by one George Estes, for instance, tried to convince Americans that the Knights of Columbus outnumbered members of the U.S. Army by five to one.[51] By that time, violence against K.C. members or members of the Order Sons of Italy in America had become quite common.[52] Even George Washington was pulled into the vortex of nativist sentiments.

America, the last of D.W. Griffith's silent epics, released in 1924, the year the Immigration Act became law, and the image of the heroic, ever-so-white Washington in the film could easily have been understood as underscoring the sentiment behind the law. This is even more plausible since *America* was made by the same filmmaker who in 1915 created *The Birth of a Nation*, a racist picture that proudly flaunted its nativism.[53]

Historians too told the glorious story of the birth and rise of the new nation, and the national currency was used to buttress the enterprise. "By 1929," Kathleen Loock found, "all historical scenes of national significance had disappeared from American paper money and with them all depictions of Columbus' great discovery."[54] Instead, the currency was graced by national heroes—most notably Lincoln, whose portrait replaced Columbus on the $5 Federal Reserve Notes, but also George Washington, Thomas Jefferson, Alexander Hamilton, James Madison, and Benjamin Franklin (for the revolutionary generation), as well as Ulysses S. Grant and Salmon P. Chase (for their decisive roles in the Civil War). The discovery of 1492 had become obsolete, though Columbus' reputation resurfaced, and Columbus Day became a federal holiday in the United States in 1937 (it had first become an official state holiday in Colorado in 1906, while earlier forms of celebration go back to the colonial period).[55] By 1937, most of the currency already consisted of small-size notes, and there had also been introduced new types, most notably Federal Reserve Notes and Federal Reserve Bank Notes. Large-size United States (Legal Tender) Notes of the post–Civil War era still had legal tender status, though mostly they had acquired additional collectors' value and were no longer seen in circulation.

A $1 United States note (Legal Tender), 1869, front, detail: Columbus vignette (American Numismatic Association Money Museum).

Collectors no doubt are aware that on the "Rainbow note" of 1869 only George Washington is represented via a portrait, whereas Columbus is part of a historical scene. Placing the discoverer within an ensemble of figures had been something of an emergency solution—no authenticated Columbus portrait existed at the time.

When Washington Irving was at work on his Columbus biography, for instance, he complained about the lack of a usable portrait that would have allowed him to describe the discoverer's features. Irving thought that an authenticated Columbus portrait would have been an ideal complement to his "pictorial" writing style; moreover, like many contemporaries at the time, Irving would draw conclusions about a person's character from outward appearances, particularly from physiognomy. Irving's first finding was a late sixteenth-century portrait by one Aliprando Capriolo. Unconvinced about the "authenticity of the likeness," he finally settled for a portrait by the Spanish artist Juan de Borgoña, knowing full well that this likeness too might have been "purely imaginary." Writing to William Cullen Bryant in December of 1851, Irving discusses more than half a dozen alleged Columbus portraits, though he adds a note of caution: "I know of no portrait extant which is positively known to be authentic."[56] It was not until the 1890s that an early sixteenth-century painting of a beardless man of learning was accorded something like official support. Until then, depictions of Columbus can be considered fantasy products, including depictions of him on the currency.[57]

Until the Civil War, most of the notes bearing depictions of Columbus had come from banks that bore Columbus in their names. Early examples are $5 notes issued by the Columbiana Bank of New Lisbon, New Lisbon, Ohio, in the 1830s. The central vignette, which depicts an agrarian scene, is flanked by portraits of Columbus.[58] In the 1840s, the Columbian Bank, Boston, Massachusetts, issued Columbus notes in several denominations: The $5 notes had as their central vignette the landing of Columbus, a motif that was also used, from the late 1850s, for the $500 notes; on the $10 notes, a portrait of Columbus appears at right; the identical portrait was used, with an additional portrait of George Washington at left, for the $100 notes in the 1860s.[59] The landing of Columbus also appeared on $1 notes issued in the late 1850s by the Bank of Columbus, Columbus, Wisconsin; on these notes, a portrait of George Washington appears at bottom left. Other denominations from this bank also bear portraits of the seafarer.[60]

A large number of banks had "Columbia" or similar denominations as part of their names, though they did not necessarily issue notes depicting Columbus: Columbia Bank, Washington, D.C. (DC-195)[61]; Columbia Bank, Boston, Massachusetts (MA-135), a non-existent bank, represented only by notes altered from those of other banks; Columbia Bank, Chatham Four Corners, New York (NY-620); Columbia Bank, Columbia, Pennsylvania (PA-80), which became the First Columbia National Bank in 1865; Columbia Bank & Bridge Company, Columbia, Pennsylvania (PA-81), formerly Columbia Bridge Company (PA-85); Columbia Bank of Pennsylvania, Columbia, Pennsylvania (PA-82), was chartered, but did not go into operation; Columbia Bank, Portage, Wisconsin (WI-648); Columbia County Bank, Portage, Wisconsin (WI-650); Bank of Columbia, Washington, D.C. (DC-65); Bank of Columbia, Columbia, Kentucky (KY-55); Bank of Columbia, Hudson, New York (NY-1040); Columbian Bank, Elizabethtown, Illinois (IL-235); Columbian Bank, Boston, Massachusetts (MA-140); Columbus and Tombigby Transportation Co., Columbus, Mississippi (MS-45); Commercial Bank of Columbus, Columbus, Mississippi (MS-50); Bank of Columbus, Columbus, Georgia (GA-105). The Bank of Columbia, Georgetown, Maryland (MD-228), never issued notes bearing a depiction of Columbus; established in 1793, the bank in 1801 became a D.C. bank (DC-65), when Georgetown became part of the District.

Still other banks put Columbus on their notes, even though there was no reference to the seafarer in the banks' names: For instance, the Bank of Grenada, Mississippi, and the Bank of Wilmington and Brandywine, Wilmington, Delaware, in the 1830s emitted $100 notes bearing as their central vignette Columbus standing, with his crew and Native Americans at a huge cross.[62] A framed portrait of a Renaissance-type Columbus flanked by two females appeared on $1 notes from the Bank of Oswego, Oswego, New York, during the 1840s and 1850s. The same portrait was also put on $1 notes from the Bank of New Jersey, New Brunswick, New Jersey, in the early 1850s. Framed portraits of Columbus also appeared on $2 notes from the Newport Bank, Newport, Rhode Island, in the 1820s and 1830s, from the Brunswick Bank, Brunswick, Maine, in the late 1840s, from the Mechanics & Traders Bank, Portsmouth, New Hampshire, the Warwick Bank, Warwick, Rhode Island, the White River Bank, Bethel, Vermont, and the Bank of Brattleboro, Brattleboro, Vermont, in the 1850s, and from the Monadnock Bank, Jaffrey, New Hampshire, in the 1850s and 1860s.[63] Finally, the Boylston Bank, Boston, Massachusetts, in the 1840s and 1850s issued $10 notes with portraits both of George Washington and Christoph Columbus; Washington (flanked by a winged angel) and Columbus were likewise put on $20 notes from the Miners Bank of Pottsville, Pottsville, Pennsylvania; and in the 1860s, the Columbian Bank, Boston, Massachusetts, issued $100 notes with the identical double fare.[64]

After the era of private money, representations of Columbus—portraits as well as historical scenes—also appeared on federal currency. The $1 United States note of 1869 is not the only example, though its ideological message, the "Columbus-Washington-Connection," proved tone-setting. It also had a spectacular comeback on the back of the $5 Federal Reserve Note, series 1914, and on the back of the Federal Reserve Bank Note, series 1915 and 1918. Ourdan's vignette after Schussele's painting is at left. At right, however, is a different vignette, Charles Burt's engraving of F.O.C. Darley's *The Landing of the Pilgrims*. Thus, the suggested chronological and causal relationship is different from the 1869 note. With George Washington out of the picture (the note's front shows a portrait of Lincoln), the narrative no longer tells of Columbus discovering America for the *Americans*. This narrative had been appropriate in the aftermath of the Civil War, when Washington's image suggested a unity and commonality in *spirit*, a message that could hardly offend the defeated South.[65]

At mid-century, as sectional conflict was coming to a head, both the South and the North had consistently laid claim to Washington's legacy, albeit in different fashions.[66] By the early twentieth century, however, the meaning of "American" had changed. For many of the elites, it now meant Anglo-Saxon. Given this kind of revisionism, the arrangement on the notes connected the discovery of America in 1492 and the beginning of successful Anglo-Saxon colonization of the North American continent in 1620: The Pilgrims landed on the American shore because Columbus had discovered the New World for *them*. The narrative's conclusion is also telling. Lincoln's portrait on the face is both a reminder of the great "test" of the nation's values and institutions, the Civil War, and a celebration of the commitment, by the nation's "savior," to unity and equality.[67]

Another image of Columbus appears on the $5 National Bank Notes, Original Series (1863–1875) and Series 1875 (1875 to 1902), and the $5 National Gold Bank Notes, Original Series. The vignette on the front is like the one on the United States note, and it is also called "Columbus in Sight of Land." The engraving is by Charles Burt, though, after Charles Fenton's design. On the back is a version, engraved by Walter Shirlaw, of John Vanderlyn's *The Landing of Columbus at the Island of Guanahani, West Indies, October 12, 1492*, the monumental history painting from the national Capitol that shows the seafarer and discoverer standing in a triumphant pose on the beach of Guanahani, surrounded by his men.[68] The $1000 United States notes (Series of 1869, 1878, 1880) likewise depict Columbus. In these instances, he is shown in his study, seated, his legs crossed, and dressed in what were thought to be contemporary garments—a tunic, tights, and cloak. He is holding a piece of paper in one hand, while he contemplates the earth on the ground to his right. Next to the terrestrial globe is a map and a magnifying glass. The vignette, placed at left on the note's face, conveys an image of learning and erudition, together with Columbus' abilities as navigator, his visionary courage and genius, and his conviction that the earth was not flat. Columbus' virtues, the note suggests, lived on in DeWitt Clinton, United States Senator, Mayor of New York City, and Governor of New York, in which capacity he was largely responsible for the construction of the Erie Canal, finished in 1825. His portrait is in the note's center.[69]

As for Columbus, his return to America's money came on the coinage in the epic year 1892, on a half-dollar struck to honor the World's Columbian Exposition, held in Chicago to commemorate the 400 years of modern America's existence. The coin is generally considered the first United States commemorative coin. Artistically, there is not much to write home about. Both the obverse (designed by Charles Barber) and the reverse (created by George Morgan) display the academicism fostered by the Mint in Philadelphia. From the start, there was controversy over whether Columbus' likeness was accurate or not. Especially the question whether he sported a beard led to many heated arguments. Designers at the Philadelphia Mint looked at a silver medal struck for the Columbian Historical exposition in Madrid; a Columbus statue, also in Madrid; and Lorenzo Lotto's painting of a Renaissance man identified as the navigator. In the end, it was thought that Lotto's portrait of 1512, which had served for the Spanish medal, was to be the choice for the American half dollar. Yet neither this likeness (which shows a clean-shaven man with an almost monk-like appearance who holds, in one hand, a conically projected map of Brazil) nor a plumper one by Sebastiano del Piombo were taken from life. Instead, they are thought to be copied after the sketch of an unknown artist working in Rome about 1500.[70]

If the 1892 half-dollar was "a great disappointment" as a work of art, the official medal for the World's Columbian Exposition was its exact opposite. The obverse, the creation of Augustus Saint-Gaudens, shows an exuberant Columbus striding ashore on an island in the New World. Yet unlike in Ourdan's vignette on the 1869 note, on Saint-Gaudens' obverse the other participants are kept away from the center. The medal is dominated by a transfigured Columbus, arms extended, palms turned upward, and eyes to the sky. With all the details centered around the powerful emotions of the discoverer, the composition becomes a complete entity, breathing, as Vermeule describes it, "mastery of the human figure over a limited area made interesting by variations in surface planes." Saint-Gaudens also created a reverse design, though his models were rejected, the combined result, the sculptor's son later explained, of Victorian naughtiness and prudery.[71] The rejection disabused Saint-Gaudens from any involvement with United States coins and medals for years to come. By the time of the quincentennial of Columbus' discoveries in 1992, even Saint-Gaudens' artistic legacy appears to have been gone. The year of 1992 brought a set of three commemorative coins—a half-dollar capturing the landing (on the obverse) and Columbus' three ships (on the reverse); a dollar with a standing Columbus on the obverse and a jarring juxtaposition of the *Santa Maria* and the space shuttle *Discovery* on the reverse; and a half eagle bearing a Columbus bust against a Western hemisphere map on the obverse and a chart with compass rose and Columbus' coat of arms on the reverse.[72]

8

National Myths

Currency notes tell a different story. The replacement, in 1929, of Lincoln's portrait for Columbus' reflects the renegotiation of American national identity against the background of international politics. By 1929, the United States no longer was a debtor nation but had become a foremost creditor nation. It was only fitting, therefore, that the nation's self-representation as a world power extended to the currency. Standardizing currency portraiture began in 1913, following the passage of the Federal Reserve Act. This piece of legislation, it should be noted, marked the culmination in a process, begun around 1870, in which monetary politics ceased to be the subject of hypnotizing public interest and seemingly endless debates in Congress and became the exclusive domain of technocrats far removed from the legislative process. Monetary politics, Roy Kreitner summarizes the process, was "beaten down, tamed … placed in the context of the kind of expertise that could dampen conflict."[1] Thus it was experts, not lawmakers, who selected Lincoln's portrait for the $5 note. The image used was Charles Burt's, who had taken it from Anthony Berger's photograph, catalogued as Ostendorf-92, and already in use for the $100 Legal Tender notes, series of 1869, the "Rainbow" notes, and the $500 Gold Certificates, series of 1870 and 1875.[2] The image continued to be used on small-size currency through the series of 1995, when the portrait was modified and enlarged.[3]

The series of 1914 notes were large-size notes; their backs showed an engraving of Schussele's painting *Columbus, Discovery of Land*. The identical engraving, by Joseph Ourdan, had appeared on the face of the $1 United States note from 1869, when, as we have seen, it provided an example of the "Columbus-Washington Connection." Then, the combination (the Founding Father of the new nation and an American of the present together with the discoverer of the continent and of a European past) provided ideological stability and comfort for a nation ravaged by the Civil War, much as it continued to be an important element in the American popular imagination. All this was gone by 1929, when historical scenes of national significance disappeared from American paper money and with them all depictions of Columbus' great discovery. Lincoln's portrait continued to be put on the $5 Federal Reserve note, series of 1928, but the Columbus vignette on the back was replaced by a picture of the Lincoln Memorial.

While Columbus disappeared from the currency, Washington, in contrast, abided. Let's, therefore, return to the question about the uniqueness of the "Rainbow note" of 1869. When the note was first issued, its illocutionary force aimed at the manufacturing of consent. Possessing the notes could make one an American, much as the notes identified one as an American. As a congressional representative from Michigan declared in

1874: "As surely as our flag represents … the unity of these States, just so surely, sir, do the United States Treasury Notes represent the cost of life and blood and treasure, the priceless value of that unity of States."[4] The theory of value and identity drawn from nationalism and patriotic labor was taken up also by the Northern press of the time. In a typical dispatch, the *New York Herald* in 1862 cheered the "general joy and satisfaction" with which Americans welcomed a currency standing on the good faith of the nation. The greenbacks, which then were backed at one and the same time by a government loan and by gold, were represented as "a currency as secure as the nation itself" and thus as a proxy for the "patriotism of the people, who, under no circumstances, will depreciate them."[5]

Patriotism is trumpeted even more loudly from another post–Civil War type of currency, the National Bank Notes. In March 1863, Lincoln's Treasury Secretary, Salmon P. Chase, invited banknote designs that would be "national in their character." The new notes were emitted from December 1863. Their designs were hailed as conveying, in the words of John Sherman, Senator from Ohio, "a sentiment of nationality."[6] Altogether, the new notes were emblematic of the consolidation of the state's authority following the North's victory in the Civil War. The notes still displayed features that retained for them a measure of the local and regional. A measure, but not too much. They might proclaim that they were from New York, or North Carolina—or the Nevada Territory, in time. But they all looked alike. They all displayed the same scenes and, from by the beginning of the 1880s, they were all coming from a single printer, the Bureau of Engraving and Printing in Washington, D.C. Even when the notes were still contracted out, the sentiment of nationality was clearly identified.

National Bank Notes were a wartime expedient. The climate of opinion clearly was such that victory of the Union was anything but self-evident. Hence, people distrusted their money, which for the most part was not backed by anything. The only assets worth talking about were those of the private banks. To enlist these banks in the war effort, the National Bank Act was passed in February 1863. On March 28, Secretary Chase received a letter from his chief clerk, Spencer M. Clark, concerning the role of currency design. The new notes, Clark explained, ideally would use panoramic scenes extending across their faces, each scene providing a patriotic, uplifting imagery. "The advantage of such a currency," the letter said,

> would be that a series properly selected, with their subject titles imprinted on the notes, would tend to teach the masses the prominent periods in our country's history. The laboring man who should receive every Saturday night, a copy of the "Surrender of Burgoyne" for his weekly wages, would soon inquire who General Burgoyne was, and to whom he surrendered. His curiosity would be aroused and he would learn the facts from a fellow laborer or from his employer. The same would be true of other National pictures, and in time many would be taught leading incidents in our country's history, so that they would soon be familiar to those who would never read them in books, teaching them history and imbuing them with a National feeling.[7]

In this passage, Secretary Chase's chief clerk not only speaks to anti–British sentiments in his reference to General Burgoyne.[8] He also identifies two central points about the potential power of imagery on paper currency in constructing a collective national identity. First, because of the pervasiveness of paper currency in the kind of market economy that was spreading across the American continent, images on paper money were guaranteed a much larger audience than images carried by other media. These images thus were particularly effective in conveying messages to the poor and illiterate with whom the state had difficulty communicating through other means such as newspapers or schooling. Second, images on paper currency were considered particularly effective tools of propaganda because people could not refrain from encountering them in their daily transactions. By providing a frequent reminder to people that they were members of what nationalists considered a common, homogeneous community, the currency could be expected to work as a much more effective vehicle of nationalist messages than even flags or anthems.[9]

This is also the way the National Monetary Commission saw it when it reviewed Salmon P. Chase's proposal of the national banking act. Listing the economic benefits of the proposed currency, they did not forget to mention its ideological surplus value—"the stimulation of the patriotism of the people which would arise from the closer touch with national affairs…."[10] Among the signal moments of American history that were printed from this motive on National Bank notes (and on the National Gold Bank notes of California) were, in chronological order, Columbus in sight of land; the Landing of Columbus; Presentation of an Indian Princess representing America to the Old World; De Soto discovering the Mississippi in 1541; Sir Walter Raleigh in England in 1585, exhibiting corn and tobacco from America; Franklin capturing electricity with a kite and a key; the Battle of Lexington on April 19, 1775; the surrender of General Burgoyne to General Gates at Saratoga on October 17, 1777; Washington resigning his commission; Commodore Oliver Perry leaving his flagship during the Battle of Lake Erie, September 10, 1813; and, surprisingly, General Winfield Scott entering Mexico City in 1847 during the Mexican-American War.[11]

A number of artworks from the Rotunda of the United States Capitol likewise was deployed on National Bank notes. Lawmakers in Congress saw the originals at regular intervals and it is safe to assume that off and on they even heeded them—John G. Chapman's *Baptism of Pocahontas* (engraved by Charles Burt for the back of the $20 note), Robert W. Weir's *Embarkation of the Pilgrims* (engraved by W.W. Rice for the back of the $50 note), Peter Frederick Rothermel's *Landing of the Pilgrims* (engraved by Charles Burt for the back of the $1 note), John Trumbull's *Washington Crossing the Delaware* (on the face of the $50 note, with a vignette of Washington praying at Valley Forge at right), and his *Jefferson presenting the Declaration of Independence to John Hancock at the Continental Congress* (on the back of the $100 note, in John Girsch's rendering).[12] Trumbull's rendering of the scene in Congress, which dates from 1826, is a perfect example of visualizing the new political order in the spirit of the Enlightenment. The way in which the delegates are gathered together suggests that the revolution obtained legitimacy and authority through rational argumentation.

Trumbull's artwork is a post-hoc construction, however. There were other ways for the American revolution to advance. One such way is captured by Alexander Anderson's engraving titled *Celebration of Independence*. The engraving was used, *inter alia*, as illustration in a popular history book, John Warner Barber's *Interesting Events in the History of the United States*. In Anderson's engraving, a tumultuous mob is shown toppling the equestrian statue of George III from its pedestal. The gilded lead statue, which showed the king in the garb of a Roman emperor, had been put up in August 1770 following the repeal of the hated Townshend Acts earlier that year. Then the statue was a suitable symbol of the easing of tensions and, as well, an articulation of the Englishness of New Yorkers. A mere six years later, the statue was torn down and decapitated; the head was paraded around the town to the beat of the fifes and drums of George Washington's soldiers and sailors, who had joined the jubilant crowd of civilians.

Celebration of Independence represents various disenfranchised groups expressing their political views through a tort action of political iconoclasm or image-wrecking. Historically, the toppling of the statue was only one among a number of similar actions. Several liberty poles were raised and subsequently destroyed, and a marble statue of the British parliamentarian William Pitt the Elder was likewise decapitated. Other symbolic assaults included the destruction of royal portraits or the removal by angry crowds of the King's coat of arms from courthouses, churches, taverns (lovingly recreated in Washington Irving's "Rip Van Winkle"), and shops. All these actions show that within the oral and popular culture, anger was a completely unbridled source of definition, much more so than the anger expressed in formal prose by major figures like John Dickinson or Thomas Jefferson. It is also a matter of record that popular uprisings occurred quite frequently in eighteenth-century America, although at first they were mostly geared to local issues of the moment, such as land title disputes, customs enforcements, and so on. It was only after the Stamp Act controversy of 1765 that the politics of the street became a regular and dominant force in the colonial challenge to imperial policies, anticipating the political elites' opposition to British rule.[13]

A comparison between Trumbull's and Anderson's renderings of the American Revolution demonstrates the use of pictures as visual arguments in attempts to define social and political goals and ideals. In these processes, pictures are always arguments directed against other pictures circulating in society. Whereas Trumbull visualized the glorified image of a revolution guided by reason, Anderson staged the founders' nightmare, the extremes of political fervor, what the founders conceived of as democracy's shadow. To George Washington, ever the strict father, the political iconoclasm at Bowling Green had "much the appearance of riot, and want of order, in the Army, that he disapproves the manner."[14] Washington wanted this revolution to be an orderly one, and he refused to condone even the desecration of the king's statue. He, like other revolutionary leaders such as John Adams or Alexander Hamilton, also strained at the rabble-rousing spirit unleashed by figures like Thomas Paine.

In the course of the nineteenth century, Washington's self-image achieved the status of memory and myth. Accounts of his role in the French and Indian wars were instrumental in this development. Understood as the result of the competition between Britain and France, these accounts glorified "Young Washington" as "prudent and brave," and as someone who "could be relied on."[15] The anti-hero, Washington's counterpart, was the haughty British General Braddock, who by ignoring the advice of the experienced American frontierspeople wantonly lost the battle of the Monongahela in 1755. "Washington and his troops," Jesse Olney, a teacher from Connecticut, wrote in a schoolbook history in 1836, "were the only part of the army that effectually resisted the enemy."[16] Such rhetoric, as well as a painting related to the event, contributed greatly to romanticizing Washington as "the greatest man in America."[17] Even more useful were the encounters in Lexington and Concord in April 1775, which marked the beginning of the Revolution, creating the first martyrs. Even the battle of Bunker Hill, which the Americans lost, was reinterpreted as a victory, as British losses had been substantial. Washington's distinguishing himself at the battles of Trenton in December 1776, and of Princeton in early January 1777, gave rise to further glorification, again by Olney: "The bold and successful movements of Washington excited the admiration of both Europe and America. Joy and hope now began to revive the drooping spirits of the nation. The people everywhere hailed Washington as the *Savior* of his country."[18]

The romantic view of Washington as the heroic savior of his country speaks loudly and clearly from Emanuel Gottlieb Leutze's monumental oil painting *Washington Crossing the Delaware*. The hero's apotheosis is evident from his resolute pose, erect, with one foot solidly planted on the boat's rim, metaphorically anchoring the cause of the American Revolution. If the boat provides a visual analogy to the ark of the covenant, the general's gazing onto the distant shore underscores his resolution and optimism, at the same time as it symbolizes the strength and glorious future of "these United States," read, territorial expansion under the aegis of manifest destiny. The painting's performative function as "visual ideology" is heightened by the still unfurled flag which, together with the figure of the general, is both centrally placed on the canvas and gloriously backlit, creating a unifying and centering symbol, both visually and metaphorically. Altogether, therefore, Leutze's canvas works not only as a visual embodiment of the energy and drive as well as the ideals of an America on the go, but also mediates the disjunctions and contradictions of a nation teetering on the brink of civil strife and the break-up of the Union.[19]

It will be hard to find a better-known picture in antebellum America than *Washington Crossing the Delaware*. The artist began work on it in 1850. A copy of it was placed on exhibition in New York during October 1851, to reviews that were uniformly superlative and exclusively nationalistic in tone. The *New York Evening Mirror* of November 7, 1851, called it "the most effective painting ever exhibited in America." Leutze had originally intended the painting for the United States Capitol. However, Congress refused to purchase it, possibly because the worthy lawmakers were unaware of or lukewarm to the artist's intentions. Leutze sought to embody a sense of the spiritual fraternity between German liberals (especially Ferdinand Freiligrath) and their struggles in the Revolution of 1848 and the mid-century democratizing impulse that was heir to American revolutionary ideals. Thus, Leutze's Washington is not the avatar of stability from the early republic so much as the romantic revolutionary.[20]

Leutze's original was destroyed in a fire, though a copy of the painting made it to America, where it was purchased by the International Art Union. In 1852, it was on display at the United States Capitol, drawing huge crowds. The canvas eventually landed in the Metropolitan Museum of Art, New York, an exhibition context which, by activating premier public space, bestows on the painting the imprimatur of an officially certified visual argument. As part of America's cultural memory, the painting accomplishes nothing less than the apotheosis of Washington in a key event in the history of the United States. The image of the crossing of the Delaware River on December 25, 1776, prior to the Americans' attack on the Hessians at Trenton, is, in David Hackett Fischer's words, "one of the folk-memories that most Americans share."[21] Leutze's artwork became the most famous of all American paintings. At one point, it even traveled through the country. (It also traveled through Europe.) Engravings, embroiderings, copies by other artists, and studies also contributed to the painting's popularity, as did reinterpretations. Not all of these reinterpretations proved successful. George Caleb Bingham's version, for instance, took many years to complete (1856–1871), but the scene he depicted remained utterly static. His Washington stands at the apex of a pyramid of figures, on horseback, with the actors rather resembling the figures of Bingham's better-known frontier paintings such as *Daniel Boone Leading the Settlers* (1851).[22]

Compositions of Leutze's picture in new circumstances range from a tableau ending the first act of John Brougham's *The Miller of New Jersey* (1856) to a dramatic scene in the silent film *Janice Meredith* (1924), an adaptation of Paul Leicester Ford's bestselling novel of the same title (1899), or Howard Fast's novel *The Crossing* (1971), which became the basis for an historical TV film that went on air in January 2000.[23] Leutze's masterpiece also inspired more serious artists in the twentieth century. In 1932, Grant Wood placed three Daughters of the American Revolution in front of the painting to show how far these matrons had strayed from its spirit. Larry Rivers' *Washington Crossing the Delaware* in 1953 featured a blurred Washington and an anxious soldier, a perfect fit for a period when heroism seemed unfashionable. Equally unheroic is Peter Saul's pop-art-inspired *Washington Crossing the Delaware* (1975), in which a dazed-looking general holds up a comically small flag while he is riding his charger into the river. Other contemporary artworks include Edward Sorel's satirical drawing *Nixon Crossing the Delaware* (1973) or Robert Colescott's *George Washington Carver Crossing the Delaware* (1973), which altogether dispenses with the hero in a powerful comment on American racism.[24]

In contrast to these modern and postmodern examples of questioning fixed or transcendent categories of meaning, Washington's heroic crossing persists in any number of recreations, usually done by schoolboys, though the annual event on the Pennsylvania side of the Delaware River has gone on under the title of an "officially recognized Bicentennial project" sine 1976. The bicentennial of Washington's birth in 1932 likewise provided an opportunity to recycle Leutze's masterpiece, this time on a set of twelve commemorative plates. The plates were rather flat, too flat to hold any quantity of Liebig's Extract of Beef, which in the late nineteenth century was advertised with a rendering of Leutze's painting. The message on the advertisement was clear: Liebig's Extract of Beef was an example of scientific achievement comparable, in its own realm, to Washington's river passage. The Inaugural Centennial also paid tribute to the fame of Leutze's picture, in the form of a huge float for the Civil Parade held in New York on May 1, 1889, in the presence of President Benjamin Harrison.[25]

By the mid–1920s, the colonial craze had reached a new height. Once the Metropolitan Museum had recognized that the decoration of the contemporary American home demanded the trappings of Washingtoniana, retailers were only too happy to supply collectible items, including windowshades with paintings of Washington crossing the Delaware. "Junk snuppers" might have paid for their fads and fancies with $50 National Bank notes, whose fronts were graced by Alfred Jones' engraved version of the crossing.[26] Jones' was a daunting task, considering that he had to compress in fine lines on a steel plate what Leutze could accomplish on a huge canvas by means of the extensive use of light and color, size, space, and paint. From hindsight, Jones' rendering of

A $50 National Bank note, 1863 to 1901, face with vignettes "Washington Crossing the Delaware" and "Washington at Prayer," 7.42 × 3.125 in. (American Numismatic Association Money Museum).

Leutze's painting, Louis Delnoce's reworking of the Valley Forge legend as well as his earlier *Apotheosis of Washington* vignette—used, for instance, on $10 notes from the Oil City Bank, Oil City, Pennsylvania, as late as 1864—reveal a profound nostalgia for the time when the Founder was alive.[27] Such nostalgia was no Gilded Age invention; Americans had bemoaned the passing of the founders' generation and their supposedly selfless commitment to public virtue ever since the 1820s. But the quickening pace of capitalist expansion after the Civil War intensified the attachment many Americans felt to what they believed was a simpler past. Nostalgia clearly set the tone in late nineteenth-century accounts of Washington's romantic life. While such accounts meant to convey the humanity of the Father of His Country, by all accounts the love of Washington's life was Martha, and, thanks to the efforts of the Daughters of the American Revolution, by the late 1890s their wedding anniversary had become a day to be commemorated.

The celebration of the first first couple's wedding anniversary reawakened artistic as well as public interest.[28] A number of paintings—by Jean Leon Gerome Ferris or John Ward Dunsmore, for example—depicted the Washingtons. In 1896, the United States Treasury introduced a new back design for the $1 Silver Certificate, graced by the dignified portraits of Martha Washington and George Washington. Martha Washington's portrait was designed by Thomas F. Morris after a painting by Charles François Jalabert, and engraved by Charles Burt. George Washington's portrait was engraved by Alfred Sealey after Gilbert Stuart. Burt's head of Martha Washington also appeared as the central feature on the $1 Silver Certificates, series 1886 and, slightly modified, series 1891, making Martha Washington the first and only named woman to appear on the primary portrait of United States currency.[29]

As for pre-federal money, a double portrait of Martha Washington and George Washington appeared on a $50 note issued by the Georgia Rail Road and Banking Company, Augusta, 1840s–1850s. Its elaborate central vignette shows an Indian woman standing, Liberty seated with pole and cap, agricultural products, and a bust of George

Washington. Martha Washington's portrait is at left, below the denomination.[30] George and Martha also share the stage on a $4 note from the Bank of Washington, Washington, North Carolina. Issued during the 1850s and 1860s, the note shows the Stuart portrait at left, above the denomination, while Martha Washington's portrait is at right, below the denomination.[31]

The back design of the $1 Silver Certificate, series 1896, warrants a closer look. Clearly its rhetoric conveys Washingtonian refinement and knowing one's place. The design is, therefore, a good example of the way elite society appropriated Washington for the purpose of increasing its legitimacy, but the notes also set the stage for society's highest strata to crown the Father of Our Country the father of their own good taste, with Martha as a sidekick, a founding mother to go with the founding father. As the *Indiana Democrat* wrote on February 20, 1901: "Persons fortunate enough to possess a one-dollar Silver Certificate have an excellent picture of Martha Washington, the wife of the Father of His Country."[32]

The $1 Silver Certificate, series 1896, is the first note in the "Educational Series," a deliberate effort on the part of the state in the manufacturing of consent. The note's face, designed by Will H. Low and engraved by Charles Schlecht, is known as "History Instructing Youth." An allegorical figure of History is pointing out to an equally allegorical Youth the principal sights of Washington, D.C.—the Washington Monument (which had finally been dedicated in 1885) and the Capitol—and presumably telling the narratives behind them, including the story of the United States Constitution, which appears at right. Today, the note is a much-sought-for collector's item because of its superb engraving. Other denominations too embodied ideas and values that were considered important for connecting with the citizenry. The face of the $2 Silver Certificate, for instance, is graced by a vignette known as "Science Presenting Steam and Electricity to Commerce and Manufacture." The note, which was engraved by George F.C. Smillie after a design by Edwin H. Blashfield, is among the most famous of all United States currency issues—and by general consent one of the most perfectly designed. Another engraving by Smillie, Electricity as the Dominant Force in the World, features

A $1 Silver Certificate, series of 1896, back, with portraits of Martha Washington and George Washington, 7.42 × 3.125 in. (American Numismatic Association Money Museum).

prominently on the $5 Silver Certificate, series 1896, the third and last of the Educational series. Critics have thought that the note looks a bit overwrought, with "a touch of Wagner and Beethoven in its highly dramatic imagery," but ornate art and architecture had reached a high point in the 1890s, and the theme may have been a good choice.[33]

As Theodore Kemm wrote in the late 1960s, the series 1896 Silver Certificates "are truly the most beautiful notes ever issued by our government."[34] Yet for all its emblematic garnish, the "Educational Series" did not merely serve the self-representation of America's cultural elites. The notes must also be seen as efforts, on the part of the state, to advance official ideologies and to seek legitimacy at a time of mass immigration. (Perhaps for this reason alone, the Educational notes were exclusive products of the Treasury Department's Bureau of Engraving and Printing, i.e., no private companies were involved.) Like the "Pledge of Allegiance," originally composed by Colonel George Balch in 1887 and revised by Francis Bellamy in 1892, the notes were employed in the manufacturing of consent. The fundamental political question of the time, we have seen, was how to assimilate a heterogeneous mass of people who were Americans not by birth but by immigration.

Immigrants, Eric Hobsbawm argued, provided a body of rather "*doubtful members of the national community*; all the more doubtful because [...] they could actually be classified as foreigners."[35] Tellingly, William McKinley in his inaugural address of March 4, 1897, urges "the spread of knowledge and free education" as the royal road to "a safer, a better, and a higher citizenship." The promotion of these goals, he said, must be undertaken "with the zeal of our forefathers."[36] The nationalist messages conveyed by the currency provided a frequent reminder to people that they were to be members of what nationalists from all social strata considered an ethnically united community. Authorities relied on the mass immersion in the nationalistic iconography on the currency to mold people's identity and their perceived destiny, to teach what is expected from them, and, not to forget, to connect to the spirit of the age in an attempt to increase the state's legitimacy with its citizenry.[37]

As regards the visual rhetoric of the notes in the "Educational Series," it is unequivocally gendered. While the notes display a multiplicity of allegorical figures, historic persons are depicted either as holders of public office—Presidents George Washington (on the back of the $1 note) and Ulysses S. Grant (on the back of the $5 note, next to General Philip Sheridan)—or as inventors (Robert Fulton and Samuel F.B. Morse on the back of the $2 note). Unsurprisingly, they are all men. And they are depicted through portraits. In contrast, women appear as full-size figures, albeit as allegories. In the notes of the "Educational Series" thus are repeated the organizational structures of viewing that were typical of the gender hierarchy of the time—public and active versus private or domestic and passive. Male protagonists are coded as image carriers of the *vita activa*, while females appear as mere showpieces, passive objects to be looked at. Put differently, insofar as women occupy a positive space in the symbolic constitution of the United States, it is in figurative symbols of liberty and republican virtue, an iconography that underscores their passivity in public forums. Liberty as well as republican virtue evoke a purity of status or innocence of experience under masculine protection, categories that preclude independent female activity.[38]

Martha Washington is no exception in this regard. Jared Sparks, historian, educator,

Unitarian minister, and one-time President of Harvard College, set a precedent in his *Life of George Washington*, when in 1839 he summed up her account in these words: "Affable and courteous, exemplary in her deportment, remarkable for her deeds of charity and piety, unostentatious and without vanity, she adorned by her domestic virtues the sphere of private life, and filled with dignity every situation in which she was placed."[39] Martha Washington's portrait, on the back of the $1 Silver certificate, also presents her as adornment, George Washington's wife, the avatar of domesticity. In contrast, George Washington confronts the viewer as president, whose "awe-inspiring air" identifies him as the Father of His Country.[40] The two portraits are also rigidly separated by the central numeral—"1," which is also spelled out as an embellished "ONE"—hinting at the gendered classification of separate spheres for men and women. Thus, the ensemble presents a seamless fit in a pictorial tradition that accepted real women only as the wives of their better-known husbands and that applied the opprobrium "masculine" to politically or intellectually active women. "I do not wonder," Abigail Adams had written in 1814, "learned [women] are considered as black swans."[41]

9

Value and the Paternal Image

Some women, understandably, saw things differently. "How blest the maid," twelve-year-old Anne Kimball of Newburyport, Massachusetts, embroidered on her sampler in 1803, "Whose useful hours successive as they glide / The book, the needle, and the pen divide." Indeed in America at the time, there was a great deal of controversy about how much training in "the book and the pen" young women needed, but the general agreement was that "the needle" was the foremost tool in their education. Some young women, especially from middle-class urban families, were sent to private academies, but even there, their "accomplishments" mostly meant fine needlework, whether they liked it or not. Fifteen-year-old Maria Crowninshield apparently did like it. She embroidered an allegorical image of female education while a student at the Ladies' Academy in Dorchester, Massachusetts, which she enthusiastically described as a "delightful mansion of happiness." Her needlework, in neoclassical style, depicts a temple of learning in which a young girl in flowing robes reads from a book held by her instructor, while a goddess crowns her with a wreath.[1]

Female reformers such as Hannah Moore or her more radical colleague, Mary Wollstonecraft, would have shuddered at such pious acquiescence and submissiveness, though the pattern of excluding women from the public sphere plagued the fledgling republic from its inception. "We know better than to repeal our Masculine systems," John Adams had responded to his wife's express desire, in March 1776, that the revolutionaries "would remember the Ladies, and be more generous and favourable to them than your ancestors." So sure was Abigail Adams' husband of the viability of the patriarchal system and so convinced was he of the necessity to keep all kinds of marginalized groups in place that he added:

> As to your extraordinary Code of Laws, I cannot but laugh. We have been told that our Struggle has loosened the bands of Government every where. That children and Apprentices were disobedient—that schools and Colledges were grown turbulent—that Indians slighted their Guardians and Negroes grew insolent to their Masters. But your letter was the first intimation that another Tribe more numerous and powerful than all the rest were grown discontented.[2]

The patriarchal Thomas Jefferson, when thinking of a healthy republican family, also meant "women fulfilled their true nature by sacrificing themselves for the comfort and well-being of their families." In Jefferson's view, the family home was a refuge, a place where the patriarch could be secure in the love of those who depended on him.[3]

Among the revolutionary leaders, only Thomas Paine addressed women's rights in a different fashion. "Man with regard to [women], in all climates, and in all ages," he wrote in 1775, "has been either an insensible husband or an oppressor." Paine's contribution for the *Pennsylvania Magazine* also details the exclusion of women from public life: "[M]an, while he imposes duties upon women, would deprive them of the sweets of public esteem, and in exacting virtues from them, would make it a crime to aspire at honor." Still, women do not seize their rights in Paine's writings. They remain the supplicants of a masculine world of patriarchs. "'Be not our tyrants in all,'" runs Paine's imagined version of this supplicating voice. "'Permit our names to be sometimes pronounced beyond the narrow circles in which we live....'"[4] There is hardly a better example of the "narrow circles" in which women lived then than William Blackstone's commentary on marriage: "By marriage, the husband and wife are one person in law: that is, the very being or legal existence of the woman is suspended during the marriage [...] incorporated and consolidated into that of the husband: under whose wing, protection, and *cover*, she performs every thing; and is therefore called in our law-french, a *feme-covert*."[5]

The "incorporation" of the woman's existence into that of the husband cannot be separated from the economic order that based value on property. As Mary Poovey argues, "a woman's sexual infidelity challenged not only the security of the paternal relation and the man's exclusive right to property, but also the illusion that women were 'fixed' as reproductive (not sexually autonomous) beings, as dependent (not socially autonomous) subjects, and as uniformly 'other' to man...."[6] Women's otherness constitutes one term in the structural opposition in which the exchange between men and women is usually cast. Based as this exchange is on possession and desire, women are mere objects to be exchanged, functionally equivalent to commodities and money, which likewise circulate among men. Their worth is not intrinsic but derives from their valuation by the male subject, his "imprint," which becomes the standard or *étalonnage*, in relation to a third. The French word *étalon*, as used by the feminist and cultural theorist Luce Irigaray, designates a stallion, a standard of measure, or a currency (*étalon-or*), thus pointing to the parallelism between sexual and financial exchanges. If femininity, for Irigaray, is premised on exclusion from control over money, language, and the gaze, masculinity is characterized by their possession. The masculine thus is the standard of value, in relation to which the feminine acquires significance and worth. This standardization, which divides the social order into what Irigaray calls masculine "producer subjects" and feminine "commodity-objects" makes the grounding of value in the paternal image so problematic.[7]

Martha Washington on the $1 Silver Certificates of 1896 is quite literally a "*femme couverte*" who, upon entering marriage, had received a "cover," to the effect that she was at the same time "protected" and "hidden."[8] Moreover, the word "ONE," spelled out over her portrait, not only evokes the many dissolving into one—*E pluribus Unum*—, but also a cruelly ironic reworking of Blackstone's commentary on marriage. The fragile and highly ambivalent gender idyll on the $1 Silver Certificates of 1896 did not last long, though. The patricians on the defensive who had hoped to be able to bring the new, non–Anglo-Saxon immigrants into the fold of ethnic unity, soon stoked their passions around other campfires, most notably, immigrant restriction. The $1 Silver Certificates of later series, 1923 and 1928 (one of the first of the new small-size notes), altogether dispensed with Martha Washington.

A $2 Silver Certificate, Series 1899, front, 7.42 × 3.125 in. (American Numismatic Association Money Museum).

Whereas the wife vanished from the currency (she lived on in the pages of *The Woman's Home Companion* or *Good Housekeeping*, and she made a comeback on a 4 cents postage stamp in 1922), the husband had been honored in his own right already on earlier issues. George Washington's portrait was centrally placed on the front of the $2 Silver Certificates, Series 1899, between two allegorical figures, Mechanics (male) and Agriculture (female). Washington's portrait was engraved by George F.C. Smillie, then chief engraver at the Bureau of Engraving and Printing. Unlike in Stuart's original and unlike in Alfred Sealey's engraving, Washington is looking towards the viewer's right, into the future.[9]

Washington had looked towards the viewer's right already on $1 notes of the Elm City Bank, New Haven, Connecticut, beginning with the 1850s. But these notes were lone exceptions. What lends importance to the $2 Silver Certificates of 1899 is that they were issued in the year of the centennial of Washington's death. The right-looking Smillie engraving was kept for most of the later federal issues, including the $5 National Bank Notes, series 1882, issued 1908–1916 in two types, "Date Back" and "Value Back."[10] The engraving's iconic status is, however, owed to the various $1 notes, beginning with the $1 Federal Reserve Bank Notes, series 1918, the redesigned United States (Legal Tender) notes, series 1923, and the redesigned Silver Certificates, series 1923, the last series of large-size notes.[11]

Silver Certificates could be exchanged for silver coins. The silvery tint on the notes' front, in imitation of the precious material, was not really necessary. It would have made sense had there been no backing by silver. It is rather the absence of such backing that stimulates the desire manifested on currency notes in the form of material imitations. Still, overdetermination also prevailed on the National Gold Bank notes of California, which were printed on yellow-tint paper in imitation of gold and bore depictions of various gold coins on their backs. The notes were issued from 1870 to 1875. They were originally introduced as an aid to California bankers who had found their business operations impaired by the ever-increasing amounts of gold coins struck at the two Western mints then in operation. While the National Gold Bank notes were fully

A $1 Silver Certificate, Series 1923, front, 7.42 × 3.125 in. (Heinz Tschachler).

redeemable in cold coins, they also constituted an attempt to disabuse Californians from payment in gold.[12]

Long before the appearance of Silver Certificates, the federal government issued Gold Certificates. Their backs were a bright golden-orange, symbolic of the gold coins the notes could be exchanged for. Washington's portrait appeared on the $20 notes, series 1905–1907, known as "Technicolor Notes" for their colorful backs. The portrait, engraved by Alfred Sealey after Fairman's print of Stuart's painting, is facing towards the viewer's left. Below the portrait is Washington's name, probably the first instance of inscribing an individual's name in this place.[13] Federal Reserve Bank Notes are but little known. Technically, they are National Bank notes, though they were issued only by one of the twelve Federal Reserve Banks and they could also be redeemed only there. One-dollar Federal Reserve Bank notes, series of 1918, bear a frameless portrait of George Washington, like the one used on the $2 Silver Certificate, series of 1899. The portrait, an engraving by George F.C. Smillie, again is looking towards the viewer's right. The notes' backs showed a patriotic eagle grasping a flag—hence the nickname "Green Eagle Notes."[14]

Clearly the image of Washington on the "Green Eagle Notes" was to inspire patriotism at a time when the United States engaged their "relentless enemy in a life-and-death struggle." At such a time, a syndicated writer noted, "what Washington did and said, and caused to be done, [was] taking on a new and solemn meaning."[15] Ten years later, new currency notes also were taking on a new and solemn meaning. Earlier notes, the "Green Eagle Notes" included, were of considerable size—7.42 × 3.125 inches. Notes issued after 1928 are much smaller—6.14 × 2.61 inches. The new size is easier to handle and store, even though at first some banks printed and gave away "wallet stuffers" to make up for the inconvenience.[16] The change in size also saved the Treasury millions of dollars, though it did nothing to stave off the Great Depression. It was much later that the measure, which was intended to align America's currency with international standards, was interpreted as a crisis symptom and President Herbert Hoover as the nation's master of thriftiness.[17]

The reduction in size had been recommended already by Treasury Secretary

A $1 Federal Reserve Bank note, Series 1918, front and back, 7.42 × 3.125 in. (American Numismatic Association Money Museum).

Franklin MacVeagh. MacVeagh served from 1909 to 1913, though his recommendation was not realized at the time. Currency design did not become an issue until 1925, and MacVeagh's recommendation was finally accepted by Treasury Secretary Andrew W. Mellon in 1927 and implemented for notes of the series of 1928, to the delight of Herbert Hoover. Hoover was then facing the thankless task of having to steer the nation through the Great Depression. Although luckless, Hoover was hardly the do-nothing president that Franklin Roosevelt and the Democrats made him out to be in the 1932 campaign. Hoover did in fact call for programs such as the Reconstruction Finance Corporation (RFC) that would provide federal loans to banks, railroads, and agricultural organizations, and, in July 1932, he even signed the Relief and Reconstruction Act, which authorized the RFC to finance $1.5 billion in "self-liquidating" public works and to loan $300 million to the states for relief.

The Relief and Reconstruction Act did too little, and it came too late. The Depression cannot therefore be separated from the steadfast refusal of federal aid to the unemployed and needy, a politics that sacrificed people in need on the altar of the integrity of the federal budget. What Hoover did to stave off the Depression was like applying a poultice to cancer: The president convened a series of conferences in the White House, to which he invited the leaders of major industries and labor unions. The main purpose of these conferences was to urge industries and workers (and, later, private and local groups, as well as the Red Cross) to act voluntarily to ameliorate the crisis. "We could no more legislate ourselves out of a worldwide depression," Hoover, stalwart defender of rugged individualism that he was, insisted, than we could "exorcise a Caribbean hurricane by statutory law."[18]

The reduction of currency notes in size—from "horse blankets" to "pocket change"—was not the only directive issued by Treasury Secretary Mellon. Mellon also acted on a committee recommendation to fundamentally redesign the visual order on existing notes. Redesigning (and restructuring) the notes indeed had become a matter of great urgency. When the committee first met, in 1925, the currency consisted of altogether 39 classes of notes, in 11 denominations. Moreover, each note had its own design. It had been common practice to leave redesigns—including the selection of portraits—to artists and engravers. The result was total chaos. A pantheon consisting of George Washington, a Sioux chief, a backwoodsman, Benjamin Franklin, T.A. Hendricks, Michael Hillegas, and many others only led to one logical conclusion—that the visual arrangement on America's currency was being made completely without rhyme or reason.[19]

In the end, however, the currency reform was not nearly substantial enough. To be sure, the notes had been reduced in size, the number of classes and types had been cut, and the visual order had been revamped. Yet there were still many classes of small-size notes. Legal Tender (United States) notes came in denominations of 1, 2, 5, and 100 dollars (the only note that is still current); Silver Certificates came in denominations of 1, 5, and 10 (all obsolete since 1963); National Bank notes in denominations of 5, 10, 20, 50, and 100 (all obsolete now); Federal Reserve Bank notes in denominations of 5, 10, 20, 50, and 100 (also all obsolete now); Federal Reserve notes were first distributed in 1913 as large-size notes; small-size notes originally came only in denominations of 5 and higher and were redeemable in gold between 1929 and 1933.[20] On the plus side of the ledger, the flood of arbitrarily selected pictures had been curbed: Between 1861 and 1900 more than 160 different types, classes, and varieties of bank notes were put in circulation. By 1929, the number was cut in half; as of 1930, only 15 were left. As for visual symbols, following the currency reform there were only a few select examples of "national" architecture left, a scene from the nation's history (the signing of the Declaration of Independence), and, most notably, the portraits of "the Presidents of the United States."[21]

Limiting portraits to those of "the Presidents of the United States" was the work, again, of Secretary Mellon's special committee, which had decided that such portraits "have a more permanent familiarity in the minds of the public than any others."[22] The word "presidents" is, strictly speaking, a misnomer. The committee's decision "was somewhat altered by the Secretary of the Treasury," the United States Bureau of Engraving and Printing (USBEP) explains, to include Alexander Hamilton, the fledgling nation's first Secretary of the Treasury (on the new $10 bill); Salmon P. Chase, Secretary of the Treasury under Lincoln and credited with promoting the National Banking System (on the new $10,000 bill); and Benjamin Franklin, one of the signers of the Declaration of Independence and, together with John Adams and John Jay, of the Paris Peace

Treaty of 1783 (on the new $100 notes, the "Benjamins"). "All three of these statesmen," the USBEP concludes, "were well known to the American public."[23] One understands the sentiment. "No people," President Calvin Coolidge said in an address delivered before the National Education Association in 1926, "can look forward who do not look backward."[24]

Choice of the iconic portraits of "the Presidents of the United States" thus seems to be based on their offering a firm footing in the midst of social and economic chaos, tendering comfort and solace and confirming the sociologist Michael Schudson's belief that "the past is constantly being retold in order to legitimate present interests" and to elaborate present ideals and realities. But were the worthy committee members really that confident about the Presidents' purported "more permanent familiarity in the minds of the public"? With George Washington, they could not have gone wrong. Even in popularity polls—another invention of the 1920s—the Father of His Country ranked as the greatest idol amongst all the heroes, living or dead. Still, when college students were asked to identify the three greatest figures of all time, they settled on Jesus Christ and Napoleon Bonaparte, closely followed by Henry Ford.[25] It is tempting to see this ranking as the reason why all the portraits on the new notes came with name tags. But adding a name below a portrait actually was in compliance with a law passed in 1889.[26] The result can be observed, per Washington's portrait, already on $20 Gold Certificates, series of 1905, the "Technicolor notes," and, per a very modest and inconspicuous portrait on the back of $5 National Bank notes issued from 1908, which had "Washington" printed above the head. (On $2 Silver Certificates, series of 1899, Washington's portrait is still nameless.)

One can only speculate about the reasons for currency designs or redesigns, as the Bureau of Engraving and Printing does not usually justify its decisions.[27] One decision at least is comprehensible even without justification—the use of "portraits of the presidents" to distinguish different denominations. The measure is not without its problems, though. Denominations always form a ranked order. Thus, the question is who is to represent which value? And, consequently, who is valued more highly than others? This uncomfortable question plagued authorities in the former German Democratic Republic, when they were planning to introduce higher denomination bills in the 1980s. Who was to be put above Karl Marx? (Marx's portrait had been on the 100 Mark note, the 100 MDM.)[28] In the United States, a portrait of the nation's founder was selected for the $1 note.

George Washington was the nation's first president, admired as "a citizen, first in war, first in peace, first in the hearts of his countrymen," and rehabilitated by William Carlos Williams as "The Pap of Our Country" in 1925.[29] Moreover, Washington's portrait was the best known among presidential portraits, and the $1 note the most widely used piece of currency. The original selection for the $2 note was James Garfield, possibly because of the sentiment for martyred presidents. In the end, Thomas Jefferson was chosen, though there does not appear to be an explanation for the switch.[30] Abraham Lincoln was selected for the $5 note, as he stood next to Washington in the ranks of American heroes. The $10 note depicts Alexander Hamilton; Andrew Jackson appears on the $20 note and Ulysses S. Grant on the $50 note.

The largest denomination notes now being printed are the $100 notes, colloquially known as "Benjamins" for their portrait of Benjamin Franklin or "C notes," the Latin "C" representing 100. All other larger-denomination notes (only Federal Reserve notes were issued)—the $500 note depicting William McKinley, the $1,000 note depicting Grover Cleveland, the $5,000 note depicting James Madison, and the $10,000 note depicting Salmon P. Chase—were last printed in 1945 and, pursuant to an executive order issued by President Nixon, have not been issued since July 1, 1969. "Use of these large denominations," a press release by the Treasury Department and the Federal Reserve System explained, "has declined sharply over the last two decades and the need for them appears insufficient to warrant the added cost of production and custody of new supplies."[31] The largest ever United States note, the $100,000 Gold Certificate carrying Woodrow Wilson's portrait, in an engraving by George F.C. Smillie, was printed only between December 1934 and January 1935. It never appeared in general circulation and was only used in transactions between Federal Reserve Banks and clearinghouses.

Back designs of the new Federal Reserve notes are closely associated in each case with the person depicted on the face of the notes. The $2 note has Jefferson on the face and a picture of his Monticello home on the back. The $5 note couples Lincoln and the Lincoln Memorial. The $10 note brings together Hamilton and the Treasury Building. The $20 note features Andrew Jackson and the White House, the $100 note (issued both as a Federal Reserve and a United States note) Franklin and Independence Hall. Other currency notes refrain from recreating in miniature the functional majesty of government. Instead, they have plain back designs, usually the denomination, in numerals and spelled out, and implications of currency security. The exception of course is the one dollar note, which first appeared in its familiar form, that is, with the Great Seal of the United States as the central feature of the back design, in 1935.[32]

The first of the new small-size notes were issued on July 10, 1929. Prior to the date of issue, press releases had been trumpeting forth the importance of identifying each portrait with a certain denomination. "The public will learn to know its money by the pictures on it," the *New York Times* wrote on June 5, 1927. "This will make it much harder for the crooks, who will find that they cannot change a '1' to a '100' and hope to pass the bill. The tell-tale portrait will stand in the way."[33] Reduced size, a simplified design, and the strict sequentiality of the notes thus served not only to bring down production costs but also to prevent counterfeiting. This was certainly true. Once holders have memorized a portrait on a certain note, they will quickly notice any marked difference in design. In contrast, to notice differences when the most prominent design elements are pictures of buildings or complicated patterns is much more difficult.

"Every conscious perception," the anthropologist Clifford Geertz noted, "is an act of recognition, a pairing in which an object (or an event, an act, an emotion) is identified by placing it against a background of an appropriate symbol."[34] The new currency notes were such "appropriate symbols" because people were expected to rely on them to encompass, and to make sense of, their experiences. Yet the information campaigns' mantra, that the public was "to learn to know its money by the pictures on it," soon became the target of ridicule. In an article published in the *Chicago Daily Tribune* on July 9, 1929, a James Gibbon confided that of course he knew who Washington, Jefferson, Lincoln, and all other through Madison were, as their faces were only too familiar from cigar cases and crossword puzzles. He did, however, have no idea what Chase looked like, nor had anyone been able to help him:

> We know Sam Chase who lives in Lake Forest, but he says he isn't the one. Then we used to know an Elmer Chase who was in our class [...] We lost a tooth now and then to Elmer but we kept his right eye permanently black. If the picture of this Chase on the ten thousand dollar bill has a black eye then it's Elmer. Otherwise the counterfeiters have us licked....[35]

Chase, needless to say, was Salmon P. Chase, Treasury Secretary under Lincoln; his portrait appeared on the $10,000 Federal Reserve note. Washington's portrait appeared on $1 United States Notes and Silver Certificates, Series 1928, with similar fronts to the large-size Series 1923 notes.[36] More like current $1 bills were Series 1935 and 1957 Silver Certificates—the former distinguished by the first appearance of the Great Seal, the latter by the first appearance of the national motto, "In God We Trust." $1 Federal Reserve Notes have been issued only after the discontinuation of the Silver Certificates, beginning with the series of 1963. Again, from Series 1963, only Federal Reserve notes have been issued. Most of the designs have been kept from previous series, though since the 1990s measures have been taken to improve currency security. These measures include the use of color-shifting ink for numerals, a fluorescent security thread, and micro-printing on water-marked paper. As of 2008, the portraits too got a face-lift. They are now larger, unframed, and positioned off-center. (For Jackson, a younger portrait is now used.) There have been exceptions to the refurbishing of the currency, though. Names are still being added below the portraits, and both the $1 and $2 bills have remained entirely unchanged—the former since 1963, the latter since 1976, the year of the bicentennial.[37]

The new design seems here to last, "fixed in a single, changeless pattern," as Richard Doty put it.[38] Another commentator even derided the enlarged portraits on the refurbished bills as "hydrocephaly on money."[39] Numismatists, collectors, and artists generally speak in the cause of *variatio delectat*, an aesthetic principle that leaves ample room for innovation, openness, even ambiguity and mysteriousness. Understandably, therefore, the new designs were not warmly welcomed among these people, even though portraits on currency notes have been enlarged all over the world.[40] What is more puzzling is the continuity of "presidential" portraits since 1929. Banknote design in general is a complex and sometimes opaque process. Decision-making is often nebulous, and the committees responsible for it are frequently composed on an ad-hoc basis. What is known is that form and content of banknote design are driven by safety concerns, stylistic conventions and, not to forget, costs. The latter factor is especially true of money that is used worldwide. Globally used paper money, Jacques Hymans suggested, "involves much higher transaction costs, including the cost of informing end-users of the changes and the cost of collecting the old bills for replacement. These costs may induce the hegemon to maintain its money's traditional 'look.'"[41]

There is another reason for the visual design of currency notes generally being more "conservative" than that of stamps and other securities. Currency notes are commonly regarded as a "state's calling cards," mirroring the values the state represents, most notably stability, continuity, and resilience to crises.[42] This is especially true for U.S. currency. At the time of the currency reform in the 1920s, substituting portraits of historical heads of state for the female allegories in classical garb had been quite an international trend.[43] In the years to follow, however, heads of state, generals, and other statesmen gave way to representatives of official culture (composers like Verdi or Strauss, for instance). Internationally, that is. United States currency remained unaffected by these changes, which prompted depictions of work or leisure activities as well as non-state actors (Werner von Siemens, Le Corbusier), or else of individuals who made significant cultural or scientific contributions (Albert Einstein, Viktor Kaplan, Angelika Kauffman). Most likely these changes in banknote design reflect certain cultural shifts—a change in legitimation, from state to society to individual; changed goals in life, from devotedness to state and fatherland to material success to a post-materialist focus on quality of life and cultural or scientific aspirations.[44] On United States currency, in contrast, the state as actor prevails, conveying to citizens the value of federal, that is, state-produced money and programs. With the economy in a recession from 2007 to 2009, the state, in an act of seeking legitimacy, attempted to allay fears and reassure the citizenry that indeed their money was worth something. One way to accomplish this was to remind people of the nation's grand old men—its "fathers," as it were—, thus providing retrospective assurance and moving the source of power back to the state.[45]

The central place accorded to presidential portraits also left little space for backdrops or sceneries. Allegorical figures were not the only casualties in the shift towards the "single, changeless pattern." Scenes from the nation's history likewise disappeared. (The one exception is the reduced version of Trumbull's "The Signing of the Declaration of Independence," which was put on the back of the $2 Federal Reserve note, series of 1976, in recognition of the bicentennial.) The new pattern is not merely "single" and "changeless," it is also simpler. Historical scenes or allegorical arrangements are much more complex than portraits. Allegories place human subjects within a mythological context, overloading them with signifiers of abstractions such as liberty or justice. Historical scenes generally depict key events such as a decisive battle, a nation's founding, or the discovery of its land. Portraits, in contrast, are at one and the same time signifiers and signifieds. While a portrait is not the same thing as the person represented, it nevertheless is *like* the person portrayed and so contains in itself that person. Put differently, the individualized presence in a portrait at the same time suggests a formal distance. This is a necessary condition, for individuality suggests equality, but that must be rendered inconceivable. Therefore, portraits are made to appear rigid, stiff, even mask-like. Only in this way can the subject be seen at once from up close and far away. Portraits, then, are not mirrors but forms of appropriating and interpreting, sense-making and meaning-construction that generate a reality of their own.[46]

Part IV

A More Permanent Familiarity

The "dead presidents," as U.S. bills are colloquially known, link to the ability to discern human faces. It is only a matter of seconds for us to filter out a face from the multiplicity of daily encounters. This fact may help explain that portraits have traditionally been valued more highly than allegories or representations of historical events. Portraits also have been used as political symbols throughout history. Alexander the Great wanted his image to be known to everyone in the lands he conquered, and he handpicked his own artists to carry the project through. The Roman Caesars, beginning with Julius and Augustus, likewise made mandatory the public display of their own likenesses. In Renaissance England, Queen Elizabeth I had approved images of herself distributed throughout the kingdom. (She even ordered that unauthorized portraits that allegedly failed to do her justice be removed. Moreover, pictures of the "Diva Elizabetha" often replaced images of Christ, the Holy Mary, and other religious icons.)[1]

Each of these historical figures knew that whoever wished to rule had to be present, no matter the size of the territory they ruled over. Of course rulers could travel, and many of them did just that. But rulers could also be present, omnipresent that is, through pictures, which made available a vicarious experience of their rule. The visual presence of political power is, however, not restricted to monarchies or other regimes. It is just as strong in republics, where members of the community need to be *convinced* of the legitimacy of the existing order. In the newly independent United States, visualizing the legitimacy, value, and authority of the new institutions unfolded in a slow and complex process of reformulating and adapting older, mainly aristocratic traditions. In this process, America's political culture was born, that is, the ensemble of cultural values and practices that frame its political institutions, define the normative ideas on which the rule of law is based, and generally provide for meaning and orientation. "Republics," Eugene Miller and Barry Schwartz argued, "must be sanctified as well as rationalized for their subjects; and state portraits are conspicuous among the symbols of power that sanctify republican rule."[2] Rulers throughout the ages made ample use of the visual presence of power, especially after printing technology became more advanced and more widely available. Printing technology made the visual presence of political power ubiquitous. The persistence of dollar bills in a "fixed in a single, changeless pattern" also is ample proof of this orientation.[3]

10

Patriotic Extravaganzas

The currency reform became an issue in 1925, when Treasury Secretary Andrew W. Mellon issued a directive that called for the reduction of currency notes in size. Two years later, Mellon acted on a committee recommendation to fundamentally redesign the visual order on existing notes. The redesign was to be implemented for notes of the series of 1928, to the delight of thrifty Herbert Hoover. Hoover's predecessor in office, President Calvin Coolidge had a different, albeit related, agenda. In December of 1924, Coolidge signed the so-called "bicentennial bill," with February 22, 1932, designated as the official bicentennial birthday. The year-long celebration of the two-hundredth anniversary of George Washington's birth became the most extensive celebration ever held for a national leader.[4]

The bicentennial celebration was marked by some truly outrageous activities. Sol Bloom, the New York congressman whom President Hoover appointed to the directorship of the Bicentennial Commission, drew on his earlier career as a public relations man and musical entrepreneur to create a patriotic extravaganza, enlisting celebrities right and left. Jimmy Doolittle, an aviator, loaded into his mail plane a middle-aged great-great-great grandniece of the first president and flew over every part of the nation where Washington had actually traveled, covering 2,600 miles between dawn and dusk on July 25, 1932. Bloom also organized public events, masquerades, radio shows, and patriotic concerts, he had Washington's name and face put on souvenirs and trinkets, and he had streets and buildings named after him. Framed cardboard versions of Gilbert Stuart's "Athenaeum" portrait were issued, finding their way into virtually every schoolroom in America. Millions of pages of print were also published, including hundreds of playlets tailored for production in schools or pageants. Teachers' manuals were crammed with ideas for instilling patriotism in the young through engaging in elaborate rites—disguising as postage stamps, snipping five-pointed stars out of scraps of old bedsheets, crossing let's pretend rivers muffled in tablecloths or, for young girls, playing at Betsy Ross making the Stars and Stripes for George Washington.[5]

Bloom also got on the front page with his efforts, per congressional mandate, to select an unimpeachable likeness of the Father of His Country. The chosen likeness would have "official sanction and be issued in hundreds of thousands of copies as part of the observance of 1932."[6] Whatever the image finally picked, it would appear on stamps, a bicentennial medal, a commemorative quarter, be distributed to the country's schools and, even more important, it would serve as the official logo for the United States George Washington Bicentennial Commission. In order to find a definitive portrait, a special "portrait committee" was established, though the committee, a mutually despising company composed of art critics and historians, could not agree on a single portrait. Finally, Houdon's bust of 1785 gained a majority and was duly photographed.[7]

Jean-Antoine Houdon, Washington bust, 1785, 25 × 18 × 18 in. (Dallas Museum of Art, gift of Ronald E. Fritz).

Secretary of the Treasury Andrew Mellon lost no time in making one of the commission's "authentic" photographs the model for artists competing for the design of a new circulating coin, the Washington Quarter. The coin debuted on August 1, 1932. Although it was trumpeted as the numismatic plum of the decade, only some six million pieces of it were minted and distributed that year, as the nation's economy was in such a slump that additional pieces were not needed in commerce. Since then, however, the Washington Quarter has been circulating in numerous combinations of metals, the loss of its silver, in 1965, included. Though intended as a commemorative, the Washington Quarter has become *the* twenty-five-cent piece used by Americans, one of the most popular coins ever produced by the United States Mint. New quarters are minted each year with the date changed but nothing else. The Washington Quarter may have become Americans' day-to-day coin, but critics never regarded it as providing an artistic "statement." As Cornelius Vermeule wrote, John Flanagan's portrait of Washington was merely "a symptom of the frozen, conservative classic naturalism that affected U.S. governmental sculpture in the generation from 1932 to 1950." The designs and models submitted by Laura Gardin Fraser had been much more vibrant, and they were preferred by nearly everyone except the Treasury Secretary, who had the last word in the decision. It also did not help that, perhaps as compensation, Fraser was the winner of the competition for the Bicentennial medal authorized by Congress.[8]

The Bicentennial of the nation's founding in 1976 spawned its own remarkable activities. Robert Arneson for instance sculpted Washington as a wine-bibbler with a glazed-ceramic portrait head titled *Can You Suggest a '76 Pinot Noir,* thus probing a patrician, and to some extent superficial, dimension of his subject in a bold and humorous way. Likewise, in 1976, Arneson created a ceramic sculpture *George and Mona in the Baths of Coloma,* in which the apparently naked Father of His Country casts a lecherous smile upon a fetching Mona Lisa. The two icons are sitting together in a pool of water. Arneson later claimed, ironically, that the low level of water symbolizes the declining value of the dollar. The sculpture no doubt does have something to say about America's money. To Mark Thistlethwaite, "Washington's green countenance, scored with lines, purposely suggests the form in which Stuart's portrait is seen daily: the 1796 'Athenaeum' image on the dollar bill."[9]

Washington Quarter (Bicentennial Quarter), obverse, diameter 24.3 mm (Heinz Tschachler).

There is hardly a better way to bring to the fore the "sacredness" of an object than to desecrate or vilify it. In 1779, for instance, the provisional government of Pennsylvania commissioned a Washington portrait, both to show the respect due the general and to give an impetus to emulation. A few years later, the portrait was mutilated by unknown perpetrators. The act was duly seen as "a deed of darkness [...] for the sons of Lucifer," as if they had desecrated a religious icon.[10] Today, the discourse is different, though the taboo against mutilation or disfigurement is still valid. It also applies to the national currency, the vehicle for the nation's most cherished icons. U.S. Code, Title 18, Section 333, says: "Whoever mutilates, cuts, defaces, disfigures, or perforates, or unites or cements together, or does any other thing to any bank bill, draft, note, or other evidence of debt issued by any national banking association, or Federal Reserve bank, or the Federal Reserve System, with intent to render such bank bill, draft, note, or other evidence of debt unfit to be reissued, shall be fined under this title or imprisoned not more than six months, or both." Prosecution and jurisdiction of such misdeeds are the duties of the United States Secret Service.[11]

The artist Mark Wagner, a Pennsylvania resident, is well aware that technically it is illegal to destroy bills, though for fifteen years he has been slicing into thin ribbons (he calls it "dissecting") one-dollar bills, the national monetary icon and, according to Wagner, "the single most popular piece of paper on the planet."[12] Wagner says he has never had any problems with law enforcement, and so he continues to use money as simply material, which means taking an object of public value (currency) and transforming it into an image of personal value. The transformation involves making intricate collages entirely from deconstructed bills (he spends about one thousand dollars a year on his main art supply), fragments of bills that he glues together to create portraits, still lifes, fantastical beasts, allegorical scenes, abstractions, even three-dimensional objects such as a push broom, its bristles made of 88 one-dollar bills, thus recasting George Washington in every roll. "It's only natural that Washington's 'Head of State' should grow a body and start walking around and doing stuff," Wagner said at one point. The result is a series of altogether 35 collages, titled "Washington at Large." In one of the collages, three Washingtons (the Stuart heads from the one-dollar bill) are shown in a box at the opera or theater; in another, Washington, casually dressed, is shown crossing Brooklyn Bridge, though his progress is barred by a one-dollar bill held across the walkway; still another collage has Washington in a small dinghy rowing towards a lighthouse; and last but not least, there is Washington in work clothes pushing a lawnmower, thus bringing forth, guess what? "Greener Grass."[13]

Wagner's work is collected by dozens of institutions including the Museum of Modern Art, the U.S. Federal Reserve Board, and the Smithsonian Institution. It has been shown extensively, including at The Metropolitan Museum, The Getty Research Institute, and the National Portrait Gallery. It's been seen in *Time*, *Newsweek*, *Harpers*, and *Art in America*, as well as on CBS, PBS, and the silver screen. Some of his works sell for tens of thousands of dollars. But is it art? People have the dollar bill in their hands on a daily basis, they worry about it, though no one, Wagner claims, is aware of what it looks like. Through defamiliarizing the national monetary icon, Wagner's works ask viewers to reconsider the piece of paper Americans value so much, pointedly and playfully exploring the intersection of wealth, power, the division of wealth, value, and American identity. Unsurprisingly, Grant Wood's *American Gothic* also is among his collages, and so is Leonardo's *Mona Lisa*, which is transformed into *Money Lisa*.[14]

In each act of dissection, mutilation, disfigurement, defacement, or desecration there is at least an implicit acknowledgment, on the part of the iconoclasts, of the intended "sacredness" of the object. This is also true of less dramatic forms of violations, such as when currency notes are colloquially referred to as "dead presidents," "Benjamins," "Abes," and what not. Various joke notes, personalized notes, fantasy notes, and overprints also turn pieces of currency against themselves, a strategy known as *détournement*.[15] In 2008, when the financial crisis reached a low point, a political cartoonist altered the iconic Stuart portrait on the one-dollar bill into a sour-looking Washington with a clinical thermometer in his mouth. More subversive examples of *détournement* result from visually altering genuine notes into pornographic images or vehicles of political messages. The inscription "gay money," for instance, drew attention to the gay community as a serious economic factor, as do so-called "queer dollars." In the more recent past, there have been "Occupy Wall Street" notes (in 2012), "Koch Bucks / Blood Money" (in 2011), and "Bush Bucks" (in 2006). "Zero Dollars" appeared between 1978 and 1994. In *Sweet Funk*, a 1963 oil painting by Phillip Hefferton, Washington's face from the one-dollar bill is transformed into a brick wall, literally monumentalized.[16]

My personal favorite among subversive interventions against conventions of mainstream or official (state-sanctioned) culture is a cartoon speech balloon coming from Stuart's dollar bill portrait saying, "I Grew Hemp!"[17] The cartoon is, however, a harmless joke when compared to a 1994 acrylic painting by Alfred J. Quiroz. The artwork, which is titled *George Washington Inspects the Hemp Crop* and is now privately owned, sets a happy Washington between a guffawing gentleman with a clay pipe and a grinning, corncob-pipe-puffing slave. It is apparent that the three men have indulged in the consumption of marijuana. The painting not only parodies the numerous representations of Washington as a gentleman farmer; its subversive scorn also targets representations of him as a tedious unsmiling prig. And, as someone under the influence, Washington appears utterly unheroic.[18] Moreover, Quiroz's painting may have served as inspiration to Thomas Pynchon, in whose novel *Mason & Dixon* (1997) the title characters visit Washington at Mount Vernon, where they are invited to sample the retired President's newest cash crop—a patch of marijuana he has planted in the back. The Father of His Country gives signs that he has already done so, as he stares into the shiny buttons of Jeremiah Dixon's coats and, additionally, threatens Charles Mason, the British surveyor, with a ghoulish vision of cannibalism.[19]

Subversive practices, such as tampering with the Fairman vignette or caricaturing George Washington as a consumer of marijuana, make visible the difference between sacred and profane, between being and appearance. Subversive practices are also irritating, as they question or even negate claims to legitimacy. They challenge traditional concepts and beliefs, much as they set in motion the "invention" of something new or different. Purveyors of Washington's greatness no doubt know that the veneration and deification of him as the Father of His Country constitutes a social or institutional object, a fact only by human agreement. Phrased differently, George Washington is the Father of His Country because people believe and accept him to be that. To simply declare him as the Father of His Country is not enough, no matter how sophisticated or worthy the criteria for greatness are. The metaphorical father acquires meaning when he is used to "frame" present-day events, or else to "key" such events to moments in the past associated with him. Keying present-day events to the past is, Barry Schwartz explains, "an act of recognition, a pairing in which an object (or an event, an act, an emotion) is identified by placing it against the background of an appropriate symbol." George Washington has been such an "appropriate symbol," a frame for American values, aspirations, and experience, for more than two hundred years. By the same token, the Father of His Country "frames" present events when they are convincingly "keyed" to his life.[20]

"Framing" is evident from various web documents that could be found in a variety of versions on private or officially instituted websites, including those of American schools. In the early 2000s, Kenston High School of Chagrin Falls, Ohio, had on its website a document titled "The Dollar Bill."[21] The document, after giving kudos to the Father of His Country, boldly declared, "what is on the back of that dollar bill is *something we should all know*." Such as, for instance, the uncapped pyramid, which symbolizes "[t]his country was just beginning. *We* had not begun to explore the West or decided what we could do for Western Civilization." What visitors to the website also should all know was that the American eagle, "a symbol for victory," was selected for two reasons: "first, he is *not afraid of a storm*; he is strong and he is smart enough to soar above it. Secondly, he wears no material crown. *We had just broken from the King of England*." And, it should be added, the exalted title of Father of His Country had been transferred from George III to George Washington. Oddly, the halo surrounding the ring of stars is explained as an assemblage of clouds. For the author of the document, they are the "clouds of misunderstanding [as they are] rolling away. Again, *we were coming together as one*." The document did not originate with Kenston High School. Its author was one Mary Alice McLarty, an Attorney at Law operating out of Dallas, Texas, whose political persuasions may be inferred from the document's subtitle: "Proud to be an American—a dying tradition," rendered by Kenston High as "Let us all remember."[22]

"Why didn't we know this?" the document asks, referring to the symbolism on the back of the one-dollar bill. "Your children don't know this and their history teachers don't know this. Too many veterans have given up too much to ever let the meaning fade. Many veterans remember coming home to an America that didn't care. Too many veterans never came home at all. Tell everyone what is at the back of the one-dollar bill and what it stands for, because nobody else will." Rhetoric of this kind articulates the ideology of the political Right who believes that Vietnam was lost because the young and the Left had betrayed the country through resisting what to them mistakenly seemed an unjust cause. "The Dollar Bill" is no longer available as of 2017, neither from Kenston High nor from Mary Alice McLarty. Perhaps its message is no longer as topical as it was in the early 2000s. Then, the Great Seal's eagle with olive branch and arrows was interpreted in the following way: "This country wants peace, but *we will never be afraid to fight to preserve peace*." And while the eagle "also wants to face the olive branch [...] *in time of war*, his gaze turns toward the arrows."[23] The question is, in time of what war? The War of Independence? Alternatively, the War of 1812? Maybe the Civil War? Or else events of the more recent past? World War II maybe? Or the Cold War of the 1950s, which also saw the acceptance of the national motto or the addition of the phrase "under God" to the Pledge of Allegiance. But in the early 2000s, the phrase "*in time of war*" most likely referred to "America's new war," the "War against Terror" in the wake of the attacks of 9/11.

The United States Department of the Treasury also featured the Great Seal's symbolism on its website in the early 2000s, telling visitors that it "reflects the beliefs and values that the Founding Fathers attached to the new nation and wished to pass on to their descendants."[24] The document also is no longer available as of 2017. At present, the USBEP's website contains a much terser description, borrowed from a 1996 Department of State pamphlet titled *The Great Seal of the United States*:

> *Obverse Side of the Great Seal:* The most prominent feature is the American bald eagle supporting the shield, or escutcheon, which is composed of 13 red and white stripes, representing the original States, and a blue top which unites the shield and represents Congress. The motto E Pluribus Unum (Out of many, one), alludes to this union. The olive branch and 13 arrows denote the power of peace and war, which is exclusively vested in Congress. The constellation of stars denotes a new State taking its place and rank among other sovereign powers.
>
> *Reverse Side of the Great Seal:* The pyramid signifies strength and duration: The eye over it and the motto Annuit Coeptis (He [God] has favored our undertakings) allude to the many interventions of Providence in favor of the American cause. The date underneath is that of the Declaration of Independence and the words under it, Novus Ordo Seclorum (A new order of the ages), signify the beginning of the new American era in 1776.[25]

We can describe the role of the Treasury Department in terms of a gatekeeper, shaping and even constructing America's stories or, rather, mythologies, from the nation's past. Just how carefully the Treasury is planning its promotional and marketing activities, and just how much eagerness, aptitude, and even dedication to national mythology there is on the part of those responsible for launching these stories can be seen from a survey about new website features the Bureau of Engraving and Printing sent out to subscribers to its email list in October 2008. The survey, which was conducted by PBS, is one of the longest and most complex undertakings of its kind I have ever seen. Its apparent purpose was to gauge the efficacy of Internet efforts towards educating people about the redesigned United States currency.[26] Another government agency maintained a special website for children. Called "Brain Food," the site offered "Cool Facts," including facts about the national currency. Again, the rhetorical strategies in the website for children were designed to "naturalize" the national currency so that its reproduction becomes automatic.[27]

Strategies of naturalization are crucial for the formation of patriotic citizens. The symbolic processes and practices involving the national currency position individuals (those visiting the site) so that they will recognize themselves and each other in precisely the terms specified by the state. After all, the Bureau of Engraving and Printing *is* a state apparatus, and the verbal and visual images on the currency function as representatives of the state and speak to their origins in the Department of the Treasury. By another Treasury strategy, displays were provided at numismatic conventions, and sheets and souvenirs were sold. Mark W. Olson, who was then Federal Reserve Board Governor, called this strategy "educational outreach."[28] Educational outreaches are not merely a matter of state apparatuses such as the Bureau of Engraving and Printing, the Federal Reserve, or the Secret Service, but are also on the agenda of ideological state apparatuses or their representatives, such as teachers and educators. For instance, in the late nineteenth century so-called "training currency," make-believe dollar notes, were widely used by business schools and textbooks.[29]

A contemporary example of educational outreach is a book by Barbara Johnston Adams titled *The Go-around Dollar*. In this book, which is listed under juvenile literature, the author provides plenty of information about dollar bills. At the same time, she tells a story of a single dollar bill changing hands as it is passed from one person to another: Matt finds a dollar on his way home from school and uses it to buy shoelaces from Eric. Eric spends the dollar on gum at the corner store. Jennifer, who happens to be the next customer, receives it as part of her change from a five-dollar bill, and then forgets it in her jeans so that it lands in the washing, and so on. The book thus can be seen as a variant of the money-tracking games I will discuss in the concluding chapter. The book's title, *The Go-around Dollar*, evokes the "spatial" character of paper money, that is, the circular trajectory from its place of issue to note-holders and back again to its place of issue for redemption. When in *The Go-around Dollar* the bill ends up in a picture frame as the first dollar earned by a new store, this is just as well, as dollar bills are no longer redeemed. What was once concrete has been withdrawn from the symbolic representation of the world of values. A bank or government note does not normally "tell" the story of its manifestations. This is what constitutes its quality and its effectiveness, which can be unmade only in the representational spaces of other media, such as the arts, which are under no constraints to approach things through a biographical model.

Although *The Go-around Dollar* is designed for children, its target audience is adults, or more precisely, parents who will read it to their children. This is an important point as children generally have their consumption mediated by their parents. Supposing that the parents are patriotic citizens, reading the book to their children can be expected to elicit the same or a similar response on their part. At the very least, the children will have a measure of exposure to where dollars bills originate (the Bureau of Engraving and Printing), how and where they are put into circulation (the Federal Reserve Banks, which send them to commercial banks), and what pictures and other pieces of information are on them (a portrait of George Washington, the Great Seal). They will also learn that dollar bills are legal tender for all debts, private and public, that counterfeiters sometimes make fake bills, that a special ink is used on genuine ones, that the Treasury Department will replace most damaged bills, and that occasionally people will keep a bill because it has a special meaning for them.[30]

Overall, *The Go-around Dollar* will build "brand loyalty" to the national currency. "Brand loyalty" in this instance means "a collective agreement not merely on meanings but on the importance of certain meanings."[31] Meanings belong to signs. They are the signifieds to the signifiers. But why use signs at all? What is their cultural work like? As Dean MacCannell explains, "signs mediate historically real social relations, and these relations are typically not between social equals."[32] Signs are, therefore, crucial in the state's construction of political hegemony, that is to say, the acceptance as a cultural norm of the ruling elites' worldview—their beliefs, explanations, perceptions, norms, values, and mores.[33] This is usually achieved by teaching the citizenry what is expected from it, and, as well, by connecting to the spirit of the age. Hegemony is, however, not always fully perceived by the men and the women living in the culture. Also not always fully perceived is that certain signs are special insofar as they "*permit humankind to subordinate itself to its own semiotic productions* by existing in a position of superiority to both addresser and addressee."[34] In this instance, the privileged elites and the common people, rulers and ruled, are "coparticipating in a semiotic production in which they are mutually complicitous in the exaltation of an iconic image."[35]

Politicians and educators, government officials, policy makers, and other cultural elites, by virtue of their direct involvement in the production of particular representations and thus in controlling the effect of the sign in the mind of the users, are somehow superior to the people at large. But even these forces of propriety maintain their superiority only by subservience to iconic sign production which, MacCannell contends, is the key to the icon's power to unite producers and consumers in a "cult."[36] As a result, certain articulations of the iconic sign are antecedent to any interpretation or reading that might subsequently be performed. As regards the national monetary icon, it is not just my subjective opinion that the money in my pocket is money. It really is cash, with an out-in-the-world objective value, which people can use to pay for goods and services. But it is only money because we all accept that it is money. There is no intrinsic physical property that makes it money. On the contrary, money only exists because society collectively assigns this particular function to pieces of metal and paper and calls them coins and bank notes. In other words, money is a fiction that, because of the lack of alternatives, we habitually believe in. Yet like all fictions, the fiction is highly fragile.

11

Dollar Bill Y'all

No one will be fooled all the time. The "dead presidents" on modern dollar bills, together with the obligatory cultural memory they tap into and activate, are also symptoms of a profound crisis of patriarchy.[1] Consider: Women have been entering the labor market in ever-larger numbers; they possess and use dollar bills on which they are not represented. True, there are monetary tokens on which women are depicted—$1 coins like the Anthony or the Sacagawea dollar—but these tokens have never been popular. Coins that do not circulate contribute nothing to stability and continuity. Nor are paper notes whose value is no longer backed by anything substantive and whose aesthetic design openly belies the economic logic of money. The metaphorical fathers on the currency therefore function as protective spirits—to maintain the belief that money as well as the acquisition of it, is a male prerogative. Patriarchy and monetary economy are, then, two sides of a coin. The "portraits of the Presidents" communicate a quasi-universal picture of patriarchal authority, based on property ownership, and the state's welfare; at the same time, they conceal the fact that from the Constitutional Convention onward, America's "national subjectivity" has always been construed as "white" and "male." From the beginning, the power of white males derived from the difference between one's own citizenship and that denied to other constituencies (women, African Americans, Native Americans). This difference has become fragile. With the ideology of separate spheres as well as traditional constructions of masculinity eroding, fears and perceptions have come to the fore among white males that affirmative action, quotas, and preferences might bring gains for racial and ethnic groups and women, but only at their expense.[2]

When Barack Obama, upon entering the first term of his presidency in January 2009 gave what commentators called a "dad speech," he did not expressly mention male prerogatives and privileges. He did, however, stress men's responsibilities, adding that the time had come "to set aside childish things." Shortly before the inauguration, the Fatherhood Educational Institute in Chicago nominated him "Father of the Year 2009," acknowledging his continuous support of fatherhood and family. Five years later, President Obama at a rally in Kansas City explained that also the time had come to print faces of women on the nation's currency.[3] The president's words must have rung sweetly in the ears of "Women on 20s," an advocacy group incorporated in January 2014, whose agenda is, primarily, to lobby the administration for a redesign of the $20 bill to bear the portrait of a woman, to be released by 2020—the anniversary of women's suffrage.[4]

"Women on 20s" is aware of the symbolic power that emanates from the currency. As is explained on the organization's website,

> Because our money sends a message both at home and abroad about what and whom we value as a nation, we believe wholeheartedly that we have to get that message right, not just as an afterthought to a security overhaul, but in a calculated and timely way. Keeping an Andrew Jackson bill in wide circulation means we celebrate and elevate historic figures who used and condoned violence against personal enemies and populations of marginalized people.[5]

In May 2015, "Women on 20s" sent out a petition calling upon President Obama to order the Treasury Secretary to redesign the current $20 bill—taking off Andrew Jackson's portrait and ensuring that the new bill reflects "the remarkable accomplishments of an exemplary American woman who has helped shape our nation."[6] The "exemplary American woman" who was finally selected as the face for the new $20 bill is Harriet Tubman (c.1822–1913). Born into slavery, Harriet Tubman escaped to the North and became a conductor in the Underground Railroad, helping slaves to escape to freedom. During the Civil War, she was active in the Union cause, serving as a nurse, a cook, and a scout, gathering intelligence.[7]

The Treasury Department, too, decided that the contributions of women to the nation's progress ought to be acknowledged on America's currency. On June 18, 2015, Treasury Secretary Jacob L. Lew announced plans to redesign the $10 bill by 2020, the anniversary year, to bear the portrait of a woman. He did not disclose any names, though he said that Hamilton's portrait would stay, while the reverse side of the bill would feature five suffragists.[8] Since, the $5 and $20 bills too have been slated for redesigning—with Harriet Tubman's portrait on the latter's front (the White House and an image of President Andrew Jackson is to go on the reverse).[9] All bills were scheduled to be released in time for 2020, though a December 2016 article suggested that Secretary Lew might have the presses cranking sooner. This would have been an effort to pressure the incoming Trump administration away from reversing the plan.[10]

Design changes are at the sole discretion of the Treasury Secretary. There is, however, no evidence that Secretary Lew had taken any action by the time he handed the keys over to his successor, Steven T. Mnuchin, in January 2017. At the time it also was not yet known how the Trump administration would approach the currency redesign, though there was considerable concern about a rollback. For Susan Ades Stone, executive director of Women on 20s, reversing the decision would be "a slap in the face of women." But not only were the "Tubmans" (colloquialism for the not-yet-released $20 bills) thought to be at risk. So much more was at stake, officials at Women on 20s announced in early January 2017, calling to partner with the Women's March, scheduled to take place in Washington, D.C., on January 21, to rally support both for the Tubman $20 and for women in general.[11]

Two and a half years into the Trump presidency, all indications are that Harriet Tubman will not become the face on the $20 bill until after President Trump leaves office. Plans to unveil the Tubman in 2020, an initiative by the previous treasury secretary, Jacob Lew, would be postponed until at least 2026, and the bill itself would not likely be in circulation until 2028. The delay is the decision of Secretary Mnuchin, who appears to have been concerned that the President might create an uproar by canceling the new bill altogether. Even so, Secretary Mnuchin is on record for telling CNBC, "People have been on the bills for a long period of time. This is something we'll consider. Right now, we've got a lot more important issues to focus on." This may well be so, but symbols are nevertheless important (if they weren't, the present book would not have ben written).[12]

Activists from Women on 20s were disappointed but hopeful that the delay would avoid meddling with President Trump. In June 2019, NPR reported that the Treasury Department was about to launch an investigation into the circumstances leading to the delay in the production of the new $20 bill. One can only speculate whether this action is in any way connected to the Harriet Tubman Tribute Act (HR 1083), which U.S. Senator Jeanne Shaheen introduced in February, or to her calling on the Treasury Department to offer clarity on the status of the $20 bill. The legislation, if passed, would direct the department to place Tubman's likeness on $20 Federal Reserve notes printed after December 31, 2020.[13]

The last word in the matter has not been spoken, though it may not even come from Secretary Mnuchin but from President Trump. Given President Trump's notorious unpredictability, however, there is no certainty about the "Tubmans" (or any other redesigns); all we know with a measure of certainty is that identity politics is not one of President Trump's political priorities. Additionally, Trump is on record as expressing great admiration for Andrew Jackson, calling him, through a spokesman, "an amazing figure in American history—very unique in many ways" and, on the occasion of a visit to Jackson's plantation home, "the people's president," whose victory "shook the establishment like an earthquake."[14] It is also a matter of record that right after his inauguration President Trump hung a portrait of Andrew Jackson in the Oval Office, as "inspiration."[15]

The planned redesign of the $20 bill was officially announced in April 2016. In response, Donald Trump said that bumping Andrew Jackson on the $20 was "pure political correctness," and suggested that Harriet Tubman be put on the $2 bill instead. For Trump, Jackson "had a great history" and so, he added, it would be "very rough" to take him off the bill.[16] Remarks of this kind reveal the extent to which selection of portraits for the currency is influenced by politics. This was no less the case in the late nineteenth century, when the validity of the female form as a symbol of the nation was profoundly questioned. "What is it that we have the ugliest money of all civilized nations?" *Galaxy* magazine provocatively asked in June 1876. The attack continued by insinuating that American coins "do not even look like money." The reason then given was the female figure of Liberty stamped on the silver dollar—a muscular woman in a seated position, with a shield resting at her right side and a cap and pole in her left hand. It would be far better, the article concluded, to place the portraits of Franklin and Washington on the national currency. The controversy over the Seated Liberty Type coin demonstrates the gendered division between realism and classicism on the coins and currency: Realist iconography then was largely a male domain, whereas allegories were usually female.[17]

In light of the ugly opinionating in *Galaxy* magazine, a portrait of a woman on the currency would be a big step up from attitudes prevailing a century or so ago. Senator Shaheen, for her part, is convinced that the image of a woman on the currency would instill in Americans a better understanding of the impact women have made in the country's history.[18] Senator Shaheen sees the currency redesign as a chance to teach the citizenry, and this may well be the motivation of the federal government. On the other hand, the government may also see it as a chance to respond to the spirit of the time and, in an attempt to seek legitimacy with its citizens, produce a currency design that strengthens identification between the state and the people. There is, however, a more fundamental question: Would a portrait of a woman on the currency make any substantive difference? Would it help undermine or terminate the real power of men in society?

The presidential election of 2016 is a point in case here. It is "not customary to have women lead or even to engage in the rough-and-tumble of politics," Hillary Clinton writes in her memoir of her unsuccessful campaign. "It's not normal—not yet. So when it happens, it often doesn't feel quite right. That may sound vague, but it's potent. People cast their votes based on feelings like that all the time."[19] The statement shows that Hillary Clinton was well aware of a basic problem, one that Uri Friedman formulated in *The Atlantic* right after election day—that "to win in a presidential system, women must contend more directly, and on a larger scale, with sexism and stereotypes."[20] What this means is nothing less that Donald Trump defeated Hillary Clinton not so much because she stood for the establishment, intellectualism, or an exaggerated concern for questions of feminism, gender, and diversity, which would have made her the "wrong" woman. This is far too easy. Hillary Clinton lost the election because of her being a woman.

The point, Annette Gordon-Reed wrote in her review of *What Happened*, is that not just Hillary Clinton but "any woman who had been the first to run for president with the backing of a major party would have encountered some of the gender-based scrutiny Clinton faced."[21] They would have encountered that scrutiny for at least two reasons. One is that many Americans, especially white men, felt that women had up-ended their world and that they now had a chance to vent their anger and frustration. The other reason is that Americans' expectations for their political leaders have been set by generations of male politicians and shaped by generations of male pundits. Hillary Clinton sought the highest office in a country whose ideal woman is located somewhere between *How to Marry a Millionaire* and *Sex and the City*, and fulfillment in Melania Trump. Unable to escape the gender trap, she was always perceived first and foremost as a woman, and only secondarily as a serious politician. In the televised debates with Donald Trump, for instance, Trump presented himself as the one to bring back "jobs," at the same time as he insinuated that she "only talks," is "all talk."[22] Altogether then, as a woman running for the presidency Hillary Clinton lacked the freedom to nonchalantly ride over social ideals of male power. Instead, she kept tapping into prevailing attitudes towards women, especially about the role of women in a matrix of feelings and the collective unconscious of a large part of the American electorate.[23]

By the time of Trump's inauguration, "misogyny was everywhere," Rebecca Solnit wrote in the *London Review of Books*.[24] International Women's Day was not too far off, though predictably the White House did not take much notice.[25] Far better to celebrate Mother's Day, which honors the mother of the family, as well as motherhood, maternal bonds, and the influence of mothers in society. Mother's Day, unlike International Women's Day, is a much closer fit to the model of femininity that has been enshrined in the United States since its beginning. The model sees women in terms of sexual utility, passive and insignificant in public life except as the wives of political figures. Mother's Day is observed worldwide. In the United States, a Mother's Day for Peace was suggested by Julia Ward Howe, author of the *Battle Hymn of the Republic*, in 1872. Some local observances honoring mothers are on record for the 1870s and 1880s, but a national holiday did not emerge until the early 1900s. In 1908, an Anna Jervis held a memorial for her mother at St. Andrew's Methodist Church in Grafton, West Virginia. Although Congress rejected her proposal to make Mother's Day an official holiday, by 1911 all states observed the holiday. Three years later, President Woodrow Wilson signed a proclamation designating Mother's Day, held on the second Sunday in May, as a national holiday.[26]

Ordinarily, what is the norm remains unmarked. But with women's suffrage established in 1920, the norm, the male norm that is, became unstable. Four years later, President Calvin Coolidge recommended Father's Day as a national holiday, calling for love and respect for fathers, as well as appreciation for the vital contributions of fathers to families and to society. The first modern Father's Day church-service celebration was held in 1908 in Fairmont, West Virginia, at Williams Memorial Methodist Episcopal Church South, now known as Central United Methodist Church. Unofficial support of Father's Day from such figures as William Jennings Bryan was immediate and widespread. Woodrow Wilson was personally feted by his family in 1916. In 1966, Lyndon B. Johnson made Father's Day a holiday to be celebrated on the third Sunday of June. Richard Nixon officially recognized it as a national holiday in 1972. Seven years later, Jimmy Carter decided to declare Father's Day officially.[27]

President Carter publicly acknowledged the importance and value of fatherhood in America, a sentiment that only increased in the decades to follow, reinforced for instance by the *Cosby Show*, which aired for eight seasons on NBC between September 1984 and April 1992. The *Cosby Show* provided the very model of proper parenting, earning its protagonist, Cliff Huxtable, the honorary title of "Greatest Television Dad."[28] No such title ever went to Jack Butler, the protagonist of 20th Century–Fox's 1983 comedy film *Mr. Mom*. Jack Butler (played by Michael Keaton) is an unemployed auto worker who becomes a stay-at-home dad taking care of three young children. Although the film carefully reflects societal changes that demanded that fathers play a bigger role in raising children, it has been criticized for rehashing the clichés of "men's work" and "women's work," confirming and reinforcing gendered differences.[29]

There is a gendered difference also in what money signifies. As the psychologists Adrian Furnham and Michael Argyle have shown, "women think of money in terms of the things into which it can be converted, while men think of it in terms of the power its possession implies."[30] For men, the two authors claim, money means happiness, excitement, respect, and reverence, its possession adding to their self-esteem, independence, and power. For all these reasons, men are more prepared to take financial risks and to speculate. Women, in contrast, seem rather afraid of money. For them, money often spells fear, depression, anger, panic, helplessness, even shame. And because they think of money as a means of purchasing things or making new relevant experiences, women tend to be more careful spending money. Above all, however, women seem to have difficulties talking about money, about how much they are making or about how much they are spending. Women, Furnham and Argyle contend, usually were and often still are kept in the dark about the household's financial situation. It does not come as a surprise that for many women, money is the currency of power and domination.

Do people see Stuart's portrait on the dollar bill in this way? The data is woefully inadequate on the ideological work that coins and currency do in people's minds and people's paying attention to and becoming aware of specific design elements. Among the few studies on the performativity of monetary tokens are the ones by Hans de Heij on users' perceptions of euro notes. De Heij's conclusion is telling: While most people answered that the core symbols are historic buildings, the original intention—to promote different periods; to symbolize openness and connectedness—is way below their radar.[31] For modern Americans, Stuart's enduring "Athenaeum" portrait of 1796 is the form in which George Washington is seen daily, indelibly connected to the one-dollar bill, the national monetary icon, the quintessential male face. Stuart was commissioned to paint it after the success of his first portrait of Washington in 1795, the much admired "Vaughan" portrait. Martha Washington convinced the 64-year-old president to sit again because, according to artist Rembrandt Peale, she "wished a Portrait for herself; [George Washington] therefore consented on the express condition that when finished it should be hers."[32]

It was not to be. Stuart, who preferred the 1796 portrait to his earlier Washington, purposely left it—and that of the first lady—unfinished so that he could use it as a model for the numerous copies that the first president's admirers commissioned.[33] Two of the copies—Stuart called them his "$100 bills"—are in the U.S. Capitol in Washington, D.C. One, the "Edward Pennington" portrait, is hung in the office of the President of the Senate; the other, the "Thomas Chestnut" portrait, is hung in the main corridor of the Senate Wing. This is the one Gideon Fairman used as model for numerous engravings done between 1805 and 1820. In 1830, one of Fairman's engravings was used for a special print of George Washington's Farewell Address of 1796.[34] A small stipple engraving, known as the "Phillips" portrait, is owned by the John S. Phillips Collection of the Pennsylvania Academy of the Fine Arts, Philadelphia.

After Stuart's death, the two original paintings were purchased for the Boston Athenaeum library, which owned them for more than 150 years. Although the "Athenaeum" portrait depicts features rendered puffy and distorted by a set of badly fitting false teeth, it soon became *the* Washington, familiar and widely celebrated, and endorsed even by the American Academy of Fine Arts. As John Neal wrote in his novel *Randolph* (1823): "[T]hough a better likeness of him were shown to us, we should reject it; for, the only idea that we now have of George Washington, is associated with Stuart's Washington." Neal shrewdly added, "If George Washington should appear on earth, just as he sat to Stuart, I am sure he would be treated as an imposter, when compared with Stuart's likeness of him, unless he produced his credentials."[35]

We do not know where Neal got his concept of Washington or what he knew about Stuart or about the art of portrait painting. Yet Neal's words, irreverent as they may have been, are a clear testimony to the iconic status the "Athenaeum" portrait had achieved by the time of the centennial of Washington's birthday. The "Athenaeum" was commonly believed to be the most authentic visual likeness of Washington, making possible a seemingly visceral experience. Rembrandt Peale's efforts to establish his own "Porthole" portrait as the most authentic portrait of all times came to nothing.[36] By the 1840s, the "Athenaeum" had eclipsed all previous portraits of Washington and had become the default template for all kinds of printed matter, books, newspapers and periodicals, stamps, bank notes, much as it was used also on three-dimensional objects, from porcelain or glass vessels to grandfather clocks and other artifacts.[37]

This is no different today. The aura of dignity, moral stature, serene composure, and sublime, visionary nature that Stuart ascribed to the ageing and ailing George Washington still captures viewers' attention, dominating America's visual conception of him. Copies of the "Athenaeum" are hung in countless corridors and offices, while millions of prints were distributed to American schools for the bicentennial of Washington's birth in 1932.[38] Following the Bicentennial, traditional commemorative rituals of this kind have been in decline. Yet there are other, more quotidian, perhaps even banal, forms of iconic reminders, not the least of which appears on the most frequently printed currency. Billions of reproductions of the "Athenaeum" have appeared on one-dollar bills. The banknote engravers—Alfred Sealey or George F.C. Smillie—did not use the "Athenaeum" as a model directly, relying instead on the "Phillips" portrait, which Gideon Fairman, who had begun as a blacksmith before he turned to copper and steel engraving, had pulled from the "Athenaeum" in 1805.

For modern Americans, George Washington is indelibly connected to the one-dollar bill. The portrait on the note's face is the work of George F.C. Smillie. In his version, Washington is facing to the viewer's right—in contrast to the works of Stuart, Fairman, and Alfred Sealey. Smillie also came up with a lyre-shaped frame or medallion.[39] The result can be found not just on the one-dollar bill. It also became the schoolroom Washington, gazing down on students throughout the day, as well as the TV Washington, serving as the patron saint for Peter Jennings' economic coverage on the ABC evening news. The face on the dollar bill also advertises big February sales in department stores and used-car lots. Reproductions of it have made it onto T-shirts (worn, for instance, by students at George Washington University), buckle belts, chocolate wraps, paper tissues, travel posters, government websites—and book covers.[40]

Popular print imagery too has appropriated the iconic representation of Washington (based on Stuart's painting) that appears on the one-dollar bill. This widely disseminated and perhaps most familiar likeness of Washington, Mark Thistlethwaite has shown in his analysis of the form, content, and context of several diverse images from recent years (editorial cartoons, advertisements, magazine covers, etc.), "provide pictorial scenarios that elevate, humanize, and deflate him." Thistlethwaite also claims, justly I think, that such familiar usage of a national foundational leader and hero appears to be "uniquely American." George Washington's image may be used or abused, yet he always serves as a potent visual synecdoche for the nation, its economy, and its consumerist culture. As Thistlethwaite aptly summarizes, "Washington's dollar bill visage has been transformed to function as the nation's personification of late capitalism." Unsurprisingly, therefore, businesses love George Washington. Washington sells. You can even sell cigars in his name.[41]

The one-dollar bill no doubt is the most familiar note among United States currency. About sixty percent of the nation's paper bills are of this denomination, to a total of over eleven billion notes. The one-dollar bill is also the most widely produced note. One third of all notes printed each year are one-dollar notes, altogether some two billion pieces. One possible reason for this is that their approximate life span is only some eighteen to twenty months, though other denominations, from twenty up, last relatively longer.[42] Certain notes seem to last a great deal longer, especially those stuffed under mattresses, both within the United States and abroad. I am saying "abroad" deliberately here because it is estimated that between one-half to two-thirds of the value of all U.S. currency in circulation is outside of the United States, to a grand total of approximately $700 billion. The great majority of these dollars exists electronically, but almost a third is printed, some seven billion notes, each weighing exactly one gram and measuring 2.61 inches wide by 6.14 inches long by 0.0043 inches thick. For this reason alone, we may reasonably assume that most people worldwide will know something about dollar bills.[43]

Gideon Fairman, *George Washington* (Phillips Portrait), stipple engraving, n.d., 5¼ × 4¾ in. (courtesy of the Pennsylvania Academy of the Fine Arts, Philadelphia. John S. Phillips Collection, Accession number 1983 x 169).

Much has been written about the current $1 bill, and justifiably so. The note is truly unique. No other piece of currency, American or non-American, communicates such abundant information about the nation's history, the structure of the nation, and its highest goals and aspirations. The note's ceremonial load (what the French scholar Jean-Joseph Goux has termed its "emblematic proliferation") is of a rare visual opulence that at the same time preserves and protects its status as an iconic sign. As Goux writes,

> The State (and its Treasury), God (and our faith in him), the Father (founder), the dead and sacralized Language (Latin): all these powerful, central signifiers converge, combine, and intensify each other so as to provide the one-dollar note with its force. It is the State in all of its foundational stability that guarantees the value of the bill, under the authority of the Treasury. By design [...] the American bill, through the almost Roman austerity that characterizes its engraving, remains strongly marked by the emblems of civil religion: that is, by the imaginary realm of guaranteed value and fixed standards. The value of the bill still refers to a certain depth, a certain verticality. Somewhere, a treasure is present, a reserve, a fund, upon which this bill is staked. There exists an underlying, protected value, which the State holds, preserves, and guarantees by its institution, and which this bill represents.[44]

The rhetoric in this passage clearly suggests that Goux views the one-dollar note as an icon its own right. An icon makes possible the seemingly direct experience of the represented object. It is like the object it visualizes, in this case "the State in all of its foundational stability," which it contains in itself. Its "central signifiers" (the State, God, the Father) give it a special power ("its force") to show or manifest what it represents, "an underlying, protected value." The note also reveals something hidden, "the imaginary realm of guaranteed value and fixed standards," which in turn should provide a stimulus to moral behavior, for instance as American patriots. Finally, there is something sacred to it, "a certain depth, a certain verticality" that demands veneration and thus unites producers and consumers in a "cult."

Dollar bills are widely recognized, they are subject to contextual spread and representational use, they have—so far—survived over time, are used in rituals, have accumulated all kinds of associations, are capable of triggering memory and nostalgia, and, not to forget, are objects whose meaning people fight over, or use to negotiate identity. Finally, and perhaps most importantly, dollar bills are rich in their metonymic resonance, that is, in the embodiment of associated ideas that allows the bills to deliver meanings beyond their utilitarian function as a means of payment into every context in which they appear. This "cult" establishes the one-dollar bill as America's national monetary icon, with Washington's image signifying in much the same way as the Queen's head on the British pound.[45]

Altogether, the current $1 bill is an impressive testimony to the power of conviction inherent in a bank note's visual design. Numismatists distinguish three divisions in a currency note's visual design—*inscriptio* (mottoes, proverbs, and sayings), *pictura* (visual symbols), and *subscriptio* (legislative acts). On the one-dollar bill the division appears in its complete form. The formal division, its quasi-mythological disguise, the allegorical mode of representation, and the abundance of historic-philosophical messages direct any interpretation towards the unique relation between image and text. The inscriptions and mottoes establish an independent level of meaning, at the same time as they impact on the visual content, which is dominated by motifs of rebirth and beginnings—the American Eagle, the repeated use of the numeral 13, and the pyramid as a symbol of step-by-step progress, the gradual perfection towards the "more perfect Union" envisaged by the Constitution.

The one-dollar note also resurrects the duality, known from the classical tradition of coinage, of head and tail.[46] One side bears the idealized picture of the "ruler"; the other side bears the number, the indication of the note's value, which is plentifully garnished with ornaments (including the "spider webs," sung by Allen Ginsberg), emblems of the state, mottoes, and inscriptions. The two sides form a wholeness, which corresponds to the personal wholeness of the nation's founder. The two sides are also complementary, mutually reinforcing and rounding out the note's assertion of value. As the German scholar Jochen Hörisch expressed the point, the two sides become "the embodiment of value." The number acquires validity and recognition through the authority emitting the note (the United States of America), returning both to the head (George Washington). Thus, the face of the nation not only maintains the "illusion of money"; it also makes the one-dollar bill "more valuable" than, say, subsidiary coins of the same denomination.[47]

On the current one-dollar bill, the face of the nation looks to the viewer's right, into the future. On older notes, Washington often looked towards the viewer's left, into the past.[48] The difference is far from trivial. In the western world, time's arrow conventionally moves from left to right. But on the current one-dollar bill, Washington not only looks to the future; he also looks at us, as if "the father of his country" had assumed the role of the eye of providence. And beginning with the Series 1928, when the "portraits of the Presidents of the United States" were first printed on all currency notes, Washington's portrait has been the foundation of the aesthetic-theological-mythological scheme to strengthen the dollar from the outside, constituting an authority that guarantees permanence and stability. Security features, emblems of statehood and other signs likewise enhance the notes' meaning and significance, strengthening the dollar from the outside and lending value beyond the notes' material value. The function of all these enhancements is a psychological-rhetorical one, which, by building trust and confidence in the currency, echoes the magical origin of symbols.[49]

To build trust and confidence in the currency is essential, though it cannot be understood in a purely rational manner. Trust and confidence in the currency is, rather, a fiction that, because of the lack of alternatives, we habitually believe in, must believe in, just as in religious life we must believe in God. On the current one-dollar bill, in any case, trust in God is transferred onto the currency. The money-makers' trust in God seems contagious. The note's visual aesthetics is transferred onto the economic value of the currency, which in turn is transferred onto the political value of the state. The enormity of this process warrants a closer look at the emblematic-esoteric density of the quasi-religious pictorial space on the one-dollar bill. The bill's face or front (sometimes also called "recto" or "obverse") displays a holy sobriety: Most prominent is the central portrait of mutton-jawed George Washington, the first president of the United States. Other iconographic details include the numeral "1" (which stands for the bill's nominal value, its denomination) and the seals of the Treasury Department and of the Federal Reserve Bank (for the two institutions guaranteeing its value). In addition, there are the facsimile signatures of the Treasurer of the United States and of the Secretary of the Treasury.

The note's denominational value is expressed both through the numeral "1" (in each of the four corners as well as to the left of Washington's portrait) and the inscription "ONE DOLLAR," one placed under the portrait, the other to the right of the portrait. A serial number with a prefix and suffix letter to identify it also appears on the note's face. Furthermore, on the face is indicated the series of which the note is a part (series year 2003, for instance, means that a change in the Office of the Secretary of the Treasury had occurred in that year).[50] The prefixed letter may be an "F," meaning that the note was issued by the Federal Reserve Bank in Atlanta.[51] The letter is also in the center of a small circle to the left of the portrait; the name of the issuing bank is spelled out on the rim of the circle. The inscription "FEDERAL RESERVE NOTE" in the upper frame indicates both the note-issuing institution and the legal basis for the emission, that is, the note's type or class. The phrase "This note is legal tender for all debts, public and private" summarizes the dominant fiscal theory. In addition, just to make sure there is no mistaking the semiological relation, the inscription "THE UNITED STATES OF AMERICA" has been placed above the portrait. Thus, the presence of the United States as a fiscal and/or monetary community is established in word and image.

The back ("verso" or "reverse") of the current one-dollar note at first sight repeats the various functional attributes. At the top is spelled out "THE UNITED STATES OF

AMERICA," the fiscal and/or monetary community within which the note is a legal tender. At the bottom is the note's nominal value, spelled out in capital letters, "ONE DOLLAR." The note's value also appears as a numerical symbol in each of the four corners. In each instance, the "1" is crossed or overwritten by the notation "ONE." An even larger "ONE" is placed in the note's center. So far, so good. But on the note's back is also unfurled what has been termed its "esoteric political theology," which covers, buttresses, and provides a foundation for the note's functional attributes. Their primary vehicles are the two large circles arranged to right and left of the large "ONE" placed in the note's center. The two circles—which at first sight may trigger bewilderment—represent the two sides of the Great Seal of the United States. The left circle (representing the Seal's reverse) shows the famous image of the pyramid with the all-seeing eye at the top, surrounded by a gloriole of light, and the year 1776, the year the United States was founded, written in Roman numerals at the base, MDCCLXXVI. Significantly, the pyramid has thirteen steps, representing the thirteen original colonies. It does not have a peak but is so to speak uncapped. This means that in 1776 nation-building was not yet finished, though the direction seems clear: Below the pyramid a banner proclaims the dawn of a new age, "NOVUS ORDO SECLORUM." The phrase "ANNUIT COEPTIS" above the pyramid provides the divine imprimatur.

The circle at right (representing the Seal's obverse) is dominated by the American eagle, its outstretched wings symbolizing rebirth as well as victory (originally over the English king). It is also a heraldic eagle. On its breast is a shield with a white bar, the sign of the United States Congress; additionally, there are thirteen vertical stripes, each for one of the original colonies. A bundle of thirteen arrows in the eagle's left claw symbolizes the nation's readiness to defend itself; the olive twig with thirteen leaves in its right claw stands for peace and peaceableness. In the eagle's peak is a banner inscribed with "E PLURIBUS UNUM," the famous motto that emphasizes the Union of the thirteen original colonies. Above the eagle thirteen five-pointed stars float in a circle of clouds, surrounded by a gloriole of light in the form of a hexagram.[52]

12

Money and Faith

The purportedly "esoteric" political theology on the back of the one-dollar bill originates from the Revolutionary era. Work on the Seal (and on the mottoes) began as early as 1774, when Thomas Jefferson realized the importance of creating symbols to represent the new order of the ages. On July 4, 1776, right after the signing of the Declaration, Congress likewise felt that a seal would somehow legitimize the historic endeavor of breaking away from England. A committee of three distinguished men was appointed—Franklin, John Adams, and Jefferson. The honorable committee soon suggested several designs, among them one that showed Moses dividing the Red Sea, alluding to the themes of the escape from slavery, the entry into the Promised Land, and the glorious future of the United States as a redeemer nation. In 2014, Ridley Scott's monumental film epic, *Exodus: Gods and Kings*, likewise made use of the biblical story; the film overwhelms through its images, but this is where the parallels end.[1] The original seal design in question had as its motto a maxim by Oliver Cromwell, "Rebellion to Tyrants Is Obedience to God." The design did not go down well with the Congress; other designs hardly fared better, most likely for their presumed radicalism. Thus, a call went out to Pierre Eugene du Simitière, a Swiss-born artist with considerable knowledge of heraldic devices.

Du Simitière made two contributions to the Seal of the United States, the motto "E pluribus unum" and the all-seeing eye of Providence, which at the time was both a common artistic motif and a Masonic symbol. The motto was probably borrowed from *The Gentleman's Magazine*. The magazine, which was founded in 1731 in London (it was discontinued only in 1922), was widely read in the North American colonies. It carried the motto on its title page. "E pluribus unum" is the best known of all-American mottoes. It was first used on New Jersey state coinage in 1786 and has been on the currency since, ditto on commemorative coins, the President's Seal, and numerous other ceremonial emblems. Interpretations of the motto vary greatly. At first the phrase referred to the union of the thirteen original colonies; the interpretation of the motto as the union of many people (or peoples) into one is much more modern. Horace and Cicero are customarily listed as the motto's originators, as the motto can be found respectively in the second volume of the *Epistles* (2:218) and in the first volume of *De Officio* (17:55–56). An entirely new interpretation has been offered by W.C. Harris. Harris argues that the motto is neolatin, created in order to find a new philosophical foundation for the problem, discussed already by Plato and Plotinus, of the relation between the one and the many (or else, between plurality and equality).[2]

Neither the motto "E pluribus Unum" nor the all-seeing eye of Providence made for a design that Congress found acceptable. Another committee went to work, now with a young Philadelphia lawyer named William Barton, a skillful draughtsman and with a passing knowledge of heraldry. From his attempts survived the eagle (not a bald eagle but a small white eagle with its wings and feet spread, though nevertheless intended as "the symbol of supreme power and authority and signifies the Congress"), as well as the unfinished pyramid, symbol of a solid foundation with work yet to be done.[3] The committee turned over Barton's work to Charles Thomson, the secretary of Congress. Thomson took ideas from all three committees. From Du Simitière he took a shield and the motto "E pluribus unum." From another former consultant, Francis Hopkinson, he took red and white stripes, now on the shield of the eagle, and an olive branch and bundle of arrows, each now in one of the eagle's talons. From Barton's design, Thomson took the eagle, now promoted to a central place in the design and transformed into the native American bald eagle with its wings extended downward as if in flight.

On June 20, 1782, Congress finally adopted the seal. Since then, the founders' deistic mythology has provided fuel to new conjectures and conspiracy theories. These conjectures and theories are strangely pervasive even today, thanks largely to a former Vice President, Henry A. Wallace, who in the 1930s became the originator of a design change that put both sides of the Great Seal on the one-dollar bill. The Seal's obverse (face), which shows the American eagle holding the United States coat of arms, had already appeared, *inter alia*, on the back of the $50 National Bank notes of the Second Charter period, and on the backs of two Gold Certificates. One was the $20 of the series of 1905 and later (the "Technicolor" note). The other was the $1,000 of the series of 1907 and later. The two Gold Certificates were produced and put into circulation through 1922.[4]

As for putting the two sides of the Great Seal on the one-dollar note, Henry A. Wallace made the claim in his behalf in two letters written in, respectively, 1951 and 1955. As he remembers, he had accidentally stumbled upon a reproduction of the Seal. "In 1934 when I was Sec. of Agriculture I waited in the outer office of Secretary [of State Cordell] Hull and as I waited I amused myself by picking up a State Department publication which was on a stand there entitled 'The History of the Seal of the United States.'" Secretary Wallace appears to have been so impressed by the phrase "Novus Ordo Seclorum" as meaning the New Deal of the Ages that he took the publication to President Franklin D. Roosevelt, suggesting that a coin be put out with the Seal stamped upon it. The President, it seems, was struck the most with the image of the All-Seeing Eye, a Masonic rendering of God as the Great Architect of the Universe. He also quite liked the idea that the foundation of the new order of the ages "had been laid in 1776 but that it would be completed only under the eye of the Great Architect." George Washington might have liked the idea himself, as he likewise belonged to a Masonic lodge. Yet America's first President may not have been particularly taken with the idea of putting the Seal on a dollar *note* rather than on a coin.[5]

President Roosevelt, being the great stickler for details that he was, may have appreciated a Masonic symbol on the back of the one-dollar bill, though his relation to the Masons was by no means untroubled. At the time, Freemasons had reached a zenith of power and influence, yet the old rituals had been lost and their activities had become rather degenerate. In order to avoid the drinking and womanizing, the President made sure to be away from Washington whenever the lodge brothers had their annual meeting and parade. Roosevelt was too shrewd and troubled a politician to be associated with the Masons. Since they still constituted a considerable segment of political and social elites, however, it was opportune to somehow keep them happy. In view of all this, the suggestion to print the Great Seal on the back of the one-dollar bill was a true godsend for the President.[6]

When the new design was ready, the President at first hesitated to use the Great Seal, likely because the suggested design offended his aesthetic sense. Consequently, he suggested that the positions of the reverse and obverse be switched. The reverse should appear at left, over the words "The Great Seal," and the obverse at right, over the words "of the United States." Reversing the positions of the reverse and obverse was quite a breach with accepted heraldic practice. Moreover, Roosevelt was also responsible for introducing the word "Great" in the phrase "The Great Seal" as it is now found under the left circle on the back of the one-dollar note. What followed is legend. As of 1935, the Great Seal has been printed in its entirety on the backs of one-dollar notes, at first on $1 Silver Certificates and, beginning in 1963, on $1 Federal Reserve notes. Altogether, if it had not been for Secretary Wallace's amusing himself while waiting in the outer office of Secretary of State Cordell Hull, the one-dollar notes would look quite different, and the mottoes would have been virtually forgotten—"but for one of those quirks of fate."[7]

Other quirks of fate led to the appearance on America's currency of what eventually became the national motto. Its making, Brian Burrell noted, is owing to "the well-timed efforts of a few well-connected men. And it did not happen all at once." In 1861, Treasury Secretary Salmon P. Chase received a letter from the Rev. M.R. Watkinson of Ridleyville, Pennsylvania. In the letter Watkinson, who was deeply concerned about the fate of the Union in those days of the Civil War, proposed that God be invoked on the country's coinage. "What if our Republic were now shattered beyond reconstruction? Would not the antiquaries of succeeding centuries rightly reason from our past that we were a heathen nation?" Secretary Chase took the suggestion seriously enough to send a directive to the director of the United States Mint. "No nation," Chase wrote, "can be strong except in the strength of God, or safe except in His defense. [Therefore, the] trust of our people in God should be declared on our national coins." The Director of the Mint, James Pollock, was a prominent member of the so-called National Reform Association, a group of radical Protestant denominations that was petitioning Congress to "reform" the Constitution to indicate that the United States was created as and remained a Christian nation. Pollock leapt at this chance, though Secretary Chase did not like any of the suggestions he received—"God, Liberty, Law" (Watkinson's suggestion), "Our Country, Our God," "God Our Trust," "Our God, and Our Country," "God and Our Country"—and came up with his own suggestion, "In God We Trust."[8]

Mottoes like "In God We Trust" reveal the desacralization of the nation, their function being to compensate for the erosion of religious bonds and social cohesion in an increasingly anonymous society. Secretary Chase did not invent the motto out of thin air, though. On the contrary, it had been in the air for quite some time, at least since Francis Scott Key in 1814 composed the song "Star-Spangled Banner." Americans ordinarily hear only one verse of the song, so they do not generally know this, but it is in the final stanza of the fourth verse that Key included the words, "and this be our motto:

'In God is our trust.'"[9] The verse no doubt was better known in nineteenth-century America than it is today. Given the heightened religious sentiment generated by the Civil War, it was used on a number of notes in 1863 and 1864, though it does not seem to have inspired support for a new national motto. That appears to have been the work of a group known as the Huntington Bible Company, who adopted the phrase "In God We Trust" as their battle-cry in 1862 and whose enthusiasm had made it quite popular by the time Chase suggested it for the new two-cent piece.[10]

The religious inscription was authorized in 1864. The new two-cent piece, which was the first coin to bear it, remained in circulation until 1873.[11] The motto lasted much longer, and was a standard feature on many coins by the early twentieth century. Still, it was not mandated by law, and it appeared on paper money only as part of the Florida state seal printed on National Bank notes issued in Florida, series of 1875 (the first use of this motto on a federal note) and 1882, and on the silver dollars shown on the back of the $5 Silver Certificate of 1886, the "Silver Dollar Note."[12] In the nineteenth century, to have "God" written on the government's money may have had the additional advantage of serving as a palliative against the pains of the newly introduced income tax. In the long run, however, the legality and the propriety of a reference to God on the currency never ceased to be a sticky issue, with the public as much as with the authorities. As Albion Tourgée observed,

> The force of authority in monetary science is greatly impaired by a general tendency to make the Almighty responsible for pet projects. The truth is that God has nothing more to do with money than with bicycles. He furnishes the raw material and the man who makes and uses both—and that is all.[13]

Tourgée's caustic remark dates from 1898. A few years later, President Theodore Roosevelt's decision to leave the motto off two new coins because to him it came "dangerously close to sacrilege" provoked a heated debate in Congress. In the end, the pro-motto faction won, and the motto was restored to all coins on which it had previously appeared. It has been in continuous use on the one-cent coin since 1909, and on the ten-cent coin since 1916. It also has appeared on all gold coins and silver dollar coins, half-dollar coins, and quarter-dollar coins struck since July 1, 1908.[14]

After a period of relative quiet, the motto question resurfaced again in the 1950s, when a renewed religious fervor met with the specter of a Communist threat. In 1953, while attending a service at a Christian Science church in Chicago, an Arkansas businessman allegedly noticed that the phrase "In God We Trust" was on the coins in the collection plate, but not on the paper money. The pious man appears to have been scandalized by the fact that the nation's paper currency did not carry this important message. He was also apparently well connected, including to Senator William J. Fulbright, and he used his connections to get his suggestion worked into a bill that was passed by the 84th Congress and signed into law by President Eisenhower in July 1955. Under this law, the United States Department of Treasury was to gradually work the motto—it was established as the national motto by the Act of July 30, 1956—into all new currency plates. The $1 Silver Certificate of 1957 became the first note on which the motto was used. The notes were first released on October 1, 1957—to considerable confusion, as the Series 1935 notes without the motto were also being printed at the same time. This fact caused much dismay among the Christian Right, who petitioned Congress to discontinue these "godless" notes. As of September 15, 1961, therefore, a series 1935-G was printed with the motto. Models were made also for other denominations, though they were never printed, since the Bureau of Engraving and Printing finally discarded its old flatbed presses. The new sheet-fed rotary presses from 1963 were used to print $1 Federal Reserve notes bearing the motto on their backs, printed in prominent letters above the word ONE. All other denominations likewise bear the motto beginning with the Series of 1963. The first $1 Federal Reserve Notes bearing IN GOD WE TRUST were produced in February and delivered in March 1964.[15]

On the one-dollar bill the motto "In God We Trust" is placed above the word "ONE." It is tempting to read this as a ringing endorsement of the one God, all the more urgent in the face of the actual inconvertibility of the bills. If the profession of monotheistic faith was to symbolically compensate for the "financial atheism" of the dollar, restoring faith in the fiat, it even suggests a divine origin of the fiscal contract between state and citizens.[16] The images of rebirth in the Great Seal's obverse only reinforce such an interpretation. A kind of rebirth had taken place in 1776, a rebirth that apparently had received God's imprimatur—spelled out as "ANNUIT COEPTIS," "He [God] has favored our undertakings." The grammatical form of the unfinished past suggests that God has already approved of the undertaking, *annuit coeptis*, and he will continue to do so, hence that there is indeed hope.[17] Indeed, the phrase "IN GOD WE TRUST" can be taken to mean that God has empowered or authorized the state to fulfill the obligations and promises articulated on the one-dollar bill. Of course, this is easier said than done. For, "IN GOD WE TRUST" notarizes the completion of the monetary cycle to the point when the notes' only backing is trust in the state. As Karl Marx wrote in *Grundrisse*, historically, gold-money became "sublimated into its own symbol first in the form of worn coin, then in the form of subsidiary metal currency, and finally in the form of a worthless token, paper, mere *sign of value*."[18]

Now that all paper dollars are mere signs of value, the phrase "In God We Trust" at the same reveals and conceals the social construction of the nation's currency, that is, the fact that people ascribe value to a medium whose material value is irrelevant to its monetary function. The purely symbolic nature of the currency necessitates both the state's guarantee and its forced exchange.[19] In this context, the national motto functions as a kind of spell, like the ontotheological answer, valid through the eighteenth century, "The Lord gave, and the Lord hath taken away; blessed be the name of the Lord."[20] In the world of money, to call on God for help has a clear psychological and rhetorical function—to generate trust and confidence. The phrase "In God We Trust" thus constitutes the aesthetic-theological-metaphysical attempt to back the (increasingly shrinking) value of the currency. It also helps maintain the faith among Americans that the dollar is *their* money and that they can have trust and confidence in it, much as they can have trust and confidence in their fellow Americans.

Trust and confidence were the work of "magic" symbols already on coins in classical antiquity. But those coins usually were struck form precious metals. And they were inscribed with not just any words but with noble and lofty ones, including, later, "Liberty" or "E Pluribus Unum." Still, money is the epitome of the ordinary. Noble metals and lofty words, the conservative romanticist Adam Müller wrote in his theory of money, are intended to make us forget that sobering fact.[21] Phrased differently, precious metals and lofty words are to nobilitate the associations and social relations that money brings about, thus manufacturing consent—"E PLURIBUS UNUM." I do not possess coins struck from "noble metals," though I always carry a one-dollar bill in my wallet, for good luck. I also look at it from time to time, noticing that I can trust it and that I can spend it at its denominational value. Thus, my one-dollar bill "functions" as money, and as long as that is the case, there is no need for me to "read" it. Yet "reading" it, I cannot help noticing that the phrase "In God We Trust" is placed above the word "ONE." What is the purpose of dragging the hereafter into this world? For Kenneth Burke, "money is modernity's 'god term' [...] a 'technical substitute for God,' in that 'God' represented the unitary substance in which all human diversity of motives was grounded."[22]

Mark Taylor, too, has analyzed the nexus between money (actually, capitalism) and religion. Describing capitalism as an "ontotheological political economy," Taylor argues, "The God in whom ontotheology trusts is ONE." References to ONE-ness abound on the one-dollar bill. Already the motto "E PLURIBUS UNUM," "From Many, One," testifies to it. The motto appears in many sites, including the Great Seal, depicted on the back of the bill. And there is the designation "ONE," which in varying form can be found in twenty-five instances—as notation at the center of the bill's back, four times in each corner, written over the numeral "1," which appears four times, and once spelled out at the bottom, in the phrase "One Dollar." On the bill's front, "One Dollar" appears twice; there are also eight notations of "ONE," and five arabic numerals "1." An additional connection to ONE-ness is the motto, "In God We Trust." As Taylor concludes, "[t]he God in whom we (but who is this 'we,' this 'magisterial *wir*'?) trust" is "*the God named ONE*."[23]

Drawing out Taylor's deconstructivist approach a bit further, we might ask why monotheism is at its most glaring on the smallest denomination, the one-dollar note. That note is not likely to circulate among the rich and affluent. Is it that those who possess the least are the ones who are most in need of protection? Or is it, in a more general sense, that the most iconic note has been selected to dispel the anxieties that arose in the wake of the erosion of religious cultures. The idea, put forth by the German philosopher, writer, and artist Eva Meyer,[24] seems not too far-fetched, considering that the abandonment of the gold standard constitutes the economic equivalent of the death of God. "God functions in religious systems like gold functions in economic systems," Mark Taylor argues in a more recent book. "God and gold are believed to be the firm foundations that provide a secure anchor for religious, moral, and economic values. When this foundation disappears, meaning and value become unmoored and once trustworthy symbols and signs float freely in turbulent currents that are constantly shifting."[25] The situation is truly paradoxical. The buttressing of religious convictions with the help of money at the same time is a consequence of the loss of religious convictions caused by money.

A good example of this paradox is a letter Bill Dannemeyer, congressional representative from Southern California, wrote to his constituency. Dannemeyer left no doubt that the termination of the Bretton Woods Agreement, which resulted in the inconvertibility of the dollar into gold, was a symptom of a *religious* crisis. "It is not an accident," he declared, "that the American experiment with a paper dollar standard, a variable standard, has been going on at the same time that our culture has been questioning whether American civilization is based on the Judeo-Christian ethic or secular humanism. The former involves formal rules adopted from God through the vehicle of the Bible. The latter involves variable rules adopted by man and adjusted as deemed appropriate." What Dannemeyer omitted in his letter was that the "desacralization" of the dollar was the direct result of the decision, by his fellow Republican Richard Nixon, to unilaterally terminate the convertibility of the dollar into gold. He also did not say that Nixon's decision was not motivated by the decline of Christian America so much as it was the logical consequence of the exploding costs of America's military engagements, not least in Vietnam.[26]

The Dannemayer episode shows that if God is dead, the future looks even bleaker than it is. To imagine differences that are considered non-negotiable by virtue of their "intrinsic" character thus is all the more tempting. In November 2005, for instance, a FOX News/Opinion Dynamics poll found that over 90 percent of registered voters nationwide wanted the motto "In God We Trust" to remain on U.S. currency and coins.[27] Possibly, these people trust that God has empowered the state to fulfill the promises and obligations articulated on the currency, in particular the paying back of debts. In addition, they may trust that God will continue to provide money. There is even a certain justification in saying that the motto engages the people managing the currency, as they are the ones who will be held accountable for the fiscal disasters threatening to hit the nation. After the banking crash of 2008 threatened to undermine even the fundamental belief in capitalism's power to heal itself, the meaning of the canonical phrase took an altogether new turn. People now could trust that God, too, "finally takes on the entire burden of guilt," as Walter Benjamin sarcastically wrote in 1921.[28] In each case, the currency is quite literally "faith-based," with the trust in question blending secular monetary and divine categories. In this, the phrase "In God We Trust" is not only symptomatic of the fact that the great confidence game of capitalism is alive and well; it also echoes the Christian tradition that saw debts as sins and that construed the relation of a sinner to God in terms of a customer to a shopkeeper or banker (a thought that is still found in John Bunyan).[29]

In light of an out-of-control national debt and an upward-spiraling budget deficit, the appearance of God's name on the currency takes on a new meaning, from establishing the United States as a Christian nation visibly different from the atheist Soviet Union to a cry for help—if not a gesture of mourning.[30] As Jean-Joseph Goux noted almost thirty years ago, "The inconvertible signifier that circulates today, that floats, that always postpones its 'realization,' guarantees the monetary function in the realm of pure symbolicity, but only by mourning the loss of the unlocatable (or floating) standard and the uncertain reserve value, secured by nothing."[31] At first sight, the "loss"—Joachim Schacht called it the loss of "God's death mask"[32]—is not even apparent. It is concealed, or rather gilded over, by all the insignia of the state's officialdom with which United States coins and currency have become embellished—abstract symbols, scenes from the nation's history, or "portraits of the Presidents," the stand-ins for the fathers who have become absent in modern society.

A beginning had been made in 1909, when the government abandoned the Indian-head penny in favor of the Lincoln penny. Thereafter, each coin in turn was changed to bear the image of a politician. The first portraits were those of the Founding Fathers, but gradually, images that are more contemporary began to appear. Paper bills that had carried scenes from the nation's history or allegorical images similar to those on coins likewise switched to portraits of politicians. The numismatic practice of switching to portraits of presidents and politicians speaks to the power of the image or, more precisely, the visual image, which has become "the basic currency for all forms of political, social, and cultural practices."[33] In this context, their "hard images" give "soft currency" a good name by magically transforming worthless pieces of paper into priceless tokens.

The transformation of something worthless into something priceless grew out of a traditional practice of the institutional church, the ceremonious consumption of the communion wafer. The wafers, I am reminded as I am writing this on Corpus Christi Day of 2017, often took the form of a stamped coin, constituting a kind of *fiat* money backed by the priest, whose words—"*crede ut edes, et edes*" ("Believe that you eat the flesh of Christ in the wafer, and you do eat it")—magically transformed worthless bread into the priceless body of Christ.[34] The belief that bread was not simply a mere symbol but rather the truest being (a *realissimum*) fell apart in the early modern period. Around 1600, in the age of the baroque, the severing of signifier and signified, of "*les mots et les choses*," began to take hold. The restructuring of language is captured in Hamlet's response to Polonius' question what he was reading: "words, words, words." Hamlet mentions neither a book title nor a topic as he no longer trusts in the backing of words in anything real or substantantive. It is no coincidence that the same suspicion was brought to bear on paper money. Paper bills were new at the time, and what bothered people was that their backing was often also merely "words, words, words."[35]

The creation of value from mere high hopes in the future, that is, from nothing, also applied to the sale of indulgences in the early sixteenth century. Indulgences, the chief target of Martin Luther's white rage, were papal dispensations of sins that were confirmed by paper certificates. Papal agents gave these printed slips of paper in exchange for coins, that is, for material wealth. Indulgences thus were the equivalents of modern paper money (including checks, bills of credit, bank notes and other financial instruments), except that they drew on the currency of heaven rather than earth.[36] In contrast, the bills of credit issued by the Province of Massachusetts Bay in 1691 did draw on the currency of earth. They rested on the belief that phrases like "shall be in values equal to money" had an objective correlative. They were, of course, backed by something, by public land, together with the mineral resources, hopefully gold, hidden in it. Public land and other assets were looked at as a kind of security, an equivalent that justified the almost unlimited increase of the paper money supply.

The arrangement was truly advantageous. One no longer had to lug around gold or other hard assets. As Goethe wrote in the second part of *Faust*: "Such currency, in gold and jewels' place, / Is neat, it bears its value on its face."[37] For the magic to work, two conditions were necessary: First, imagination, for it was indispensable to imagine the real values backing the paper money. Second, trust and confidence that the backing is genuine, not fake. Paper notes therefore had to be authenticated by a higher authority, as for instance the Massachusetts Provincial Assembly. The Massachusetts Provincial Assembly, however, never possessed enough assets for backing the currency in full; consequently, the denominational value was never realized in financial transactions, neither in Massachusetts nor in other colonies that likewise emitted paper bills for similar purposes—to pay soldiers recruited for military expeditions or to pay for weaponry and ammunition.

During the Revolutionary era paper money was issued for similar purposes, with even more drastic consequences. In the era of private banking, paper bills also could be exchanged for gold and silver at par only in the rarest instances; notes from other states were even considered as "foreign" money and were exchanged at even lower rates.[38] The introduction of a federal paper currency in the Civil War era altered the situation, though it took a while for it to be effective. At first, the value of the newly introduced "greenbacks" fluctuated, in tandem with the war effort. When the Union was winning, the notes rose in value, as in August 1863, after Gettysburg and Vicksburg, when they hit eighty-two cents a dollar. By June 1864, when the war was costing the Union over two million dollars per day, they were valued at thirty-five cents on the dollar. Their value rose again in spring of 1865, as the Union forces seemed more certain of winning the war.[39]

When the Civil War was over, Wall Street "bulls" like Jay Gould and Jim Fisk would speculate on the performance of the greenbacks against gold. At one point, they drove the premium for gold up to 150 (meaning that 150 paper dollars were required to purchase $100 in gold), which was up more than 20 points from the "normal" rate and so high that gold was literally sucked out of banks, many of which became insolvent. At the height of the crisis, President Ulysses Grant stepped in, ordering the sale of $4 million in federal gold. In no time, the price of gold fell to 135 and the bubble burst, ruining any number of people.[40] Altogether, it took ten more years for the greenbacks being once again accepted at face value. Once they were, the mania for backing again made itself felt. The Resumption Act, which John Sherman helped steer through Congress in 1875, held that the United States would be paying out gold in exchange for greenbacks as of January 1, 1879. The same view—that the national currency needs gold backing—keeps adding fuel to the myth of Fort Knox. It also nourishes the ritual freight of all paper currency. The appearance of money must be seconded by the notion that the bills are backed by more than what they purport to be.[41]

By virtue of this seconding notion, the current one-dollar bill still refers to a certain depth, a certain verticality, its ever-diminishing value notwithstanding. As Jean-Joseph Goux suggested, "[s]omewhere, a treasure is present, a reserve, a fund, upon which this bill is staked. There exists an underlying, protected value, which the State holds, preserves, and guarantees by its institution, and which this bill represents."[42] "Treasure" is only one possible translation of the French word *trésor*, which can also mean "treasury" and "thesaurus," a treasury of words. Still, the primary sense intended by Goux is a repository or reserve of wealth in the form of money or precious metal. The pertinence of "treasure" is owed to the shift, so central to Goux's extensive reading of André Gide's novel *The Counterfeiters* (*Les faux-monnayeurs*, 1925), "from a society founded on legitimation by representation to a society dominated by the inconvertibility of signifiers, that refer to one another like tokens in infinite slippage, with no standard or treasury to offer the guarantee of a transcendental signifier or referent."[43]

In Gide's novel the monetary metaphor registers the fact that language, especially literary language, can no longer be compared to gold money, or even to paper money that is representative of gold. Reading the metaphor to itself registers the shift from representative paper money, which can be converted to precious metal, to fiat money, which is inconvertible and circulates only as forced currency.[44] Thus, the treasure to which the current one-dollar note bears witness, its protected value, is gold, the "Lord of commodities," to repeat Marx's phrase. In the word "Lord" the two realms of Christian doctrine come together, the secular one of economic exchange (in which the dollar is a monetary token), and the divine one of the exchange of gifts (in which the dollar is an infinitely large and archaic gift, which obligates the recipient to give back something, or at least to be grateful). In earlier Christian thinking, the gift figured as the Holy Grail, the container of Christ's blood. It was a gift of boundless wealth, pictorialized in grail-like cornucopias, which appeared in allegorical depictions of commerce in seventeenth-century paintings.[45] Cornucopias also were popular images on nineteenth-century bank notes.[46]

The two realms—the secular one of economic exchange and the divine one of the exchange of gifts—are held to be mutually exclusive. Therefore, the object that appears as both money and gift is granted a privileged status. This status is provided by the manifestation of money as an ideal *and* a real thing, an instance of value impressed into a material thing. The pagan gods and goddesses appearing on bills issued by private banks highlighted this. These figures were not unproblematic, as they also deflected from the Christian One, who might have considered greed as sinful. On the other hand, they restored the ancient practice of touching the deity. Every time someone held a piece of paper money in their hands, they would touch the deity, in hope that its power would be transferred, and encourage people to proceed on.

People always choose the gods that are socially needed. Since the pagan gods and goddesses are no longer seen as capable of blessing and protecting the currency of a Christian nation, the Christian One comes in. Pagan gods and goddesses are acceptable as allegories; representations of the Christian deity, however, run up against the Biblical ban on graven images, especially in protestant America. Thus, only the name of the deity appears on the currency—"In God We Trust." Additionally, God is represented by the phrase "annuit coeptis," the mark of approval of what the nation's founders had undertaken. In the Latin phrase, the subject is unmarked, though it can be construed as meaning that a gift—the new nation, together with its republican form of government—was bestowed by God's grace or, in the diction of the Founders, through God's providence. With the sacred smuggled so blatantly into what purportedly are secular institutions, it is no surprise that Americans of religious persuasion saw George Washington as the executor of God's plan. A dictum common during the early years of the nation said "Providence" had left Washington childless so that the nation might call him "Father." A funeral oration even proclaimed that Washington was a "Gift from God," raised up from youth "for the salvation of his country." In 1814, the youthful Ralph Waldo Emerson conceived the idea in the following way: "The God of Israel heard our groans and cries / And bade to life a WASHINGTON arise." It was not only Northerners who were consistent on this point; many Southerners too came to see Washington as "the man designed by heaven" to follow through.[47]

The two phrases—"In God We Trust" and "annuit coeptis"—are as central to the symbolic arrangement on the current one-dollar bill as is Washington's portrait. The tension between the verbal image of the Lord God, whose claim is to a superior status, and the visual image of the secular Lord, George Washington, whose claim likewise is to a superior status, is enormous, though. Washington's status has the imprimatur of history and myth. The lyre-shaped frame surrounding his portrait can be read symbolically, as OMEGA, the final letter in the Greek alphabet. The "Ω" represents the end of things or the glorious future the United States is looking forward to and working towards—in contrast to ALPHA, which represents the beginning of things, "A," hence God. Within this framework, Washington's portrait is symbolically linked with the future, at the same time as it is suggested that the Founding Father's spirit is still guiding the nation's destiny. In summary, then, both the visual and the verbal images on the current one-dollar bill re-connect Americans to the belief of the early Protestant settlers that piety and economic success were sure signs of salvation in the hereafter. Both, it is worth mentioning, were a matter of faith, and required moral limits.

Today, moral limits are no longer allowed to get in the way of success, though politicians keep repeating that "trust" is essential to free enterprise. Theoretically this makes sense, as investors should not play in the stock market if they cannot trust corporate executives to do right. Yet popular books and films like *Wall Street* or *The Wolf of Wall Street* suggest that the opposite is true, or at least that there is no guarantee that this will happen. All we have is a promise in which we must believe. We must have faith in those taking our money. We must believe that corporate executives will do what they have promised. That is why God is so important to free enterprise. "Both religion and the market are based on similar principles of unquestioned belief," the political scientist Ronnie Lipschutz remarked. God can be considered as a given fact, and so can the market economy. Both require vast quantities of trust. And there is no salvation outside of either.[48]

If the entreaty to unquestioned belief is given weight and depth through God's name, the name's appearance on the currency is also limiting. The quasi-religious practices associated with paper dollars are valid only for those who possess them. Until recently, this used to be the high-rolling rich, who often have been lampooned by comically suggesting that they light their cigars or stoke their fires with high-denomination paper bills. Now that money is becoming ever more ethereal, those in possession of dollar bills increasingly are the less affluent. As those who possess the least are the ones who are most in need of protection, most likely they are also the ones to protect the national motto, aside from those for whom patriotism sells.

The dollar was adopted as the national currency of the United States of America in 1785. The Coinage Act of 1792, shepherded into law by Alexander Hamilton, defined the dollar as a "unit of account," that is, as a measuring rod for the means of payment (or medium of exchange) Congress had created. In effect, this meant that one had to give $19.39 in exchange for a troy ounce of gold and a correspondingly lesser amount for silver. Almost two hundred years later, the dollar still stood at $35 to the ounce. Between then and the mid–1990s, it sank to roughly $400 per ounce of gold. Today, the price for gold fluctuates between $1,100 and $1,700, that is, to less than one-tenth of what it had been before President Nixon closed the gold window in 1971.[49]

The real losers, as always, are the taxpayers. Yet the word "taxpayers" may be misleading, as it suggests that all people are equally hit. This is decidedly not the case when dealing with inflation. The inflation rate, Jack Weatherford explains, "is merely a numerical index, but it is an average based on quite different life circumstances. It lumps together the billionaire and the pauper, and therein lies a great inequality." Billionaires invest their money, which will yield higher returns during inflation. A loss of fortune therefore does not really amount to much for the billionaire. For the average wage earners and pensioners, however, the loss of purchasing power comes out of their lifestyles, not out of their investments. Any loss thus represents a substantial decrease in purchasing power that is not made up for through increasing investment yields.[50] The "inflation tax," as Weatherford calls it, "constitutes the most retrogressive of all forms of taxation because it hurts the poor the most." The poor are more likely to be living from fixed incomes, and they use more cash—and "not from virtue, but because they are refused credit," as the French writer Anatole France noted about a century ago. Today, middle and upper-class consumers use plastic money and checks; the poor live in what Weatherford has termed the "cash ghetto," using government-printed paper dollars supplemented by food stamps, vouchers, and other forms of near-money issued by the federal government.[51]

The poet Allen Ginsberg too did not have much of a living moneywise. Yet money, or rather America's currency, is at the center of a poem he wrote in 1958—"American Change." The poem bears the epigraph "*S.S. United States*, July 1958," suggesting that it was written during the poet's voyage home from a trip to Europe. During his stay in Europe, Ginsberg had met Ezra Pound in Italy, and he may have taken inspiration for the poem from Pound's attacks on money-mad materialism. "American Change" was first published in 1963 in the collection *Reality Sandwiches*. The poem's form constitutes a meditation on the figurative and literal meanings and values of the national currency. Without their value as American currency, the coins and bank notes were only souvenirs when the speaker was at sea, but as the poem plots the speaker's return to New York, he removes the change from his pocket and revalues it. Thus the change becomes money "looked on, after a long time far from home in mid / Atlantic on a summer day," providing "memory in my aging hand," a reminder for instance of the Statue of Liberty ("I ride enfolded in money to you") or else, much more mundanely, of a "gas lot in Paterson where I found half a dollar gleaming in the grass."[52]

"American Change" retains the long, surging lines reminiscent of the poetry of Walt Whitman, which Ginsberg had already used in "Howl," "A Supermarket in California," and "America." The verse-form, in what is called the "breath-unit line," leaves the rhythms of the money experience open to discovery, turning them into sensory perceptions that at the same time are absorbed and offered to readers in the form of a "reality sandwich." Each of the poem's five stanzas is organized according to the particular piece of currency the speaker takes as his subject matter. Stanza 1 is devoted to the Indian-head nickel; in stanza 2 the speaker explores the cultural meanings of a dime; stanza 3 is occasioned by a quarter, and a five-dollar bill is the subject matter in the fourth stanza. The final stanza is devoted to a meditation and description of the ubiquitous one-dollar bill: "Washington again, on the Dollar, same poetic black print, dark / words, The United States of America, countless numbers." Lifting Washington's image off the picture and transferring it to the medium of poetry, the metaphorical father is given a genuinely ekphrastic rendering.[53]

The "change" in the poem is highly ambiguous, as Ginsberg uses it in at least two senses, as the money one gets back when making a payment with more money than it costs and as something becoming different. The ambiguity ultimately reduces the literal value of money. From "Howl" onward, Ginsberg's poetry had concerned itself with both the materialist and the visionary consequences of contemporary social injustice. Thus, as the visionary potential of the country fades in the poem, so does material value. In the midst of the third stanza, the speaker counts the coins he has thus far described—a nickel, dime, and quarter—and states: "Quarter, remembered quarter, 40¢ in all—What'll you buy me when I land—one icecream soda?"[54] Altogether, the "change" signifies the betrayal of the American dream by "an America gone mad with materialism, a police-state America, a sexless and soulless America," as Ginsberg noted in 1959.[55] Money-mad materialism, Ginsberg believed, robs the imagination of cultural currency as it emphasizes the importance of actual hard currency itself. In "American Change," the country's economic and imperialist expansionism increases the national wealth at the same time as it devalue the individual spirit, whose fate is much like that of the buffalo in the first stanza, reduced to a "hoar body rubbed clean of wrinkles and shining like polished stone." The gleam is deceptive, just as it is when the speaker reveals that the nearly baroque illuminations on the dollar bill are merely safeguards against counterfeit currency rather than artistic renderings of the creative imagination.

The "green dollars" in Ginsberg's poem evoke the famous "greenbacks," as the federal currency has been known colloquially since 1861. In that year, the Union government decided to use a second color on currency notes to deter counterfeiters. Different colors had been tried since the 1840s, with red and orange long enjoying great popularity—until it was discovered that green was much more of a challenge to photographers than any other tint. Still, counterfeiters could remove the colored tints, make any number of copies, and then restore an imitation of the colored parts. However, in 1857 an ink was developed that could not be erased without destroying the paper. The company of Rawdon, Wright, Hatch and Edson first used this ink—the Patent Green Tint—on state bank bills. Thanks to the promotional efforts by its subsequent owner, the American Bank Note Company, the ink has been in use on American paper money ever since.[56] Today's dollar bills no longer look "green," the one and two-dollar bills excepting. Beginning in the 1990s, all other denominations have been redesigned. This had become a dire necessity because of near-perfect fakes—some $100 notes were being forged so superbly that American authorities respectfully dubbed them "super notes."[57]

Security was by no means the only reason for uploading the redesigned notes with all kinds of political and ideological messages. Almost all the redesigned notes communicate patriotism, using symbols such as the torch carried by Statue of Liberty, the Liberty Bell, the quill pen the Founding Fathers used to sign the Declaration of Independence with, the American eagle and, not to forget, the flag. The notes also function as the nation's collective memory, bound up inseparably with the "portraits of the Presidents of the United States." The only difference from earlier notes is that the new portraits are more colorful and slightly off-center. European bank notes, in contrast, have been following different trends. Abandoning insignia of the state's officialdom, they rather show representatives of the arts and sciences (Strauss, Verdi, Kaplan, Heisenberg, etc.), of sports, and of women, from Angelika Kaufmann to Clara Schumann. These trends mark a significant cultural shift, from legitimating currency notes by means of the state (often through mythological-allegorical figures) to society (represented by social groups or classes) to individuals (artists and writers, scientists, composers, etc.). The shift reflects changing goals in people's lives, from loyalty and submissiveness to state and fatherland to a post-materialist focus on quality of life and self-improvement.[58]

The advanced statefulness in European countries can do without "portraits of presidents." Seen in this light, the "portraits of the Presidents of the United States" are an anachronism, put into circulation by the state as actor and providing retrospective assurance from remembering the nation's grand old men—its "fathers," as it were. The term "state as actor" means, for instance, that new notes are not just put into circulation haphazardly. Already the design requirements are tightly controlled, and new notes are usually released with much fanfare, a great deal of promotional effort, and buttressed by official websites and other media. Thus, when in April 2004 the new $50 note was unveiled at the Bureau of Engraving and Printing's Western Currency Facility (WCF) in Fort Worth, Texas, the occasion was also used for the grand opening of the WCF's new Visitor Center. The Center, which can welcome 500,000 guests annually, provides free tours of the production facility five days a week. The tours are offered in English, Spanish, Chinese, Japanese, French, German, or Portuguese. Guests may learn about the technology and history of United States currency through interactive displays, and purchase money-themed items and souvenirs in the gift shop.[59]

Promotional efforts of this kind make clear that currency notes are print matter of the greatest officialdom imaginable. Currency notes, the German Bundesbank declared, are not simply "objects of everyday use"; they are, rather, "advertising media" that "reflect key values" such as "stability, continuity, and resistance to crises." Thus, currency notes may legitimately be considered a "state's calling cards."[60] The United States Bureau of Engraving and Printing also sees it in this way. Design requirements stipulate that currency notes must be identifiably "American," much as they must bear "dignified images" which reflect the strength of the American economy. Altogether, the "new symbols of Freedom" are key points of identification, and they as it were make the notes suggest, "This dollar note is for you!" By getting Americans to identify with the new notes, it is hoped, they will develop "brand loyalty"—not just to the national currency but to the government as well. As Treasury Secretary John W. Snow announced on his department's website, "the President's economic policies" are to ensure "more of those dollars stay in the pockets of American families."[61]

Rhetoric of this kind still enjoys widespread recognition and acceptance. We should be wary, though. The rhetoric is part of a "politics of symbolism" that resonates strongly with the self-image of a large portion of the American people—white, male, middle-class Americans, the very segment that is most contested and fought over during elections and the ones who are hardest hit by the economic policies of various conservative administrations. During the administration of George W. Bush, the Nobel-prize winning economist Paul Krugman aptly dubbed these policies as "bad economics wrapped in the flag."[62] Krugman's vitriolic comment dates from 2003. By that time, the American middle class already was more of a phantom rather than a sociological fact.[63] Still, in 2008 President George W. Bush chose to present his economic recovery plan seated in front of Gilbert Stuart's portrait of George Washington, that is, in front of the face of the nation and, figuratively speaking, under the gaze of the Father of His Country, who is peering over his successor's shoulder.[64]

Neither the politics of symbolism nor the sense of tradition that speak from the photograph should surprise European observers. Behind the writing desk of Austria's presidents, for instance, also hangs a picture of a ruler—Maria Theresa, the Habsburg empress. Whether this is fitting for a republic remains an open question.[65] What truly amazes European observers is that in the United States there is hardly any national debate about or public outcry against the culture of poverty an ever-increasing number of Americans is subjected to.[66] The absence is truly puzzling and may well be related to cultural attitudes towards wealth. "For the average American," Walter Sombart observed in the late 1800s, "being successful means first and foremost becoming rich." Thus, he added, "the greater intensity put into his labor by the American worker is only the extension of his fundamentally capitalist disposition."[67]

When Sombart wrote this, Americans still sought to realize the American dream of success, fame, and wealth through thrift and hard work. Since, expectations have been steadily declining. The Aspen Institute and *The Atlantic* found in 2015 that 75 percent of Americans believed that the American dream was "suffering." If this is a measure of how badly expectations have been undermined, the percentage of those who say that they are "just getting by" should also be a matter of concern. According to Federal Reserve surveys, fully one third of Americans say that. And about 13.5 to 14.3 percent of the population—43.1 to 45.7 million people—are considered to live in poverty.[68] These levels of economic distress may very well have contributed to the election of Donald J. Trump, who during his campaign consistently emphasized the lack of good jobs in America and promised, however simplistically, to create many more and better ones.

The promise of good jobs may have worked as an effective soporific, but what also made possible Trump's success was the lure of "get rich quick." As Sherry A. Dillon, an attorney at Morgan Lewis, said at the president-elect's press conference on January 11, 2017, "many people voted for [Trump] precisely because of his business success."[69] Indeed, and with his choice of inauguration prayer leaders, the event of January 20, 2017, became a perfect staging of Trump's own *The Art of the Deal*, if not of Andrew Carnegie's "Gospel of Wealth."[70] Yet then and now success, fame, and wealth seems to be a form of self-empowerment, and for as long as self-empowerment is a culturally shared goal, to wait for a moral outcry against economic and social inequality is gratuitous, as the rich are merely more successful in doing what most people want to do and always have wanted to do. As the writer and humorist Fran Lebowitz said, Trump is "a poor person's idea of a rich person"—living in a vulgar gold splendor the poor man would embrace if he had "made" it.[71]

Epilogue: "Where's George?"

The belief, among Americans, that the dollar was *their* money and that therefore they could have trust in it was massively shaken when in August 1971 President Nixon decreed that redemption, the convertibility of paper to gold, be stopped. With the "gold window" closed, America's currency was no longer pegged to a specific value in any commodity. It would "float" relative to all other currencies, forever exposed to the whims of currency traders on Wall Street, and in London and Tokyo. Few people cared at the time; if they did, such as a delegation of worried Europeans gathered at the G-10 summit in Rome, they were likely to hear Treasury Secretary John Connally's retort: "The dollar may be our currency, but it's your problem."[1] Nixon's decision did away with the ratio, established at the Bretton Woods conference of 1946, of 35 dollars to an ounce of gold. The hope then was that the ensuing devaluation of the dollar would contain the exploding deficit. It did not, though the United States still owns a considerable amount of gold, some 8,133.5 tons. Although the book value is only about $44 per ounce, the market value is staggering. Even at a mere 1,140 USD per ounce (December 12, 2016), we are talking some $345,832,000,000 here, that is, some $346 billion dollars, most of which is safely stored away at Fort Knox.[2]

In the early 1970s, most Americans considered the gold standard irrelevant. The dollar reigned supreme in the world, and most currencies were based on it at seemingly permanent rates. Yet in March 1972, the dollar was devalued to $38.00 per ounce of gold. The following year it was devalued again, to $42.22. Oil price shocks and a global recession took their toll, as did shifts in international competitiveness. By 1995, the price of an ounce of gold had increased to $400.00. The consequences were truly dramatic. As Vjacheslav Belov wrote in 1992, since the 1970s the dollar has been losing the "planetary gleam" it had since the 1944 fall of the British Pound. "From 80% of world currency reserves, it has fallen to 52%, its buying power versus the deutschmarks and yen fallen 65%, the number of countries who peg their currencies to the dollar halved."[3] After a ten-year interval in which the dollar became popular again as a foreign currency reserve, the dollar's downward trend resumed in 2001, falling to a bare 60 percent of world currency reserves in 2010, at the same time as its share in the foreign-exchange market also declined.[4] Unsurprisingly, many Americans have come to realize that the dollar is not only their money but also their problem, a problem that is compounded by the dollar's dwindling purchasing power.[5] The question is, then, whether it helps to have a deified George Washington on the one-dollar bill.

When Gilbert Stuart was at work on his portraits of Washington, it was commonly believed that it was possible to deduce a person's character from his or her face. Thus, focusing on the face was a prerequisite for a claim to moral exemplariness. But Washington is also a "representative man," thought to embody the nation's most cherished ideals and virtues. Through his portraits, these ideals and virtues are experienced and thought of as the real presence of forces that are the source of the power that resides in it. Washington's portraits thus evoke loyalties and attachments not merely to the historic Washington but to the larger collectivity he represents. Viewing his likeness brings people into contact with something great, even sacred, and allows them to reaffirm those principles upon which the society is based. This is no doubt the function of Stuart's portrait of 1796, which from the beginning was an object of veneration, at one and the same time exemplifying and stimulating moral behavior. Washington's iconization is not therefore a matter of the historic person alone (though it does, of course, matter), but also of the artist's ability to represent both his object's physical presence and his dignity, seriousness, and moral strength.[6]

For any object to be used as an icon, easy and universal recognition is essential. Recognition doubtless underwrites one of the latest monetary actions of the U.S. government, the minting of new $1 circulating coins bearing portraits of the presidents in the order in which they served. In compliance with the Presidential Coin Act of December 22, 2005 (the act had been introduced because of the failure of the $1 Sacagawea coin to gain widespread circulation), the U.S. Mint has minted and issued four presidential coins per year, beginning with Presidents Washington, Adams, Jefferson, and Madison in 2007. Each coin in the ten-year initiative has a reverse design featuring a rendition of the Statue of Liberty. Edge-incused inscriptions bear the year of minting or issuance, "*E Pluribus Unum*," "In God We Trust," and the mint mark.[7] Many conservative lawmakers opposed the original plan of placing "In God We Trust" on the coin's edge, believing it was a step towards removing it altogether. In response to the criticism, Congress in late 2007 approved a bill that provides for moving the motto to a more prominent position on the obverse or reverse. On December 26, 2007, President George W. Bush signed into law the Consolidated Appropriations Act, which gave the U.S. Mint until 2009 to put God back in plain view.[8]

Presidential $1 coins are legal tender. Beyond that, they were intended as "a great educational tool for citizens of all ages." Hence, many events were staged to attract attention. For one thing, the Mint embarked on a ten-city Presidential Coin education tour beginning in Chicago in January 2007 and ending in Charlotte, South Carolina, in early February. Historians were invited to give talks, and local residents were able to see the new coins up close and personally even before the first coin's official release. Take-home educational materials from the Mint were also made available. Businesses, consumer groups, media outlets, and schools received special material, including brochures, a release schedule, informational take-ones, collector boards, bookmarks, program tent cards, a variety of posters, durable door/window clings, and a CD-ROM containing web-based tutorial and computer-based presentations for employee training. "Presidential $1 Coin e-Newsletters" were sent out regularly.

Whenever a new Presidential $1 coin was introduced, the Mint staged a ceremonial launch event, which included a coin exchange and an official ceremony with the

Mint's Director and other dignitaries (the George Washington $1 Coin event was held on February 15, 2007, in New York City's Grand Central Station). To ensure adequate supplies for commerce and collectors, the coins were shipped to banks and other financial institutions in rolls and bags. The question is, has the program paid off? According to information released by the U.S. Mint, by May 2007 nearly half a billion George Washington and John Adams $1 coins had been ordered for circulation. In addition, public awareness of the new coins had tripled from 15–20 percent in November 2006 when the designs were first unveiled to approximately 60 percent in March 2007. On the other hand, in a Harris Poll, 75 percent of the respondents claimed that they had not seen a presidential dollar coin in circulation, and only 13 percent said that they preferred it to the paper dollar.

The poll also noted that the coins were least used in the Eastern United States. The coins were also not much sought after by collectors, one reason being their low material value, another their somewhat startling visual appearance. Thus, in December 2011, Secretary of the Treasury Timothy F. Geithner directed that the U.S. Mint suspend minting and issuing circulating Presidential One Dollar Coins. Regular circulating demand for the coins was to be met through the Federal Reserve Bank's existing inventory of circulating coins minted prior to 2012 (estimated at 1.4 billion, that is, more than 40 percent of the coins minted). The U.S. Mint was to continue to offer several products that contain Presidential $1 Dollar Coins, including new entries, though in reduced numbers and only for collectors; they still do, though several items are unavailable or appear to be sold out. Small wonder, then, that not even Senator John McCain saw in the Presidential $1 coins viable alternatives for the paper dollar.[9]

The Presidential Coin Act stipulates that for former presidents to be honored, they must have been deceased for at least two years before issue. This means that former presidents Jimmy Carter, Bill Clinton, George W. Bush, and Barack Obama, as well as current president Donald J. Trump, as yet are ineligible to have a coin issued in their honor. The last president who was eligible was Ronald Reagan. After honoring him in

George Washington $1 Coin, obverse and reverse, diameter 26.49 mm (Heinz Tschachler).

2016, the series ended, at least for the time being. (George H.W. Bush, who passed away on November 30, 2018, now would be eligible, too.) In the meantime, the nation's past presidents are being commemorated in another ongoing series, this time of medals. There are two types of these medals, congressional gold medals and bronze duplicates (90 percent copper, 10 percent zinc), which are produced with an authorization from Congress and are for sale to the public.

The George Washington commemorative medal features on its obverse a portrait of America's first president with the inscription "GEORGE WASHINGTON PRESIDENT OF THE UNITED STATES 1789" centered along the border of the medal. The reverse shows the "PEACE AND FRIENDSHIP" symbol—two hands clasped in token of amity. On the cuff of the left wrist are three stripes with buttons, each button carrying the American eagle; the other wrist is bare. Above the hands, the pipe of peace and the tomahawk are crossed over each other, a clear echo of the numerous "Peace Medals" issued during the War of Independence and the early republic. The medal, which is three inches in diameter, was designed by Pierre Simon Duvivier (obverse) and John Reich (reverse); it is minted at the Philadelphia Mint, and sells for $39.95.[10]

Neither the changes in currency design nor the trend in coinage are accidental. The Presidential Coin Program in particular is proof that what Benjamin Franklin could only dream about in 1785 has now come true—that America place images of her honored great on the money, thus creating "monuments against perishing and being forgotten." Franklin's dream has even been surpassed by the creation, also under the Coin Act of 2005, of the First Spouse $10 Gold Coins as the pure gold collectible counterparts of the circulating Presidential $1 coins.[11] Following an observation by the British historian Eric Hobsbawm, currency design indeed is "highly relevant to that comparatively recent historical innovation, the 'nation,' with its associated phenomena: nationalism, the nation-state, national symbols, histories and the rest."[12] Behind these phenomena, we sense deliberate exercises in social engineering that are to perfect the nation-state as much as they are to make citizens recognize the form of government as representative and managed.

The fate of the Presidential $1 coins goes to show, however, that the project of constituting Americans is by no means as easy to manage as the state's elites envisage it. While the manufacturing of consent has always been a source of antagonism, this is so most notably today. For in our day and age, "the nation" clearly has ceased to be the single or even the dominant point of reference for constructing identities. Of course, the state still co-opts dissent (the recent "Make America Great Again" slogan being a perfect example), and there is still plenty of repression, but it is not nearly as total or totalizing as it was a hundred years ago. The results are often frantic and sometimes pitiful efforts by state apparatuses to endorse and enforce and, on occasion, advertise and promote through educational outreach, the national symbolic. The Presidential $1 coins, for instance, were introduced to the public with much fanfare. No less festive was the introduction, in 1982, of a half-dollar coin commemorating the 250th anniversary of Washington's birth. The coin was designed by Elizabeth Jones, chief sculptor and engraver at the Mint. Its obverse shows a uniformed Washington astride a horse. The head is taken from Stuart's Athenaeum portrait, the garment from a Trumbull painting. The legend "GEORGE WASHINGTON / 250TH ANNIVERSARY OF BIRTH 1982" appears above and below the rendering of Washington. On the reverse is a reconstruction of Washington's birthplace, under the legend "UNITED STATES OF AMERICA / IN GOD WE TRUST."

The Washington was the first commemorative coin issued since 1954. Not only was it an instant success; it also marked a new start for America's commemorative coin program. The program had begun with the 1892 Columbus half-dollar. From its inception, it reflected a general trend away from local places, people, and events towards events, persons, and places of national significance. Commemorative coins have recognized, paid homage to, or celebrated Major General Lafayette, the Pilgrim Tercentenary, the Sesquicentennial of American Independence in 1926, Daniel Boone, the Old Spanish Trail, the Battle of Gettysburg, the Korean War, Olympic Games, the bicentennials of the United States Congress and of the Bill of Rights, and, most recently, the Bald Eagle. Altogether, some 82 commemorative types appeared between 1982 and the end of 2006, most of them in a style that does not make an artistic statement so much as it borrows from the past, with the purpose of educating Americans about America.[13] A notable exception from postmodern self-referentiality is the George Washington Death Bicentennial of 1999. This half-eagle gold coin brought back from obscurity Laura Gardin Fraser's design from 1932. Although Fraser's design—intended for the quarter—had been twice chosen in the contest, Treasury Secretary Andrew Mellon unjustly rejected it, choosing instead a design by John Flanagan, the very design that Allen Ginsberg would sarcastically dismiss as "some idiot's design of the sexless father."[14]

It is inconceivable that Ginsberg would have similarly disparaged the bronze medal the Irish-born sculptor Augustus Saint-Gaudens produced in 1889 to commemorate the centennial of Washington's first inauguration in 1789. On its face, Saint-Gaudens' medallion features a dignified bust of Washington in profile and a bundle of fasces, a symbol of the Republic. The bust is almost a half-figure and in "Continental costume," that is, in "plain" coat, neckband, and lace shirt. The strongly defined profile in high relief is reminiscent of the work of Italian masters of the 15th century, most notably Pisanello. The inscription PATER PATRIAE is laid across the portrait, the perfect symmetry deliberately broken by the fasces at right. The medal's reverse is dominated by an American eagle, with wings spread, bearing the arrows, olive branch, and shield with E PLURIBUS UNUM. An extended inscription is alongside the coat-of-arms of New York State, which had commissioned the medal. Two thousand copies were struck in 1889, and they were sold at the exhibition in honor of Washington's inauguration for the deliberately affordable price of two dollars. The medallion's relief format reflects Saint-Gaudens' beginnings as a cameo cutter during the 1860s, while its memorial subject is typical of much of his signature work that followed his return to the United States in 1875, including the superlative marble *The Angel of Purity* of 1902. Above all, the 1889 medal firmly established the Early Renaissance format in Saint-Gaudens' medallic work, and his organization of obverse was present in medals and coins by his students for two generations to come.[15]

Saint-Gaudens' Washington medal is artistically convincing, far more so than the prosaic Lafayette commemorative dollar. This inconspicuous silver coin was first struck in 1900, coinciding with the unveiling, at the International Show in Paris, of Paul Wayland Bartlett's equestrian statue in honor of the French Major General. The Lafayette dollar will nevertheless be remembered for the jugate busts of Washington and Lafayette on the obverse, thus for the first American to appear on the nation's coinage, appropriately the first President.[16] The distinction of the first regular issue United States coin to portray an actual historic figure goes to the Lincoln cent in 1909 (the coin received new back designs in 2009 to commemorate the 200th anniversary of Lincoln's birth); next came the Washington quarter of 1932, the Jefferson nickel of 1938, and the Roosevelt dime of 1946. The Lincoln cent of 1909 had superseded the 1864 "copper" cent with the head of Liberty in an Indian bonnet (hence called "Indian Head" cent). Created by engraver-sculptor Victor David Brenner, the coin came into existence on the initiative of an enlightened Theodore Roosevelt seeking "moderation and seriousness of purpose" in the arts.[17]

Augustus Saint-Gaudens, *George Washington Inaugural Centennial Medal*, 1889, bronze, diameter 4.37 in / 11.1 cm (Philadelphia Museum of Art: Gift of the McNeil Americana Collection, 2011, 2011-91-27).

In December 1904, President Roosevelt had written to Treasury Secretary Leslie M. Shaw, "I think our coinage is artistically of atrocious hideousness. Would it be possible, without asking the permission of Congress, to employ a man like [Augustus Saint-Gaudens] to give us a coinage that would have some beauty?"[18] Roosevelt pursued his quest for classically inspired currency and retained the services of the great artist. In so doing, he ushered in the Golden Age of American numismatics. In 1907, Saint-Gaudens' redesigned $10 and $20 gold coins emerged from the U.S. Mint to instant acclaim. As collector Howland Wood wrote in the December 1907 issue of *The Numismatist*, "At last it has come—art in our new coinage." And in the January 1908 issue, Mint Director Frank A. Leach "hail[ed] the innovation with much interest and satisfaction," adding his hope that "the efforts at improvement and artistic realization be continued until we have a series of coins worthy of the great nation they represent."[19] And, one should add, a series of currency notes that are equally worthy of the great nation they represent. The one-dollar bill with George Washington's portrait on it certainly belongs to such a series, no matter that it has become "fixed in a single, changeless pattern."[20]

The iconic face of the nation not only maintains the "illusion of money." As a personalized quality mark, it also is essential in cultural regulation, constituting a promise of value that helps maintain trust and confidence both in America's money and in the community at large. Phrased differently, Washington's portrait on the one-dollar bill works as a symbol of national consensus and continuity to which all citizens might defer. And, to repeat a point made earlier, Washington's iconic portrait enables the seemingly direct experience of the represented object, in this case the Father of His

Country. Icons also bring to mind an absence, they visualize the invisible, which in this instance is the good and morally sound character of the nation's first president. Thus, Washington's portrait on the one-dollar bill offers a model for and stimulus to moral behavior. Viewing his portrait also brings people into contact with a larger whole and allows them to reaffirm the principles upon which the nation is based, including, of course, the risk-taking ethos of American capitalism. Overall, then, there is something sacred to Washington's portrait on the one-dollar bill, "a certain depth, a certain verticality" that demands veneration and that rallies people in its defense.[21]

There are other ways as well to draw from the commemoration of the Father of His Country a feeling of strength and confidence. One way is to track him, which is what several million Americans have been doing, if only for a pastime and (at least at first) on the ubiquitous one-dollar bill. The fun started in December 1998, when a database-programming consultant named Hank Eskin, who then lived in Brookline, Massachusetts, set up a website called Wheresgeorge.com, which invited players to purchase a small rubber stamp for $14.95 and use it on their dollar bills. The stamp says "Wheresgeorge.com" and allows people to track that bill's journey by its serial number on the web. (The stamp is no longer sold, so players must create their own stamps, have one made, or simply write on the bill.) The game, which was started as a pastime and because it had not been done yet, became hugely popular. By 2007, there were over 100 million bills being tracked and located, to a total value of over $560 million. By January 2017, some 268,916,641 bills had been entered, at a total value of $1,445,964,784. Most of the bills were and still are of the $1 denomination, some 225 million of them, or 73.57 percent of all bills, followed by the $20 and the $5. Altogether, WheresGeorge currently has over 8 million registered users, of whom over 6 million have entered bills. Californians seem to be addicted to the diversion the most: By January 23, 2017, California players had entered 25,211,097 bills, though the top-scoring place by ZIP code is Wattsburg, Pennsylvania, with some 2,220,408 bills entered. The top-scoring individual user reportedly entered more than 2 million bills.

"Wheresgeorge" is a competitive game, the point being to get the most "hits" from the most interesting places. (In 2007, the bill with the most "hits" had been registered thirteen times. At present, the overall hit rate is about 11 percent, with the average time for a hit about 27 days.) Understandably perhaps, people try to cheat. To prevent cheating, the game's creator continually updates the validation process for bills being entered into the system, weeding out serial numbers that are obviously false or bills entered repeatedly by someone trying to claim a higher hit ratio. "We do like to be sure that the bills actually enter circulation," remarked Eskin, who is also excited about the many new words that have sprung up among enthusiasts. A "boomerang" is a bill that was entered in one city, traveled to some place far away, and then returned to the original city. A "sleeper" is a bill that takes more than a hundred days to get a hit. A "Naked George" is a hit with a user note saying the bill was spent or received at a strip club or massage parlor. "I didn't think it would be as addicting as some people are finding it," Eskin also said. "It's something out there on the Internet that's not porn, and it's not selling anything. It's pure fun. I think people appreciate that."[22]

As if to prove Eskin's estimation, imitators of the game sprang up around the world. Germans played "*Wo ist mein Geld*?" ("Where's My Money?"), but they were also able

A $1 note, front and back, as entered into "Wheresgeorge.com" (photographs courtesy Carina Rasse, 2016).

to track euros, on a different site. There are also the British, tracking their "doshes," or their "lizzies," the Canadians tracking their "willys," the Russians their rubles, and the Japanese their "*osatsus*" (which means, simply, "bills")—and there are others, lots of them.[23] The thrill of actually seeing where money goes has always motivated people to write messages on bills or stamp them with, say, a cartoon horse, to see if they would come back. "Georgers" and their imitators simply engage in making money less anonymous in a more modern medium. They also may have been inspired by the movie *Twenty Bucks*, in which the journey of a $20 bill is the theme binding together the lives of, *inter alia*, a homeless woman, a would-be writer, a stripper, and two thieves. While the film, which was directed by Keva Rosenfeld, was released only in 1993, the original screenplay apparently dates from the Great Depression.[24]

Yet who are the "Georgers"? Most likely they are Americans, though even that is not a foregone conclusion. I myself would consider myself a "Georger," if only because, had the paper dollar been phased out, this book would not have been written, or only in the form of a dithyramb. Thus, thanks are owed to another group of "Georgers," those who have consistently stood up against plans to phase out the one-dollar bill, from "Save the Greenback" in the 1990s to "Americans for George" in the 2010s. Armchair psychology would have it that most of these people are social conservatives whose identity has been shaped by a predominantly white and Christian milieu and deference to male dominance. To them, the demographic rise of nonwhite minorities, the emergence and solidification of women's rights, and the changing attitudes towards sexual orientation, especially among the younger generation, must be dismaying. The seductive conservatism on the one-dollar bill, then, would serve to unite aficionados in circuits of convention and conventional feelings, constituting them as respondents to rather than as performers of cultural products.

Upon closer inspection, however, "Georgers" rather seem an elusive quarry, just like the namegiver himself, George Washington.[25] There does not appear to be any reason for women not to be "Georgers," or else for African Americans. No one really knows where "Georgers" live, whether they live in rural or urban areas, for instance. Are they predominantly affluent? Or are they rather people who may be described as "broke and patriotic," poor but still seeing their country as the "last hope" for themselves and the world?[26] Still others may simply have become the dupes of special interest groups in Congress and the Treasury Department—groups at the beck and call of paper companies producing banknote paper, perhaps, or the cotton industry, which produces fabrics used in the paper dollar, or else of ink suppliers, which all had been rallying behind "Save the Greenback" in the 1990s.

When plans to phase out the one-dollar bill resurfaced in the 2010s, certain interest groups found a willing publication medium in *The Washington Examiner*, which had "DOLLAR BILL UNDER THREAT" as its headline on the title page of the weekend edition for April 27–28, 2012. From its beginning in 2005, *The Washington Examiner* was a free tabloid meant to be a "conservative counterweight" to what the paper's owner, Philip Anschutz, saw as the liberal bias of *The Washington Post*. *The Washington Examiner* soon became influential in conservative political circles, endorsing John McCain in the 2008 presidential election (and Mitt Romney for the 2012 Republican presidential nomination).[27] Yet despite its alleged "right-wing tilt" on its editorial pages, the paper also built a reputation as "one of the best local sections in DC,"[28] which is as good an explanation as any for so prominently displaying "Americans for George's" resistance to the phasing out of the one-dollar bill.

"Americans for George" was created as a public affairs campaign by the firm of kglobal, a division of Zenetex. The firm says that they had been approached by a group of pro-dollar bill businesses after the COINS Act was introduced in the House of Representatives in August 2011. The group soon metamorphosed into a coalition of more than one hundred American small businesses that promoted the dollar bill and the perils associated with replacing it with a coin.[29] Later in 2011, the Washington, D.C., based public opinion research firm Lincoln Park Strategies teamed up with "Americans for George," providing quantitative and qualitative data for the campaign. The firm began by conducting a national survey of 800 interviews, testing likely voters' attitudes on the issue of dollar bill vs. dollar coin. The result was overwhelmingly in favor of the "Georges." Opposition to the dollar coin not only brought members of both parties together, but it also united all areas of the country. Eighty-two percent of voters in the

South, 71 percent of voters in the Northeast, and 74 percent of voters in the West said they wanted to keep the paper bills in their pockets as opposed to carrying around extra change.

Focus groups across the country too showed that the public was firmly behind the one-dollar bill: 76 percent of Pennsylvania voters, for instance, opposed removing the bill from circulation and replacing it with a coin; 54 percent were strongly opposed to the idea; 77 percent of those polled felt the dollar coin was unnecessary or unwanted; 76 percent believed the bill was more convenient to carry and use than the coin; and 70 percent said the bill carrying Washington's portrait was "*more American*" than a coin. "Sentiments against the dollar coin are strong across Pennsylvania and the rest of the country," said Stefan Hankin, president of Lincoln Park Strategies. "Our research shows people's resistance to the dollar coin spans from everyday usage to the feeling that politicians should be spending their time on more important issues." The poll also found that unlike most political topics, support for the one-dollar bill spans partisan and demographic groups. Eighty-two percent of Pennsylvania's Democrats, 79 percent of the state's Republicans, and 59 percent of its Independents opposed the proposed legislation that suggested a potential savings by eliminating the "Georges."[30]

"Americans for George," thanks to a coordinated media campaign, were mentioned in nearly every major news publication, including *The New York Times*, *The Washington Post*, *USA Today*, and *The Washington Times*, as well as dozens of regional outlets. It is hardly a good idea, therefore, to say that all of the more than 80 percent of Americans who allegedly are in favor of keeping the bill are conservatives, Christian nationalists, and whatnots. Postings and tweets that point to the one-dollar bill's "national symbolism, much of which dates to the founding of the nation," talk about the bill as a "uniquely American icon," or want George Washington's "memory live on via the #dollarbill!" also cannot in good conscience be lumped together under labels such as "socially conservative," "Christian nationalist," or "white or male."[31] In fairness, it seems more accurate to describe "Georgers" as people who still think in terms of "We Americans," who see themselves as part of a larger whole, and who are proud to be American rather than proud to be "different." While these people are nostalgic for an America that never existed, they seem united not by any specific ideology so much as by a compound of old-fashioned values and traditions, last seen perhaps in the patriotic politics of Franklin D. Roosevelt, of a desire for commonness and "unity of purpose" rather than societal disintegration and divisiveness, and with it respect for a man at the nation's founding whose like they do not expect to see again.[32]

"Americans for George" are not George Washington's only "adopted political heirs." There appear to be many more people who still believe that the Father of His Country "was and would continue to be there for them."[33] A statement of this kind points to a deeply felt need for protection and care, spawned, the philosopher Martha Nussbaum has suggested, by fearfulness.[34] An inconclusive list of "fearfuls" would contain people who choose to name a plaza outside a new federal building after George Washington; people who leave "Happy Birthday" posts on the George Washington Facebook site; people who bake George Washington meatloaves, creating an edible icon; people who get excited about news of strands of Washington's hair recently found in an almanac from 1793; people who are willing to spend $21.95 for a "Founding Fathers currency set" consisting of a Series 2017 $1 note from the Federal Reserve Bank of New York and a Series 2013 $2 note from the Federal Reserve Bank of San Francisco; or people who around Father's Day 2018 disseminated on social media a Lansdownesque image of George Washington inscribed with "America, I am your father." The post drew any number of likes and comments, such as "Happy almost Father's Day to the Father of our Country," "I wish he could come back," "if you could only see your country today," or "we NEED him instead of this guy we got now."[35]

Likewise among Washington's "adopted political heirs" would be people who scatter the ashes of loved ones on the grounds of Mount Vernon; the visitors who leave the premises loaded with Mount Vernon Folk Art Christmas Tidings and other souvenirs; descendants of Revolutionary War officers in the Society of the Cincinnati who some years ago donated to the Mount Vernon Ladies' Association a bronze copy of Houdon's marble statue in the Virginia State Capitol; the 150 or so uniformed "soldiers" (actually schoolchildren) who still meet every Christmas Day afternoon on the banks of the Delaware River, in Pennsylvania's Washington Crossing Historic Park, to recreate that fateful day in 1776 by rowing across the river in "authentic reproductions" of the boats used in Washington's surprise attack on Trenton (high winds scuttled the reenactment in 2017).[36]

A secure place on the list of Washington's "adopted political heirs" also belongs to that faithful representative braving scorn and derision to deliver the Farewell Address to an empty House or Chamber. Mark S. Wilson also would make the list, for carving an Americana Totem Pole in red pine, for display at the Yankee Doodle Country Store in Canastota, New York. The mixed-media column features familiar symbols of American democracy including a bald eagle, the Liberty Bell, and the Constitution. Below the scroll, Washington sits atop an original flag of the U.S.A. and a white pillar of justice. And, last but not least, an "adopted political heir" no doubt is an ambitious young man by the name of Dennis Rudenko, who is planning to build an innovative seven-story building in the San Francisco area, whose front will resemble the quarter dollar. As the Ukrainian entrepreneur said, the quarter dollar is "the longest-serving, unchanged coin design that every American has in his or her pocket," and it depicts "America's first president."[37]

All these people, in one way or the other, have taken the Father of His Country into their minds—internalized him as an object, as psychoanalysts put it. Clearly for these people Washington's hallowed face offers a sense of dignity, a model for the nation as a whole—for its citizens individually or for all of them acting together. "Georgers" also would like to know *how* the Father of His Country would think, and judge, and proceed, because they know that the first form of self-government is governing ourselves. Defending Washington's memory at once articulates an ethical imperative and documents a political ethics. In this context, Gilbert Stuart's portrait on the lowly paper dollar revives the portrait's former status as a religious icon. Religious icons are hung, not only in churches but also, and often primarily, in homes. So were "likenesses" of the Father of His Country, as the Russian diplomat Pavil Svinin noted while traveling through the United States in the early years of the nineteenth century.[38] Svinin no doubt had personally encountered religious icons in his home country. The functional parallels between religious icons and Washington's portrait were not lost. In 1963, the year the popular TV series *Father Knows Best* was discontinued, the artist Tom Wesselmann produced a pop-art-style collage titled *Still Life*. The work places a Stuart-like portrait of Washington next to a TV set, suggesting a religious icon being placed next to the modern equivalent of the domestic fireplace.[39]

Wesselmann's artwork cannot be accused of encouraging uncritical veneration. Nevertheless, the promise of value that Washington's image provides always has been crucial during times of crisis. The first of these crises occurred during the revolutionary period and the early republic, when republican elitism collided with loyalist sentiments, democratic radicalism, and a motley group of fractious states. In the years before and during the Civil War, Washington was seen at the same time as the guarantor of unity and the leader of the first revolution. In the late nineteenth century, the specter of mass immigration led authorities to use Washington's likeness on the currency to bring "doubtful members" of the community into the national fold. During the nativist climate of the post–World War I era, the prevailing sense of white supremacy was reinforced, and male fears assuaged by "the more permanent familiarity" of presidential portraits on the currency. In the present crisis, with a country divided along the rift lines of class, ethnicity, age, and gender, and stymied by congressional gridlock and a perpetual adolescent in the White House, we are seeing an increased investment in patriotic symbols on the currency, at the same time as the actual use of currency is increasingly confined to the "cash ghetto," whose inhabitants, following a slang expression, have to "squeeze every dollar until the eagle sh*ts."[40]

Crises are times when beliefs, convictions, or moral values are no longer commonly held or broadly shared. At the same time, the demand for mythic stories or grand narratives is most intense and the moral inspiration from even the crudest myth most deeply felt during times of crisis. The currency, I have tried to show in these pages, is one of the many ways in which the state tells its stories to its citizens. "Monetary space is sovereign space," the British sociologist and political scientist Geoffrey Ingham stated. Unsurprisingly, the pictures on America's coins and currency have been routinely used by the United States government to disseminate stories of national heroes (and villains).[41] While these repetitive images contribute towards building a national identity, none of the stories springs up spontaneously or "naturally." On the contrary, they are always constructed, propagated, and passed on with a view to the maintenance of power. As George Gerbner noted, "Those who tell stories hold the power in society."[42] For the state, this power consists in manufacturing consent, that is, in conveying beliefs, convictions, or moral values that will be broadly shared. It is the manufacturing of consent, the ingraining in the popular unconscious of a set of values and beliefs, that allows the state to imagine the people under its dominance, the geographic territory under control, and the nature of historical legitimacy.

One of the stories told and retold in the United States is the father narrative, the "dad story," as it were. Allen Ginsberg is not the only one to evoke that narrative, even though he did so in a rather melancholy way, "O Washington—O Father." Ginsberg was a child of the 1950s, a time when fatherhood occurred within broader cultural norms, described by Wini Brines as a "moralistic national family ideology."[43] Those years are also inseparably connected with the name of Dwight D. Eisenhower. Eisenhower had been a soldier—lovingly called "Ike" since World War II—before he became president in 1952. His conservative and paternalistic attitude must have felt comforting to Americans frightened by the possibility of a nuclear Armageddon. Eisenhower, like his predecessor in office, Harry Truman, indeed projected an image of quiet and serene authority and paternal confidence, enough for President Kennedy to call him for advice during the Cuban missile crisis. Yet if Eisenhower was considered the undisputed "father" of a nation imagined as a family, the cracks in the family fabric were already becoming obvious. It is well to remember, then, that whatever his qualities, the Eisenhower *image* stemmed from sophisticated media work. It was the image, not content, that decided the elections, first in 1952 and then again in 1956.[44]

Eisenhower's opponent in both elections was Adlai Stevenson, a Democrat. Stevenson could never project the image of the nation's "father." Rather, he was seen as too serious and cerebral, if not as patronizing and condescending. John Alsop, a journalist, famously described him as an "egghead," adding that all the eggheads were for Stevenson but there were simply not enough of them.[45] About a half year into Eisenhower's second term, Americans got to know a different "father." In September 1957, the President sent some 11,000 National Guards to the little town of Little Rock, Arkansas. Their job was to escort nine African American school children through the gauntlet of angry white faces. State police had denied the school children entry into a "white" high school—at the behest of the state governor, who simply ignored the Supreme Court's ruling that racial segregation was unconstitutional.[46] In the long run, however, not even Eisenhower could bring back the traditional roles of fatherhood that had been lost since the time of the Founders—of irreplaceable caregiver, moral educator, head of family, and family breadwinner. It is no coincidence that during these eventful years, Eisenhower relegated the role of the nation's father to God. In July 1955, he signed a law that made it mandatory for the motto "In God We Trust" to be printed on the currency. A year later, the motto became the national motto, and on October 1, 1957, the first dollar bills with the motto were released.

If God made it onto the nation's currency, Eisenhower did not make it, and neither will Barack Obama or Donald J. Trump, at least not during their lifetimes. Federal law prohibits this and, it is safe to say, Republicans in Congress also would rather be dead than see a portrait of the first African American president on the currency. Attempts to put a portrait of Ronald Reagan on the currency also flopped, though bronze medals of both Reagan and Obama have been issued. Produced with an authorization from Congress, these as well as other medals commemorate the nation's past presidents.[47] On the currency, however, George Washington's iconic portrait endures. The bills are real; stories and pictures, however vivid, are abstractions, symbols for things that could be touched once, for words once spoken and feelings that once stung the heart. The memories embedded in such symbols are not without their force, though. They foster a sense of community. They offer a firm footing in the midst of social and economic chaos. They tender comfort and solace to those who feel orphaned, and they strengthen the bonds of union to the national community. Activities as diverse as "Wheresgeorge," "Save the Greenback," or "Women on 20s," therefore once again confirm the "more permanent familiarity" attested by the Bureau of Engraving and Printing in the 1920s. Yet as I've said, bank notes and coins are social or institutional objects, facts only by human agreement; thus, they function only because people believe them to be money. Members of a society must have confidence or trust in them, just as they must have confidence or trust in God.

As long as there is trust or confidence in the nation's currency, in money, mammon or, borrowing from Friedrich Schiller, in the earth-god reigning supreme,[48] the face of the nation unambiguously and undistortedly emanates character and strength. The bills carrying the portrait of the "Father of His Country" no doubt tap into deeply felt needs and desires. As David Blankenhorn has suggested, "having a father may foster anger, but having no father fosters even greater anger. [...] Perhaps the demonization of the Old Father largely reflects the fact that, for the most part, he no longer lives among us."[49] Needs and desires of this kind only strengthen the one-dollar bill. How else can we explain its resilience against attempts to replace it with a coin? Economic reason—as John McCain noted, the switch from paper bills to coins would save some $4.4 billion in currency production costs over the next 30 years—apparently is no match against people's emotions. To date, not a single one of the attempts to enact such legislation have been reported out of the committees of jurisdiction. And opinion polls have shown consistently that few Americans are prepared to give up their beloved "Georges."

With the "Father of His Country's" home on the one-dollar bill safe, the Bureau of Engraving and Printing too shifted gears. As of August 2012, $1 Lucky 777 currency notes went on sale, at $5.95 apiece. At the same price, potential Chinese customers could choose between $1 Fortune 8888 and $1 Prosperity Forever 168 notes. As of February 2017, $1 Happy Birthday notes have been on offer. More affordable, if less flashy, are uncut $1 currency sheets, which run from 5 to 50 subjects, from $18.50 to $86.00. The priciest item is the "America's Founding Fathers Currency Set," first released in 2013 with a Series 2009 $1 note bearing Gilbert Stuart's portrait of George Washington and a Series 2003A $2 note bearing the portrait of Thomas Jefferson, also after Stuart—each intended to propagate the idea of "a dignified image that reflects the strength of the American economy."[50]

Contrary to the late Senator McCain's conviction, abolishing the lowly paper dollar is more than simply "taking one form of currency that disappears and is worn out and has to be discarded, [and replacing it with] another form of currency that lasts forever."[51] Yes, it does cost about 18 cents to produce a coin, compared to about 5 cents to make a dollar bill. And yes, unlike $1 notes that circulate for about two years, $1 coins last approximately 30 years.[52] And yes, paper money connects to the disappearing world of industrial capitalism, together with the printing press that made possible paper money's cheap and easy reproduction. But in April 2012, "Americans for George" spoke out vociferously against replacing "all that national symbolism, much of which dates to the founding of the nation, with a mere scrap of metal alloy," against replacing "a uniquely American icon with a nondescript piece of spare change," and expressly wished that Washington's "memory live on via the #dollarbill!"[53] And even if the 87-some percent of Americans that according to *The Washington Examiner* then opposed replacing the $1 note with a $1 coin are an exaggeration or, worse, fake news, official reports also are not in the worthy senator's favor: In fiscal year 2015, production of $1 notes still totaled some 2.451 billion notes, which roughly corresponds to the yearly average since 1980 (production peaked in FY 2000 with roughly 5.2 billion notes printed); and by December 31, 2016, the number of $1 notes in circulation was at 11.4 billion (out of a total of 38.1 billion notes).[54]

All this means that the balance between economic interests (currency efficiency in the name of budgetary discipline), the interests of a specific capitalist phase (industrial capitalism), and the interests of a liberal society (commemoration and convenience) cannot be achieved by legislative measures alone. Culture—in the sense of "*both* the meanings and values which arise amongst distinctive social groups and classes [...] *and* [...] the lived traditions and practices through which those 'understandings' are expressed and in which they are embodied"[55]—is as much an ordering moment as the rule of law. Phrased differently, culture at least some of the time trumps politics and the economy. Or, cultural notions trump political and economic notions. Thus, for as long as the values, customs, beliefs, practices, and stories that constitute the way of life of a people are alive and respected, we can reasonably assume that Americans' beloved "Georges" will continue to offset the traditional numismatic hierarchy, which puts paper in last place among available monetary substances. And we can just as reasonably assume that the Father of His Country's face will continue to legitimate, make visible, and consecrate the stories that keep a big country and a diverse people united. Had he not lost his year-long battle against brain cancer, perhaps even thrifty John McCain might have come to see it in this way.

Chapter Notes

Prologue

1. Hamilton, "Report on Establishing a Mint," 154 and, for "freaks of fortune," Jonathan Levy's eponymous book (Boston, MA: Harvard University Press, 2012).

2. Foucault, *The Order of Things*, 175–76. On money as a cultural issue, see Viviana E. Zelizer, *Economic Lives: How Culture Shapes the Economy* (Princeton, NJ: Princeton University Press, 2010).

3. Miller and Schwartz, "The Icon of the American Republic," 521–23; for "innermost essence," see Pavil Svinin, commenting on Rembrandt Peale's *Patriae Pater*, qtd. *ibid.*, 528; for "the icon acts," see Marie-José Mondzain, *Image, Icon, Economy: The Byzantine Origins of the Contemporary Imaginary*, trans. Rico Franses (Stanford, CA: Stanford University Press, 2005), 106. On sacred objects in general see Maurice Godelier, "What Mauss Did Not Say," in *Values and Valuables: From the Sacred to the Symbolic*, ed. Cynthia Werner and Duran Bell (Walnut Creek, CA: Altamira Press, 2004), 3–20, especially 17. For semioticians, "iconic" denotes a way of representation that makes possible the seemingly direct experience of the represented object. In contrast, "indexical" denotes an actual relation between a sign and the represented object, whereas "symbolic" means that the relation between sign and represented object is completely arbitrary. For a description and further discussion of the triadic scheme of signs, see Charles Sanders Peirce, *Philosophical Writings*, ed. Justus Buchler (New York: Dover Publications, 1955), 98–119.

4. On August 25, 2018, John McCain passed away at age 81 after a long battle with brain cancer. For a summary of the law he proposed in 2015, see McCain's Senate website at http://www.mccain.senate.gov/public/index.cfm/2015/7/senators-john-mccain-mike-enzi-introduce-the-usa-act-to-save-billions-in-taxpayer-dollars, July 19, 2015, accessed August 28, 2018. For the proposed law's progress, see U.S. Congress, S.1888, USA Act, https://www.congress.gov/bill/114th-congress/senate-bill/1888, July 29, 2015, accessed August 28, 2018. The CAGW (Council for Citizens Against Government Waste) is a private, nonpartisan, nonprofit organization that works "to eliminate waste, fraud, abuse, and mismanagement in government through research and public education activities." Founded in 1984, CAGW is the legacy of President Ronald Reagan's Private Sector Survey on Cost Control, also known as the Grace Commission. CAGW claims that today it represents more than a million members and supporters nationwide. See http://cagw.org/about-us/mission-history, n.d., accessed August 28, 2018. The Dollar Coin Alliance describes itself as "a coalition of small businesses, mass transit agencies, budget watchdogs, trade associations, and private companies devoted to saving American taxpayers billions of dollars by modernizing our currency to the $1 coin." See http://www.dollarcoinalliance.org, n.d., accessed August 28, 2018.

5. Etymologically the words "specie" and "species" converge in the medieval appellation for God, who was construed as the supreme or true species, "*la vraie espèce*." From the twelfth century onward, "species" meant a sign, a manifestation, or a revelation of God in consecrated bread and wine. Medieval theologians developed the argument further, to include human beings and, as well, other (or lesser) "species." From the end of the fifteenth century onward, the word "specie" signified a means of payment, in specie, "*en espèces*," that is, what one could see, as in merchandise. In contrast, paper money was not "specie" but, as a famous son of the Scottish Enlightenment, James Steuart, wrote in 1767, "a species of what is called credit." *An Inquiry into the Principles of Political Economy*, qtd. in Eagleton and Williams, *Money: A History*, 177. For a discussion of Steuart's pre-classical monetary theory, see Douglas Vickers, *Studies in the Theory of Money, 1690–1776* (Philadelphia-New York: Chilton, 1959), 240–90. On the etymology of "specie" and "species," see Daniel de Coppet, "Une monnaie pour une communauté mélanésienne," in *La Monnaie souveraine*, ed. Michel Aglietta and André Orléan (Paris: Odile Jacob, 1998), 159–211, here 192–96.

6. See David L. Ganz, "Reconsidering the Small-Sized Dollar Coin," *The Numismatist* 101:3 (March 1988), 441–49.

7. Even fewer people, I suspect, will have seen the Susan B. Anthony statue in the United States Capitol in Washington, DC. The statue is difficult to find, standing as it does in a rarely visited niche. John R. Gillis, "Memory and Identity," in *Commemorations: The Politics of National Identity*, ed. the same (Princeton, NJ: Princeton University Press, 1994), 3–24, here 23*n*35.

8. None of all this deterred the National Susan B. Anthony Mouseum & House in Rochester, New York, to host a ceremony on July 2, 2019, to commemorate the 40th anniversary of the coin's release. The event coincided with the opening of the exhibit "More than a Coin: 40 Years of the Susan B. Anthony Dollar," on display at the institution's visitor center. For more information, go to https://susanb.org/40-years-of-the-susan-b-anthony-dollar/.

9. Gene Hessler, "It's Easier Being Green," *The Numismatist* 104:2 (February 1992), 221.

10. Frank Annunzio, qtd. in Ganz, "Reconsidering the Small-Sized Dollar Coin," 447.

11. United States Mint, "Native American $1 Coins," 2014, http://catalog.usmint.gov/coin-programs/native-american-dollar-coins/, February 9, 2016.

12. See Marjie Lundstrom, "Sacagawea dollar coin? Californians just aren't buying the idea," *Sacramento Bee* (September 21, 2002).

13. United States General Accounting Office, "Financial Impact of Issuing the New $1 Coin," April 7, 2000, p. 3, http://www.gao.gov/assets/90/89684.pdf, December 12, 2016, and "New Dollar Coin: Marketing Campaign Raised Public Awareness but Not Widespread Use," September 2002, p. 36, http://www.gao.gov/assets/240/235565.pdf, December 12, 2016. Currrent production costs for the $1 and $2 denomination are at 5.5 cents per note. Notes of higher denomination cost more to produce because of security features. (The $100 denomination costs 14.3 cents per note.) Federal Reserve Board, "How much does it cost to produce currency and coins?" January 4, 2016, http://www.federalreserve.gov/faqs/currency_12771.htm, December 12, 2016. Economizers have set their sights also on circulating coins, most notably on the penny (1¢) and the nickel (5¢), which—respectively at 1.7 cents and 8 cents—cost more to produce than their nominal values. See U.S. Mint, *2014 Biennial Report to the Congress*, December 14, 2014, p. 2, https://www.usmint.gov/about_the_mint/PDFs/2014-rd-biennial-report.pdf, December 12, 2016. Although production costs fell in fiscal year 2014 due to the falling price of copper, one of the primary metals used to make coins, the Mint continues to lose money on pennies and nickels. It now costs $1.62 to make a dollar's worth of nickels, and $1.66 to make a dollar's worth of pennies. By contrast, it costs only 36 cents to make a dollar's worth of quarters, and 40 cents for a buck of dimes. Paper dollar bills are even more cost-effective. Christopher Ingraham, "It cost 1.7 cents to make a penny this year, and 8 cents to make a nickel," *The Washington Post*. December 15, 2014, https://www.washingtonpost.com/news/wonk/wp/2014/12/15/it-cost-1-7-cents-to-make-a-penny-this-year-and-8-cents-to-make-a-nickel/?utm_term=.79afa89e6c9c, December 12, 2016.

14. See "Coin Coalition" and "Save the Greenback," both in *Wikipedia*, respectively August 10, 2017, http://en.wikipedia.org/wiki/Coin_Coalition, August 21, 2018, and September 4, 2018, http://en.wikipedia.org/wiki/Save_the_Greenback, September 21, 2018, and Tschachler, *The Greenback*, 56–57. The Coin Coalition also advocated the abolition of the penny. A 1989 bill to that purpose was, however, actively opposed by "American for Common Cents" (A.C.C.), a lobbying group that was funded mainly from Jarden Zinc Products, one of the nation's largest producers of zinc, supplying the U.S. Mint with penny planchets. Later attempts to phase out the penny also led nowehere, thanks again to A.C.C. and any number of Lincoln-loving people. David Owen, "Penny Dreadful," *The New Yorker*, March 31, 2008, www.newyorker.com/magazine, February 22, 2015; Michael Nottelmann, "Make Sense of Our Coinage," *The Numismatist* 125:8 (August 2012), 99–100, here 99. The website of Americans for Common Cents is still active, at http://www.pennies.org.

15. "Americans for George," April 27, 2012, https://www.facebook.com/amerforgeorge, December 12, 2016; see also Howard Fischer, "Americans for George support clean crisp dollar bill," *Verde Independent* (Phoenix, Arizona), October 25, 2011, http://verdenews.com/main.asp?SectionID=1&SubSectionID=1&ArticleID=44453, September 19, 2014; and Harry Bradford, "Most Americans Against Replacing Dollar Bill with Coin," *The Huffington Post*, October 19, 2011, http://www.huffingtonpost.com/2011/10/19/majority-americans-dollar-bill-coin_n_1019704.html, December 9, 2016.

16. A similar bill was introduced to the U.S. Senate by Senator Tom Harkin (D-IA) in June 2013 as S. 1105: United States Congress, "Currency Optimization, Innovation, and National Savings Act," June 6, 2013, https://www.congress.gov/bill/113th-congress/senate-bill/1105?s=2&r=1916, May 26, 2019. For the COINS Act, see United States Congress, "All Bill Information (Except Text) for H.R. 2977—Currency Optimization, Innovation, and National Savings Act," September 20, 2011, https://www.congress.gov/bill/112th-congress/house-bill/2977/all-info, December 9, 2016; Marc Lacey, "Hoping to Save Money for the Government, Some Seek an End to the $1 Bill," *New York Times*, November 5, 2011, http://www.nytimes.com/2011/11/06/us/some-seek-to-replace-the-dollar-bill-with-the-dollar-coin.html, December 9, 2016; Joseph Straw et al., "Congress considers getting rid of dollar bills for $1 coins to save money," *New York Daily News*, December 3, 2012, http://www.nydailynews.com/news/national/ax-dollar-bills-save-money-congress-article-1.1211013, July 31, 2014.

17. Representatives Lacy Clay (D-MO) and Carolyn Maloney (D-NY), qtd. in Straw et al., "Congress considers getting rid of dollar bills for $1 coins to save money."

18. United States General Accounting Office (now Government Accountability Office), "Financial Impact of Issuing the New $1 Coin," and "New Dollar Coin," 36. For the GAO's annual reports, see http://www.gao.gov/duplication/action_tracker/U.S._Currency/action1, accessed January 19, 2016. An independent economic study conducted by John Dunham & Associates in November 2011 also

found that a transition to dollar coins would increase annual costs to private businesses by $220 million, lead to thousands of job losses, and result in other capital expenses and costs to banks, money-transfer companies and other financial firms. "Leave the $1 Bill Alone," *The Numismatist* (May 2012), 33.

19. Pete Kasperowicz, "House GOP wants to cash out dollar bill," *The Hill*, September 27, 2011, http://thehill.com/blogs/floor-action/house/184155-house-senate-prep-for-next-money-battle-dollar-bill-vs-dollar-coin, August 18, 2012.

20. United States Congress, "Currency Efficiency Act of 2011," n.d. https://www.congress.gov/bill/112th-congress/senate-bill/1624?q=%7B%22search%22%3A%5B%22Currency+Efficiency+Act%22%5D%7D&r=1, December 9, 2016.

21. United States Congress, "All Bill Information (Except Text) for H.R.2977—Currency Optimization, Innovation, and National Savings Act," web document.

22. For McCain's address to the CAGW and the Dollar Coin Alliance, see "Remarks by Senator John McCain on the COINS Act," July 22, 2013, http://www.mccain.senate.gov/public/index.cfm/2013/7/post-07c47691-ef21-8e6e-14ce-c0537f4eb206, January 19, 2016. That the *USA Act* is likely the last attempt to replace the $1 note with a coin is supported by the May 21, 2019 report by the Government Accountability Office (formerly General Accounting Office), which says that the financial benefit of such a replacement has decreased and the GAO is no longer tracking this action; instead, the GAO recommends that the Treasury be allowed to alter the metal composition of all coins. See U.S. GAO, "Annual Report on Duplication and Cost Savings," May 21, 2019, https://www.gao.gov/duplication/overview, retrieved May 25, 2019.

23. Heathcot-Amory and Archbishop of Canterbury, qtd. in Helleiner, "National Currencies and National Identities," 1409, 1413.

24. Irene Haskill et al., *Human Geography of the UK* (London: Routledge, 2001), 190; Gabriele Metzler, "'Abolish the pound and you abolish Britain,'" *Die kulturelle Seite der Währung*, ed. Bernhard Löffler (München: Oldenbourg, 2016), 169–97. For an illustration of the "Keep the Pound / Stuff the Euro" photograph, see Tschachler, *Americans for George*, 11.

25. Max Hastings, "Splendid Isolation," *New York Review of Books*, October 12, 2017, https://www.nybooks.com/articles/2017/10/12/dunkirk-churchill-splendid-isolation/, November 1, 2017.

26. Michael Aglietta and André Orléan, eds., *La monnaie souveraine* (Paris: Odile Jacob, 1998), 31.

27. European Commission, qtd. in Helleiner, "National Currencies and National Identities," 1409. In a recent study, economists, historians, and bankers identified the core problem with the Euro in the philosophical differences between the founding countries of the Eurozone, particularly Germany and France: Whereas the former sees the legal basis for the Euro as a set of fixed rules, the latter rather sees it as a flexible framework, to be overseen by national governments. See Markus K. Brunnermeier et al., *The Euro and the Battle of Ideas* (Princeton, NJ: Princeton University Press, 2016).

28. Théret, "L'euro en ses tristes symbols. Une monnaie sans âme ni culture," *Le Monde diplomatique*, Décembre 2001, 4–5. An English-language version is available to subscribers at http://mondediplo.com/2001/12/.

29. An overview of the denominations and design elements of the euro notes can be found on the website of the ECB, the European Central Bank. For an overview of the entire design competition with its altogether 44 submissions, see Admirable Design, "The euro banknotes that never were!" N.d., http://www.admirabledesign.com/-Designs-de-l-euro-, September 22, 2014.

30. The original series had been designed by Austrian Robert Kalina; revisions for the new series are by Reinhold Gerstetter. Refurbishing the notes began in 2013; it is to include seven Euro denominations, 5, 10, 20, 50, 100, 200, and 500, and is expected to be completed by 2020. See European Central Bank, "New Euro Banknotes," http://www.new-euro-banknotes.eu, retrieved February 9, 2016 (no longer available in this format, but see "Europea series of euro banknotes," http://www.ecb.europa.eu/euro/banknotes/europa/html/index.en.html, retrieved August 28, 2018); see a. Stefan Hampl's marvelous analysis of the new Euro bills: "EU-ropa Regina: Die Bildpolitik der neuen Euro-Banknoten," in *Der schöne Schein. Symbolik und Ästhetik von Banknoten*, ed. Stefan Hartmann und Christian Thiel (Regenstauf, Germany: Gietl-Verlag, 2016), 193–24.

31. Hessler, "It's Easier Being Green," 221.

32. Anti-*Oedipus* (1972; London: Athlone, 1997) is part of a two-volume work by Gilles Deleuze and Félix Guattari, titled *Capitalism and Schizophrenia*; the second volume, *A Thousand Plateaus* was published in 1980. On the the relevance of *Anti-Oedipus* within the context of monetary communication, see Jochen Hörisch, *Kopf oder Zahl*, 73–74.

33. Cunliffe, *George Washington*, 14.

34. Brookhiser, *Founding Father: Rediscovering George Washington*; *George Washington Reconsidered*, ed. Don Higginbotham (Charlottesville: UP of Virginia, 2001). Marcus Cunliffe, too, traces the "lineaments of the real man," in four chapters, "George Washington, Esquire," "General Washington," "President Washington," and "The Whole Man."

35. Washington, Cunliffe argues (*George Washington*, 16), occurs "in any or all of the four following guises: a) *the Copybook Hero*; b) *the Father of His People*; c) *the Disinterested Patriot*; d) *the Revolutionary Leader*."

36. Doty, *Encyclopedic Dictionary of Numismatics*, 83, 246, 218; Nussbaum, *History of the Dollar*, 52; Federal Reserve Board, "How much does it cost to produce currency and coins?" (web document).

37. Kenneth S. Rogoff, *The Curse of Cash: How Large-Denomination Bills Aid Crime and Tax Evasion and Constrain Monetary Policy* (Princeton, NJ: Princeton University Press, 2016). Rogoff's plan is to start with the 100s, then the 50s, then the 20s, leaving smaller bills in circulation for the foresee-

able future. Just for the record, Rogoff served as an economist at the International Monetary Fund (IMF) and at the Board of Governors of the Federal Reserve System; at present, he is a Professor of Economics at Harvard University—see https://en.wikipedia.org/wiki/Kenneth_Rogoff, and Peter Coy, "This Harvard Economist is Trying to Kill Cash," *Bloomberg Businessweek*, September 7, 2016, http://www.bloomberg.com/news/articles/2016-09-07/harvard-economist-kenneth-rogoff-is-trying-to-kill-cash, September 29, 2016.

38. Tietmeyer, qtd. in Bernhard Löffler, "Währungsgeschichte als Kulturgeschichte?" *Die kulturelle Seite der Währung*, ed. Bernhard Löffler (München: Oldenbourg, 2016), 3–35, here 23, my translation. The concept of "monetary rhetoric" ("*Rhetorik des Geldes*") belongs to Gottfried Gabriel, *Ästhetik und Rhetorik des Geldes*, 10. For a general discussion of currency images as accompanying measures for building trust see Gabriel's "Aesthetics and Political Iconography of Money," 420–22. For "functional encroachments" ("*funktionale Übergriffe*," my translation), see Hörisch, *Kopf oder Zahl*, 74.

39. Hörisch, *Kopf oder Zahl*, 200–201, my translation. On the interconnections between literature and the economy see Marc Shell, *The Economy of Literature* (Baltimore, MD: Johns Hopkins University Press, 1978). Generally on art and money, see Shell's eponymous book.

40. Faus*t* I, verse 382–83. On "money holding together the world in its core" as a literary theme, see Jochen Hörisch, *Gott, Geld, Medien. Studien zu den Medien, die die Welt im Innersten zusammenhalten* (Frankfrt am Main: Suhrkamp, 2004), 7–30. Hörisch also spends a great many pages on Goethe's fascination with monetary matters, on his familiarity with Adam Smith, and on his tenure as Secretary of the Treasury at the Weimar court. *Ibid.*, 90–107.

41. On the "ideological evolution" of monetary form, see Rizzo, "'Show Me the Money!'" (web document). For "traces" of the past in the present, see Peter Burke, *Eyewitnessing: The Uses of Images as Historical Evidence. Picturing History Series* (Ithaca, NY: Cornell University Press, 2001), 13.

42. On the "Natural History" paradigm, see Pamela Regis, *Describing Early America: Bartram, Jefferson, Crèvecoeur, and the Rhetoric of Natural History* (DeKalb: Northern Illinois University Press, 1992).

43. Hans Gebhardt, *Numismatik und Geldgeschichte* (Heidelberg: Universitätsverlag Winter, 1949), especially 17–21. For an overview of the current state of research see two articles by Christian Thiel, respectively titled "Der schöne Schein" and "Banknoten im Blickpunkt der Wissenschaft."

Part I

1. Nathaniel Niles, in Charles S. Hyneman and Donald S. Lutz, *American Political Writing Writing during the Founding Era, 1760–1805*, 2 Vols. (Indianapolis, IN: Liberty Fund, 1983), Online Library of Liberty, http://oll.libertyfund.org/titles/hyneman-american-political-writing-during-the-founding-era-1760-1805-2-vols, 1:273, February 13, 2018. Samuel Davies, "On the Death of His Late Majesty King George II," *Spreading the Gospel in Colonial Virginia: Sermons and Devotional Writings*, ed. Edward L. Bond (Lanham, MD et al.: Lexington Books, 2004), 398–413, here 398.

2. Weems, *The Life of George Washington*, 80.

3. Jefferson, "The Declaration of Independence as Adopted by Congress," 377. For an analysis of Jefferson's ideas in 1776, see Gary Wills, *Inventing America: Jefferson's Declaration of Independence* (Garden City, NY: Doubleday, 1978); for a reading of the Declaration in the context of English common-law practice, see Ferguson, *The American Enlightenment*, 126–130. "[H]orrors of civil discord," George Washington, letter to Robert McKenzie, October 9, 1774, in George Washington, *Writings*, ed. John Rhodehamel, 160 (subsequently abbreviated as *WWR*).

4. On the stormy protests articulated in all forms of media, see Stephen D. Solomon, *Revolutionary Dissent: How the Founding Generation Created the Freedom of Speech* (New York: St. Martin's Press, 2016); for Robert A. Ferguson, the American Revolution is first and foremost a "literary pursuit" (*The American Enlightenment*, 1–21).

5. The denominations on the notes—for instance, "One Dollar and Two Thirds of a Dollar"—is a result of the confusion in the British currency system. One pound was worth 20 shillings; a guinee, a larger gold coin, was worth one pound and one shilling; one shilling was equal to twelve pence; and each penny was divided into four farthings. It was not until 1971 that Britain's currency went metric. Weatherford, *The History of Money*, 181.

6. For an illustration of a Maryland note, see Tschachler, *Political Fatherhood*, chapter 2; for descriptions, see Doty, *America's Money*, 46–47, and the website of University of Notre Dame, Special Collections, "Colonial Currency," n.d., http://www.coins.nd.edu/ColCurrency/CurrencyText/CC.html, accessed February 24, 2017.

7. Newman, *Early Paper Money*, 445. The phrase was recommended by George Mason to the Virginia Assembly in 1776, as part of the commonwealth's seal. The Seal was planned by Mason and designed by George Wythe, who also signed the Declaration of Independence. "Thus always to tyrants" is a shortened version of the phrase "Sic semper evello mortem tyrannis" ("Thus always I bring death to tyrants"). The phrase is sometimes said to have originated with Marcus Junius Brutus during the assassination of Julius Caesar on March 15, 44 BC, though according to Plutarch, Brutus either did not have a chance to say anything, or if he did, no one heard what was said. See *Plutarch's Lives*, the translation called Dryden's, corr. and rev. by A. H. Clough (New York: Colonial Company, 1905), 5: 320–28. For an illustration of the Virginia issue, see Tschachler, *Political Fatherhood*, chapter 2.

Chapter 1

1. Jefferson to Henry Lee, May 8, 1825, *Writings*, 1500–1501 and, for "extract consensus at all costs," Ferguson, *The American Enlightenment*, 6.

2. Michel Foucault, "Politics and the Study of Discourse," *The Foucault Effect: Studies in Governmentality*, ed. G. Burchell, C. Gordon and P. Miller (Chicago: University of Chicago P / London: Harvester Wheatsheaf, 1991), 53–72, qtd. 59.

3. Ferguson, *The American Enlightenment*, 188–189; for "Only children can be orphans," see *ibid.*, 37.

4. For the extent to which American propagandists depicted Washington as a virtuous replacement for the "tyrant" George III, see Paul K. Longmore, *The Invention of George Washington* (Berkeley: University of California Press, 1988), 202–11. On the colonial renunciation of George III as a deeply traumatic experience, see Winthrop D. Jordan, "Familial Politics: Thomas Paine and the Killing of the King, 1776," *Journal of American History* 90 (September 1973), 294–308.

5. The "god of the clan," Émile Durkheim wrote, can be "nothing else than the clan itself, personified and represented to the imagination under the visible form of the animal or vegetable which serves as totem." *The Elementary Forms of the Religious Life* (New York: Free Press, 1965), 236.

6. Albanese, *Sons of the Fathers*, 144.

7. Benjain Rush, qtd. in Bryan, *Washington in American Literature*, 25.

8. Levi Allen to George Washington, January 27, 1776, *Founders Online*, National Archives, http://founders.archives.gov/documents/Washington/03-03-02-0141, retrieved January 26, 2017.

9. Henry Knox to George Washington, November 26, 1777, *Founders Online*, National Archives, http://founders.archives.gov/documents/Washington/03-12-02-0407, retrieved January 26, 2017. Among the possible Roman sources of Knox's eulogy are Cicero (*Phillipicae* XIII: 19, 40f.), Ovid (*Fasti* 2, 127–44), and Horace (*Carmen Saeculare* III 5, 2ff.). Andreas Alföldi has traced the genealogy of "*patriae pater*" in Roman antiquity in *Der Vater des Vaterlandes im römischen Denken* (Darmstadt, Germany: Wissenschaftliche Buchgesellschaft, 1971), especially 80–101. *Pater patriae*, Alföldi has shown, originated in the time of Romulus; the honorary title was in common usage during the republican era, reaching a new peak under Caesar (following the end of the civil war) and Augustus, when it became both an honorary title and a political concept. Among Augustus' followers, numerous coins were struck bearing the inscription *Patri patriae* (*ibid.*, 95).

10. The denomination on the notes that have been preserved is of the value of 9d (*Pence*, that is, 3/4 of a shilling or 1/8 of a dollar); the notes were issued in Waterford, Virginia. Newman, *Early Paper Money*, 444. As regards the Lansdowne portrait, versions of it appeared on $10 notes issued in the 1830s, respectively by the Commercial Bank of Florida, Apalachicola, and the Piscataqua Bank, Portsmouth, New Hampshire. The 1830s have gone down as the Jacksonian era, when the restraint of classical republicanism was shattered by "majority rule," Jackson's populist agenda of providing average citizens (the "common man") with greater power. On the notes referred to, Washington is at right; at left is the figure of a standing Indian. For illustrations, see Haxby, *Standard Catalog of U.S. Obsolete Bank Notes*, FL-5-G12, and NH-280-G48 (all subsequent references are abbreviated as Haxby).

11. United States Bureau of Engraving and Printing (USBEP), "U.S. CURRENCY FAQs," qtd. in Tschachler, *The Greenback*, 19.

12. The overall number of non-circulating Washington pieces is conservatively estimated at 2,500 different ones, with over 650 through 1883, and "literally thousands" since. Most of these pieces were issued at anniversaries of Washington's birth, presidency, death, and other major events. While these pieces are not money, they have become valuable among collectors. Nordham, *George Washington and Money*, 112–13 and *Vignettes and Memorabilia*, 61–71; Bowers, *Garrett Collection*, 167–77 and, for illustrations, color plate 14, following 120.

13. Bowers, *Whitman Encyclopedia of Obsolete Paper Money*, 1:141; subsequently abbreviated as *Whitman*. Andrew Jackson is perhaps second in popularity after Washington, but he is featured nearly always as a portrait, not posed or in action. *Ibid.*, 143. For a sample sheet produced by Fairman, Draper, Underwood & Co. in 1830 and showing various Washington vignettes, see Tomasko, *The Feel of Steel*, 8.

14. Rare exceptions are Muscalus, *An Index of State Bank Notes That Illustrate Washington and Franklin* and Nordham, *George Washington: Vignettes and Memorabilia*, especially 72–77 (chap. 9), and *George Washington and Money*, 99–114. For a brief citation of numismatic research on Washington, see Bowers, *Obsolete Paper Money*, 476; in 2006, Bowers could name only one collector of bank notes bearing Washington's image. *Ibid.*, 479. It is rather beyond paper money, the doyen of American numismatics noted, that "the field of Washingtonia, sometimes called Washingtoniana, is a wildly popular numismatic specialty." *Whitman*, 1:141–42. For the George Washington Numismatic Association, located in Washington, PA, and part of the Pennsylvania Association of Numismatists, visit http://pancoins.org/coin-clubs/pa-coin-clubs-western-region/, accessed April 18, 2017.

15. Louis J. Tellkampf, "Method for Correcting the Currency without the Aid of a United States Bank," *Hunt's Merchants' Magazine* 6:1 (January 1842), 65–71, qtd. 65, italics in original. The essay was prompted by John Tyler's veto, in 1841, of a bill that would have resurrected the Bank of the United States. See Tschachler, *The Monetary Imagination of Edgar Allan Poe*, 156–59. For "natural" money, see Karl Marx, *Capital (A Critique of Political Economy)*, trans. Cedar Paul and Eden Paul (London-Toronto: J. M. Dent, 1930), 65.

16. On the "hierarchy of materials" ("*Materialhierarchie*"), see Klüßendorf, "Gold—Silber—Kupfer—

Aluminium—Papier. Materialhierarchien in der Münz- und Geldgeschichte Botschaft," *Anzeiger des germanischen Nationalmuseums* 110 (1995), 107–14. Klüßendorf's hierarchical scheme is unhistoric; it has no place for plastic or electronics as means of transferring and storing value, and it also does not relate the dominance of specific materials to specific phases in economic development. On the "ideological evolution" of monetary form, see Rizzo, "'Show Me the Money!'" (web document).

17. On the distinction between "aesthetics of materials" ("*Materialästhetik*") and "aesthetics of symbols" ("*Symbolästhetik*"), see Gabriel, "Aesthetics and Political Iconography of Money," 420–22.

18. Comics, too, have been classified as "not quite art." Roger Sabin, *Comics, Comix, and Graphic Novel: A History of Comic Art* (London: Phaidon, 1996), 8. I am grateful to my colleague René Schallegger for pointing this out to me.

19. Rhys Carpenter, *The Esthetic Basis of Greek Art* (Bloomington: Indiana University Press, 1962) 21, qtd. in Vermeule, *Numismatic Art in America*, 10.

20. Qtd. in Goodwin, *Greenback*, 150.

21. Hamilton, "Report on Establishing a Mint," 154.

22. On the interconnections between language and the economy see Shell, *Money, Language, and Thought: Literary and Philosophic Economies from the Medieval to the Modern Era* (Baltimore, MD: Johns Hopkins University Press, 1982). On the role of money and language as unifying forces in culture and society, see Gabriel, *Ästhetik und Rhetorik des Geldes*, 129–30, and his "Aesthetics and Political Iconography of Money."

23. Gabriel, *Ästhetik und Rhetorik*, 42–43.

24. The terms "iconography" and "iconology" originate from Erwin Panofky's *Meaning in the Visual Arts* (1955; Chicago: University of Chicago Press, 2008). In German-speaking Europe, the two practices are respectively called "*Bildwissenschaft[en]*" (Klaus Sachs-Hombach) and "*Bildkritik*" (Gottfried Boehm). For an overview of German-language scholarship, see Marion G. Müller, "Ikonografie und Ikonologie, visuelle Kontextanalyse, visuelles Framing," in *Die Entschlüsselung der Bilder. Methoden zur Erforschung visueller Kommunikation. Ein Handbuch*, ed. Thomas Petersen and Clemens Schwender (Köln: Herbert von Halem Verlag, 2014), 28–55, here 29–34. Panofsky's pioneering study notoriously lacked a social dimension, was indifferent to social context. More recent studies have amended this, by asking, for instance, for whom an image has meaning. See especially, W. J. T. Mitchell, *Iconology: Image, Text, Ideology* (Chicago: University of Chicago Press, 1986), his *Picture Theory*, and Larry J. Reynolds, "American Cultural Iconography: Vision, History, and the Real," *American Literary History* 9 (1997), 381–95.

25. There are hardly any studies on the actual perception of coins and currency. Notable exceptions are empirical studies done by Hans de Heij. *Designing Banknote Identity*, for instance, is a study of users' perceptions of Euro notes. The results are telling. Most people see the historic buildings as the notes' core message; very few pay attention to their intended meanings—different historic periods, symbols of openness and connectedness.

26. The classic source for all numismatic vocabulary is Friedrich von Schrötter's *Wörterbuch der Münzkunde*. Richard Doty's *Encyclopedic Dictionary of Numismatics* is the most useful guide to numismatic terminology in English. Also useful is Philip Grierson's book *Numismatics*, as well as the American Numismatic Society's "Introduction to Numismatic Terms and Methods." For paper money terminology, see Q. David Bowers, *Whitman Encyclopedia of U.S. Paper Money*, especially 1–45 and 868–71.

27. Fred Smillie, chief engraver at the U.S. Bureau of Engraving and Printing in the years 1912–1915, qtd. in Tomasko, *Images of Value*, 18.

28. For detailed accounts of the process of designing, engraving, and printing bank notes, see Bowers, *Obsolete Paper Money*, 7–76, 197–211, 261–67, and 424–26, and Tomasko, *The Feel of Steel*, 67–122; also useful is Tomasko's "primer" on bank note engraving in Stahl, *Money on Paper*, 3–16.

29. Regarding "redemption," in the English language the word has been used as an economic term since the mid-sixteenth century, though the specific ecclesiastical sense of it dates back much earlier, to 1340. Then it meant deliverance from sin and its consequences by the atonement of Jesus Christ. "Redemption" is also used in the Jewish "seder" ceremony during the feast of Passover, describing what God did for the Israelites when he freed them from slavery in Egypt.

30. Fabio Mugnaini, "Messages sur billets de banque: La monnaie comme mode d'échange et de communication," *Revue Terrain* 23 (Oktober 1994), 63–80; O'Donnell, *Standard Handbook of Modern United States Paper Money*.

31. Nussbaum, *History of the Dollar*, 24–26; Doty, *Dictionary of Numismatics*, 135.

32. Doty, *America's Money*, 10–14, 22–29, and, for the Pine Tree shilling, *Dictionary of Numismatics*, 256–58. For full-color illustrations of colonial coinage, see Bowers, *Garrett Collection*, plates 2–7 and, for further analysis and description, *ibid.*, 105–20.

33. On the money supply in pre-federal America, see Mossman, *Money of the American Colonies and Confederation*, 32–37.

34. Vermeule, *Numismatic Art in America*, 6–9 and, for "provide democracy with instruments of visual beauty," *ibid.*, preface. Cornelius Vermeule is a former director and curator at the Museum of Fine Arts, Boston. The domination of Liberty is owed to the fact that justice emblems dropped out of sight after Independence. Elizabeth M. Nuxoll identified two reasons for the change. Justice had appeared on debt certificates, most of which were in the hands of speculators by the 1790s, while those who provided goods and services during the Revolution were left empty-handed. Thus, Justice became "a code word for repayment of the public creditors (usually defined as those currently holding the debt certificates, not the original holders)." With Justice rejected, Liberty's popularity was reinforced by the

French Revolution. See "A Generation of Numismatic Cooperation: Findings on the Notes and Coins of the Confederation through the Papers of Robert Morris," *American Journal of Numismatics* Second Series 9 (1997), 55–87, here 65. On the Justice motif on the 1779 Continental Currency, see Newman, *Early Paper Money*, 44.

35. The full text of the Mint Act of April 2, 1792—"An Act establishing a Mint, and regulating the Coins of the United States," *Statutes at Large*, 2nd Congress, 1st Session, chapter XVI—is available online from the Library of Congress: "A Century of Lawmaking for a New Nation: U.S. Congressional Documents and Debates, 1774–1875," http://memory.loc.gov/cgi-bin/ampage?collId=llsl&fileName=001/llsl001.db&recNum=369, accessed May 19, 2017. See Section 9 for the value respectively of the dollar and the eagle, http://memory.loc.gov/cgi-bin/ampage?collId=llsl&fileName=001/llsl001.db&recNum=371. As a courtesy to the government, the *Columbian Sentinel* published the Act in its April 21, 1792, issue. To view the high-resolution, four-page issue and the full text of the Act, visit https://www.money.org/blog/ColumbianCentinel, retrieved August 17, 2017.

36. Qtd. in Vermeule, *Numismatic Art in America*, 29. For Stuart's "lost sketch" see Wells, "Strokes of Genius," 45–46.

37. The Mint agreed to exchange any Spanish or Mexican coin at the rate of 25 cents for 2 reales, but only for two years and for the new Flying Eagle copper-nickel cents. The venture provided a windfall seigniorage that paid for the entire mint operation for 1858. Krooss, *Documentary History of Banking and Currency*, 1: 233, and Doty, *America's Money*, 33–35. On the origin of the dollar sign in the Spanish dollar's iconography, see Tschachler, *The Greenback*, 22–23. Readers of Robert Louis Stevenson's classic of 1883, *Treasure Island*, might recall the old pirate's parrot aboard the *Hispaniola* incessantly screaming "pieces of eight, pieces of eight."

38. The law also established values at which these coins were to circulate. For instance, the Spanish dollar would be worth 100 cents, and its French equivalent 110. For a history of foreign coins in America, see Mossman, *Money of the American Colonies and Confederation*, 53–77, Raphael E. Solomon, "Foreign Specie Coins in the American Colonies," *Studies on Money in Early America*, ed. Eric P. Newman and Richard G. Doty (New York: American Numismatic Society, 1976), 25–42, and David A. Martin, "The Changing Role of Foreign Money in the United States, 1782–1857," *Journal of Economic History* 37 (1997), 1009–1027; for a typical guide to coinage from the era, see John Thompson's *Coin Chart Manual* (New York: W.W. Lee, 1849).

39. In all likelihood, the saying originated from *Niles' Weekly Register*, a mercantile and financial magazine, which on March 9, 1822, reported that American eagles, "being worth ten dollars and eighty five cents in silver, for the British Mint, have nearly all taken wings and flown away" (23). A few years earlier, *Niles'* had carried a report about two ships sailing from Boston to England, carrying away $500,000 in specie, expected to fetch from 28 to 34 percent advance, compared with Bank of England notes. Because of such shipments, the magazine noted, "money is scarcer in Boston than in any other part of the United States." *Niles' Weekly Register*, July 15, 1815, 352.

40. Vermeule, *Numismatic Art in America*, 53 and, for an overview of neoclassicism on Unites States coinage, 40–57.

41. *Ibid.*, 58.

42. *Ibid.*, 72–74 and, for an overview of neoclassicism of U.S. coinage from the Civil War through 1892, 58–81. On the wooden medals and plaques, see Donald G. Tritt's eponymous book, available as an e-book to members of the American Numismatic Association at https://www.money.org/uploads/pdfs/DiePedWoodenMedals8.26.pdf, retrieved August 17, 2017.

43. Vermeule, *Numismatic Art in America*, 90 and, on the coinage of 1892, 82–89.

44. *Ibid.*, 2 and, for detailed description and analysis of the "artistic revolution" set in motion by Theodore Roosevelt, 102–30. On the "Renaissance in American money," see also Doty, *America's Money*, 169–73.

45. There have been exceptions, such as the "African-American Liberty," a $100 high-relief gold coin with raised edge-lettering, issued in 2017 to mark the mint's 225th anniversary. The coin was criticized as too politically correct and aesthetically unappealing. At present, the gold coin sells for $1,690 apiece; a silver medal version is available for budget-minded collectors. See United States Mint, "American Liberty 225th Anniversary Gold Coin," 2017, https://catalog.usmint.gov/american-liberty-225th-anniversary-gold-coin-17XA.html?cgid=gold-coins#_ga=2.211605779.767910792.1496049593-381926292.1494498521&start=1, May 28, 2017.

46. Vermeule, *Numismatic Art in America*, 3–9.

47. *Ibid.*, 3 and, on the "return of commemorative coinage," 217–34.

48. Gary Marks, qtd. in Louis Golino, "Modern U.S. Coin Design," *The Numismatist* 130:6 (June 2017), 32–37, qtd. 35. The CCAC, the Citizens Coinage Advisory Committee, is primarily tasked with approving designs that should appear on coins and medals. The CCAC also was the originator of the hugely successful State Quarters Program.

49. GovMint.com, "How Are Coins Made," https://www.govmint.com/coin-authority/post/how-are-coins-made/, accessed September 6, 2018.

50. For a history of the term "style" and its proper application, see C. H. V. Sutherland, "What is Meant by 'Style' in Coinage," *American Numismatic Society Museum Notes* 4 (1950), 1–12.

51. Vermeule, *Numismatic Art in America*, 5 and, for a descriptive overview, Q. David Bowers, *A Guide Book of Modern United States Dollar Coins* (Atlanta, GA: Whitman Publishing, 2016).

52. The word "cash" meaning coin or specie may be derived from the French word *casse* (modern French *caisse*, for cash desk or paying agency) or else, from Portuguese *caixa*, for chest or strongbox. There

is also an Indian word *karsha*, meaning "copper coin." Doty, *Dictionary of Numismatics*, 47; Eagleton and Williams, *Money: A History*, 141.

53. The "legal tender" quality of money is discussed in full in Hurst, *A Legal History of Money in the United States*, 40–45.

54. Standish, *The Art of Money*, 129.

55. The terms "empty value," "forced currency," and "fiction of value" belong to Jean-Joseph Goux, *The Coiners of Language*, 128.

56. For the father as the "general equivalent of subjects," see Goux, Introduction to *Symbolic Economies*, 3–4. The notion that each face is singular at the same time as it reflects God's face, Dieter Lau found, originated in the Christian tradition, specifically in the patristic and classical literature. Most of these faces were in hands, hence Augustine's dictum, "*Nummi Dei sumus*," we are God's coins, meaning God's seal imprint, our proper place being in God's treasure chest. In contrast, the proper place of coins bearing the face of the prince is in secular treasure chests. See "Nummi Dei sumus. Beiträge zu einer historischen Münzmetaphorik," *Wiener Studien. Zeitschrift für Klassische Philologie und Patristik* 93 (1980), 192–228. On trust as the basis of a money economcy, see Georg Simmel, *The Philosophy of Money*, trans. Tom Bottomore and David B. Frisby (1978; third edn. London-New York: Routledge, 2004), 178, and Joseph A. Schumpeter, *History of Economic Analysis* (London: Allen & Unwin, 1954), 688–95. For money as an "illusion," see Schmölders, *The Psychology of Money and Public Finance*, esp. part 2. The German economist saw money as altogether an "illusion," insofar as members of a community erroneously believe that the money is "theirs," and that therefore they can trust "their money."

57. "These were the times when the demand for Washington's image was most intense [...] and the moral inspiration from even the crudest likeness most deeply felt." Miller and Schwartz, "The Icon of the American Republic," 537.

Chapter 2

1. Foucault, *The Order of Things*, 175–76: "La monnaie n'emprunte point sa valeur de la matière don't elle est compose, mais bien de la forme qui est l'image ou la marque du Prince." Hobbes, *Leviathan*, reprinted from the Edition of 1651, with an Essay by the late W. G. Pogson Smith (Oxford: Clarendon Press, 1909; 1929), 193, 194 (Book II, chapter xxiv).

2. Rizzo, "'Show Me the Money!'" (web document).

3. The absence of precious metal was not merely an American phenomenon. From the eighteenth century, note-issuing banks emerged all over the western world, in an effort to meet the growing demand of currency in economic transactions and investments. And as in the United States, notes were being issued by private banks, under varying degress of government control. René Brion und Jean-Louis Moreau, *A Flutter of Banknotes. From the First European Paper Money to the Euro*, trans. Ian West and Matthew Clarke (Antwerp: Mercatorfonds, 2001), 8.

4. Newman, *Early Paper Money*, 13.

5. "Had there been no paper," Richard Doty argues, "we would now be speaking of the numismatic history of a much smaller, and a much lesser country." *America's Money*, 11.

6. I discuss the issue of confidence in Chapter 6 of my *The Greenback*, especially 166–177.

7. Alexander Del Mar, *The History of Money in America: From the Earliest Times to the Establishment of the Constitution* (New York: Cambridge Encyclopedia Company, 1899), 80.

8. Qtd. in James Thomas Flexner, *George Washington*, 4 vols. (Boston: Little, Brown & Co., 1965–1969), 1:310.

9. "[A] new bond of union," qtd. in Charles A. Kromkowski, *Recreating the American Republic: Rules of Apportionment, Constitutional Change, and American Political Development, 1700–1870* (New York: Cambridge University Press, 2002), 157–58; on this and on colonial paper money in general, see Tschachler, *The Greenback*, 31–33, 94–98. On the consolidation of governmental authority as part of the historic process of nation building, see Wilbur Zelinsky's pioneering studies. European history has in store an interesting historic parallel: After a treaty of customs and commerce between Austria and Prussia had been concluded in 1853, further negotiations should be opened on a universal German coin convention. Negotiations for the convention failed, however, as Prussia insisted on silver currency. Carl Ludwig von Bruck, Austria's treasury secretary from 1855, reached a resumption of the negotiations under the premises of a common silver currency, which was explicitly discussed in terms of an ideological "glue" ("*Kitt*") for a pan-German union. The negotiations were now successful and the treaty contract, the Wiener Münzvertrag, was signed on January 24, 1857. Gabriel, *Ästhetik und Rhetorik des Geldes*, 129–31 and, for further analysis and discussion, Wilhelm Zich, "Der Wiener Münzvertrag vom 24. Januar 1857 und Carl Ludwig von Bruck," Ph. Dissertation, U of Vienna, Faculty of History and Culture Studies (Historisch-Kulturwissenschaftliche Fakultät), 2009, http://othes.univie.ac.at/7155/, October 24, 2016.

10. Joseph J. Ellis, *After the Revolution: Profiles of Early American Culture* (New York: W. W. Norton, 1979), 175, and, for further discussion, Harlow Giles Unger, *Noah Webster: The Life and Times of an American Patriot* (New York: Wiley, 1998). The original title of 1783 was *The First Part of the Grammatical Institute of the English Language*; it was changed to *The American Spelling Book* in 1786, and again in 1829 to *The Elementary Spelling Book*. It was the most popular American book of its time; by 1837, it had sold 15 million copies, and some 60 million by 1890.

11. Qtd. in Irvin, "Benjamin Franklin's 'Enriching Virtues': Continental Currency and the Creation of a Revolutionary Republic," *Common-Place: The Interactive Journal of Early American Life* 6:3 (April 2006), http://www.common-place.org/vol-06/no-03/irvin/, September 11, 2014.

12. *Ibid.* For a complete list of mottoes and emblematic legends, see Newman, *Early Paper Money*, 484–87.

13. Samuel Dexter, *Reminiscences of Samuel Dexter* (Boston: Henry W. Dutton & Son, 1857), 95, https://archive.org/stream/reminiscencesofs-00sarg#page/94/mode/2up, October 14, 2014.

14. Kahler, *The Long Farewell*, 134. Kahler's partial listing of funeral rites runs to approximately 400 for the period December 18, 1799 through March 9, 1800. *Ibid.*, 10–13, 137–49. For an overview of the many forms of observances commemorating Washington's death see a. Schwartz, *American Symbol*, 93–103, and Eliassen, "George Washington, Death, and Mourning."

15. Of this plethora of verse and oratory, a few survive in manuscript, some in the collected works of recognized poets, such as Susanna Rowson, in volumes of Washingtonia and, last but not least, in the University of Freiburg's database "Poems on American Presidents, 1789–1865," Universität Freiburg, n.d., https://presidents.ub.uni-freiburg.de/index.php, July 14, 2017. For "Lady Washington's Lamentation," which is in the possession of the Peabody Essex Museum, Salem, Massachusetts, see Cavitch, "Remembering George Washington," 263. For a discussion of the 346 funeral orations known to have been printed, see Bryan, *Washington in American Literature*, 55–64; for poetic eulogies, see 154–56; for *Washingtons Ankunft in Elisium*, see *ibid.*, 180 and, for the text of the sketch, *Early American Imprints, Series I, 1639–1800*, ed. Charles Evans, no. 39020, Readex, 2017, http://www.readex.com/content/early-american-imprints, October 18, 2017.

16. Max Cavitch cites a poem in which a Pennsylvanian woman, lamenting the king's death, "joins a Nation's sigh." Her "Nation," in 1760, of course was England. "Remembering George Washington," 272*n*18.

17. Penn*sylvania Gazette*, January 8, 1800, qtd. in Schwartz, *American Symbol*, 81.

18. See, for instance, Jacob French's "Mount Vernon Hymn": "What solemn sounds the ear invade, / What wraps this land in sorrow's shade, / From herein the awful mandate flies, / The Father of His Country dies." Qtd. in Elliassen, "Death, and Mourning," 585.

19. Representative Clairborne, in *Annals of Congress*, 1799–1801, 858–59, qtd. in Miller and Schwartz, "The Icon of the American Republic," 529. The statue was to have been an equestrian one; Congress gave the prestigious commission to artist Joseph Wright, who constructed a preparatory bust, then did a portrait, but did not live to complete the statue. Chernow, *Washington*, 508–509.

20. Haxby, RI-560-G14, G16, G18, G34, G42, G52, and G66, and, for further description and analysis, Bowers, *Obsolete Paper Money*, 47–48, and Wick, *George Washington, an American Icon*, 69–70 and 152–54. The notes were non-interest-bearing bills of credit ("promissory notes") issued in denominations of 1, 2, 3, 5, 10, 20, and 25 dollars. The paper had come from Philadelphia. Three original copperplates (respectively of four "one dollar" notes, one "twenty-five dollar" and three "three dollar" notes, and one "ten dollar" and three "five dollar" notes, inscribed with the date 1803) are still owned by the Washington Trust Company in Westerly. It is possible that Doolitle's engraving (after an etching by Joseph Wright) is second only to a "commander-in-chief" portrait engraved by a John Norman in 1799. David McNeeley Stauffer, *American Engravers Upon Copper and Steel*, 3 vols. (1907; repr. London: Forgotten Books, 2013), 2:388.

21. Roger H. Durand, "An Introduction to Obsolete Currency," *America's Currency, 1789–1866*, ed. William E. Metcalf, Coinage of the Americas Conference, Proceedings No.2 (New York: American Numismatic Society, 1986), 57–63, here 60.

22. Foucault, *The Order of Things*, 175–76.

23. Qtd. in Eliassen, "Death, and Mourning," 586.

24. All qtd. in Chernow, *Washington*, 568.

25. Washington, "First Inaugural Address (30 April 1789)," *WWR*, 733. For further discussion of Washington's political philosophy, see Morrison's eponymous book and Nicholas P. Cole, "George Washington and Republican Government: The Political Thought of George Washington," *A Companion to George Washington*, ed. Edward G. Lengel (Malden, MA: Wiley-Blackwell, 2012), 430–46.

26. The coat George Washington wore on the occasion also was a political statement. Its color, brown, was a clear marker of independent republicanism. Moreover, the cloth was home-made, coming from the Hartford Woolen Manufactory, which had been founded by Jeremiah Wadsworth, a former supplier to the Continental Army. Washington was pleased. As he wrote to Henry Knox a mere two weeks before the inauguration, "The cloth & Buttons ... really do credit to the Manufactures of this Country." Qtd. in Gene Tempest, "The President's New Clothes," *American Experience*, February 16, 2017, https://medium.com/americanexperiencepbs/the-presidents-new-clothes-fda9dd72f1e6#.nmsxwrcvc, February 17, 2017. Edward Lengel disputes this account, adding that when Washington visited the manufactory in the fall of 1789, he found that its products were "not of the first quality" (*First Entrepreneur*, 181).

27. MacNeil, *The President's Medal*, 14; George Fuld, "Washington Inaugural Buttons and Helpful Resources," *The Numismatist* 124:11 (November 2011), 46–49; on Washington's aversion to practices that were too "monarchical" for a democratic nation, see Mudd, "Image and Republican Sovereignty," 39, and Stahl, "Capping Liberty."

28. Hamilton, "Report on Establishing a Mint," 154, emphases added.

29. Ann*als of the Congress of the United States*, Second Congress, First Session, 69–72 (January 12, 1792), and 483–88 (March 24, 1792), qtd. in Cunningham, *Popular Images of the Presidency*, 164.

30. Amer*ican Apollo*, qtd. in Tuckerman, *Character and Portraits*, 73.

31. Edward C. Halper, "Aristotle and the Liberal State," in *Aristotle's Politics Today*, ed. Lenn E. Goodman and Robert B. Talisse (Albany, NY: State U of New York Press, 2007), 33–44, here 39–42.

32. Isabella Woldt, "Freiheit," *Handbuch der politischen Ikonographie*, ed. Martin Warnke, Uwe Fleckner, and Hendrik Ziegler, vol. 1 (München: C. H. Beck, 2011), 372–380.

33. William Barton to the Continental Congress, qtd. in Aron, *Why the Turkey Didn't Fly*, 16. When Barton wrote this, in 1782, there was no president; the government of the United States was that of the Articles of Confederation, and the Continental Congress was both the executive and legislative branch. Barton introduced the eagle, but the ultimate source for the national bird, Cornelius Vermeule found, was the Flavian relief set over the door of the Church of the Twelve Apostles (Santi Apostoli) in Rome. The Flavians were emperors of the first century AD. As the followers of Nero, they first engaged in rebuilding the imperial city—hence rebirth seems a legitimate meaning also for the American eagle. Vermeule, *Numismatic Art in America*, 45.

34. Washington had almost made it onto the redesigned five-cent piece in 1909, when the artists of the Mint produced a series of patterns with half-figure busts of him on the obverses. Vermeule describes these patterns as "pedestrian" (*Numismatic Art in America*, 117). The Washington nickel was never produced, though. In 1909, the Mint decided that the cent needed redesigning first; the redesigned nickel had to wait until 1913, when it appeared as the Indian Head or Buffalo nickel. Next in line was the dime, which was redesigned in 1916 and became known as the "Mercury" dime. The quarter did not get a facelift until 1932, the bicentennial of Washington's birth.

35. See United States Department of Veterans Affairs, "Celebrating America's Freedoms," n.d., http://www.va.gov/opa/publications/celebrate/eagle.pdf, January 14, 2016. For illustrations of the coins, see Yeoman, *A Guide Book of United States Coins*.

36. Vermeule, *Numismatic Art in America*, 13–15 and 53–55 (quotations 14, 15); Princeton University Library, "Capping Liberty: The Invention of Numismatic Iconography for the New American Republic," 2012, http://rbsc.princeton.edu/capping-liberty/exhibition/item/3021, April 26, 2017.

37. Linda K. Kerber, *Women in the Republic* (New York: Norton, 1981) and, for further analysis of renderings of Native Americans on the currency, Tschachler, *The Greenback*, 81–87 and "From 'Wildman' to 'True Native American,'" 8–28.

38. Williamson, *Annals of the Congress*, qtd. in Miller und Schwartz, "The Icon of the American Republic," 38–39*n*7 and, for further discussion and anlysis, Mudd, "Image and Republican Sovereignty," 30–32, and Garson, "Counting Money." R. W. Julian offers a useful and eminently readable overview in "All about the Dollar," *The Numismatist* 120:12 (December 2007), 40–52. For a detailed description of the coins issued during the mint's first six months of operation, see Pete Smith et al., *1792: Birth of a Nation's Coinage* (Dallas, TX: Heritage Auctions, 2017).

39. George Washington to William Grayson, *Founders Online*, National Archives, modified June 13, 2018, http://founders.archives.gov/documents/Washington/04-03-02-0182, retrieved July 25, 2018.

40. Thomas Jefferson to George Washington, *Founders Online*, National Archives, modified June 13, 2018, http://founders.archives.gov/documents/Washington/05-11-02-0319. Henry Voigt was the chief coiner at the Mint.

41. On the diverse coin shipments, see Bowers, *Garrett Collection*, 185; for Washington's letter to Congress of November 19, 1794, see *The Writings of George Washington*, ed. Fitzpatrick, 34:28.

42. Edmund Randolph to George Washington, *Founders Online*, National Archives, modified June 13, 2018, http://founders.archives.gov/documents/Washington/05-17-02-0050, retrieved July 25, 2018.

43. Florence Seville Berryman, "Dunsmore's Epic of the American Revolution," *Daughters of the American Revolution Magazine* 60:11 (November 1926), 644–54, and 61:1 (January 1927), 25–33.

44. Raymond H. Robinson, "The Marketing of an Icon," in *George Washington: American Symbol*, ed. Barbara L. Mitnick (New York: Hudson Hills Press, 1999), 109–21, here 110–16.

45. Paul Johnson, *George Washington: The Founding Father* (New York: Atlas Books/Harper Collins, 2005); Albanese, *Sons of the Fathers*, especially Chapter 1, "Our Fathers Who Trod the Wilderness," 19–45.

46. Jefferson, "The Declaration of Independence as Adopted by Congress."

47. Garson, "Counting Money," 23–25, and Mossman, *Money of the American Colonies and Confederation*, 144–50.

48. Washington to Congress, November 16, 1780, qtd. in Felt, *Massachusetts Currency*, 190.

49. *Rivington's Gazette*, May 12, 1781, qtd. in Stephen M. Bivens, "Paper Bullets," *The Numismatist* 101:8 (August 1988), 1382–90, qtd. 1388.

50. Silverman, *A Cultural History of the American Revolution*, 366.

51. Qtd. *ibid.*, 601.

52. Letter to Jabez Bowen, January 9, 1787, *Founders Online*, National Archives, modified June 13, 2018, retrieved July 25, 2018, http://founders.archives.gov/documents/Washington/04-04-02-0428; letter to Thomas Jefferson, August 1, 1786, *Founders Online*, National Archives, modified June 13, 2018, retrieved July 25, 2018, http://founders.archives.gov/documents/Washington/04-04-02-0174.

53. Alexander Del Mar estimated that the total issue of $200,000,000 of Continentals yielded the government what might have been purchased in coin for $36,000,000. A similar ratio applied to the paper issues of the various states. Together with federal and state debts, the total estimated actual cost of eight years' war was some $140,000,000—a real bargain when compared with the $9,194 million that the Civil War would cost. Del Mar, *Gold Money or Paper Money* (New York: Anson D.F. Randolph, 1863), 23. J. W. Schuckers, *Finances and Paper Money of the Revolutionary War* (Philadelphia: J. Campbell & Son, 1874; repr. New York: S. J. Durst, 1978), 109, estimated the cost of the Revolution from $170,000,000 to $180,000,000.

Chapter 3

1. Qtd. in Bray Hammond, *Sovereignty and an Empty Purse: Banks and Politics in the Civil War* (Princeton, NJ: Princeton University Press, 1970), 92–93.

2. On the debates and the final passage in the Constitution, see Hurst, *A Legal History of Money in the United States*, 8–14 and 135–36.

3. For an overview, see George Fuld, "Early Washington Medals," *American Journal of Numismatics*, Second Series 14 (2002), 106, Table 1.

4. Cunningham, *Popular Images of the Presidency*, 164–65. For further description and discussion, see Russell Rulau and George Fuld, *Medallic Portraits of Washington* (Iola, WI: Krause, 1985), 37–37, and George Fuld, "The Washington Manly Medal Revisited," *The Numismatist* 121:10 (October 2008), 48–55

5. "Washington Before Boston" pieces are still produced today. During the first years of the Civil War, the medal, as well as several others from the "Comitia Americana" series were restruck in a copper/tin alloy used primarily for casting bells, hence "bell-metal." See Craig Sholley, "The Curious Tale of the Comitia Americana Gunmetal Restrikes," *The Nunismatist* 131:8 (August 2018), 63–71.

6. "Triumpho" is a verb and should not be translated as "triumphant." More appropriately, it means "I triumph" or even "I rejoice greatly." "Georgius Triumpho" therefore would be something like "I, George, rejoice [in a triumph gained]." Martin Purdy, "More on George," *The Numismatist* 130:1 (January 2017), 14.

7. There is a caveat, though. According to Purdy ("More on George," 14), the legend "Voce populi" also is found on Irish tokens from 1760, surrounding a bust that might (or might not) be George III.

8. Q. David Bowers, "George on My Mind," *The Numismatist* 129:10 (October 2016), 117–118, qtd. 118 and, for further description and discussion, Mossman, *Money of the American Colonies and Confederation*, 136–37. The story that the "Georgius Triumpho" tokens circulated widely in Georgia, Virginia, and Florida, but because of the distaste for the George III-like bust many were mutilated and shipped to Jamaica is apocryphal. In contrast, the story about a halfpenny authorized by the colony of Virginia in 1773 is fact-based, as is the striking similarity between the halfpenny and the "Georgius Triumpho" copper. While the inscription "GEORGIUS" is identical and in the same place on both coins, on the Virginia coin the inscription at right reads "III. REX" and "TRIUMPHO." The Virginia Halfpenny was struck in London. When the first shipload reached America, the War of Independence was underway, and the colony's treasurer did not dare to issue the coins without explicit approval from London. After the approval finally arrived, the coins instantly disappeared in chests and other hiding places. They reappeared after Yorktown, together with the coins of the new nation.

9. The coins are known as "Ugly Head" cents. Fuld, "Coinage Featuring George Washington," 168–69.

10. The coins are known as "IMMUNIS COLUMBIA"; a variant had an eagle reverse. Fuld, "Coinage Featuring George Washington," 169–70; Yeoman, *Guide Book*, 54.

11. Fuld, "Coinage Featuring George Washington," 173. Barry Schwartz renders the inscription as "I prevailed not by might, but by virtue" (*American Symbol*, 149). It has also been rendered, rather unfortunately, as "Not by force but by virtue we have won." For illustrations of Washington tokens go to University of Notre Dame Special Collections at http://www.coins.nd.edu/WashToken/.

12. For an illustration of a "Perkins Funeral Medal," see the Department of Special Collections, University of Notre Dame, "Perkins Funeral Medal—1800," n.d., http://www.coins.nd.edu/WashToken/WashTokenText/1800.html, February 17, 2017. For further description and discussion, see Ray Williams, "'He Is in Glory.' Washington medals commended the country's first official leader," *The Numismatist* 131:2 (February 2018), 67–68. Max Cavitch cites a contemporary letter in which Thomas Dwight, a United States Representative from Massachusetts, tells his wife about the acquisition, during a Washington mourning ceremony in Boston, of "four Washington medals of white metal," intended as souvenirs for his daughter, his two sons, and a nephew. "Remembering George Washington," 274*n*42.

13. The first reference work on Washington medals was James Ross Snowden's *A Description of the Medals of Washington*, published in 1861 when Snowden was in his last year as director of the U.S. Mint. A long-standard reference in the field was William S. Baker's *Medallic Portraits of Washington*, first published in 1885. For over a century, Washington medals were known by their Baker numbers. Ever since the publication, in 2016, of Neil Musante's two-volume *Medallic Washington*, it has become common to use Musante GW numbers. For a brief overview see Joseph A. Esposito, "Collecting Washington Medals: A Sampler," *The Numismatist* 131:2 (February 2018), 32–35 and, for a balance of the early Washington medals starting with the funderal issues until the death of Lafayette in 1834, Fuld, "Early Washington Medals," 126–27, Table 2.

14. Fuld, "Early Washington Medals," 105–63; Alan M. Stahl, "American Indian Peace Medals of the Colonial Period," *Money of Pre-Federal America*, ed. John M. Kleeberg, Coinage of the Americas Conference Proceedings, Number 7 (New York: American Numismatic Society, 1992), 159–80; and Vermeule, *Numismatic Art in America*, 19. On the Perkins medal, see Bowers, *Obsolete Paper Money*, 52–53.

15. The Washington portrait was designed by John G. Hancock. Hancock's design had already been used for the Washington Eagle Cents of 1791, but it was the "Ship Halfpenny" that gave it its widest circulation. For an illustration of the "Ship Halfpenny," see Department of Special Collections, University of Notre Dame, "The Washington Ship Halfpenny of 1793," n.d., http://www.coins.nd.edu/ColCoin/ColCoinText/WashSHIP.html, February 17, 2017. On English-made coins of the Confederation period,

see Fuld, "Coinage Featuring George Washington," 176–83, and 205–11.

16. Among numismatists, Hancock's designs are called "Hancock's Revenge" or, more formally, "Roman Head" pieces. Fuld, "Coinage Featuring George Washington," 190–92, and for Hancock's original submissions, 192–96.

17. See, for description and further discussion of the "Getz" coins, Fuld, "Coinage Featuring George Washington," 183–90; and Stahl, "Capping Liberty."

18. Qtd. in Irvin, "Benjamin Franklin's '*Enriching Virtues*,'" web document. For an interpretation of Franklin's currency amidst his many symbols of American identity and in the context of other national symbols from the Revolutionary period, see Lester C. Olson, *Emblems of American Community in the Revolutionary Era: A Study in Rhetorical Iconology* (Washington, DC: Smithsonian Institute Press, 1991); for a broader perspective on Revolutionary culture, see Silverman, *A Cultural History of the American Revolution.*

19. Reference to "Lord of Commodities" is to Karl Marx, *A Contribution to the Critique of Political Economy* [1859], trans. W. I. Stone (Chicago: Charles H. Kerr, 1904), 166.

20. Qtd. in Victor Annaloro, "An Argument for Presidential Portraits," *The Numismatist* 118:9 (September 2005), 56–57, qtd. 56. The *Columbian Centinel* was printed and published by Benjamin Russell of Boston, Massachusetts. Russell was a veteran of the Continental Army and, in 1812, became a founding member of the American Antiquarian Society.

21. NGC (Numismatic Guaranty Corporation) Coin Explorer, "1792 Eagle & Stars Gold Washington President $10 M," January 8, 2018, https://www.ngccoin.com/coin-explorer/early-american-washington-pieces-1783-1795-pscid-123/1792-eagle-and-stars-gold-washington-president-10-m-coinid-108388, August 1, 2018. The coin, which was last owned by the late Eric P. Newman, was sold for $1,740,000.00 by Heritage Auction in Philadelphia on August 16, 2018.

22. Two subsequent acts, respectively passed in 1837 and 1873, repeat the mandatory use of the liberty emblem and wording. The act of 1873 also stipulates that all coins bear not only the inscription "In God We Trust" but also "E Pluribus Unum," most likely to emphasize the idea of national unity after the catastrophe of the Civil War. Nussbaum, *A History of the Dollar*, 134 and, for the original passage concerning the president's representation, "The Law of the Dollar," *Columbia Law Review* 37:7 (November 1937), 1057–91, here 1071.

23. In 1796, for instance, the English firm Kemson and Sons sent samples for the struggling Federal mint in Philadelphia. Called "Repub. Ameri." pennies, the coins showed a profile bust of George Washington in presidential garments, "George Washington" around, and 1796 in the exergue. Fuld, "Coinage Featuring George Washington," 214–15.

24. Quite a few of the privately issued tokens were restrikes of Washington coinage from the Confederation period. The practice continued well into the early nineteenth century; some of these pieces ("non-contemporary Washington coinage" in numismatic lingo) were in circulation until the 1850s. Fuld, "Coinage Featuring George Washington," 216–41.

25. On the overstamping of U.S. coins by the Bank of England, see Andy Smith, "Making a Mark," *The Numismatist* 127:10 (October 2014), 3. (One such overstamped coins was recently sold at auction for $110,000.)

26. Senate Select Committee, *The New American State Papers: Public Finance, ed.* Sidney Ratner (Wilmington, DE: Scholarly Resources, 1972), 27:292.

27. The *Journals and Miscellaneous Note Books of Ralph Waldo Emerson*, ed. Merton M. Sealts, Jr., vol. 5, *1835–1838* (Cambridge, MA: Belknap P of Harvard University Press, 1965), 334.

28. A recent study by Philip F. Gura, *Man's Better Angels: Romantic Reformers and the Coming of the Civil War* (Cambridge, MA: Belknap P of Harvard University Press, 2017), invites us to see Brook Farm and similar communal experiments in this way.

29. Harry Levin, *The Power of Blackness* (Columbus: Ohio University Press, 1960), 32 and, for further discussion and analysis of Jackson's "bank war" and its reverberations in American literature, Tschachler, *The Monetary Imagination of Edgar Allan Poe*, 29–30, 71–74, 80–98, and 148–55.

30. The notes issued by private financial institutions are now "obsolete," declared invalid during the Civil War era. In contrast, all notes issued since 1861 are still legal tender; you can still use them to do your grocery shopping, although this may not be such a hot idea—among collectors, their value usually is way beyond their denominational value.

31. During Andrew Jackson's bank war, Senator Daniel Webster alluded to Washington's stand on monetary matters, particularly a national bank, in at least four speeches, the first made at Wheeling, Virginia, in 1837. Bryan, *Washington in American Literature*, 69–70.

32. E. James Ferguson, *The Power of the Purse: A History of American Public Finance, 1776–1790* (Chapel Hill: University of North Carolina Press, 1961), 118–24.

33. Alexander Hamilton, "Final Version of the Second Report on the Further Provision Necessary for Establishing Public Credit (Report on a National Bank), December 13, 1790," *Founders Online*, National Archives, last modified June 13, 2018, http://founders.archives.gov/documents/Hamilton/01-07-02-0229-0003, retrieved July 26, 2018.

34. Washington, "Farewell Address," *WWR*, 972.

35. The amount of specie in circulation was $48 million in 1813 and $28 million in 1836; again in 1836 there were some $45 million in specie in banks. Treasury Reports qtd. in Krooss, *Documentary History of Banking and Currency*, 1: 266; 2: 130. Milton Friedman and Anna Jacobson Schwartz provide slightly different figures in *Monetary Statistics of the United States: Estimates, Sources, Methods* (Cambridge, MA: National Bureau of Economic Research, 1970), 214–59.

36. For a table correlating banking, the growth of the money supply and the growth of the population for the period 1830–1860, see Davies, *A History of Money*, 484.

37. *Whitman*, 1:1–3 and, for the Cass County Bank, 1:10.

38. Journals like *Paper Money* (published by the Society of Paper Money Collectors), *The Numismatist* (the official journal of the American Numismatic Association), or *The Bank Note Reporter* (by Krause Publications) are valuable sources of information. James Haxby's four-volume *Standard Catalog of U.S. Obsolete Bank Notes* (1988; CD_ROM edn. 2009) is essential reading, as is Q. David Bowers' *Whitman Encyclopedia of Obsolete Paper Money* (8 volumes by July 2017). Gene Hessler's *The Engraver's Line* has much useful information about the people who created the artwork and designs. Roger Durand published a series of monographs in the *Interesting Notes* series, including three volumes *About Portraits*.

39. In 1702, John Coney of Boston engraved plates with a bit more artistic imagination and a different state seal. Hessler, *The Engraver's Line*, 1 and, for further discussion of the documentary style of early paper money, Lauer, "Money as Mass Communication," 114–16, and—per English and British paper bills—David Blaazer, "Reading the Notes: Thoughts on the Meaning of British Paper Money," *Humanities Research* 1 (Canberra, AUS, 1999), 39–53.

40. See Tschachler, *The Greenback*, 44–48.

41. Hurle, "Abstractions of Value," 30–36, quotation 32. On lathework see also Tomasko, *The Feel of Steel*, 70–72. Good examples of Washington-related bank notes using machine-engraving are the $1 notes issued by the Metropolitan Bank, New York, New York, in the 1850s-1860s: the notes bear a central oval portrait of Washington in a large round die, with "ONE DOLLAR" arched above. Haxby, NY-1775-G2, G2b, G2c.

42. Rizzo, "'Show Me the Money!'" (web document).

43. Doty, *Dictionary of Numismatics*, 138; and see the exhibition catalog *Money and Beauty: Bankers, Botticelli and the Bonfire of the Vanities*, ed. Ludovia Sebregondi and Tim Parks (Florence, Italy: Giunti, 2011).

44. This may strike one as quaint. If anything, the schilling should have been called the "Alpine mark," which it really was, because of numerous policies, in the past, of tying it to the deutschmark. Yet such was then the actual power and reputation of the United States that the name of its currency was adopted, in colloquial parlance, for Austria's native currency. For a bitingly satirical commentary on the iconography of the Schilling, see Robert Menasse, *Das Land ohne Eigenschaften. Essay zur österreichischen Identität* (Frankfurt am Main: Suhrkamp, 1995).

45. Eric P. Newman, "Unusual Printing Features on Early American Paper Money," *Money of Pre-Federal America*, ed. John M. Kleeberg, Coinage of the Americas Conference Proceedings No. 7 (New York: American Numismatic Society, 1992), 59–83 and, for illustrations of Franklin's "nature printing," Doty, *America's Money*, 33, and 39.

46. Muscalus, *Index of State Bank Notes*, 1–12. For the 6¼¢ notes from the Farmers Bank of the State of Delaware, see Haxby, DE-15-G8 and G12, G108, G112, and G116. The denomination of 6¼¢ was a result of the confusion in the British currency system. Since one dollar usually went for 7s and 6d, that is, 84 pence, the 6¼¢ would have been the equivalent of 5d and 1 farthing. Haxby lists neither the Baltimore Savings Institution (see *Whitman*, 8:174–76), nor the Washington County Savings Institution (see *Whitman*, 8:320–21), nor the Taylorsville Delaware Bridge Co., though several institutions issued 6¼¢ notes between the 1810s and 1830s, including the Bank of Augusta, Augusta, Georgia (GA-30-G2, from 1816), the Bank of Maryland (MD-95-G4 and G4a) and the New Hope Delaware Bridge Co. (PA-355-GW), albeit without portraits of Washington. No notes featuring George Washington are on record for Arizona, California, Colorado, Hawaii, Idaho, Montana, Nevada, New Mexico, North Dakota, Oregon, South Dakota, Washington State, Wyoming, and West Virginia, as statehood came only *after* the era of private banking.

47. Haxby, respectively DC70-G2, etc. (Bank of Commerce); RI-430-G2a, etc. (Washington County Bank); MS-25-G12, etc. (Mississippi & Alabama Railroad Company's Bank); RI-360-G12a, etc. (National Bank); VA-145-G5a, etc. (Exchange Bank of Virginia, 1850s-60s); MA-395-G10, etc. (Washington Bank, 1840s-60s).

48. *Whitman*, 1:141. Individual banks mentioned in this paragraph are listed in Muscalus, *Index of State Bank Notes* 1–12. For Haxby's classification, see respectively GA-30-G42, etc. (Bank of Augusta); MA-785-G44, etc. (Lynn Mechanics Bank); NY-1980-G4, etc. (Highland Bank); PA-185-G28, etc. (Farmers Bank); KY-175-G6, etc. (Northern Bank of Kentucky); PA-475-G20, etc. (Bank of Penn Township); RI-560-G14, etc. (Washington Bank, Westerly).

49. Ross Barrett, "Capital Likenesses: George Washington, the Federal City, and Economic Selfhood in American Portraiture," The Edgar P. Richardson Symposium: New Perspectives on Portraiture at the National Portrait Gallery, Washington, DC, September 20, and September 21, 2018, Day 1, Session 2, YouTube. November 19, 2018, https://www.youtube.com/watch?v=HvCl-PDYwH4&feature=youtu.be, November 21, 2018. Barrett, an art historian at Boston University, also shows that the notes' images tapped into a deeply rooted body of portrait images—most notably Edward Savage's *The Washington Family* and, much less known, Josef Perovani's *George Washington*—that aligned Washington not only with a successful revolution but also with the liberal economic ideals and the speculative ethos of American capitalism. I discuss Savage's artworks in my *Political Fatherhood*, chapter 7.

50. Haxby, NJ-438-G2 (and *Whitman*, 1:141); Haxby, VA-200-G60; CT-100-G90 (and *Whitman*, 2:46). Notes from the Potomac Savings Bank and the Mechanics and Traders Bank are not listed in Haxby (see *Whitman*, 8:155–56 and 2:657). Additional examples of equestrian vignettes are on record from

the Manufacturing & Banking Company, Hoboken, New Jersey ($3 notes, 1820s, Haxby, NJ-210-G34); the Fulton Bank, New York, New York ($2 notes, 1820s, Haxby, NY-1620-G8); and the Bank of Norwalk, Norwalk, Ohio ($1 notes, 1830s to mid-1840s, Haxby, OH-350-G6, G6a).

51. Haxby, NJ-340-G40; MS-135-G18 (the $100 notes are not listed in Haxby, thus see *Whitman*, 7:424). The identical vignette was used also on $5 notes from the Piscataqua Bank, Portsmouth, New Hampshire, 1830s (Haxby, NH-280-G38), and on $50 notes from the Washington County Bank, Williamsport, Maryland, 1830s–1850s (Haxby, MD-325-G24).

52. Haxby, NJ-60-G16 and G16a.

53. The notes from the State Bank in Trenton are worthy of mention also because of the production technology—Jacob Perkins' siderography, a way of transferring impressions from a steel plate to a steel cylinder in a rolling press, which made possible the almost unlimited and, above all, identical reproduction of steel printing plates. For a description of the process, which was a milestone in the development of counterfeit-proof bank notes, see Doty, *America's Money*, 82–86 and, for an illustration of a Perkins plate note, 85.

54. The note was produced by Draper, Toppan, Longacre & Co., New York. Haxby, MI-385-G12; Bowers, *Obsolete Paper Money*, 208; *Whitman*, 1:138.

55. Haxby, respectively NJ-260-G12 and G12a, and MD-100-G52. For the Mississippi banks bearing the vignette on notes issued in the 1830s, see Haxby, respectively MS-10-G16, MS-75-G14 and G14a, MS-80-G14 (illustration in *Whitman*, 7:398), MS-110-G40a, MS-120-G12, MS-140-G22, and MS-195-G12. Banks in Virginia also featured the "Washington seated" vignette, as see *Whitman*, 8:512 and 519.

56. Haxby, ME-225-G8; VT-130-G10 (illustration in *Whitman*, 5:397); NY-1550-G10, G10b; NH-190-G30 (illustration in *Whitman*, 2:627).

57. Haxby, NH-230-G6 (illustration in *Whitman*, 2:641); the identical vignette was used on $10 notes from the Northampton Bank, Northampton, Massachusetts (MA-956-G52a). Haxby (2:1227) identifies the old man as Benjamin Franklin, which makes sense. Franklin (together with Thomas Jefferson) had commissioned Jean-Antoine Houdon to create a marble statue of Washington. A Washington bust created in 1785 (it lives on on the Washington Quarter) was part of the artist's preparation. On Houdon's celebrated masterpiece, see John S. Hallam, "Houdon's Richmond Statue of Washington," *American Art Journal* 10 (November 1978), 73–80, and Tschachler, *Political Fatherhood*, chapter 5.

58. Haxby, MI-125-G6. The worthy bank was one of those inspected and found wanting in 1838. Bowers, *Obsolete Paper Money*, 247 and, for a detail, *Whitman*, 1:142.

59. Haxby, IL-740-G46; VT-70-G8 (illustration and a note not listed in Haxby in *Whitman*, 5:365); PA-700-G88 (the notes are dated July 4, 1825); IL-235-G6a; IL-520-G4a.

60. Haxby, PA-155-G64. The notes from the DC bank were issued in denominations of $5, $10, $20, $50, and $100. Haxby, DC-70-G2 to G10, and, for an illustration of a $20 note, *Whitman*, 1:141. S1 notes with the identical vignette were issued by the Hartford Bank, Hartford, Connecticut; see *Whitman*, 2:86 (not listed in Haxby). A variant of this vignette, with Liberty at left and two female allegories (possibly representing Truth and Justice) at right, appeared on $100 notes from the Sugar River Bank, Newport, New Hampshire, in the 1850s (Haxby, NH-235-G16, illustration in *Whitman*, 2:644).

61. Haxby, VT-240-G44, G4a (*Whitman*, 5:454), and VT115-G10 (*Whitman*, 5:388).

62. Haxby, NJ-60-G12a; *Whitman*, 1:141.

63. Haxby, MA-325-G12, RI-505-G6a; the latter notes reappeared as altered notes under the name of the Farmers & Mechanics Bank in Camden, New Jersey. Haxby, NJ-60-A25; *Whitman*, 1:142.

64. Haxby, DC-170–10a and 10b; the bank failed in 1862.

65. Haxby, MA-785-G148a, 148b; VT-40-G10a; LA-15-G48a and, for an illustration of the vignette, Doty, *Pictures from a Distant Country*, 25.

66. Haxby, NY-2995-G48; IN-270-G4 and G4a; ME-415-G10 (for an illustration see *Whitman*, 2:444); OH-75-G36a.

67. Haxby, CT-280-G52 and G56 (*Whitman*, 1:143).

68. Haxby, OH-75-G24; SC-50-S5a (ill. in *Whitman*, 6:429, as W-SC-170–005-S010).

69. Haxby, MD-215-G36 and NH-285-G10 (*Whitman*, 8:300, 1:143, and 2:664).

70. Haxby, DC-260-G8 (*Whitman*, 8:137). Equally unusual is the roster of portraits on notes from the Hamilton Bank, Baltimore, Maryland. Issued in denominations of $5, $10, $20, $50, and $100, they all had Hamilton at center, and Charles Carroll, George Washington, and Robert Fulton at left, and an unknown male portrait, Benjamin Franklin, and Robert Morris at right. The Bank was chartered in 1836 but lost its charter in 1840. *Whitman*, 8:228–29; Haxby, MD-80-G4, G6, and G8; of the $50 and $100 notes (G10, G12) none are known.

71. It is also possible to interpret the fusion of two and three as the Pythagorean symbol of synthesis or wedding. On the numerology of "5" see Ingrid Riedel, *Bilder in Therapie, Kunst und Religion. Wege zur Interpretation* (Stuttgart: Kreuz Verlag, 1988), 195–97. *Whitman* (1:213) provides an illustration of a generic back of Ormsby's design. Among the banks that issued such notes was the Mousam River Bank in Sanford, Maine, one of the many pseudo-banks. Similar notes were issued by the State Bank of Lecompton, Kansas Territory, except that the notes' front was graced by five cherubs arranged on an arch (the bank probably never opened). Haxby, KS-G8a (illustrations in Bowers, *Obsolete Paper Money*, 296, 304). The similarity of the five circles to the famous Salzburg Mozartkugels (balls of marzipan and praline coated in chocolate) is, of course, purely coincidental.

72. *Whitman*, 1:231, and Bowers, *Obsolete Paper Money*, 531.

Part II

1. Doty, *Pictures from a Distant Country*, 146–45. Asher Durand designed numerous denominations, from $1 to $1000, all with the identical Washington vignette. The notes went through several issues, unregistered (1829 to 1840s), registered (through 1856), and free bank (1857–66). Because the notes looked so much alike, they were all too often counterfeited or raised. Haxby, NY-1785-G2, etc.

2. George Bennet to his mother, April 15, 1783, *The Writings of George Washington*, 26:321n. Almost two centuries later, another visitor from England described Washington as essentially a figure "of the *eighteenth* century," holding a "dual citizenship," at once English and Roman. Cunliffe, *George Washington*, 160, 162 and, for further description and analysis of the "classical code" Washington followed, 161–67.

3. There is a caveat, though, formulated by Ron Chernow, in that the unremitting emphasis on *Cato* as being Washington's favorite play has obscured his love of many other plays, most notably ribald comedies such as Sheridan's *School for Scandal*. See *Washington*, 126. Ironically, *Cato* seems to have been the favorite play also of George III. Marcus Cunliffe, "The Two Georges: The President and the King," *American Studies International* 24:2 (October 1986), 53–73, here 59. On *Seneca's Morals* as a source of inspiration for Washington, see Brookhiser, *Founding Father*, 122–23.

Chapter 4

1. Cunliffe, *George Washington*, 165.

2. The token is listed as #5 in Baker's *Medallic Portraits of Washington*, revised by Rulau and Fuld in 1985 and in a 2nd edition published in 1999. Stacks replicated the obverse for their 50th anniversary storecards in 1985, using original dies from the Smithsonian Institution's National Numismatic Collection. Mark Fox, "The Washington & Independence Tokens," *The Numismatist* 125:7 (July 2012), 35–44, here 40.

3. Baker, *Medallic Portraits of Washington*, #1.

4. The vignette reappeared on $5 notes from the City Bank of New Orleans in the 1840s (Haxby, LA-20-G14b and 14c), and from the Union Bank of Louisiana, New Orleans, in the 1850s (Haxby, LA-150-G2a).

5. Haxby, respectively MI-130-G6; RI-115-G32, G44, G68 and G68a (the Mount Vernon Bank relocated to Providence in 1854), and RI-276-G62.

6. Haxby, SC-45-G16.

7. *Ibid.*, MA-190-G80. The note is a typical example of the many Patent Stereotype Steel Plate (PSSP) issues from banks in Massachusetts. The Washington vignette was engraved by Asher B. Durand. Hessler, *The Engraver's Line*, 109. The original marble statue, which dates from 1826, is the work of Sir Francis Chantrey. It was the first statue to be placed in the State House. On Webster's Federalist stand on money matters, see Bryan, *Washington in American Literature*, 69–70.

8. Haxby, respectively FL-35-G2; MI-130-G6; MI-420-G2; NJ-365-G8; GA-180-G20; VT-165-G28 (illustration in *Whitman*, 5:416); MS-195-G24; NY-1845-G16; and FL-70-G10. On the notes from the Bank of Mississippi, the vignette appears on both left and right. For the Mount Vernon Bank, see *ibid.*, RI-115-G68, G68a. The notes from the Bank of Selma are not listed in Haxby, but see *Whitman*, 7:42; also not listed are the notes from the Bank of Potomac (Haxby, DC-30 / VA-20; *Whitman*, 8:60, 370). Additionally, the Massachusetts State House statue of George Washington standing appeared on $5 notes issued by the Confederate States of America in August 1861. Friedberg and Friedberg, *Paper Money of the United States*, 242, as CS-31

9. Haxby, VT-40-G10a (*Whitman*, 1:141). For the Louisiana notes, see Haxby, LA-15-G48a, and *Whitman*, 7:276. On $5 notes issued by the Dover Bank, Dover, New Hampshire, in the 1840s to 1850, Washington modestly looks the other way, lest he be tempted by the two fetching females at right and the two allegorical figures wrapped in diaphanous scarfs at upper left. Haxby, NH-61-G16, illustration in *Whitman*, 2:567. Temptation is also evident from $50 notes from the Park Bank, New York, New York, 1850s, though again Washington chastely turns away from the semi-nude female allegories depicted on them. Haxby, NY-1865-G14 and G14a.

10. Enough nudity to support that theory was provided by $1 notes from the Bank of Syracuse, Syracuse, New York, 1840s to 1860s. Haxby, NY-2655-G2 through G2e.

11. For illustrations, see Haxby, NH-80-G4-G4c, and Bowers, *Obsolete Paper Money*, 452.

12. Haxby, CT-275-G2 to G2b; *Whitman*, 1:141. The notes are imprinted "Seropyan's Patent 1856" at the border below Washington's portrait. The "Patent" refers to certain chemical methods said to prevent counterfeiting by photographic, anastatic, photo-lithographic, transfer, and other nefarious practices. Seropyan's system, Q. David Bowers explains, was used by relatively few banks and, moreover, was found utterly useless by a committee representing New England's banks. *Ibid.*, 1:216.

13. Henry "Light Horse Harry" Lee was a major general in the Continental Army, a member of the Continental Congress, governor of Virginia, and a close friend of George Washington. Lee's eulogy was commissioned by Congress upon Washington's death in 1799. Bryan, *Washington in American Literature*, 63–64. For an illustration of notes from the Presidents Bank, see Haxby, DC-340-G2, and *Whitman*, 8:156.

14. Another dubious enterprise was the Bank of the Republic, Providence, Rhode Island, which gained a repuation from sending vast amounts of notes (including $1 notes with Washington's portrait as the central vignette) out of state, which made it difficult for the notes to ever be redeemed, leaving the bank with immediate profit. Haxby, RI-385-G2 and G2a; *Whitman*, 5:141.

15. Haxby, MA-120-G2, G2a (for an additional note, see *Whitman* 3:78); MA-645-G2 (for unlisted notes, see *Whitman* 3:347).

16. For discussions of these nefarious practices, see Tschachler, *The Greenback*, 51, 185–87; Mihm, *A Nation of Counterfeiters*; and David R. Johnson, *Illegal Tender: Counterfeiting and the Secret Service in Nineteenth-Century America* (Washington, DC: Smithsonian Institution Press, 1995).

17. Haxby, PA-540-G8 and, for illustrations, *Whitman*, 1:165, 166. On several notes from the Iron Bank, Falls Village, Connecticut, Washington nobilitates the mining and manufacturing of iron; on $3 notes from the Traders Bank, Bangor, Maine, his portrait lends prestige to forest-clearing; on $5 notes from the Somersworth Bank, Somersworth, New Hampshire, he is connected to plowing a field with horses. In 1862, the Milwaukee County Bank, Milwaukee, Wisconsin, began issuing $10 notes with a large medallion portrait of Washington at left, the denomination "TEN" arched above and below; at center is a view of Niagara Falls, as if the first president was the patron saint of the nascent tourist industry. Haxby, CT-120-G2 and G2c, G14 and G14c; ME-135-G6; NH-330-G8a and G8b (for illustrations, see *Whitman*, 2:61, 342, and 687), WI-515-G4.

18. Haxby, MA-1275-G8a; for illustrations of this and a note unlisted in Haxby, see *Whitman*, 3:330; Washington is paired with a railroad train also on $1 notes from the Bank of Cayuga Lake, Ithaca, New York, 1847, and on $5 notes from the Jefferson County Bank, Watertown, Wisconsin, mid-1850s. Haxby, NY-1070-G2; WI-820-G6 through G6d.

19. Haxby, RI-100-G46. A good example of these paintings is Lilly Martin Spencer's *Domestic Happiness* (1849), which shows a glowing couple watching their two small children sleep. A light shines beatifically on the children, happy in each other's arms. The mother holds up one arm to her husband's chest in a gesture of intimacy that links husband and wife together physically. But the story of domestic happiness was, as Anne McClintock argues, a master narrative that pasted over the contradictions of actual families, erasing their relations to the "commodity market," to "politics," and even to "history proper." McClintock, *Imperial Leather: Race, Gender and Sexuality in the Colonial Contest* (New York: Routledge, 1995), 357. Photographers also worked with articulations of family and nation. And, in the words of Laura Wexler, they too were "haunted" by the iconic image of George Washington. Wexler, "Techniques of the Imaginary Nation: Engendering Family Photography," in *Looking for America: The Visual Production of Nation and People*, ed. Ardis Cameron (Malden, MA: Blackwell, 2005), 94–117, here 103. See Tschachler, *Political Fatherhood*, chapter 8.

20. Haxby, GA-145-G6 and G6a.

21. Haxby, PA-475-G50a; DC-170-G8a; G8b, issued in 1862, has the famous green tint on the back. For a colorful illustration, see Bowers, *Obsolete Paper Money*, 408. A detail of the Bank of Penn Township note is in *Whitman*, 1:179. For a Mount Vernon Cemetery medallion engraved by Charles Burt, see Hessler, *The Engraver's Line*, 75.

22. Haxby, MA-565-G84a. The Washington bust was engraved by Charles Burt.

23. Haxby, DC-385; *Whitman*, 8:112–14 (Bank of Washington); Haxby, DC-60 (Central Bank of Georgetown and Washington), DC-320 (Patriotic Bank of Washington), DC-85 (Farmers Bank), DC-390 (Washington Bank), DC-395 (Washington City Bank), DC-400 (Western Bank of Washington), DC-380 (Virginia Bank of Washington City).

24. Wolka, "Caught in a Lie," *The Numismatist* 131:2 (February 2018), 65–66. For the George Washington Bank, see *Whitman*, 3:240. All other references to banks in this paragraph follow Haxby's numbering system: Washington Bank, Westerly, Rhode Island (RI-560); Washington County Banks—Calais, ME (ME-250), Williamsport, MD (MD-325), Union Village, NY (NY-2770), Richmond, RI (RI-430); Banks of Washington—Lebanon, KY (KY-160; and *Whitman*, 7:140), Washington, NC (NC-85), Washington, PA (PA-690 and PA-685 for Franklin Bank of Washington); Washington Banks—Boston, MA (MA-395), City of New York (NY-1965), Miamisburg, OH (OH-295); Bank of Washington and Warren, Sandy Hill, NY (NY-2494), Washington and Warren Bank (NY-2495); Lake Washington and Deer Creek Rail Road and Banking Company, Princeton, MS (MS-1901); Washington Banking Company, Hacksensack, NJ (NJ-180); George Washington Bank, Corning, NY (NY-710); Farmers Bank of Washington County, Fort Edward, NY (NY-865, though George Washington does not appear on any of the bank's notes); Freemen's Bank of Washington County, Hebron, NY (NY-1010); Franklin's Bank of Washington, Washington, PA (PA-685); Bank of Ohio, Guernsey branch in Washington County (OH-5).

25. Muscalus, *Index of State Bank Notes*, 2, 4, and 10; Haxby, respectively IN-435-G6, G6a, and G8 and G8a; MA-300-G4a and G10a; and RI-115-G32, G44, G68 and G68a (the bank relocated to Providence in 1854). An additional Mount Vernon Bank, operating from Mount Vernon, Ohio, is listed only in Haxby (OH-305), though it is impossible to establish whether Washington is featured on the short-lived bank's notes, which were issued only in the 1860s.

26. Haxby, NH-295-G28 and G124 and, for illustrations, Bowers, *Obsolete Paper Money*, 457. The Treaty of Paris of 1783 terminated the American War of Independence; it was signed by John Jay, Benjamin Franklin, and John Adams. In 1787–1788 Jay also contributed, with James Madison and Alexander Hamilton, to the *Federalist Papers*.

27. Haxby, MA-660-G18. $100 bills from the City Bank of New Haven, Connecticut, also carried a portrait of George Washington (Haxby, CT-265-G92 and G92c, and *Whitman*, 1:220). The notes date from the 1850s; later notes had a large red "100" overprint on the back, which served as a "counterfeit protector."

28. Haxby, TN-100-G22a and G64a; for a good illustration, see Tomasko, *Images of Value*, 33.

29. Haxby, GA-30-G112 and, for a good illustration, Tomasko, *The Feel of Steel*, 5.

30. Haxby, respectively RI-276-G62 (Commercial Bank), NJ-350-G84 and 84a (State Bank of New Brunswick), NY-1865-G18, G60 (Chatham Bank), MA-415-G22 (Brighton Market Bank), MA-550-G18 (Lechmere Bank). For a more exhaustive list, see Muscalus, *Index of State Bank Notes*, 3–10.

31. Haxby, LA-105-G78a, and TN-210-G26, G80, G120, G160, and G238. Also noteworthy are the $1000 notes from the Continental Bank in New York City, 1850s, which showed both an engraving of the surrender of Cornwallis and a Stuart portrait of Washington at right. See *Ibid.*, NY-1550-G20 and 20b. For a more exhaustive list, see Muscalus, *Index of State Bank Notes*, 3–10.

32. Leisering, "DDR-Banknoten," 141–48. Officials from the New Orleans Canal and Banking Company suffered a similar dilemma, though their solution was different: When $5000 notes were first issued in the 1850s, Washington's portrait, which had graced the bank's $1000 notes, was quietly dropped. *Whitman*, 7:322.

33. The notes were so-called "merchant scrip," not bank notes. In 1835 (a year before Wisconsin was constituted as a territory), a Bank of Wisconsin opened in the house occupied by John Jacob Astor's American Fur Trading Company. The Bank of Wisconsin then was the first bank west of Lake Michigan. Astor was part of Green Bay, Wisconsin. For the Bank of Wisconsin, see Haxby, WI-245. For illustrations of the scrip notes, go to Denly's of Boston, https://www.denlys.com/inventory/display.asp?table=%5BInventory%20-%20Obsoletes%5D&state=WI, accessed March 27, 2017. For local history, go to "Brown County Historic Sites—Green Bay," *Industory*, July 13, 2010, http://industory.pivotrock.net/historicsites/old_combined_page.html, accessed July 15, 2014. For the Tecumseh Bank (which never opened), see Haxby, MI-440-G4.

34. Haxby, respectively FL-85-G10 and G12; GA-60-G24; GA-160-G172; and GA-215-G8.

35. Emily Pearce Seigerman, "Libertas Americana: How an Infant Hero Replaced a Classical Goddess," *The Numismatist* 130:7 (July 2017), 37–39, and, for a more general discussion, Max M. Edling, *A Hercules in the Cradle Cradle: War, Money, and the American State, 1783–1867* (Chicago: University of Chicago Press, 2014). In 1783, the German writer Christian Friedrich Daniel Schubart published a poem titled "Die Freiheit Amerikas" ("America's Freedom"), which merges Hercules with George Washington into the guardian spirit of liberty: "Und Flammen sprüht! Doch Herkules-Washington, / Der Freiheit Schutzgott, stämmte den starken Arm / Ihr kühn entgegen…" Qtd. in Frey, "Washington in American Fiction," 25.

36. Bowers, *Obsolete Paper Money*, 129–34; Haxby, NY-1705; CT-270 (for the Eagle Bank of New Haven); GA-180-G60 and *Whitman*, 6:155 (for the Bank of Hawkinsville). An illustration of a $100 note from the Marble Manufacturing Company is in *Whitman*, 1:53. As Bowers observes, "fraudsters often called on the leading bank-note companies to create notes that today are high examples of engraving art"—in this instance, a note produced by the partnership of Durand & Wright, New York. On the "hermeneutics of suspicion" (German "*Unterstellungshermeneutik*"), see Gabriel, *Ästhetik und Rhetorik*, 90: "*Die politische Ikonographie ist der 'natürliche' Tummelplatz für 'Unterstellungshermeneutiker'*" ("political iconography is the 'natural' playground for hermeneutists of suspicion").

37. Doty, *America's Money*, 98.

38. The incident is retold in John Jay Knox's *History of Banking* and qtd. in Bowers, *Obsolete Paper Money*, 542. Stephen Mihm likewise makes ample use of it in *A Nation of Counterfeiters*, 184–85. For an illustration, see Tschachler, *Americans for George*, 45. For the $20 notes from the Merchants' Bank (Haxby, NY-1745-G108, G-110, G110a), see Tomasko, *Images of Value*, 34–35.

39. Charles Francis Adams, "The State of the Currency II," 515.

40. Aaron White, qtd. in Bowers, *Obsolete Paper Money*, 471.

41. Goodwin, *Greenback*, 186.

42. Edgar Allan Poe, *Poetry and Tales*, ed. Patrick Quinn (New York: Library of America, 1984), 380.

43. Poe, "Diddling Considered as One of the Exact Sciences," in *Poetry and Tales*, 607–17, quotations 607, 608.

44. Philip B. and Peter W. Kunhardt, p. *T. Barnum: America's Greatest Showman* (New York: Knopf, 1995), vi, and Claude Richard, "Poe and the Yankee Hero: An Interpretation of 'Diddling Considered as One of the Exact Sciences,'" *Mississippi Quarterly* 21 (Spring 1968), 93–109.

45. On Barnum's exhibition of Joice Heth, see Benjamin Reiss, *The Showman and the Slave: Race, Death, and Memory in Barnum's America* (Cambridge: Harvard University Press, 2001).

46. *Ibid.*, 135–67.

47. The nation, somewhat belatedly, thanked P. T. Barnum in its own way. In order to honor the centennial, in 1936, of the incorporation of Bridgeport, the U.S. Mint launched a commemorative half-dollar picturing the city's most famous resident on the reverse.

48. Peale, "Washington and His Portraits," qtd. in Gustavus Eisen, *Portraits of Washington*, 1:299. (Eisen reprints the entire lecture in vol. 1, 297–323.) The lecture Peale delivered to the New York Historical Society on June 16, 1857, was later referred to in *The Magazine of American History* 20 (July-December 1888), as "an illuminated illustration of a hallowed past" (485–88, quotation 488).

49. Edward Everett, "The Character of Washington," in *Orations and Speeches on Various Occasions*, vol. 4 (Boston: Little, Brown, and Co., 1868), 3–51, qtd. 50. Other references to the lecture in this paragraph are, respectively, to 52, 28, 34–35, 36, and 49.

Chapter 5

1. Thomas Jefferson, letter to Dr. Walter Jones, January 2, 1814, *Founders Online*, National Archives,

last modified June 13, 2018, http://founders.archives.gov/documents/Jefferson/03-07-02-0052.

2. John Neal, *Seventy-Six; or, Love and Battle* (1823; London: J. Cunningham, 1840), 90.

3. Sewall, "War and Washington," *Poems on American Presidents, 1789–1865*," Universität Freiburg, n.d., https://presidents.ub.uni-freiburg.de/index.php, July 14, 2016. Freneau, "American Liberty," *The Poems of Philip Freneau*, ed. Fred Lewis Pattee, vol. 1 (Princeton. NJ: Princeton University Library, 1902), 142–57, qtd. 149.

4. Joel Barlow, *The Vision of Columbus; a Poem in Nine Books* (Hartford, CT: Hudson and Goodwin, 1787), 160; Humphreys, "A Letter to a Young Lady in Boston," *The Miscellaneous Works of David Humphreys* (New York: T. and J. Swords, 1804), 196–201, qtd. 201; Snowden, *The Columbiad*, qtd. in Bryan, *Washington in American Literature*, 140. For additional examples, see *ibid.*, 120–140.

5. Irving, *Life of Washington*, chapter XXVI, 1:309–24, quotation 311.

6. Irving, *Life of Washington*, 4:517, and, for a thorough analysis of Washington's Cincinnatus image, Gary Wills, *Cincinnatus: George Washington and the Enlightenment* (Garden City, NY: Doubleday, 1984).

7. For an illustration of the lithograph, see Tschachler, *Political Fatherhood*, chapter 3; for Trumbull's paintings, see *ibid.*, chapter 7.

8. Museum of Fine Arts, Boston, http://www.mfa.org/collections/object/the-passage-of-the-delaware-31231, accessed August 18, 2016. For Lang's engraving of 1825, which was etched by William Humphreys, go to Library of Congress, http://www.loc.gov/pictures/item/98501385/, accessed August 18, 2016.

9. Jefferson C. Harrison, qtd. in Martha N. Hagood and Jefferson C. Harrison, *American Art at the Chrysler Museum: Selected Paintings, Sculpture, and Drawings* (Norfolk, VA: Chrysler Museum of Art, 2005), 46, no. 21.

10. Chrysler Museum of Art, Learning Resource, "Colonial and Revolutionary America, 1610–1776," https://chrysler.org/index.php?s=colonial+and+revolutionary+america&search=, accessed May 24, 2018.

11. A fully illustrated version of the pages to follow has appeared in *The Numismatist* of February 2018.

12. In 1853, Emanuel Gottlieb Leutze, better known for *Washington Crossing the Delaware*, painted the Monmouth scene on a canvas 24 feet wide and 15 feet high; the artwork, titled "Washington Rallying the Troops at Monmouth," is now hung in the Roger W. Heyns Reading Room, Charles Franklin Doe Memorial Library, University of California, Berkeley, CA; see "Portraits in Revolution," AmericanRevolution.com, http://www.americanrevolution.com/gallery/other_images/legacy_images/emanuel_leutze/washington_rallying_troops_at_monmouth, accessed July 27, 2018.

13. Haxby, NJ-160-G16a and NJ-160-G16; Doty, *Pictures from a Distant Country*, 30, 31, and email to this author, March 23, 2010. For further discussion and on the widely used "counterfeit detectors," see Tschachler, *The Monetary Imagination of Edgar Allan Poe*, 60. The "Monmouth" vignette had been in use before, *inter alia* on $3 notes from the Washington Banking Company, Hackensack, New Jersey, in the 1820s, as well as on notes of various denominations from the Real Estate Bank of the State of Arkansas, Washington branch, in the 1830s. Haxby, NJ-180-G18; AR-5-G90, G92, and G94.

14. Niles' *Weekly Register*, February 24, 1821, 417, qtd. in Tschachler, *The Greenback*, 161*n*8.

15. Haxby, MA-995-G4, G4a; for additional, unlisted notes and illustrations, see *Whitman*, 3:184. On $3 and $5 notes from the same bank, Washington's portrait appears at left ($3 notes are unlisted in Haxby, thus see *Whitman*, 3:185; for $5 notes, see Haxby, MA-995-G16 and G16a). A different version of the Landing of the Pilgrims vignette appears on the bank's $20 notes; a Native American man is at left, Washington's portrait at right (Haxby, MA-995-G26, G26a; illustration in *Whitman*, 3: 186).

16. Haxby, respectively RI-240-G22 (produced by Carpenter Toppan), OH-295-G2, MA-595–36a, MA-910-G26, G30, and G32, G36 (with the surrender of Cornwallis at left), MD-325-G20, and NJ-280-G28. A similar vignette appeared on $2 notes from the Bank of Brattleboro, Brattleboro, Vermont, in the 1850s and 1860s. Haxby, VT-35-G26a. For additional notes, see Muscalus, *Index of State Bank Notes* 18.

17. Haxby, MS-95-G12; NY-590-G66; RI-135-G36; OH-375-G12a; OH-295-G4; IN-45-G8; KY-195-G36; DC-175-G6; ME-80-G8 and G8a; PA-335-G2a.

18. Haxby, NH-95-G16 and G16a (Granite Bank, Exeter, New Hampshire), NH-305-G4 and G4a (Rochester Bank, Rochester, New Hampshire); VT-190-G8 (Bank of Bellows Falls, Rockingham, Vermont; and see *Whitman*, 5:427), and Haxby, VT-260-G14, G14a, G14b (Bank of Newbury, Wells River, Vermont), the latter examples of the many Patent Stereotype Steel Plate (PSSP) issues.

19. Haxby, MD-215-G16; RI-30-N5; MA-280-G32 and G44; PA-590-G22 245. Post notes are bills imprinted with a statement that they were redeemable at par only at a later specified date (*Whitman*, 7:669). For an illustration of Stuart's painting of 1806, see Schwartz, *American Symbol*, Fig. 34. Today, the *Washington at Dorchester Heights* painting is on exhibit in the Museum of Fine Arts, Boston, http://www.mfa.org/collections/object/washington-at-dorchester-heights-30879, August 4, 2017.

20. Haxby, GA-245-G6 and G6a, and Doty, *Pictures from a Distant Country*, 31–32.

21. Haxby, respectively RI-280-G8a and G6; MA-160-G12a; NY-1550-G20; MA-965-G40; SC-65-G2 and 2a, G12a and 12b; MA-910-G36; MA-475-G12; and RI-325-G14.

22. *Whitman*, 1:141; Haxby (NJ-175-G6 and G6a) dates the notes from the late 1850s.

23. Haxby, MA-475-G2a, G2d, G4a, G4d, G6a, G6d, G8a, G8d, and, for the $10 notes, G10a and G10c (illustrations in *Whitman*, 3:253–54); a dif-

ferent vignette depicting the Battle of Bunker Hill appeared on $100 notes from the Merchants Bank, Newburyport, Massachusetts, 1830s to 1850s (Haxby, MA-910-G56, illustration in *Whitman*, 3:137). For the Bank of Rhode Island notes, see Haxby, RI-170-G62a.

24. Haxby, RI-430-G8a. The cameo vignette was also used on notes from a number of other banks throughout the nation, including The Home Bank, Home Bank, Connecticut (Haxby, CT-455-G8), the Bank of Ashland, Kentucky (Haxby, KY-5-G6a and G22a), the Union Bank, Concord, New Hampshire (Haxby, NH-45-G4a), the Safety Fund Bank, Boston, Massachusetts (MA-345-G8, G8a), the Bank of the State of Tennessee, Nashville (Haxby, TN-195-G12a, G154a, G226a, G250a, G290a, G330a, G370a, G410a, and G480a), and the Bank of Orange County, Chelsea, Vermont (Haxby, VT-76-G4a).

25. Haxby, DE 50-G8a. The notes were issued a mere three years after the bank's incorporation; for an illustration see *Whitman*, 8:26. For an earlier note showing the identical camp scene, see *ibid.*, 384 ($5, Bank of Charleston, Charleston, VA, Haxby, VA-30-G4a). The camp scene with officers also appeared in the 1860s on $1 notes from the J. W. Ramsay and Company's Bank of Tarrytown, Tarrytown, New York (Haxby, NY-2665-G2). For the notes from the National Bank, see Haxby, RI-360-G28a and G28b, and *Whitman*, 5:203; for the Union Bank, see Haxby, PA-505-G2a; for the Bank of Phoenixville, see Haxby, PA-515-G6a; and for the Bank of Rhode Island note, see Haxby, RI-170-G56a, and *Whitman*, 5:77.

26. Haxby, NY-710-G2a, G2b, G2d; CT-395-G2c (for an illustration see *Whitman*, 2:241).

27. For the Smithfield Exchange Bank, see Haxby, RI-465-G50 and G50a, and *Whitman*, 5:67; for the Bank of Black River, see Haxby, VT-185-G2 and G2a, and *Whitman*, 5:423–24, and for the Battenkill Bank, Haxby, VT-130-G2, and *Whitman*, 5:396. For the Cuyler's Bank of Palmyra, see Haxby, NY-2165-G6 series for the $5, and G8 series for the $10. For the Bank of Albion, see Haxby, NY-115-G10; for the Bank of Rutland, Haxby, VT-200-G20a, for The City Bank of Columbus, Haxby, OH-170-G12, G12a, and for the Haverhill Bank, Haxby, MA-670-G54; MA-785-G244. For the Bank of Lansingburgh, see Haxby, NY-1180-G68, G68a, G68b, and for the Bank of the Republic, Haxby, MA-335-G12a; illustration in *Whitman*, 3:67.

28. Richard Henry Stanton, Representative from Kentucky (D), qtd. in Smorag, "From *Columbia* to the *United States of America*," 78. See, for further discussion, Mark E. Neely, Jr., et al., *The Confederate Image: Prints of the Lost Cause* (Chapel Hill: University of North Carolina Press, 1987), and Carla Mulford, "George Washington, the South, and the Poetics of National Memory," in *George Washington's South*, ed. Tamara Harvey and Greg O'Brien (Gainesville: UP of Florida, 2004), 316–65.

29. Haxby, NC-60–4B and 4Ba.

30. Haxby, NC-85-G6 and G8a.

31. Haxby, GA-210-G6 and G6a. The notes from the Mississippi Mutual are not listed in Haxby, thus see *Whitman*, 7:354. Northern banks also used the identical vignette, as on $3 notes from the Manufacturers and Traders Bank, Portland, Maine (Haxby, ME-475-G52, illustration in *Whitman*, 2:474). A slightly different version ("Navigation" seated on bales of goods and barrels on a wharf, with ships in the background, "Agriculture" with a sickle and a harvest scene in the background) appears on $1 notes from the non-existent Merchants Exchange Bank, Washington, DC. *Whitman*, 8:141 (the notes are not listed in Haxby).

32. Haxby, LA-75–14a, 14b, 14c. For an earlier note not listed in Haxby, see *Whitman*, 7:249.

33. Haxby, GA-90-G4a. The Washington vignette had been used before, on $2 notes from the Merchants and Mechanics Bank, Washington, DC (DC-285-G4). For the notes from the Louisiana State Bank, see *ibid.*, LA-80-G54b.

34. Haxby, GA-270-G78a. A few years later, the notes' producer, the National Bank Note Company, slightly altered the vignette for the Banco Boliviano, La Paz, Bolivia. It now showed a portrait of Simon Bolívar, while a mountain scene replaced the U.S. coat of arms. Tomasko, *The Feel of Steel*, 23.

35. See Karsten Fitz, *The American Revolution Remembered, 1830s to 1850s* (Heidelberg: Winter, 2010), 101–102.

36. The song is from 1863, became immensely popular, and was sung on both sides in the Civil War.

37. Matthew Karp, *This Vast Southern Empire: Slaveholders at the Helm of American Foreign Policy* (Cambridge, MA: Harvard University Press, 2016), 78, 80. On the dismay, among leading American statesmen, over the war's unsavory origins, see Peter Guardino, *The Dead March: A History of the Mexican-American War* (Cambridge, MA: Harvard University Press, 2017). On Lincoln's role in the uproar caused by the war against Mexico, see Sidney Blumenthal, *A Self-Made Man: The Political Life of Abraham Lincoln, 1809–1849* (New York: Simon and Schuster, 2017).

38. Bryan, *Washington in American Literature*, 239.

39. For further discussion and biographical details see Scott McDermott, *Charles Carroll of Carrolltown: Faithful Revolutionary* (New York: Scepter, 2002). Following the War of Independence, Carroll served as state senator of Maryland. In this capacity, he became acquainted with Eleanor "Nelly" Custis, one of George Washington's adopted grandchildren, who in 1797 attracted unwanted attention when she danced with him in what was then called the Federal City. And when Nelly's brother, George Washington "Washy" Custis, implied a romance between Carroll and Nelly, George Washington sharply upbraided his adopted grandson. Richard Norton Smith, *Patriarch* 301 and 318, and Donald Jackson, "George Washington's Beautiful Nelly," *American Heritage* 28:2 (February 1977), http://www.americanheritage.com/content/george-washington'-beautiful-nelly, February 23, 2018.

40. Haxby, GA-15-G8; PA-475-G65a and G56b; MA-510-G40; SC-95-G6; GA-325-G22; and CT-225-

G14. The Bank of Chicago was a short-lived bank opened by the spiritualist Seth Paine. The $2 notes, dated October 16, 1852, are not listed in Haxby. For a description and an illustration see Stahl, *Money on Paper*, 55 and 56.

41. Carroll's portrait appeared, *inter alia*, on notes from the Bank of the State of Alabama (Haxby, AL-5), the Bank of Tennessee (Haxby, TN-195, Design 2Ca), the Mechanics Bank, Atlanta, GA (Haxby, GA-60-G34), the Mechanics Bank, Wilmington, DE (Haxby, DE-75-G14), and the New Orleans and Carrollton Rail Road Company (Haxby, LA-110-G14, G16, G18).

42. Haxby, GA-250-G12a and G12b (for the Bank of the Empire State notes). As for Calhoun, his portrait appears at right on $5 notes issued by the Bank of South Carolina, Charleston, South Carolina, in 1861. The central vignette, engraved from an artwork attributed to Theodore August Liebler, shows two allegorical figures placing a laurel wreath on a bust of Washington. Ironically, the notes were produced by Rawdon, Wright, Hatch & Edson of New York. Tomasko, *Images of Value*, 38–39, and Haxby, SC-30-G34 and G34a.

43. Haxby, KY-175-G56 v. KY-175-G58. The policy of replacement was also adopted by the bank's branches, and on notes of different denominations, as see Haxby, KY-175-G86 v. KY-175-G88, KY-175-G128 v. KY-175-G130, KY-175-G144 v. KY-175-G146, KY-175-G176 v. KY-175-G178, KY-175-G198 v. KY-175-G200, KY-175-G222 v. KY-175-G224, KY-175-G230 v. KY-175-G232, KY-175-G252 v. KY-175-G254, KY-175-G260 v. KY-175-G262, KY-175-G268 v. KY-175-G270, KY-175-G276 v. KY-175-G278, KY-175-G308 v. KY-175-G310, and KY-175-G332 v. KY-175-G334.

44. Doty, *Pictures from a Distant Country*, 33–36, and Haxby, SC-45-G60a (for the Bank of the State of South Carolina note); for an example of a "Calhoun" note from the 1850s, see Haxby, SC-30-G34 and G34a: this $5 note from the Bank of South Carolina, Charleston, shows a portrait of Calhoun at right; at center is a bust of Washington behind a shield, flanked by two allegorical women, a native-looking Columbia and Liberty with pole and cap. For "Abolition and the Union cannot co-exist" see "Slavery a Positive Good" (1837), in *Key Concepts in American Cultural History: From the Colonial Period to the End of the 19th Century*, 2nd edn., ed. Bernd Engler and Oliver Scheiding (Trier, Germany: Wissenschaftlicher Verlag Trier, 2007), 586.

45. Haxby, MA-1130-G165a; for a good illustration, see *Whitman*, 1:186.

46. Haxby, PA-365-G14, R10 (raised to $5), R15 (raised to $10). Haxby erroneously identified General Slemmer as General Clemmer, an error that flitted about in the numismatic literature for years. For good illustrations of the notes from the Bank of Montgomery County see Stahl, *Money on Paper*, 59, and *Whitman*, 1:176.

47. See James M. McPherson, *The War That Forged a Nation: Why the Civil War Still Matters* (Oxford: Oxford University Press, 2015).

48. John Sherman, qtd. in Helleiner, "National Currencies," 1411.

49. Doty, *America's Money*, 164.

50. Salmon P. Chase, "unnational circulation," letter to John Sherman, 1864, John Sherman's *Recollections*, qtd. in Bowers, *Obsolete Paper Money*, 441.

51. United States notes (the "greenbacks") were backed by federal borrowings and a 30 percent gold reserve; National Bank notes were secured by government bonds that had to be deposited with the Treasury Department; Gold and Silver Certificates were secured by gold and silver deposits.

52. Alexander Hamilton, letter to James Duane, representative in Congress of New York, September 1780, *The Works of Alexander Hamilton*, ed. Henry Cabot Lodge (New York: Putnam's, 1904), 1:225. For a more detailed account of America's banking system through the Civil War, see my *The Monetary Imagination of Edgar Allan Poe*, esp. chap.5, "Fables of Circulation."

53. Madison, "To the People of the State of New York [*The Federalist*, no.10, 1787]," *The Heath Anthology of American Literature*, ed. Paul Lauter et al. (Lexington, MA-Toronto: D. C. Heath, 1990), 1013–18, qtd. 1018.

54. Just as ineffective was Madison's essay on money and finance in Philadelphia's *National Gazette*. In it, Madison remembered the ill-begotten Continentals, calling them "omens of public bankruptcy" as they had been issued in such large quantities that they soon after gave rise to a "distrust of the *public ability* to fulfill their engagements." The *National* Gazette, which was published by Madison's friend Philip Freneau, produced the essay in two installments, respectively on December 19 and 22, 1791. Madison had originally written it during the years 1778–1779, as he was observing the rapid decline in value of the Continental currency; its title then was simply "Money." Ralph Louis Ketcham, *James Madison: A Biography* (Charlottesville: University of Virginia Press, 1990), 85–86. An edited and annotated version of "Money" appeared in *The Papers of James Madison*, vol. 1, *16 November 1751–16 December 1779*, ed. William T. Hutchinson and William M. E. Rachal (Chicago: University of Chicago Press, 1962), 302–10.

55. In James Alexander Dallas, *Documentary History of Banking and Currency in the United States*, 1:189. The decision in Congress was a narrow one. The bill providing for a renewal of the charter was defeated by a single vote in the House of Representatives; in the Senate it was lost by a tie. William O. Scroggs, *A Century of Banking Progress* (Garden City, NY: Doubleday, Page, 1924), 14–15.

56. James Alexander Dallas, in *Documentary History of Banking and Currency*, 1:215.

57. Daniel Walker Howe, *What Hath God Wrought: The Transformation of America, 1815–1848*, Oxford History of the United States, vol. 5 (New York: Oxford University Press, 2007), 835.

58. Lincoln, "Speech on the Subtreasury," Springfield, Illinois, December 1839, *The Collected Works of Abraham Lincoln*, 1:164. On Lincoln's role in the

Harrison campaign, see Robert Gray Gunderson, *The Log-Cabin Campaign* (Lexington: University of Kentucky Press, 1957), 212–16.

59. The Illinois state bank, like other banks, was bringing its bills into circulation at its most distant branches. The purpose of this practice was to make redemption of the bills difficult, though it was an insult to the moral sense of many Illinoisans. Lincoln nevertheless defended the bank, and he did so in a way that many Whig grandees would take note. Gabor S. Boritt, *Lincoln and the Economics of the American Dream* (1978; Urbana and Chicago: University of Illinois Press, 1994), 15–18, 29. For the end of the bank in 1842, see *ibid.*, 51–61.

60. Lincoln, "Fragment: What General Taylor Ought To Say," *The Collected Works of Abraham Lincoln*, 1:454, emphases added.

61. For "sound and uniform currency," see Lincoln, "Speech on the Subtreasury," *The Collected Works of Abraham Lincoln*, 1:164. For "power of regulation" see Charles Francis Adams, "The State of the Currency II," 506.

62. Eric Helleiner, "Historicizing Territorial Currencies: Money and the Nation-State in North America," *Political Geography* 18 (1999), 309–39, here 310*n*1.

63. Eric Helleiner, *The Making of National Money: Territorial Currencies in Historical Perspective* (Ithaca, NY: Cornell University Press, 2003), 123–39; Dodd, *The Social Life of Money*, 211–68. On state monopoly over money as a universal phenomenon, see David Glasner, "An Evolutionary Theory of the State Monopoly over Money," in *Money and the Nation-State: The Financial Revolution, Government, and the World Monetary System*, ed. Kevin Dowd and Richard H. Timberlake (New Brunswick, NJ: Transaction Publishers, 1998), 21–45.

64. For "banal nationalism," see Michael Billig's eponymous book (London: Sage, 1995) and, for further discussion and specifically on paper money, Lauer, "Money as Mass Communication," 127–28, and Jan Penrose, "Designing the Nation: Banknotes, Banal Nationalism and Alternative Conceptions of the State," *Political Geography* 30 (2011), 429–40.

65. Senator John Sherman, qtd. in Helleiner, "National Currencies and National Identities," 1416.

66. Qtd. in Goodwin, *Greenback*, 68.

67. Qtd. in Bowers, *Obsolete Paper Money*, 12.

68. Lauer, "Money as Mass Communication," 121–22; United States Bureau of Engraving and Printing (USBEP), "*BEP* History. Papers Prepared by the Historical Resource Center, 2004," n.d., http://www.moneyfactory.gov/images/BEP_History_Sec508_web.pdf, December 5, 2014.

69. W. L. Ormsby, qtd. in Bowers, *Obsolete Paper Money*, 285. Thus, a view of the Niagara Falls would form a part of the design to designate an institution in that part of the country; similarly, the Bunker Hill Monument might be used for banks in Boston.

70. In 1859, some 9,916 different genuine notes *and* some 5,400 different kinds of counterfeit notes in circulation were listed. For a detailed treatment of counterfeiting in antebellum America, see Bowers, *Obsolete Paper Money*, chapter nine, 157–76, and Mihm, *Nation of Counterfeiters*, 209–304. The expression "bearing a common impression" belongs to Samuel P. Chase, qtd. in Mihm, *Nation of Counterfeiters*, 312.

71. "Abraham Lincoln" and "Ode Recited at the Harvard Commemoration," qtd. in Butter, *Der "Washington-Code,"* 97–98; for "Prairie King," see *ibid.*, 95. For the full texts of these and other sources used here, see "Poems on American Presidents, 1789–1865," Universität Freiburg, n.d., https://presidents.ub.uni-freiburg.de/index.php, July 14, 2017.

72. "Ode on the Death of President Lincoln" (1865), qtd. in Butter, *Der "Washington-Code,"* 96; for "principles of Washington," see Schwartz, *American Symbol*, 197.

73. Qtd. in Schwartz, *American Symbol*, 197.

74. Schwartz, *American Symbol*, Fig. 40.

75. Rutherford Hayes, qtd. in Casper, "The Washington Image," 600. For Washington as an object of nostalgia, see George B. Forgie, *Patricide in the House Divided: A Psychological Interpretation of Lincoln and His Age* (New York: W. W. Norton, 1979).

76. For an illustration of a Demand Note as well as for further discussion, see Tschachler, *The Greenback*, 110, and *The Monetary Imagination of Edgar Allan Poe*, 13–15. On the proposed nickel five-cent coins, see Vermeule, *Numismatic Art in America*, 64. The proposed coins were never realized; in their stead, "Shield" type nickels were struck from 1866 to 1883. Yeoman, *Guide Book of United States Coins*, 124.

77. Alfred Mitchell, *The Coloniad: A Narrative in Verse on Washington's War*, qtd. in Bryan, *Washington in American Literature*, 142.

78. John R. Thompson, "Inauguration of the Equestrian Statue of Washington … Opening Ode," qtd. *ibid.*, 164.

79. Henry Wise, qtd. *ibid.*, 79–80. The Richmond statue monument was commissioned by the state of Virginia in 1849; its unveiling took place two years after Henry Kirke Brown's bronze equestrian statue had been installed in New York's Union Square Park. On the Great Seal of the Confederation, see Miller and Schwartz, "The Icon of the American Republic," 521.

80. Richter, *The Quaker Soldier*, and "Rebels," qtd. in Bryan, *Washington in American Literature*, 165. For a fuller treatment of the role of Washington in prewar controversy, see Bryan, "George Washington: Symbolic Guardian of the Republic."

81. For Confederate stamps, see Hessler, *The Engraver's Line*, 156. For bank notes, see Haxby, VA-170-G2a and G12a (Bank of the Commonwealth), VA-195-G41 (Traders Bank), and VA-50-G8a, G8b, and G16a (Pittsylvania). For the Texas warrant, see Wells, "Strokes of Genius," 43. For the $5 CSA note, see Friedberg and Friedberg, *Paper Money of the United States*, 242, cited as CS-31. The note shows the same Massachusetts State House statue of George Washington standing that had appeared on various antebellum notes from the 1830s. The notes of the Traders Bank were issued in December 1861 when the Civil War was in Progress (*Whitman*, 1:258).

This was not an unusual practice: Florida seceded from the Union and joined the confederacy in January 1861. No longer constrained by the U.S. Constitution and desperately needing money, the State of Florida issued its own currency during the Civil War from 1861 to 1865. A portrait of George Washington graced the $1 notes. For an illustration, see *Whitman*, 6:455. For a descriptive listing of state-issued notes and other Florida currency, see Ronald J. Benice, *Florida Paper Money: An Illustrated History, 1817–1934* (Jefferson, NC: McFarland, 2008).

82. Friedberg and Friedberg, *Paper Money of the United States*, 239 (CS-6). The Union in 1861 likewise produced $50 notes, but with Justice at center (*ibid.*, 41). Each of the two sides probably saw good reasons to appeal to Justice. Private banks had done the same; in their case, Justice likely was to foreground the straight dealing of the note-issuing institution. For the Pittsylvania notes and generally on the problems bedeviling Southern banks during the Civil War, see Doty, *America's Money*, 126–40.

83. Doty, *Pictures from a Distant Country*, 189.

84. Holzer, "Beyond Face Value: Slavery Iconography in Confederate Currency," Civil War Center / Louisiana State University, *Beyond Face Value: Depictions of Slavery in Confederate Currency*, 1996–2007, http://www.cwc.lsu.edu/BeyondFaceValue, September 11, 2008. I discuss renderings of African Americans on the currency in *The Greenback*, 87–91.

85. Holzer, "Beyond Face Value" and, for description and illustration, Haxby, AL-65-G16, G16a and G16b. $1 notes from the Southern Bank of Tennessee, Memphis, 1853, show George Washington on horseback inspecting fields worked by slaves (Haxby, TN-125-G2), as do $1 notes from the Farmers and Merchants Bank, Washington, DC, 1851 (Haxby, DC-235-G2); $10 notes from the Farmers and Mechanics Bank of Carroll County, Westminster, Maryland, show the identical vignette (Haxby, MD-310-G10).

86. The scrip notes from the 1870s are from the Reconstruction era and were issued directly by the state government. *Whitman*, 6:457. For a pre-Civil War note with a similar arrangement—portrait of Washington at right, slaves at work at left, see Haxby, SC-15-G6a. The note in question is a $20 note issued by the Farmers and Exchange Bank of Charleston in the 1850s. The notes were printed by Rawdon, Wright, Hatch & Edson in New York.

87. Jefferson Davis, *The Rise and Fall of the Confederate Government* (New York: D. Appleton, 1881), 1:78.

Chapter 6

1. Haxby, RI-435-G38, with ill. The Citizens Union Bank was organized in 1832. For the Bank of North America note, see *ibid.*, PA-465-G248.

2. Haxby, MS-60-G18 and G20. The vignettes were also used, *inter alia*, on $5 notes from the Bank of West Union, West Union, Ohio, 1830–1840 (OH-440-G52a), and the Chippeway County Bank, Sault de St. Mary, Michigan, 1838 (MI-390-G4), though no notes from this bank were officially issued. On Juno Moneta, see *Wörterbuch der Münzkunde*, 397–98 and, for a depiction of the goddess on a Roman *follis* coin, Doty, *Dictionary of Numismatics*, 217–18.

3. Haxby, TN-55, Design 5C, G36a, G68a, G96a. $5 notes from the Bank of Chattanooga, Chattanooga, Tennessee, displayed an almost identical arrangement, as did $50 notes from the Holyoke Bank, Northampton, Massachusetts, and $100 notes from the Ocean Bank, Kennebunk, Maine, and from the Maritime Bank, Bangor, Maine. *Ibid.*, TN-10-G2, G2a, R15, and G46, G46a; MA-950-G24, G24b, G24c (illustrations in *Whitman*, 3:157); ME-375-G16; notes from the Maritime Bank are not listed in Haxby, thus see *Whitman*, 2:331.

4. Walter Benjamin, "One Way Street," *One Way Street and Other Writings* (London: Verso Press, 1978), 61–94, qtd. 87. Cf. a. Emily Gilbert's use of Benjamin's essay for her analysis of the iconography of Canadian paper money: "'Ornamenting the Façade of Hell': Iconographies of 19th-Century Canadian Paper Money," *Environment and Planning D: Society and Space* 16 (1998), 57–80.

5. Benjamin, "Capitalism as Religion," 291; for a useful collection of essays re-reading Benjamin's fragment see Dirk Baecker, ed., *Kapitalismus als Religion* (Berlin: Kulturverlag Kadmos, 2003), which also reprints the text. A year before Benjamin wrote his fragment, Sinclair Lewis published *Main Street*. The tenth chapter of the novel includes a conversation between the heroine, Carol, and the town handyman, Miles Bjornstam, who is of Swedish descent. Bjornstam, lamenting the power of bankers, points out that in America the dollar sign has "chased the crucifix clean off the map" (New York: New American Library/Signet Classics, 1980, 115). This statement is not only a good example of the spread of the "capitalism as religion" theme but also, at least for those familiar with secret symbols, of the idea that the dollar sign was derived from the image of a serpent hanging from a cross, as on the obverse of early Joachimsthalers.

6. Benjamin, "Capitalism as Religion," 289; see a. Bolz, "Der Kapitalismus—eine Erfindung von Theologen," in *Kapitalismus als Religion*, ed. Dirk Baecker (Berlin: Kulturverlag Kadmos, 2003), 187–207. Also note that in the German language, "debt" and "guilt" converge in one word, "*Schuld*."

7. David Wells, the Special Commissioner of Revenue, in 1869 estimated the costs incurred directly by the Union government as $4,171 million, with directly incurred costs for the Confederacy of $2,700 million. A remaining sum of $2,323 million, not divided between North and South, included such items as pensions, state and local government debts, and losses to shipping and industry, making a total war cost of $9,194 million, which in today's money is more than the cost of the war in Iraq. Davies, *A History of Money*, 487.

8. For instance, on a $3 note from the State of Florida, the Stars and Stripes on a naval vessel was

altered to resemble the new Confederate flag. Wendell Wolka, "Does that Flag Still Wave?" *The Numismatist* 129:6 (June 2016), 79–80, here 79.

9. Galbraith, *Money*, 95. I have also drawn in this paragraph on Mihm, *Nation of Counterfeiters*, 319–21, and 328–30.

10. Robert J. Kravitz, *A Collector's Guide to Postage and Fractional Currency*, 2nd edition (Williston, VT: Coin and Currency Institute, 2012); Nordham, *Vignettes and Memorabilia*, 75–76; and Doty, *America's Money* 140–42.

11. 31 USC 413, qtd. in Tschachler, *The Greenback*, 68. USC 31:413 has since been revised; it is now 31:5114(b). On Superintendent Clark, see Benny Bolin, "Spencer M. Clark, Cornerstone of the Bureau of Engraving and Printing," *Paper Money* 27 (1988), 77–80. For an illustration of the Spencer Clark fractional note, see Tomasko, *The Feel of Steel*, 94. For illustrations of other fractionals and further discussion, see Bowers, *U.S. Paper Money*, 783–803. As regards stamps, the "Athenaeum" on the 1847 postage stamp got there via a "pre-existing engraving, probably from an engraver's sample book." Peter T. Rohrbach and Lowell S. Newman, *American Issue: The U.S. Postage Stamp, 1842-1869* (Washington, DC: Smithsonian Institution Press, 1984), 68. Earlier stamps with more limited circulation (the 1842 "City Dispatch" stamps and the later "postmasters' provisionals") bore similar "Athenaeum" Washington images. See *ibid.*, 45, 46. For an overview of stamps honoring George Washington, see Nordham, *Vignettes and Memorabilia*, 78–100, for images, see *Scott Specialized Catalogue of United States Stamps and Covers*, ed. James E. Kloetzel (Sidney, OH: Scott Publishing, 2017). Per John E. Ferling's findings, Washington's face is the most widely featured one throughout U.S. postal history, more than all other presidents combined. See *The First of Men: A Life of George Washington* (Knoxville: University of Tennessee Press, 1988), 100.

12. Tuckerman, *Character and Portraits*, 33–34.

13. Likenesses of George Washington were printed on the $100 Compound Interest Treasury Notes from 1864–1865 and the $100 Interest Bearing Treasury Notes from 1863 (both engraved by Owen G. Hanks), and on the $500 Interest Bearing Treasury Notes from 1861 (engraved by Alfred Sealey). Friedberg and Friedberg, *Paper Money of the United States*, 37 (design no. 38, notes 193–193b), 40 (design no. 44, note 199), 43 (design no. 54, note 209). The "Guardian" vignette on the $100 note features a woman standing behind a flag-draped cannon, holding a shield, with another nearby shield inscribed "IN GOD IS OUR TRUST." Bowers, *U.S. Paper Money*, 626–27.

14. Felt, *Massachusetts Currency*, 46 and, for a full account, 30–50.

15. Act of December 10, 1690, qtd. in Curtis P. Nettels, *The Money Supply of the American Colonies Before 1720* (Madison: University of Wisconsin Press, 1934), 254. The designation "indented bill" refers to the wavy line cut between a numbered note and its stub kept in a book at the place of issuance; the method was supposed to make redemption safer, as were the notes' borders that were cut in a particular way. Andrew McFarland Davis, *Currency and Banking in the Province of the Massachusetts Bay* (1901; repr. New York: A. M. Kelley, 1970), gives extensive details of the entire issue. On the origin of the bills' "Standing Indian" figure in the iconography of the European Middle Ages, see Tschachler, "The Wildman in the New World," 11. On their technical status as "bills of credit," see Mossman, *Money of the American Colonies and Confederation*, 97–98.

16. Borrowing from the English system, the calendar through 1752 commenced annually on March 25 and concluded 365 days later, on March 24. Historians refer to this as the Julian calendar. As of 1752 the year was set in the American colonies to commence with January 1 and end with December 31, the reckoning in place ever since, called the Gregorian calendar.

17. Ernest Bogart, *Economic History of the American People*, 172, qtd. in Galbraith, *Money*, 51.

18. Nussbaum, *History of the Dollar*, 15.

19. Newman, *Early Paper Money*, 9–10. It is not clear, Donald Kagin notes, but references are made in various colonial documents to the use of some sort of paper money prior to 1652. In 1656, a bank began issuing forms of credit under a royal permission but was soon forced to close. In 1686, the Massachusetts Council approved of a bank that would issue bills of credit. A rolling press was purchased, but the scheme was abandoned two years later, and the bills were never issued. In the end, the exigencies of the frontier led to the world's first emission of paper money in 1690. Kagin, "The First Attempts at Paper Currency in America," *The Numismatist* 86:4 (April 1973), 543–52, here 549.

20. Doty, *America's Money*, 36.

21. Galbraith, *Money*, 45.

22. South Carolina followed in 1703, Connecticut, New Hampshire, New Jersey, and New York in 1709, Rhode Island in 1710, and North Carolina in 1712–1713; eventually all thirteen original colonies authorized paper money (bills of credit), Vermont last of all in 1781. Newman, *Early Paper Money*, 9–11; Felt, *Massachusetts Currency*, 50–51.

23. Robertson, "The Aesthetics of Authenticity," 36–42 and, for detailed accounts of the process of designing, engraving, and printing, Bowers, *Obsolete Paper Money*, 7–76, 197–211, 261–67, and 424–26, and Tomasko, *The Feel of Steel*, 67–122; also useful is Tomasko's "primer" on bank note engraving in Stahl, *Money on Paper*, 3–16. For an illustration of a banknote printing machine, see Bowers, *Garrett Collection*, 211.

Part III

1. On "precision" as, not just a component of machines but as a "phenomenon" that fundamentally reshaped our social, mercanntile, scientific, mechanical, and intellectual landscapes, indeed made the modern world possible, see Simon Winchester, *The*

Perfectionists: How Precision Engineers Created the Modern World (New York: Harper, 2018), passim.

2. The American Bank-Note Company (the firm of Jocelyn, Draper, Welsh & Co. used that name years before the 1858 merger into the ABNCo.) charged at least $150 to $200 for one-time use of a "principal vignette" (more if it was to be used by only one customer), while the price tag for engraving four bank notes on steel was $500. Tomasko, *The Feel of Steel*, 14; for a brief history of banknote engraving from the pioneer days of craftsmen like Benjamin Franklin, Paul Revere, Robert Scot, and Jacob Perkins to the end of the nongovernmental part of the banknote industry in the 1990s, see *ibid.*, 1–65.

3. Hessler, *The Engraver's Line*, passim.

4. Qtd. in Bowers, *Obsolete Paper Money*, 425.

5. London *Art Journal*, October 1860, qtd. in Hessler, *The Engraver's Line*, 93. Felix Octavius Carr Darley was the premier banknote vignette artist from the 1850s to the 1870s, even though he is perhaps best remembered as the illustrator of novels of James F. Cooper and works of Washington Irving.

6. Qtd. in Goodwin, *Greenback*, 150.

7. James Harvey, *Paper Money: The Money of Civilization* (London: Provost & Co., 1877). About a century and a half later, the economic historian William N. Goetzmann was to sound a similar note in his book *Money Changes Everything: How Finance Made Civilization Possible* (Princeton, NJ: Princeton University Press, 2016).

Chapter 7

1. Qtd. in Tomasko, *The Feel of Steel*, xiii. For similar statements, see William H. Gerdts' preface to Tomasko, *Images of Value*, 8–9.

2. Qtd. in Goodwin, *Greenback*, 150. Reference to John Berger is to *Ways of Seeing*, 135.

3. Using history paintings as originals for banknote engravings thus was quite profitable, with prices varying from several hundred to several thousand dollars. Hessler, *The Engraver's Line*, 3. On the creation of vignettes and portraits see Tomasko, *The Feel of Steel*, respectively 81–93 and 93–98, and *Images of Value*, 15–24.

4. Spencer M. Clark, qtd. in Bowers, U.S. *Paper Money*, 58 and, for a contemporary story on the technical aspects of operation in the Bureau, published in the *New-York Daily Tribune*, 60–66. On transferring, see also Tomasko, *The Feel of Steel*, 72–73.

5. Ginsberg, "American Change," 69. "T-Men" are law-enforcement agents of the Treasury Department. Geometric lathes are no longer in use today; they have been replaced by computer algorithms. Hurle, "Abstractions of Value," 36. On the technical aspects of modern banknote production, see Bender, *Geldmacher*, 248–55, and Thiel, "Banknoten im Blickpunkt der Wissenschaft," 64–68.

6. Gene Hessler's encyclopedia only treats "artists" among banknote engravers; even as gifted an operator of the geometric lathe as Charles Wesley Dickinson is only mentioned cursorily. *The Engraver's Line*, 105. To see at least a few of Dickinson's design, therefore, the best thing to do is to contact the Smithsonian's National Numismatic Collection.

7. Walter Benjamin, "The Work of Art in the Age of Mechanical Reproduction," *Illuminations* (London: Collins/Fontana Books, 1970), 220–27, qtd. 222.

8. Benjamin's "mistake," Adorno concluded, was to link the aura of the work of art with its "autonomy." What he did not see was that "autonomy" cannot be separated from bourgeois individualism, which as a social formation is itself the very basis of mechanical reproduction. Theodor Adorno et al., *Aesthetic Theory*, trans. and ed. Robert Hullot-Kentor (London: Continuum, 2007), 56.

9. The development from aureole to aura to gilt frame to portrait frame on bank notes thus corresponds to the larger historical movement in which religion first gives way to art, which then is displaced by economics. Mark Taylor has described this movement in terms of a dialectic without synthesis. *Confidence Games*, 25–26.

10. Benjamin, "The Work of Art in the Age of Mechanical Reproduction," 222, and, on the frame as a border defining a picture *as* a picture, Dieter Mersch, "Blick und Entzug. Zur 'Logik' ikonischer Strukturen," in *Figur und Figuration. Studien zu Wahrnehmung und Wisssen*, ed. Gottfried Boehm et al. (München: Fink, 2007), 55–69, here 58–62.

11. Lauer, "Money as Mass Communication," 126.

12. For these two positions see, respectively, Gabriel, *Ästhetik und Rhetorik des Geldes*, 9, and Robertson "The Aesthetics of Authenticity."

13. William J. Hubard, "A National Standard for the Likeness of Washington," *Magazine of American History* 4 (1880), 83–108, qtd. 85; John Marshall, qtd. in Eisen, *Portraits of Washington*, 1:xvii; John Neal, *Randolph: A Novel*, 1: 63.

14. "Rainbow notes" also existed in other denominations. All were printed on a special paper, the "blue stain" paper developed by the Willcox company in Glen Mills, Pennsylvania. The purpose of using both many colors and a special paper was to stop the counterfeiting of the new greenbacks. Wendell Wolka, "Paper Trail," *The Numismatist* 130:7 (July 2017), 81–82.

15. Bushman, "Columbus-Washington-Connection," in *America Discovers Columbus: How an Italian Explorer Became an American Hero* (Hanover, NH: UP of New England, 1992). On the "Columbus-Washington-Connection" on the national currency, see Kathleen Loock, "Goodbye Columbus, Hello Abe!" and her book *Kolumbus in den USA: Vom Nationalhelden zur ethnischen Identifikationsfigur* (Bielefeld, Germany: Transcript Verlag, 2014). On Columbus' influence on the rewriting of America's national origin myth, see Timothy Kubal, *Cultural Movements and Collective Memory: Christopher Columbus and the Rewriting of the National Origin Myth* (New York: Palgrave Macmillan, 2008).

16. Friedberg and Friedberg, *Paper Money of the United States*, 15–16, 321.

17. See, for further discussion, Schwartz, "A New Man for a New Century," 124–27.

18. Mitchell, *Picture Theory*, 104.

19. Smorag, "From *Columbia* to the *United States of America*," 74–75, and Thomas J. Schlereth, "Columbia, Columbus, and Columbianism," *Journal of American History* 79 (December 1992), 937–68. On Columbus as an American "messiah," see Daniel J. Boorstin, *The Discoverers* (New York: Random House, 1983), 232.

20. Ellis, *After the Revolution*, 175; see a. Unger, *Noah Webster: The Life and Times of an American Patriot.*

21. Irving, *A History of the Life and Voyages of Christopher Columbus*, 1:10.

22. John D. Hazlett, "Literary Nationalism and Ambivalence in Washington Irving's *The Life and Voyages of Christopher Columbus*," *American Literature* 55:4 (1983), 560–75, qtd. 573.

23. Irving, *Columbus*, 1:56.

24. *Ibid.*, 4:54.

25. *Ibid.*, 4:55.

26. *Ibid.*, 4:63.

27. As Michael S. Stevens points out, one of the key elements of Irving's *Columbus* project "was to the creation of a historical persona for Christopher Columbus that imagined his achievements as a logical and constitutive element in the emergence of the United States." Stevens, "Spanish Orientalism: Washington Irving and the Romance of the Moors," *History Dissertations*, Paper 8 (Georgia State University, 2007), 259.

28. John D. Hazlett, "Literary Nationalism and Ambivalence in Washington Irving's *The Life and Voyages of Christopher Columbus*," *American Literature* 55:4 (1983), 560–75, qtd. 567.

29. Irving's description of the landing ar Guahani also served as model for John Vanderlyn's monumental painting (now among the Americana in the U.S. Capitol) *The Landing of Columbus at the Island of Guanahani, West Indies, October 12, 1492*, which (in an engraving by Walter Shirlaw) was later used for the back of the $5 National Bank notes of the first charter period (1863–1882, and issued through 1902). Loock, "Goodbye Columbus, Hello Abe!" 88–89.

30. According to Andrew Burstein, Irving's *Columbus* generally was "the most commonly owned book" in American libraries in the mid-nineteenth century and "undeniably influenced how American school-children were taught their country's origins." Burstein, *The Original Knickerbocker: The Life of Washington Irving* (New York: Basic Books, 2007), 196. For the 1833 recommendation, by the New York State Legislature, that Irving's *Columbus* be used as a textbook for the common schools, see Andrew B. Myers, *The Worlds of Washington Irving, 1783–1859* (Tarrytown, NY: Sleepy Hollow Restorations, 1974), 73.

31. Burstein, *The Original Knickerbocker*, 205.

32. On the popularity of Irving's *Columbus*, see a. Stanley Thomas Williams, *The Life of Washington Irving*, 2 vols. (New York: Oxford University Press, 1935), 1:355, 2:304. By the time Morison's biography was published, the critical tide had changed against Irving, whose *Columbus* was seen as failed history, neither very accurate nor original enough to count as historical scholarship. Stanley Williams even went so far as to say that Irving deserved censure for his "plagiarism, if such it may be called." *Life of Irving*, 2:298. Elsewhere, Williams dismisses Irving as nothing more than the interpreter, during his twenty-one months in Madrid, of materials the Spanish historian Navarrete had spent thirty-five years gathering. *Ibid.*, 2:300; for critical discussions of Irving's diction, tone, and characterization in *Columbus*, see *ibid.*, 322–24, 296–308.

33. Pierre M. Irving, *The Life and Letters of Washington Irving*, 4 vols. (New York: Putnam, 1862–1864), 2:429–31; for membership in the Spanish Royal Academy, see Irving's letter to Prince Dolgorouki, Seville, January 10, 1829, qtd. *ibid.*, 2:366.

34. Benton, speech on the Oregon question given in 1846, in *Key Concepts in American Cultural History*, 398. I treat the links between westward expansion, divine providence, and racial doctrines of the superiority of the white race in my "'Roman Countenances' and 'Abominations.'"

35. Key *Concepts in American Cultural History*, 399.

36. *Ibid.*, emphasis added.

37. See Hobsbawm and Ranger, eds., *The Invention of Tradition*, esp. 1–13.

38. Smorag, "From Columbia to the United States of America," 76; Lawrence M. Baldwin and Michel Grimaud, "How New Naming Systems Emerge: The Prototypical Case of Columbus and Washington," *Names* 40 (September 1992), 153–65, here 161.

39. Higham, *Strangers in the Land*, 212–13, and William J. Connell, "What Columbus Day Really Means," *The American Scholar*, October 4, 2012, https://theamericanscholar.org/what-columbus-day-really-means/#, February 13, 2017.

40. Italian genetic inferiority was, of course, difficult to reconcile with the genius of Columbus, Leonardo or Michelangelo, and so at least on one occasion the problem was solved by fiat, declaring that they were actually Nordics. On this and other ramifications of bigotry, eugenics, and U.S. legislation, see Daniel Okrent, *The Guarded Gate* (new York: Scribner, 2019).

41. Marling, *Washington Slept Here*, 151–53, and, for further discussion, Rabinowitz, "George Washington as Icon," 78–79.

42. Loock, "Goodbye Columbus, Hello Abe!" 95.

43. Hobsbawm, "Mass-Producing Traditions: Europe, 1870–1914," 279.

44. Thomas F. Gossett, *Race: The History of an Idea in America* (1963; New York-Oxford: Oxford University Press, 1997), 389 and, for further description and discussion of Grant's racism, 353–63; on anti-immigration, 287–309; on the "tribal twenties," see Higham, *Strangers in the Land*, 270–77. For further discussion of Grant and Osborn, see Jedediah Purdy, "Environmentalism's Racist History," *The New Yorker*, August 13, 2015, http://www.newyorker.com/news/news-desk/environmentalisms-racist-history, February 13, 2017.

45. See Matthew Dennis, *Red, White, and Blue Letter Days: An American Calendar.*

46. Theodore Roosevelt, "Speech Before Knights

of Columbus, New York, October 12, 1915," *Works*, Memorial edn., ed. Hermann Hagedorn (New York: Scribner, 1923), 20:456–59, qtd. 456.

47. Theodore Roosevelt, "Speech at the State Republican Convention, Saratoga, New York, July 19, 1918," *The Roosevelt Policy: Speeches, Letters and State Papers*, ed. William Griffith, vol.3, *Newer Roosevelt Messages* (New York: Current Literature Pub. Co., 1919), 946–56, qtd. 946.

48. Leroy G. Dorsey, *We are All Americans, Pure and Simple: Theodore Roosevelt and the Myth of Americanism* (Tuscaloosa: University of Alabama Press, 2007), 7. For a more recent attempt to portray Theodore Roosevelt as a rather sinister figure in American history, see T. J. Jackson Lears, *Rebirth of a Nation: The Making of Modern America, 1877–1920* (New York: HarperCollins, 2009). On Stephen Miller's use of the Roosevelt quotation, see William D. Cohan, "How Stephen Miller Rode White Rage from Duke's Campus to Trump's West Wing," *Vanity Fair*, May 30, 2017, https://www.vanityfair.com/news/2017/05/stephen-miller-duke-donald-trump, August 26, 2018.

49. Theodore Roosevelt, qtd. in Dorsey, *We are All Americans, Pure and Simple*, 33.

50. Linda Gordon, *The Second Coming of the KKK: The Ku Klux Klan of the 1920s and the American Political Tradition* (New York: W. W. Norton, 2017), 41–49.

51. *Ibid.*, 60.

52. *Ibid.*, 101–102. On the Knights of Columbus, see Christopher J. Kauffman, *Faith and Fraternalism: The History of the Knights of Columbus, 1882–1982.* (New York: Harper & Row, 1982); on the Order Sons of Italy, see Dominic Candeloro, "Italian Americans," in *Multiculturalism in the United States: A Comparative Guide to Acculturation and Ethnicity*, ed. John D. Buenker and Lorman A. Ratner, rev. and exp. edn. (Westport, CT: Greenwood Press, 2005), 233–56.

53. John D. Thomas, "George Washington," *The Columbia Companion to American History on Film: How the Movies Have Portrayed the American Past*, ed. Peter C. Rollins (New York: Columbia University Press, 2004), 198–203, here 200.

54. Loock, "Goodbye Columbus, Hello Abe!" 91.

55. See Dennis, *Red, White, and Blue Letter Days.*

56. Irving to Bryant, December 26, 1851, in Pierre M. Irving, *Letters*, 4:283. A year after Irving's death, Bryant became his first hagiographer. For the Capriolo portrait, see Irving's letter to Prince Dolgorouki, February 4, 1829, *ibid.*, 2:377.

57. Vermeule, *Numismatic Art in America*, 87–88, 230, and Gene Hessler, "Capturing the True Columbus," *The Numismatist* 105:10 (October 1992): 1436–39. For a fanciful illustration by F. O. C. Darley for a projected illustrated volume of Irving's *Life and Voyages of Christopher Columbus*, see Myers, *The Worlds of Washington Irving*, 54; the illustration is available from the New York Public Library, Manuscript and Archives Division in the Duyckinck, Hellman, Seligman's collections and Washington Irving Papers.

58. Haxby, OH-320-G40.

59. Haxby, MA-140-G66, G-122, G-84, and G-118.

60. Haxby, WI-95-G2, G2a, and R5 ($3b notes raised from the G2 series); for the $2 notes, see G4, G4a, and R7 ($5 notes raised from the G4 series).

61. Classification follows Haxby, here and in the following.

62. Haxby, MS-80-G20 and DE-85-G56; for good illustrations, see *Whitman*, 7:399 and 8:46. Another bank issuing notes with the identical vignette was the Farmers Bank of the State of Delaware, Dover, Delaware (Haxby, DE-15-G90a and G90b).

63. Haxby, NY-2155-G22, G22a through G22d, NJ-345-G2a, G20a and G20b, RI-160-G20 (illustration in *Whitman*, 5:88), ME-125-G8, NH-265-G10, RI-545-G30 (illustration in *Whitman*, 5:288), VT-20-G8 (illustration in *Whitman*, 5:326), VT35-G24, and NH-135-G6 and G6b. $20 notes from the Mechanics Bank, Providence, Rhode Island, 1850s, also bore the identical vignette (Haxby, RI-340-G36).

64. Haxby, MA-120-G10, PA-575-G32, MA-140-G118 (illustration in *Whitman*, 3:90).

65. Another instance of avoiding Civil War themes is provided by the Presidential medal for Andrew Johnson, on which "peace" is symbolized by pictorial conventions that go back to the peace medals of the Revolutionary era and the early republic, which were given as tokens of friendship to Native American chiefs in alliance with the patriots and, later, the United States. Cornelius Vermeule describes the Andrew Johnson medal as follows: "Before a bust of George Washington on a Roman altar, Liberty and a thoroughly Roman Indian shake hands. The latter holds his pipe of peace, and his tools of war or of the chase are at his feet. Buffalo and an Indian on horseback gallop across the plains at the left. Gears, anchors, forging tools, and the inevitable plow lie at the Graeco-Roman Liberty's feet. The train speeding across a viaduct at the right complements the scene of galloping bison on the opposite side of the apotheosis of Washington. The Indian and Liberty clutching her flag are set on a podium that leads to the steps of the Washington Memorial, as if the whole ensemble were a monumental marble relief or a painted signboard." Vermeule, *Numismatic Art in America*, 76, and for an illustration, *ibid.*, 75.

66. See Bryan, "George Washington: Symbolic Guardian of the Republic," 63.

67. Friedberg and Friedberg, *Paper Money of the United States*, 122, 125, and 337; Bowers, *U.S. Paper Money*, 253–54, 263–64, and, for further description and analysis, Loock, "Goodbye Columbus, Hello Abe!" 90.

68. Vanderlyn's painting was inspired by the description of the landing in Washington Irving's biography. Loock, "Goodbye Columbus, Hello Abe!" 87–89 and, for illustrations, Bowers, *U.S. Paper Money*, 217, 219, and 223.

69. Loock, "Goodbye Columbus, Hello Abe!" 86; for illustrations and brief descriptions, see Bowers, *U.S. Paper Money*, 734–37.

70. Vermeule, *Numismatic Art in America*, 87–88, 230; Paul Martin Lester, "Looks Are Deceiving: The Portraits of Christopher Columbus," *Visual Anthropology* 5 (1993), 221–27, and Nancy Oliver and

Richard Kelly, "Columbus Controversy," *The Numismatist* 126:11 (November 2013), 98–99. Further research indicates that the anonymous portrait dates from 1516. See Bruno Aloi, "Ritratto di Cristoforo Colombo di Anonimo ai Musei Civici di Como," Comitato Nazionale Cristoforo Colombo, November 19, 2016, http://www.cristoforocolombo.com/ritratti-colombo/ritratto-cristoforo-colombo-anonimo-ai-musei-civici-como/, accessed April 6, 2018.

71. Vermeule, *Numismatic Art in America*, 90–92, quotation 90. Saint-Gaudens had rendered a nude boy in his initial design for the reverse. Both this and two more proposals were turned down. Instead, Charles E. Barber's uncontroversial (and cluttered) design was selected. The decision infuriated Saint-Gaudens, who later "savaged" Barber's accepted design.

72. *Ibid.*, 226.

Chapter 8

1. Roy Kreitner, "Shifting the Grounds of Monetary Politics: The Case of 1870," *Culture and Money in the Nineteenth Century: Abstracting Economics*, ed. Daniel Bivona and Marlene Tromp (Athens: Ohio University Press, 2016), 66–97, quotation 66.

2. Friedberg and Friedberg, *Paper Money of the United States*, 29 (168), and 137 (1166-i and 1166-n).

3. Bowers, *Whitman Encyclopedia of U.S. Paper Money*, 316–17 (W-1191-).

4. Qtd. in Michael O'Malley, "Specie and Species: Race and the Money Question in Nineteenth-Century America," *The American Historical Review* 99:2 (April 1994), 369–395, qtd. 383.

5. Qtd. in Mihm, *A Nation of Counterfeiters*, 315.

6. Treasury Secretary Salmon P. Chase, "national in their character"; John Sherman, "a sentiment of nationality," both qtd. in Tschachler, *The Greenback*, 110, 112. All National Banks received "charters" that were valid only for a limited time. Notes from the first charter period are known as "Series 1863," those from the second charter period as "Series 1882." Altogether, "Nationals" were issued from 1863 to 1922. Friedberg and Friedberg, *Paper Money of the United States*, 75–102, and 332, 333, 334.

7. Spencer M. Clark, qtd. in Bowers, *Obsolete Paper Money*, 406. Clark had advocated the use of panoramic scenes already during the planning stage for the Legal Tender Notes. Such scenes did not come to pass on these notes, but Clark continued to persist, including the idea in the letter to Chase. (The letter is among the Records of the Bureau of Engraving and Printing, Record Group 318, USNA.)

8. American history books of the nineteenth century commonly represented Burgoyne as the one British general from the War of Independence who was the most responsible for plundering and looting, massacres, unspeakable cruelties, and destruction—and for stirring up the native tribes against the Americans. Eugen Kotte, "USA. Konsens und Mission," in *Mythen der Nationen. Ein europäisches Panorama*, ed. Monika Flacke (Berlin: Deutsches Historisches Museum, 1988), 557–75, here 564–65.

9. Helleiner, "National Currencies," 1412–1414.

10. National Monetary Commission, qtd. in Andrew McFarland Davis, *The Origin of the National Banking System* (Washington, DC: Government Printing Office, 1910), 106.

11. Scott's campaign was, of course, a military success, but many American statesmen were dismayed about the war itself, including Henry Clay, Ulysses Grant, and Attorney General Robert Kennedy, for whom the war was definitely not "a very bright chapter in our history." See Guardina, *The Dead March*, quotation 205.

12. See, on the artworks, Ann Uhry Abrams, "National Paintings and American Character: Historical Murals in the Capitol Rotunda," in *Picturing History: American Painting 1770–1930*, ed. William Ayres (New York: Rizzoli International, 1993), 65–80.

13. Wendy Bellion, "Politics in American Art," Chicago Humanities Festival, November 1, 2015, https://www.youtube.com/watch?v=zKyvCaKpW-c0&feature=youtu.be, December 11, 2015; Ferguson, *American Enlightenment*, 112–13 and, for further discussion, Simon P. Newman, *Parades and the Politics of the Street: Festive Culture in the Early American Republic* (Philadelphia: University of Pennsylvania Press, 1997). For an illustration of *Celebration of Independence*, reproduced in John Warner Barber's *Interesting Events in the History of the United States* (1830), see Tschachler, *Political Fatherhood*, chapter 10.

14. George Washington, "General Orders," July 10, 1776, *Founders Online*, National Archives, http://founders.archives.gov/documents/Washington/03-05-02-0185, retrieved September 26, 2017.

15. Benson J. Lossing, *A Primary History of the United States: For Schools and Families* (1858; New York: Sheldon & Co., 1870), 94.

16. Jesse Olney, *A History of the United States States, on a new plan; adapted to the capacity of youth* (1836; New-Haven, CT: Durrie & Peck 1839), 108.

17. Lossing, *A Primary History of the United States*, 94. The painting, which was executed by Junius Brutus Stearns around the time of the centennial of the battle, shows a gallant Washington at right, on horseback, in the pose of a hero who, at the moment of the collapse of British resistance against French superior forces, takes command after Braddock's fatal wound. It communicates Washington's resolve in view of the imminent catastrophe (hinted at through the chaos at left) and, explicitly, presents him as the protector of American colonists. View reproductions of the painting in Herbert J. Bass et al., *America and Americans*, vol. 1, *From Exploration to Reconstruction* (Morristown, NJ: Silver Burdett Press, 1983), 181, and Matthew A. Byron, "Battle of the Monongahela," *Digital Encyclopedia of George Washington*, n.d., http://www.mountvernon.org/digital-encyclopedia/article/battle-of-the-monongahela/, April 6, 2018. A lithograph of the painting by Régnier, published in Paris c.1854, is among the holdings of the Library of Congress Prints and Photographs Division, LC-DIG-pga-02418.

18. Olney, *A History of the United States*, 144.

19. Tschachler, *Political Fatherhood*, chapter 10. On the critical reception of Leutze's epic painting and its function as "visual ideology" see Thistlethwaite, "*Washington Crossing the Delaware*: Navigating the Image(s) of the Hero," in *George Washington in and as Culture*, ed. Kevin L. Cope et al. (New York: AMS Press, 2001), 39–63. I have also drawn here on Louis Kern's conference paper, "'A New Gospel to This Continent…,'" Paper given to "American Foundational Myths," Swiss Association for American Studies (SANAS) / Austrian Association for American Studies Joint Conference, University of Zurich, November 19–21, 2000. On the emergence of the "Manifest Destiny" movement, see Albert K. Weinberg, *Manifest Destiny: A Study of Nationalist Expansionism in American History* (Chicago: Quadrangle Books, 1963), 107–29.

20. Kern, "'A New Gospel to This Continent….'"

21. David Hackett Fischer, *Washington's Crossing* (New York-Oxford: Oxford University Press, 2004), 1. I have also drawn in this paragraph from Thistlethwaite, *The Image of Washington*, 87–88, and Brumwell, *Gentleman Warrior*, 278–79. For a detailed consideration of the painting's reception, see Barbara S. Groseclose, *Emanuel Leutze, 1816–1868: Freedom Is the Only King* (Washington, DC: Smithsonian Institution Press, 1975), 40–41.

22. Bingham's *Washington Crossing the Delaware* is currently located at the Chrysler Museum of Art, Norfolk, Virginia. To view the painting, visit http://collection.chrysler.org/emuseum/view/objects/asitem/search$0040/3/title-asc?t:state:-flow=d3df6110-288f-4f8a-b652-c9a1827cd9c3, accessed August 23, 2017. Both *Washington Crossing* and *Daniel Boone* are reproduced in Thistlethwaite, *The Image of George Washington*, 260, figs. 79 and 80.

23. The film, which was directed by Robert Harmon, stars Jeff Daniels as George Washington. William McDonald, "The General, The River, The Famous Boat Ride," *New York Times*, January 10, 2000, http://www.nytimes.com/2000/01/10/arts/television-review-the-general-the-river-the-famous-boat-ride.html, March 2, 2017. For *The Miller of New Jersey*, see Bryan, *Washington in American Literature*, 183.

24. See Tschachler, *Political Fatherhood*, chapter 10. In 1999, in a climate of renewed patriotism, the New Jersey quarter came to bear the solemn inscription "Crossroads of the Revolution," relating to Washington's crossing of the Delaware River into New Jersey.

25. Marling, *Washington Slept Here*, 136; other references in this paragraph are to *ibid.*, 383, 378, 160, and 336.

26. A second vignette, engraved by Louis Delnoce after Mason Locke Weems' Valley Forge fable, shows Washington at prayer before a battle. A kneeling Washington is shown with three goddesses and a banner inscribed VICTORY above. The $50 National Bank notes were issued from 1863 until 1922. From 1870 to 1875, Washington Crossing the Delaware was also printed on the California National Gold Bank Notes. Friedberg and Friedberg, *Paper Money of the United States*, 83, 91, 101, and 135.

27. Delnoce created the *Apotheosis of Washington* vignette for the American Bank Note Company in 1862. He posed himself and his daughter, drew the artwork, and engraved the vignette. For a description and an illustration of the vignette, see Tomasko, *The Feel of Steel*, 87; for the note from the Oil City Bank, see Tomasko's *Images of Value*, 62–63.

28. Schwartz, "A New Man for a New Century," 125–26.

29. Bowers, *U.S. Paper Money*, 124–26. On possible image sources for Martha Washington's portrait, see Tomasko, *Images of Value*, 91 and 98.

30. Haxby, GA-10-G50; *Whitman*, W-GA-180-050-G060; ills. in *Whitman*, 6:100, 101 (counterfeit note).

31. Haxby, NC-85-G6 and G8a; *Whitman*, W-NC-560-004-G020 and G020a; ills. in *Whitman*, 6:352, 353.

32. Ind*iana Democrat*, qtd. in "Martha on $1," *George Washington's Mount Vernon*, n.d., http://www.mountvernon.org/george-washington/martha-washington/martha-on-1/, September 20, 2017.

33. On the other hand, the notes were so heavily engraved that they became dark from dirt and wear after much circulation. There were other criticisms, too, and so the notes were later declared a failure and were discontinued only two years after their issue. Tomasko, *The Feel of Steel*, 46, and *Images of Value*, 91–93. For "a touch of Wagner and Beethoven," see Standish, *The Art of Money*, 139. For a description of the events surrounding the production and public reception of the Educational notes, see the series of articles by Thomas Morris II, "The Life and Work of Thomas F. Morris, 1852–1898," *Essay-Proof Journal* 23:1 (1966) to 25:2 (1968).

34. Kemm, *The Official Guide of United States Paper Money*, qtd. in Nordham, *George Washington and Money*, 105.

35. Hobsbawm, "Mass-Producing Traditions," 280, 279 (emphasis in original).

36. William McKinley, "Inaugural Address," March 4, 1897. Online by Gerhard Peters and John T. Woolley, *The American Presidency Project*, http://www.presidency.ucsb.edu/ws/?pid=25827, retrieved August 23, 2018.

37. For a good example of the state-as-teacher approach to currency iconography, see *Nation-States and Money: The Past, Present, and Future of National Currencies*, ed. Emily Gilbert and Eric Helleiner (London: Routledge, 1999). For an elaboration of the state-as-legitimacy-seeker approach, see the writings of Jacques Hymans, especially "The Changing Color of Money."

38. Ferguson, *The American Enlightenment*, 180; Marina Warner, *Monuments and Maidens: The Allegory of the Female Form* (New York: Atheneum, 1985), xx, 277.

39. Sparks, *Life*, 99, here qtd. in Bryan, *Washington in American Literature* 117.

40. For "awe-inspiring air," see *ibid.*.

41. Abigail Adams, letter to Judge F. A. Vanderbilt, February 3, 1814, qtd. in Ferguson, *The American Enlightenment*, 182.

Chapter 9

1. Angela L. Miller et al., *American Encounters: Art, History, and Cultural Identity* (Upper Saddle River, NJ: Pearson, Prentice Hall, 2008), 160–63; for an illustration of *Allegory of Female Education*, from the Peabody Essex Museum, Salem, Massachusetts, see *ibid.*, 134.

2. John Adams and Abigail Adams, qtd. in Ferguson, *The American Enlightenment*, 152.

3. Annetta Gordon-Reed and Peter S. Onuf, *"Most Blessed of the Patriarchs": Thomas Jefferson and the Empire of the Imagination* (New York-London: Liveright, 2016), 119 and, for further discussion of Jefferson's "family values," 183–85.

4. Paine, *An Occasional Letter on the Female Sex*, qtd. in Ferguson, *The American Enlightenment*, 179.

5. William Blackstone, *Commentaries on the Laws of England* (1765–69), qtd. *ibid.*, 160.

6. Mary Poovey, *Uneven Developments: The Ideological Work of Gender in Mid-Victorian England* (Chicago: University of Chicago Press, 1998), 80. The sentiment even speaks from the gospels: When Jesus reminds a supplicant, "Thou knowest the commandments," the first one he lists is "Do not commit adultery," before murder (Mark 10:19; similarly Luke 18:20). In another episode, brought before Jesus is a woman "taken in adultery," who by the law of Moses is to be stoned (John 8:3–11); in this instance, Jesus diplomatically resolves the quandary by saying that whoever is without sin first cast a stone at the woman (*ibid.*. 7).

7. Luce Irigaray, *This Sex which is Not One*, trans. Catherine Porter with Carolyn Burke (Ithaca, NY: Cornell University Press, 1985), 222; I have here made use of Eva Boesenberg's reading of the passage in "Self-made Women, Spent Men? Money and Gender in U.S. American Novels since the 1980s," in *Almighty Dollar: Papers and Lectures from the Velden Conference*, ed. Heinz Tschachler, Eugen Banauch, and Simone Puff (Wien-Münster: LIT Verlag, 2010), 159–80, here 160–61.

8. The same notion is preserved in the German phrase "*unter die Haube kommen*."

9. Hessler, *The Engraver's Line*, 280–85. Prints of Smillie's engraved portrait have invariably been on offer at Heritage Auctions. For an October, 2000 auction, go to https://currency.ha.com/itm/miscellaneous/small-oval-engraved-portrait-of-george-washington-approximatel/a/30101-10401.s, accessed March 31, 2017. For descriptions of the $2 notes, see Friedberg and Friedberg, *Paper Money of the United States*, 54–55 (notes 249–258, Design 67) and 327, and Bowers, *U.S. Paper Money*, 186 (Bowers does not identify the engraver). For the 1922 postage stamp (the artwork was by Leo C. Kauffmann), see Tomasko, *Images of Value*, 98.

10. This was the second of the Series 1882. It became necessary because of a change in the security or backing of the notes authorized by the Aldrich-Vreeland Act of May 30, 1908. The Washington portrait is at left on the notes' back; at right is the U.S. Capitol. Friedberg and Friedberg, *Paper Money of the United States*, 93, and Bowers, *U.S. Paper Money*, 229–35.

11. The United States notes of the series 1923 are identical with the Silver Certificates of the same series, the type description excepting. Friedberg and Friedberg, *Paper Money of the United States* 52, 327. For the Elm City Bank notes, see Haxby, CT-275-G2a and G2b, and *Whitman*, 1:141.

12. Friedberg and Friedberg, *Paper Money of the United States*, 133–35.

13. Bowers, U.S. *Paper Money*, 484–86. Gold Certificates were first introduced in 1863. The denomination "Technicolor note" for the $20 note, series 1905–1907, is somewhat of a misnomer, as the technicolor technique was not invented until 1916.

14. *Ibid.*, 133–35.

15. Los *Angeles Times*, February 22, 1918, qtd. in Schwartz, "A New Man for a New Century," 34.

16. Bernard Schaaf, "The Shrinking Dollar or The Decline and Fall of Beautiful American Banknotes," *International Bank Note Society Journal* 24:2 (June 1985), 38–40, here 40.

17. The reduction in size indeed impacted on production costs, not least with respect to paper and ink. Tschachler, *The Greenback*, 181–82 and, for a reading of the reform as a crisis symptom, Standish, *The Art of Money*, 141.

18. Hoover qtd. in Matthew Crenson and Benjamin Ginsberg, *Presidential Power: Unchecked and Unbalanced* (New York: Norton, 2007), 149; I have also drawn here and in the preceding paragraph on David M. Kennedy, *Freedom from Fear: The American People in Depression and War, 1929–1945* (New York: Oxford University Press, 1999), 85–93.

19. William Atherton Du Puy, "Whose Pictures Should Go On Our Paper Money," *American Bankers Association Journal* 19 (March 1927), 790–91, here 790. Hillegas was the first Treasurer of the United States; Hendricks was Vice President under Grover Cleveland in 1885. Coins were organized in a similarly messy way: On some coins the numerical value was spelled out, on some it was not; on some, the value was given in Arabic numbers, on others in Roman numbers; on occasion, abbreviations such as "D" (for dollar) or "C" (for cent) were used.

20. Friedberg and Friedberg, *Paper Money of the United States*, 158–205, passim. Since 1963, Federal Reserve notes have been exlusive.

21. For an overview of the development of America's paper money since the Civil War, see Lauer, "Money as Mass Comunication," 121–24.

22. United States Department of the Treasury Bureau of Engraving and Printing (USBEP), "U.S. CURRENCY FAQs," n.d., http://www.moneyfactory.gov/faqlibrary.html, July 7, 2014.

23. USBEP, "Selection of Portraits and Designs Appearing on Paper Currency," n.d., http://www.moneyfactory.gov/document.cfm/18/118, August 15, 2001.

24. Coolidge, qtd. in Marling, *Washington Slept Here*, 261.

25. Henry Ford is customarily remembered as the Good Businessman for whom history was "more

or less bunk." Yet in the late 1920s, Ford turned his birthplace, Greenfield Village (near Detroit), into a museum of early American history. And he became an avid collector of Washingtoniana. Marling, *Washington Slept Here*, 280–81, 285–88. Michael Schudson, "the past is constantly being retold," qtd. in Schwartz, "A New Man for a New Century," 137.

26. "Legislation passed in 1889 mandates that all banknotes and other securities containing portraits include the name of the individual below the portrait." United States Currency Education Program, "The History of American Currency," n.d. https://www.uscurrency.gov/content/history-american-currency, April 6, 2017. The law now is part of 31 USC 5114(b): "The name of the individual [whose portrait appears on U.S. currency and securities] shall be inscribed below the portrait."

27. See U.S. Department of the Treasury, *History of the Bureau of Engraving and Printing, 1862–1962* (Washington, DC: Treasury Department, 1962), and Murray Teigh Bloom, *The Brotherhood of Money: The Secret World of the Bank Note Printers* (Port Clinton, OH: BNR Press), 1984.

28. See Leisering, "DDR-Banknoten," 141–48.

29. From the central chapter in Williams' collection of essays, *In the American Grain*, qtd. in Marling, *Washington Slept Here*, 295.

30. James Garfield was shot on July 2, 1881, seven months after his election to the presidency. He died on September 19, 1881. Less than a year later, his portrait appeared on $5 National Bank Notes. The notes thus are the first (albeit unofficial) "commemorative notes." The second president who was accorded this honor was William McKinley; his portrait appeared on the $10 National Bank Notes, Series 1902, likewise less than a year after his violent death in Buffalo, New York, on September 14, 1901. Friedberg and Friedberg, *Paper Money of the United States*, 98, 108, 333, 335; Hessler, "Unofficial Commemorative Notes," *The Numismatist* 105:5 (May 1992), 656–58.

31. Tschachler, *The Greenback*, 122. This was the official reason, though it is probably not too far-fetched to assume that the discontinuation of large-denomination notes was a precaution against tax fraud and money laundering. *Ibid.*, 22–23.

32. The series year is 1934, not 1935, as the series number then identified the year of the approval of the design. The design of the one-dollar note, which was done in part by Edward Mitchell Weeks from the Bureau of Engraving and Printing, was approved by President Roosevelt, and signed by Henry Morgenthau, Jr., who was then Secretary of the Treasury, and W. A. Julian, the Treasurer of the United States, in 1934.

33. The *New York Times*, June 5, 1927, qtd. in Loock, "Goodbye Columbus, Hello Abe!" 92. In March of the same year, William Du Puy had used similar arguments in the *American Bankers Association Journal*: "The thing to be desired is that the man in the street should come to recognize bills of each denomination at a glance and without reference to the number in the corner." Du Puy, "Whose Pictures Should Go On Our Paper Money," 790.

34. Clifford Geertz, *The Interpretation of Cultures: Selected Essays* (New York: Basic Books, 1973), 215.

35. "We Hope It's Elmer on the New Bill," *Chicago Daily Tribune*, July 9, 1929, qtd. in Loock, "Goodbye Columbus, Hello Abe!" 92.

36. Washington's portrait, like most other features of the front design, was retained from large-size $1 notes, Legal Tender Notes and Silver Certificates, Series 1923. Friedberg and Friedberg, *Paper Money of the United States*, 16, 52.

37. See Federal Reserve Board, "U. S. Currency Education Program (CEP)," n.d., https://www.uscurrency.gov/seven-denominations, May 22, 2015.

38. Doty, *America's Money, America's Story*, 198.

39. Standish, *The Art of Money*, 142.

40. Heij, *Designing Banknote Identity*, 46.

41. Hymans, "The Changing Color of Money," 29.

42. Deutsche Bundesbank, "Das besondere Objekt [The Special Object]. Ästhetik und Sicherheit—Weltbanknoten der Jahre 2005 bis 2009," November 24, 2010, http://www.bundesbank.de/Redaktion/DE/Downloads/Bundesbank/Geld_Kunstsammlung/aesthetik_und_sicherheit_weltbanknoten.pdf?__blob=publicationFile, December 2, 2014: Not simply "ein *Gegenstand des täglichen Gebrauchs für jedermann … als Werbeträger sollte sie ein Spiegelbild der Werte sein, die sie repräsentiert, wie Stabilität, Kontinuität und Krisenfestigkeit. […] Daher wird die Banknote gelegentlich auch als Visitenkarte eines Staates bezeichnet.*"

43. See Birger P. Priddat, "'Geist der Ornamentik,' Ideogrammatik des Geldes: Allegorien bürgerlicher Zivilreligion auf Banknoten des 19. und 20. Jahrhunderts," in *Kapitalismus als Religion*, ed. Dirk Baecker (Berlin: Kadmos Verlag, 2003), 19–34, here 29: "*…an die Stelle der allegorischen Religion tritt das kollektive Gedächtnis der Gesellschaften.*"

44. Hymans, "The Changing Color of Money," 8–12.

45. On presidential portraits and currency legitimacy, see Marcia Pointon, "Money and Nationalism," in *Imaging Nations*, ed. Geoffrey Cubitt (Manchester, UK: Manchester University Press, 1998), 229–54. Modern U.S. coins are different in this respect. Beginning with the Lincoln cent in 1909, Washington, Jefferson, Roosevelt, Franklin, Eisenhower, Kennedy, but also Susan B. Anthony, Sacagawea, Francis Scott Key, and many other non-state actors have appeared on the coinage, with an unforeseen problem—Mint officials run out of denominations before they run out of deserving people. Nottelmann, "Make Sense of Our Coinage," 99–100. John Katsion has come to similar conclusions in his study of the stories told by the images on dollar coins. Whereas the coins' designs clearly reflect various cultural shifts, the currency is much more static. See "'Symbols Are Important': Nation-States and the Images on Our Money," especially 41–44.

46. Berger, *Ways of Seeing*, 97 and, for further discussion of pictures, W. J. T. Mitchell, *What Do Pictures Want? The Lives and Loves of Images* (Chicago: University of Chicago Press, 2006).

Part IV

1. Roy C. Strong, *Portraits of Queen Elizabeth* (Oxford: Clarendon Press, 1963), 36.

2. Miller and Schwartz, "The Icon of the American Republic," 517.

3. Doty, *America's Money, America's Story*, 198.

Chapter 10

4. For a record of the bicentennial activities see the five-volume history edited by the United States George Washington Bicentennial Commission.

5. For details of some of the more outrageous activities of the Bicentennial see Marling, *Washington Slept Here*, chapter 11, 325–64.

6. *Special News Releases*, qtd. in Marling, *Washington Slept Here*, 337.

7. *Ibid.*, 337–41. The photographer was an immigrant from Austria named Max Jaffé. Houdon's bust originally stood in Washington's mansion at Mount Vernon. A copy created in 1932 is in the Indiana Statehouse in Indianapolis.

8. Vermeule, *Numismatic Art in America*, 165–69, quotation 165. Flanagan, a former assistant to Augustus Saint-Gaudens, had been forced by his commissioners to use as prototype the official photograph of Houdon's neo-classicist bust of 1785. Use of the bust, which is now at Mount Vernon, seems to have had the force of law ever since the Civil War. The 1863 two-cent patterns, a series of 1866 five-cent pattern coins, Charles Barber's Lafayette dollar of 1900, and the 1999 Washington bicentennial commemorative half eagle bore Washington portraits based on Houdon's work. In each instance, however, the resulting designs appear rather cold and lifeless. *Ibid.*, 96, 166, 229–31. For a thorough review of the issuance of the Washington Quarter see *History of the George Washington Bicentennial Celebration*, 5:175–77.

9. Thistlethwaite, "Hero, Celebrity, and Cliché," 149. The sculpture is owned by the Stedelijk Museum, Amsterdam; to view an illustration, go to http://www.stedelijk.nl/en/artwork/64-george-and-mona-in-the-baths-of-coloma, accessed September 19, 2017. On Arneson's *Pinot noir*, see H. Nichols B. Clark, "An Icon Preserved: Continuity in the Sculptural Images of Washington," in *George Washington: American Symbol*, ed. Barbara L. Mitnick (New York: Hudson Hills Press, 1999), 39–53, here 51 and, for a full-color illustration, *ibid.*, 22, plate 27.

10. Frank Moore, *Diary of the American Revolution* (New York: Charles Scribner, 1860), 2:492, qtd. in Miller und Schwartz, "The Icon of the American Republic," 533.

11. See United States Secret Service, www.secretservice.gov, accessed September 1, 2014. For convictions, see the annual reports of the Bureau of Justice Statistics, United States Department of Justice, http://bjs.ojp.usdoj.gov/, accessed October 7, 2012, and the Federal Bureau of Prisons, http://www.bop.gov/about/statistics/, accessed September 27, 2014.

12. Mark Wagner in "Art that's made of Money," CBS Sunday Morning, March 23, 2014, You Tube, https://www.youtube.com/watch?time_continue=10&v=zTahzALzLJU, September 10, 2018.

13. For an illustration of *Greener Grass*, from the "Washington at Large" series, go to http://markwagnerinc.com/washington-at-large/, retrieved September 10, 2018.

14. Mark Wagner, at http://markwagnerinc.com/; you can also follow Wagner on Instagram at https://www.instagram.com/markwagnerinc/. To see his newer work, go to http://markwagnerinc.com/dnm9hqrgbkt12mhy7hvxqrbwfg6ewv; also of interest is *Money, Power, Sex & Mark Wagner at Pavel Zoubok Gallery, September 2013*, Exhibition Catalog (New York: Pavel Zoubok Gallery, 2013), http://markwagnerinc.com/shop/money-power-sex-mark-wagner, June 24, 2018. Harley J. Spiller briefly treats Wagner within the context of "The Art of Money," *Keep the Change: A Collector's Tales of Lucky Pennies, Counterfeit C-Notes, and other Curious Currency* (New York: Princeton Architectural Press, 2015), 40–41.

15. Tschachler, *The Greenback*, 127–51, and Stefan Hartmann, "Faites vos jeux: subversive Banknoten-Fakes," in *Der schöne Schein. Symbolik und Ästhetik von Banknoten*, ed. Stefan Hartmann und Christian Thiel (Regenstauf, Germany: Gietl-Verlag, 2016), 245–76.

16. Sidra Stich, *Made in U.S.A.: An Americanization in Modern Art, the 50s and 60s* (Berkeley: University of California Press, 1987), 40.

17. Get the sticker from Santa Fe Hemp at $2.50 apiece. Santa Fe Hemp, http://www.santafehemp.com/products/i-grew-hemp-sticker, accessed January 5, 2017. Also available are rubber stamps (priced at $6.95 apiece) that make Washington say, "I grew hemp." See Doug Fine, "The Drug Peace Bumblebee," National Cannabis Coalition, July 26, 2013, http://nationalcannabiscoalition.com/2013/07/arizona-conservatives-embrace-the-drug-peace/#sthash.GJwaCRwc.dpuf, July 1, 2014; orders for the rubber stamp may be placed with IGrewHemp at http://www.igrewhemp.net/.

18. See, for an illustration and further description, Thistlethwaite, "Hero, Celebrity, and Cliché," 148, and Barry Schwartz, "Collective Memory and Abortive Commemoration: Presidents' Day and the American Holiday Calendar," *Social Research* 75.1 (2008), 75–110, here 97–98.

19. Thomas Pynchon, *Mason & Dixon* (New York: Henry Holt, 1997), 280.

20. Barry Schwartz, *Abraham Lincoln in the Post-Heroic Era: History and Memory in Late Twentieth-Century America* (Chicago: University of Chicago Press, 2008), xi. On the construction of social or institutional facts, see John R. Searle's *The Construction of Social Reality* (New York: Free Press, 1995).

21. Kenston High School, "Let us all remember," http://www.kenston.k12.oh.us/khs/current/us_dollar_bill.htm, May 5, 2002, no longer available as of 2017.

22. Mary Alice McLarty, "The Dollar Bill," 1996–2000, http://www.maryalice.com/DollarBill.html,

April 16, 2002, 2002, emphases added, and, for further discussion and analysis, Tschachler, *The Greenback*, 153–56.

23. McLarty, "The Dollar Bill."

24. USBEP, "The Great Seal of the United States on Paper Currency," n.d., http://www.moneyfactory.gov/document.cfm/18/2233, August 15, 2001. No longer available as of 2017.

25. USBEP, "FAQs," n.d., http://www.bep.gov/resources/faqs.html, August 15, 2017. Originally from Charles Thomson, secretary of Congress, to the Continental Congress, in late 1778.

26. USBEP, "Survey about New Web Site Features for Bureau of Engraving and Printing," October 6, 2008, http://research.opinionguru.com/mrlWeb/mrlWeb.dll?l.Project=a15057, no longer available as of 2017.

27. Ginnie Mae, "Brain Food: Cool Facts: Money," June 17, 2002, http://www.ginniemae.gov/homezone/brainfood/coolfacts.html, no longer available as of 2017.

28. USBEP, "The New Color of Money," April 27, 2004, www.moneyfactory.com/newmoney, no longer available as of 2017.

29. See Herb Schingoethe and Martha Schingoethe, *College Currency: Money for Business Training: Money for Business Training*, ed. Neil Shafer (Port Clinton, OH: BNR Press, 1993).

30. Barbara Johnston Adams, *The Go-Around Dollar* (New York: Simon & Schuster, 1992) is from 1992; a more recent example of educational outreach to children is Christopher Forest's *Dollar Bill in Translation: What It Really Means* (North Mankato, MN: Capstone P), which dates from 2009. Definitely not for children is Peter Davidson's *Penny: Hands I Passed Through—Things I Saw—Stories I Can Tell!* (Arnolds Park, IA: Sweet Memories Publishing, 2017), which tells the stories of the people whose hands PENNY (actually a late-1982 one-cent piece, the final penny ever minted of 95% copper) passes through.

31. MacCannell, "Sights and Spectacles," 432.

32. *Ibid.*, 425.

33. On the concept of "hegemony," see Perry Anderson, *The H-Word: The Peripateia of Hegemony* (London: Verso Press, 2017).

34. MacCannell, "Sights and Spectacles," 426, emphasis added.

35. *Ibid.*

36. *Ibid.*

Chapter 11

1. "Dead presidents" is a well-known and often-used colloquialism, though it's well worth revealing it to itself. "Fathers," Jean-Joseph Goux notes, can fulfill their privileged roles only as long as they are separated, kept at a distance from the "family," that is, the larger whole. Phrased differently, "fathers" can ascend to symbolic heights and assume transcendence only as "dead fathers," their place reduced to the "Name-of-the-Father" ("Numismatics," 18, 49).

2. See, on white men feeling unworthy and burdensome, Lionel Tiger's treatise *The Decline of Males* (New York: Golden Books, 1999). On America's "national subjectivity" as the dominion of white males, see Dana D. Nelson, *National Manhood: Capitalist Citizenship and the Imagined Fraternity of White Men* (Durham, NC: Duke University Press, 1998) and Valerie Melissa Babb, *Whiteness Visible: The Meaning of Whiteness in American Literature and Culture* (New York-London: New York University Press, 1998). On the close links between monetary systems and patriarchal authority based on property that is held *de jure* (private property over which owners have documented claims on the basis of which it can be sold, mortgaged, or loaned with a view of appropriate returns, as opposed to mere *de facto* possession, the basis of feudal relations in which mutually binding customary rules govern use and material production, reproduction, and consumption), see Heinsohn and Steiger, *Ownership Economics: On the Foundations of Interest, Money, Markets, Business Cycles, and Economic Development*, trans. and ed. Frank Decker (Abingdon, UK-New York: Routledge, 2013), especially chapters 3 and 4 and, from the perspective of literature, Eva Boesenberg, *Money and Gender in the American Novel, 1850–2000* (Heidelberg, Germany: Universitätsverlag Winter, 2010).

3. Joel Siegel, "President Obama: Put faces of women on U.S. currency," *New York Daily News*, July 30, 2014, http://www.nydailynews.com/news/national/president-obama-put-faces-women-u-s-currency-article-1.1886537, July 31, 2014. "President-elect Barack Obama Named 2009 Father of the Year," *American Chronicle* (Washington, DC), January 4, 2009, http://www.americanchronicle.com/articles/view/86742, February 8, 2009; for "Dad speech," see Joel Achenbach, "Achenblog: Obama's Inaugural Address," January 20, 2009, http://voices.washingtonpost.com/achenblog/2009/01/obamas_inaugural_address.html, January 29, 2009.

4. Wome*n on 20s*, http://www.womenon20s.org/, accessed August 28, 2018; postal address: Women on $20s, Inc., PO Box 2353, Mount Vernon, NY 10550, U.S.A.

5. Wome*n on 20s*, "$10 vs. $20," n.d., http://www.womenon20s.org/points, July 4, 2015. One could think of another reason for removing Jackson's portrait: Andrew Jackson has gone down in history for his "war" against the Bank of the United States; while the bank issued paper bills, Jackson was a declared "hard money man"—hence his portrait is not exactly a fitting choice for bills issued by the Federal Reserve.

6. Wome*n on 20s*, "The Petition," May 11, 2015, http://www.womenon20s.org/the_petition, May 18, 2015.

7. Harriet Tubman received some 30 percent of a total of more than 350,000 votes cast in the final round on April 5, 2015. Runners-up were Eleanor Roosevelt, Rosa Parks, and Wilma Mankiller. *Women on 20s*, "Results," May 18, 2015, http://www.womenon20s.org/results, May 18, 2015.

8. "Remarks of Secretary Jacob J. Lew at The National Archives," June 18, 2015, http://www.treasury.gov/P-center/P-releases/Pages/jl0082.aspx, June 26, 2016.

9. U. S. Department of the Treasury, "Introducing the new $20, $10, and $5," November 16, 2016, https://www.treasury.gov/P-center/news/Pages/Introducing-The-New-20,-10,-And-5.aspx, August 2, 2018.

10. Maya Rhodan, "The Harriet Tubman $20 Bill Could Make an Early Debut," *Time*, December 7, 2016, http://time.com/4593420/harriet-tubman-20-bill-donald-trump-design/, January 7, 2017.

11. *Women on 20s*, "Women on 20s on the March," January 6, 2017, http://www.womenon20s.org/on_the_march, January 7, 2017.

12. Alan Rappaport, "Harriet Tubman $20 Bill Is Delayed Until Trump Leaves Office, Mnuchin Says," *New York Times*, May 22, 2019, https://www.nytimes.com/2019/05/22/us/harriet-tubman-bill.html, June 24, 2019. For Symbols Matter T-Shirts, available from the Women for 20s Store, go to https://www.womenon20s.org/women_on_20s_store.

13. Wome*n on 20s*, "Mnuchin's Excuse for Delaying the Harriet Tubman $20 Bill Is Insulting," https://www.womenon20s.org/mnuchin_s_excuse_for_delaying_the_harriet_tubman_20_bill_is_insulting, May 23, 2019, and "Our Reaction to the Mnuchin Delay," http://www.womenon20s.org/, June 24, 2019. NPR, June 24, 2019, https://www.npr.org/2019/06/24/735525569/treasury-department-launches-investigation-into-delays-behind-harriet-tubman-20-, June 25, 2019. As for the Harriet Tubman Tribute Act (HR 1083), after its introduction the bill was immediately referred to the House Committee on Financial Services; to date (September 19, 2019), no further action has been taken. See Congress.gov, https://www.congress.gov/bill/116th-congress/house-bill/1083?q=%7B"search"%3A%5B"S+582"%5D%7D&r=175&s=1.

14. "President Donald Trump's Remarks at Andrew Jackson's Hermitage," March 15, 2017, YouTube, https://www.youtube.com/watch?v=thx5_2jfpiU, June 27, 2017. For Jackson as "an amazing figure in American history," see Max Greenwood, "Trump hangs portrait of Andrew Jackson in Oval Office," *The Hill*, January 25, 2017, http://thehill.com/homenews/administration/316115-trump-hangs-portrait-of-andrew-jackson-in-oval-office, January 26, 2017.

15. Maggie Haberman, "A Homebody Finds the Ultimate Home Office," *New York Times*, January 25, 2017, https://www.nytimes.com/2017/01/25/us/politics/president-trump-white-house.html?_r=1, January 26, 2017. Since the hanging of the portrait, the likeness of America's seventh president has been on every official photograph showing President Trump at work. According to *Newsweek*, the film was getting early Oscar buzz months ahead of its release. H. Alan Scott, "The Harriet Biopic Is Here and It's Already Generating Oscar Buzz," *Newsweek*, July 23, 2019, https://www.newsweek.com/harriet-tubman-biopic-here-its-already-generating-oscar-buzz-1450769.

16. Sam Frizell, "Donald Trump Says Harriet Tubman on the $20-Bill is 'Political Correctness,'" *Time*, April 21, 2016, http://time.com/4303332/donald-trump-says-harriet-tubman-on-the-20-bill-is-political-correctness/, January 7, 2017. One wonders how (if at all) President Trump will respond to *Harriet*, a Focus Features biopic released in November 2019. The film, which stars Cynthia Erivo as Harriet Tubman, follows Harriet Tubman's daring escape from the slave South to Philadelphia and her subsequent return trips to the South where she rescued her family and other slaves on what came to be known as the Underground Railroad. It also shows her involvement in the early days of the Civil War as a member of the Union Army.

17. The article from *Galaxy* magazine is also reproduced in Vermeule, *Numismatic Art in America*, 72–74. For an illustration of the Seated Liberty dollar, see Garrett and Guth, *100 Greatest U.S. Coins*, 98; for an exhaustive treatment of the controversy, see Christina L. McGinley "Coining Nationality: Woman as Spectacle on 19th-Century Currency," *American Transcendental Quarterly* 7 (1993), 247–69, here 255–58. The custom of using women as a "spectacle of nationhood" was not uniquely American, though; rather, as McGinley has shown, it reflects a long-standing habit, typical both of Europe and of the United States, which gendered nations as female.

18. Carol Lee, "Alexander Hamilton to Share Image on $10 Bill With a Woman," *The Wall Street Journal*, June 17, 2015, https://www.wsj.com/articles/alexander-hamilton-to-share-image-on-10-bill-with-a-woman-1434591472, September 6, 2018.

19. Hillary Clinton, *What Happened*, 224–25.

20. Uri Friedman, "Why It's So Hard for a Woman to Become President of the United States," *The Atlantic*, November 12, 2016, https://www.theatlantic.com/international/archive/2016/11/clinton-woman-leader-world/506945/, March 11, 2018. Sexism and stereotypes are, of course, only one obstacle to be overcome. Another, related one, is that women have always found it extremely difficult to raise funds sizeable enough for a prolonged and successful campaign. On this issue see Ellen Fitzpatrick, *The Highest Glass Ceiling: Women's Quest for the American Presidency* (Cambridge, MA: Harvard University Press, 2016), 276–77.

21. Annette Gordon-Reed, "Female Trouble," *The New York Review of Books* LXV:2 (February 8, 2018), 12–14, qtd. 13. On the wide literature addressing women and the American presidency, see Fitzpatrick, *The Highest Glass Ceiling*, 295*n*2.

22. Second presidential debate, Sunday, October 9, 2016, Washington University, St. Louis, MO. For a transcript, go to http://www.nytimes.com/2016/10/10/us/politics/transcript-second-debate.html?ribbon-ad-idx=11&rref=politics&module=Ribbon&version=origin&region=Header&action=click&contentCollection=Politics&pgtype=article, accessed October 10, 2016. Ten days later, Trump repeated the charge: Clinton only "talks" and, if elected to the presidency, would be "a mess." He, in contrast, would "run the country the way I run my company." Third presidential debate, Wednesday, October 19, 2016, University of Nevada, Las Vegas, NV. Watch the debate and read the transcript at https://www.washingtonpost.com/news/the-fix/wp/2016/10/19/the-final-trump-clinton-de-

bate-transcript-annotated/, accessed October 20, 2016. Finally, in his Inaugural Address, really a recycled campaign speech, Trump announced: "We will no longer accept politicians who are all talk and no action—constantly complaining but never doing anything about it. The time for empty talk is over. Now arrives the hour of action." Donald J. Trump, "Inaugural Address," The White House, January 20, 2017, Web, January 23, 2017, https://www.whitehouse.gov/inaugural-address.

23. As Hillary Clinton writes in her memoir, historically, "women haven't been the ones writing the laws or leading the armies and navies. [...] It's the men who lead. It's the men who speak. [...] That's been the case for so long it has infiltrated our deepest thoughts." *What Happened*, 223.

24. Rebecca Solnit, "From Lying to Leering," *London Review of Books*, January 19, 2017, http://www.lrb.co.uk/v39/n02/rebecca-solnit/from-lying-to-leering, January 29, 2017.

25. International Women's Day was introduced in 1910. It is a global day celebrating the social, economic, cultural and political achievements of women. See International Women's Day (March 8), n.d., https://www.internationalwomensday.com/About, November 29, 2016.

26. See Virginia Bernhard, "Mother's Day," *The Family in America: An Encyclopedia*, ed. Joseph M. Hawes and Elizabeth F. Shores (Santa Barbara, CA: ABC-CLIO, 2002), 2:714–15.

27. See "Father's Day," *New World Encyclopedia*⊠; January 12, 2009, http://www.newworldencyclopedia.org/entry/Father's_Day, February 8, 2009, and Len Travers, *Encyclopedia of American Holidays and National Days* (Westport, CT: Greenwood Press, 2006), vol. 1; also useful for Father's Day is Samuel, *American Fatherhood*, esp. 9–10.

28. "TV Guide's '50 Greatest TV Dads of All Time,'" *TVWeek*, January 3, 2014, http://www.tvweek.com/in-depth/2014/01/tv-guides-50-greatest-tv-dads/, January 21, 2017. For Jimmy Carter's Father's Day speech, see "Carter Proclaims Father's Day," *New York Times*, May 1, 1979, B8, qtd. in Samuel, *American Fatherhood*, 45.

29. Samuel, *American Fatherhood*, 85–86.

30. Adrian Furnham and Michael Argyle, *The Psychology of Money* (London-New York: Routledge, 1998, 2007), 40. In the following, see *ibid.*, 24–25 and 46–48.

31. Hans A. M. de Heij, *Designing Banknote Identity* and, for further discussion and analysis, "Banknote Opinion Polls," Paper, De Nederlandsche Bank Cash Seminar, 28–29 February 2008 (35pp.) and "A Method for Measuring the Public's Appreciation and Knowledge of Banknotes," Paper, IS&T/SPIE 14th Annual Symposium, San Jose, CA, 2002 (43pp.).

32. Rembrandt Peale, qtd. in National Portrait Gallery, "The 'Athenaeum' portrait," n.d. http://npg.si.edu/portraits/search?edan_fq%5B1%5D=p.edanmdm.descriptivenonrepeating.unit_code%3A%22NPG%22&edan_q=Gilbert+Stuart+washington&edan_local=1&op=Search, February 22, 2017.

33. Stuart is said to have made about 100 copies. His commercial talent, if his game can be called this, made for quite some bad blood. The Washingtons, who had commissioned him in the first place, repeatedly demanded that he deliver the portrait. Stuart always had the same excuse—it was still unfinished. In fact, he needed it as a model for the copies he sold to great profit. Stuart's business habits need to be seen in the context of an almost complete absence of copyright legislation in the nineteenth century. The works of practically all artists were ruthlessly copied, not only by the artists themselves but also by true incompetents. Tuckerman, *Character and Portraits*, 60.

34. See, for illustrations, Diane K. Skvarla and Donald A. Ritchie, *United States Senate Catalogue of Graphic Art* (Washington, DC: United States Senate, Commission on Art, 2006), 231; Thistlethwaite, "The Face of the Nation," 46.

35. Neal, *Randolph*, 1: 64; Neal's remarks were reprinted in 1832 in *Observations on American Art*. For the 1824 circular from the American Academy of Fine Arts, see Miller and Schwartz, "The Icon of the American Republic," 525.

36. See Rembrandt Peale, letter to William Dunlap, December 27, 1834, repr. in *Magazine of American History* 5 (1880), 129–32. Peale tried to regain lost ground also in his lecture tour of 1857/1858, again to no avail. One of the lectures, delivered to the New York Historical Society on June 16, 1857, was later published as "Washington and His Portraits" and subsequently reprinted in Gustavus Eisen, *Portraits of Washington*, 297–323. On the bitter controversy over the most authentic visual likeness of Washington, see Egon Verheyen, "'The most exact representation of the Original': Remarks on the Portraits of George Washington by Gilbert Stuart and Rembrandt Peale," in *Retaining the Original: Multiple Originals, Copies, and Reproduction*, ed. Kathleen Preciado (Washington, DC: National Gallery of Art, 1989), 127–39.

37. William Ayres, "At Home with George: Commercialization of the Washington Image," in *George Washington: American Symbol*, ed. Barbara L. Mitnick (New York: Hudson Hills Press, 1999), 91–107, esp. 99–103, and William M. S. Rasmussen and Robert S. Tilton, *George Washington: The Man Behind the Myths* (Charlottesville: UP of Virginia, 1999), especially 215–25.

38. Wick, *George Washington, an American Icon*, 58–62. On the "Athenaeum" as a birthday memento, see Thisthlethwaite, "The Face of the Nation," 38.

39. Smillie had engraved Washington's portrait already for the $2 Silver Certificate, series 1899 (framed), and for the $1 Federal Reserve Bank Notes, series 1918 (unframed). His lyre-shaped medallion was first used on the $1 United States Notes (Legal Tender Notes), series 1923, the last of the large size notes; it was also used on the small size notes, series 1928; additionally, it served for the large size Silver Certificates, series 1923, as well as for subsequent small size series—1928, 1934, and 1935 (with the redesigned back that has remained unchanged till today—the motto "In God We Trust" excepting),

and, finally, on the $1 Federal Reserve notes, series 1963.

40. See, for instance, the cover for Heinz Tschachler, *The Greenback: Paper Money and American Culture*, at https://mcfarlandbooks.com/product/the-greenback/.

41. Thistlethwaite, "'Where Am I?': Tracking George Washington's Dollar Bill Image," Paper given to "Rethinking National Foundations: Using/Abusing History," American Comparative Literature Association Conference, Harvard University, March 17–20, 2016.

42. On average, paper currency is lost or destroyed at the rate of $1 per year for each $1,000. The emphasis here should be on *totally* lost or destroyed. As Chuck O'Donnell explains, if clearly more than one-half of the original note remains, it will be still exchanged at its face value. Even fragments of notes are not necessarily a total write-off, for they too will be exchanged at their face value if the Treasurer of the U.S. is satisfied that the missing portions have been destroyed. *Standard Handbook of United States Paper Money*, 26.

43. According to the Treasury Department, most of the notes held outside the U.S. are $100 notes. See "A Global Currency," n.d., https://uscurrency.gov/content/global-currency, January 10, 2017. The Federal Reserve announced that as of October 20, 2016, some $1.48 trillion worth of dollar notes was in circulation, of which $1.43 trillion was in Federal Reserve notes. Board of Governors of the Federal Reserve System, "How much U.S. currency is in circulation?" October 25, 2016, https://www.federalreserve.gov/faqs/currency_12773.htm, January 9, 2017. As regards the volume of currency in circulation, by December 31, 2015, a total of 38.1 billion dollar notes were in circulation, of which 11.4 billion were $1 notes; in FY 2015 alone, the Bureau of Engraving and Printing delivered approximately 7.5 billion notes to the Federal Reserve, of which 2.425 billion were one-dollar notes. Worldwide some 180 to 190 billion notes of all kinds are in circulation, at an estimated value of $4.3 trillion (about 8.3 per cent of the money in the world). Global annual production of notes is estimated at 85 to 95 billion notes, at an estimated market value of $11.5 billion, and rising at an annual rate of 5.5 per cent; this means that by 2026, some 943 billion bank notes (as well as 179 billion coins) will be circulating worldwide, and cash will continue to be the key medium for payment and the storage of value. Board of Governors of the Federal Reserve System, "Currency in Circulation: Volume," February 5, 2016, https://www.federalreserve.gov/paymentsystems/coin_currcircvolume.htm, January 9, 2017. For global figures, I have drawn on Smithers Pira, "Fit for Circulation: The Future Lifecycles of Currency to 2026" (July 31, 2016), http://www.smitherspira.com/industry-market-reports/security/banknotes/life-expectancy-of-currency-forecasts-to-2026, and "The Future of Banknotes to 2021" (December 11, 2016), http://www.smitherspira.com/industry-market-reports/security/banknotes/the-future-of-banknotes-to-2021, both retrieved January 10, 2017. Smithers Pira is a British testing service for the packaging, paper, and print industry supply chains.

44. Goux, "Cash, Check, or Charge?" 117 and, for further description and discussion of the one-dollar note, Hörisch, *Kopf oder Zahl*, 75–78.

45. I have drawn here on my essay "'In God We Trust' or, How Dollar Bills Represent and Constitute the American Nation," in *U.S. Icons and Iconicity*, ed. Walter Hölbling et al. (Wien: LIT Verlag, 2006), 41–61, here 41–45 and, for a definition of an icon's properties, on Miller and Schwartz's "The Icon of the American Republic," 521–23. On the icon's power to unite people in a "cult," see MacCannell, "Sights and Spectacles," 416.

46. For a reference to the back of the one-dollar bill as its "coat-of-arms-side" ("*Wappenseite*"), see Gabriel, *Ästhetik und Rhetorik des Geldes*, 67.

47. Obviously, this is not the case for gold and silver coins, whose material value usually surpasses by far their denominational value. On the other hand, crisp dollar bills are known for their discernible rustling, whereas the sound of subsidiary coins is a throwaway. For the two sides of the one-dollar note becoming "the embodiment of value" ("*runden sich zum Inbegriff des Wertvollen*"), see Hörisch, *Kopf oder Zahl*, 14, 16; for "illusion of money" ("*Geldillusion*"), see Schmölders, *Psychologie des Geldes*, 145.

48. Washington mostly looks towards the viewer's left in engravings modeled after Gilbert Stuart or Gideon Fairman, such as Alfred Sealey's. Exceptions exist, though, as on various fractional notes, respectively from 1863, 1864, and 1869 (Friedberg and Friedberg, *Paper Money of the United States*, 147–152), on the $5 National Bank notes, Series 1882, back (*ibid.*, 93), on the $2 Silver Certificate, 1899 (*ibid.*, 54), the $1 Federal Reserve Bank note, 1918 (*ibid.*, 119), the $1 United States (Legal Tender) note, 1923, and on the $1 Silver Certificate, 1923 (*ibid.*, 16, 52). Nordham's account of this issue (*George Washington and Money*, 103) is flawed.

49. Gabriel, *Ästhetik und Rhetorik des Geldes*, 27.

50. Prior to 1974, the series date indicated the year in which the face design of the note was approved, with a capital letter following indicating that a minor change (for instance, a change in the signature on the face) was authorized. O'Donnell, *Standard Handbook*, 21.

51. The Federal Reserve Bank in Atlanta is one of twelve Federal Reserve Banks. For a list of all twelve, together with the twenty-four branches, see O'Donnell, *Standard Handbook*, 23–24. The "FW" in the lower right corner indicates that the note was printed at the Western Facility in Fort Worth, Texas. By 2006, a total of 294,400,000 one-dollar notes had been printed at this facility. Arthur L. Friedberg and Ira S. Friedberg, *A Guide Book of United States Paper Money: Complete Source for History, Grading, and Prices. Federal Currency Complete 1861 to Date* (Racine, WI: Whitman Publishing, 2005), 83.

52. On the history and heraldics of the Great Seal, as well as on the various mottoes, see Richard S. Patterson and Richardson Dougall's authoritative book *The Eagle and the Shield* (Washington, DC: Office

of the Historian, Department of State, 1976). On the origin of the Great Seal, see Frank H. Sommer, "Emblem and Device," *Art Quarterly* 24:1 (Spring 1961), 57–76. The phrase "esoteric political theology" ("*esoterische Polittheologie*") is from Hörisch, *Kopf oder Zahl*, 76.

Chapter 12

1. See "Exodus: Gods and Kings," *Wikipedia*, last edited September 10, 2018, http://en.wikipedia.org/wiki/Exodus:_Gods_and_Kings, January 15, 2019. On the mission of the United States as a "redeemer nation," see Ernest L. Tuveson's eponymous book (Chicago-London: University of Chicago Press, 1968).

2. Harris, E Pluribus Unum: *Nineteenth-Century Literature and the Constitutional Paradox* (Iowa City: University of Iowa Press, 2005). For *The Gentleman's Magazine*, see Burrell, *The Words We Live By*, 183, Fig. 343.

3. William Barton, qtd. in Aron, *Why the Turkey Didn't Fly*, 16. Both the thirteen-step pyramid and the all-seeing eye of Providence had been used as motifs on "Continental Currency" notes, as see Newman, *Early Paper Money*, 66, 462, 463, and University of Notre Dame, Special Collections, "Colonial Currency," http://www.coins.nd.edu/ColCurrency/CurrencyText/CC.html, accessed February 24, 2017. Technically, Barton's eagle appears in what is termed the "displayed" atttitide, that is, with wings and feet spread. Library of Congress, "The American Dollar Bill," *The Numismatist* 73 (August 1960), 1186–90, here 1189–90.

4. Bowers, *U.S. Paper Money*, 559, 484–86, 747–48.

5. On the—completely unmysterious—story of how the Great Seal came to be printed on the dollar bill, see Burrell, *The Words We Live By*, 186. On Washington's involvement with Freemasonry, see William D. Moore with John D. Hamilton, "Washington as the Master of His Lodge," in *George Washington: American Symbol*, ed. Barbara L. Mitnick (New York: Hudson Hills Press, 1999), 70–89. By a stroke of historic irony, two years after the national motto first appeared on a one-dolllar note (the $1 Silver Certificate of 1957), Donald De Lue completed a 10-foot statue of George Washington as a Master Mason for the Louisiana Lodge. The statue, which was later cast in bronze and has been replicated numerous times, shows Washington standing beside a Masonic altar; he is dressed in masonic britches, with an apron and a medallion decorated with Masonic symbols, the three-cornered hat on his left arm, and a gavel in his right hand. Mitnick, ed., *American Symbol*, 21, color plate 25.

6. Burrell, *The Words We Live By*, 185, 186.

7. *Ibid.*, 184, 186. Unsurprisingly, the "quirk of fate" has given rise to readings of the one-dollar bill's "esoteric political theology" that belong to the realm of conspiracy theories. For criticism of these and other writings, see Tschachler, *All Others Pay Cash*, 315–16. Peter Knight's two-volume encyclopedia on *Conspiracy Theories in American History* (Santa Barbara, CA: ABC-CLIO, 2003) has useful entries on "Dollar Bill," "Illuminati," and "New World Order."

8. M. R. Watkinson and Salmon P. Chase, qtd. Burrell, *The Words We Live By*, 188; on the various suggestions, see *ibid.*, 189 and, with illustrations, Vermeule, *Numismatic Art in America*, 50, 58–59.

9. Key may have taken the line from the fifty-sixth Psalm, verse four of which contains the phrase, "In God I have put my trust." Possible sources are also other verses from *The Book of Psalms*, such as 18:2, 25:2 and 20, 26:1, 71:1, and 73:28. Whatever the source used by Key, this is how the entire final stanza reads: "And this be our motto: 'In God is our trust.' / And the Star Spangled Banner in triumph shall wave / O'er the land of the free and the land of the brave." For a reading of the cultural anxieties surrounding the national anthem, see Ferguson, *The American Enlightenment*, 26–30.

10. Burrell, *The Words We Live By*, 190. For an illustration of the two-cent coin, see Yeoman, *Guide Book of United States Coins*, 121. James Barton Longacre, engraver in the U.S. Mint, was entrusted with placing the motto on the coins; for some of Longacre's drawings, including drawings for "God, Our Trust," see Vermeule, *Numismatic Art in America*, 50 and, for both patterns (an 1863 pattern had "God and Our Country" on it, surrounding a portrait of George Washington) and realized coins, 59.

11. In 2014, a large medal appeared to commemorate the sesquicentennial of the national motto on money. The medal, which was designed by Pennsylvania numismatist Tom Uram, carries the three men who played a pivotal role in the establishment of the motto on its obverse (the Reverend M. R. Watkinson, Treasury Secretary Salmon P. Chase, and James Pollock, Director of the Philadelphia Mint), while the reverse is similar to the obverse of the original 2-cent piece. The medal, which is 44.45mm in diameter, is available in silver, copper, and bronze, and can be ordered from the Pennsylvania Association of Numismatists store at http://pancoins.org/pan-store/, accessed April 18, 2017.

12. Bowers, *U.S. Paper Money*, 222, 226, and 245.

13. Albion Tourgée, *The War of the Standards: Coin* and *Credit Versus Coin* Without *Credit* (New York: Putnam, 1896), 22–23, qtd. in Louis J. Kern, "In the Land of the Dollar, but Which Dollar? The 'Crime of '73,' the Free Silver Crusade, and the Populist Dollar," in *Almighty Dollar: Papers and Lectures from the Velden Conference*, ed. Heinz Tschachler, Eugen Banauch, and Simone Puff (Wien-Münster: LIT Verlag, 2010), 45–62, qtd. 59.

14. Viviana E. Zelizer, *The Social Meaning of Money: Pin Money, Paychecks, Poor Relief and Other Currencies* (Princeton, NJ: Princeton University Press, 1997), 107–108. For later attempts to have the motto declared as unconstitutional, see Tschachler, *The Greenback*, 189–95.

15. U. S. Department of the Treasury, "History of 'In God We Trust,'" March 8, 2011, https://www.treasury.gov/about/education/Pages/in-god-we-trust.aspx, April 18, 2017.

16. The phrase "financial atheism" belongs to Jean-Joseph Goux, whose summary is pertinent: "As if an explicit affirmation of faith in God could somehow magically reverse the loss of convertibility to the unique presence of gold, the State uses this solemn motto to restore faith in the currency." *The Coiners of Language*, 134.

17. Literally, "annuit coeptis" translates as "He/she/it nods/has nodded to the undertaken," from L. *annuo, annuere, annui, annutum*, to nod. *Annuit* is either the 3sg. pres. ind. act. or 3sg. perf. ind. act. *Coeptis* comes from *coepio, coepere, coepi, coeptum*, to begin, and is a departicipial noun; hence it can also mean beginning or undertaking. "Annuit coeptis" therefore may well be translated as "He approved of our undertakings." The origin of the phrase in Virgil's *Georgica* (1:38–42), in contrast, uses the simple subjunctive, *adnue coeptis*, "may the gods approve of the building [of the Roman Empire]," which expresses a wish. The Seal of the United States thus bears the mark of God's approval of what Americans had undertaken but what had been bestowed by God's grace or, in the diction of the time, through God's providence. I am grateful to my colleague Johann Köberl (†) for providing this information. On the Roman origin of *annuit coeptis* and, as well, of *E pluribus unum*, see also Gordon S. Wood, "Rambunctious American Democracy," *The New York Review of Books* XLIX (May 9, 2002): 20–23, here 21.

18. Karl Marx, *Grundrisse: Foundations of the Critique of Political Economy* [1857–58], ed. David McLellan (London: Paladin, 1980), 149, emphasis added. There is a stage beyond the one Marx deemed final, one that he could not foresee, in the form of credit cards and other forms of electronic money, which are entirely devoid of any monetary signs. On the "spectral" character of these relational moneys, see Taylor, *Confidence Games*, 117.

19. This is why the difference between "money" and "currency" is so crucial. "Currency" (Fr. "*monnaie*"), Jean-Joseph Goux noted, is "an objective concept relating to the social organization of economic exchanges." In contrast, "money" (Fr. "*argent*") is "a subjective notion, connected with the idea of wealth." See "Numismatics," 30, 47–48.

20. Job 1:21 (KJV).

21. Adam Müller, *Versuche einer neuen Theorie des Geldes* (1816; Jena: Fischer, 1922).

22. Kenneth Burke, *A Grammar of Motives* (New York: Prentice Hall, 1945), 111.

23. Taylor, *Altarity*, 256, 259. The German Studies scholar Jochen Hörisch likewise designates money as "the leading medium of onto-semiology" ("*onto-semiologisches Leitmedium*"), a "universally shared symbolic system" in Talcott Parsons' sense. Hörisch, *Kopf oder Zahl*, 26–27.

24. Eva Meyer, *Zählen und Erzählen: Für eine Semiotik des Weiblichen* (Berlin: Medusa, 1983), 143–49.

25. Taylor, *Confidence Games*, 6.

26. Bill Dannemeyer, qtd. in Taylor, *Confidence Games*, 128. On the link between the abandonment of the gold standard and America's military engagements, see C. A. Gregory, *Savage Money* (Amsterdam: Harwood Academic Publishing, 1997), 273 and, for a general evaluation of Nixon's economy, Allen J. Matusow, *Nixon's Economy: Booms, Busts, Dollars, and Votes* (Lawrence: UP of Kansas, 1998). On the concept of "desacralization," see Michel Aglietta, *La Fin des Devises Clés. Essai sur la monnaie international* (Paris: La Découverte, 1986). In November 2005 a FOX News/Opinion Dynamics poll asked, *inter alia*, if Americans felt that Christianity was "under attack" in the United States today. 50 percent of the respondents answered yes, 37 percent answered no. Polling Report, Inc., "Religion," 2017, www.pollingreport.com/religion.htm, February 26, 2017.

27. Polling Report, "Religion."

28. Benjamin, "Capitalism as Religion," 289.

29. Late-medieval thinkers, Marc Shell found, also suggested that God is essentially a money-changing banker, sometimes understood as the creditor of life—or death: "We owe God a death," Shakespeare wrote in *2 Henry V* (3.2.229–30). Tellingly, "death" was then usually pronounced "debt." The conjunction of debt and sin had been spelled out in the Lord's Prayer. In the Vulgate Latin text of Matthew's version, we read "*Dimitte nobis debita nostra*" for "Forgive us our debts," with debts (*debita*) meaning sins. The equation provided an unmistakable monetary option for wiping out sin. Yet sin, Augustine had taught, could never be wiped out altogether, and so the need for expiatory giving would never entirely go away, requiring payments without end. Hence, "We owe God a death." Shell, *Art and Money*, 176*n*21 and, for further discussion and analysis, Peter Brown, *The Ransom of the Soul: Afterlife and Wealth in Early Western Christianity* (Cambridge, MA: Harvard University Press, 2015).

30. Benn Steil, "The End of National Currency," *Foreign Affairs* (May/June 2007), 1–10, here 7.

31. Goux, "Cash, Check, or Charge?" 115.

32. Joachim Schacht, *Die Totenmaske Gottes. Zur Kulturanthropologie des Geldes; ein Versuch* (Salzburg: Müller, 1967), 49–53. Death masks traditionally were made of gold, the "eternal" quality of which making it the perfect symbol of stability and endurance, even of a life beyond time.

33. Berndt Ostendorf et al., "Iconographies of Power: An Introductory Statement," *Iconographies of Power: The Politics and Poetics of Visual Representation*, ed. Ulla Haselstein et al. (Heidelberg: Universitätsverlag Winter, 2003), 7–9, qtd. 7.

34. In Luke (15:8–10) the human soul, as God's image (*Imago Dei*), is likened to a coin. Today, the eucharist has found another structural resemblance in the CD-ROM. Jochen Hörisch, *Ende der Vorstellung. Die Poesie der Medien* (Frankfurt am Main: Suhrkamp, 1996), 11–34, 241–43.

35. Hörisch, *Kopf oder Zahl*, 237; "*les mots et les choses*" references to an essay by Michel Foucault published in 1966, *Les mots et les choses. Une archéologie des sciences humaines* (Paris: Gallimard, 1966). The quotation from Shakespeare's *Hamlet* (c.1599 to 1602) is from Act II, scene 2.

36. Ingrid D. Rowland, "Martin Luther's Burning Questions," *The New York Review of Books* LXIV: 10 (June 8, 2017, 10–14, here 10–11.

37. Johann Wolfgang von Goethe, *Faust. Part Two*, trans. Walter Arndt, ed. Cyrus Hamlin (New York: W. W. Norton, 2000), 177 (First Act, "Pleasure Garden. Morning Sun").

38. In the 1830s, to have to pay $1.10 in paper for one silver dollar did not upset any one; the pain threshold was at $1.30. Responsibility for the misery lay with the private (actually, state-chartered) banks, who were extremely reluctant to comply with the obligation to provide gold or silver backing for the paper notes they were issuing. Tschachler, *The Greenback*, 159–61.

39. State bills (notes from private commercial banks) also traded at a discount in terms of gold and silver, though when given a choice, most people preferred to own greenbacks or, after 1863, other federal paper money such as National Bank notes. For some well-authenticated tables illustrating the fluctuating value of the greenbacks through 1865, see Krooss, *Documentary History of Banking and Currency in the United States*, 2: 280–81.

40. For a more detailed story, see H. W. Brands, *The Money Men: Capitalism, Democracy, and the Hundred Years' War Over the American Dollar* (New York: Norton, 2006), 138–58.

41. See Hörisch, *Kopf oder Zahl*, 74: "*Dem Schein des Geldes muß die Erleuchtung sekundieren, durch mehr als nur durch sich selbst gedeckt zu sein*"; on the mania for backing (German "*Deckungswahn*") as the premier element in people's trust in the currency, see Schmölders, *The Psychology of Money and Public Finance*, 153–54.

42. Goux, "Cash, Check, or Charge?" 117.

43. Goux, *The Coiners of Language*, 4.

44. *Ibid.*, 16 and chap.13, especially 124–28.

45. For a reproduction of Johann Heiss' painting *The Allegory of Commerce* (ca. 1680), see Shell, *Art and Money*, 59.

46. In or around 1860, the Citizens' Bank of New Orleans issued $5 notes showing a female figure with a staff tipped by a liberty cap and a cornucopia from the tip of which flows a seemingly endless stream of precious coins. For an illustration, see Tschachler, *The Greenback*, 194.

47. All qtd. in Schwartz, *American Symbol*, 173.

48. Nigel Dodd's most recent book is exceptional in this regard. Dodd ponders the question how money could be wrested from banks and governments and returned to the people, thus quite literally redeeming them. *The Social Life of Money*, especially 197–204, 313–81. On the structural similarities between Christian religion and market economy, see Ronnie D. Lipschutz, "In God We Trust. All Others Pay Cash," *Good Times*, July 18, 2002, http://www.people.ucsc.edu/~rlipsch/god.html, June 14, 2006.

49. Weatherford, *The History of Money*, 205.

50. *Ibid.*, 207.

51. *Ibid.*, 210 and, on the ratio between credit cards and checks to cash and similar means of payment, Tschachler, *The Greenback*, 183. The idea of an "inflation tax" gives an unexpected twist to the hypothesis, put forward by Christina von Braun in her book *Der Preis des Geldes* ["The Price of Money"]. *Eine Kulturgeschichte* (Berlin: Aufbau Verlag, 2012), that modern currencies, precisely because they are no longer backed by real assets, are "backed" by human bodies.

52. Ginsberg, "American Change," 68, 69.

53. "Ekphrastic texts," W. J. T. Mitchell explains, overcome their own semiotic "others" (*Picture Theory*, 156), meaning that in ekphrasis, the medium of language must overcome the condition of visual representation, as, for instance, in Wallace Stevens' "Anecdote of a Jar" (*ibid.*, 166–68). Page references to Ginsberg's poem are to "American Change," 69.

54. Ginsberg, "American Change," 68.

55. Ginsberg, "Poetry, Violence, and the Trembling Lambs," in *The Poetics of the New American Poetry*, ed. Donald Allen and Warren Tallman (New York: Grove Press, 1973), 331–33, qtd. 333.

56. Tschachler, *The Greenback*, 60, and—in more detail—*The Monetary Imagination of Edgar Allan Poe*, 60–63.

57. Bender, *Geldmacher*, 257–62.

58. Hymans, "The Changing Color of Money," 8–9. Worldwide, fewer than 10 percent of coins and currency bear "national" or "nationalistic" symbols and motifs. Dodd, *The Social Life of Money*, 213.

59. Tschachler, *The Greenback*, 57, and United States Treasury Bureau of Engraving and Printing, "Fort Worth Tours," n.d. http://www.moneyfactory.gov/tours/fortworthtxtours.html, July 11, 2014. The WCF is the only location other than the Bureau's Washington, DC, facility that prints the nation's currency. It prints 55 percent of all U.S. paper currency.

60. "*Visitenkarte eines Staates*," Deutsche Bundesbank, "Das besondere Objekt" ["The Special Object"], web document.

61. USBEP, "The New Color of Money," April 27, 2004, www.moneyfactory.com/newmoney, no longer available as of 2017, and, for "dignified images," "The Production Process: How Money Is Made Today," n.d., http://www.moneyfactory.gov/uscurrency/theproductionprocess.html, March 13, 2015.

62. Paul R. Krugman, *The Great Unraveling: Losing Our Way in the New Century* (New York: W. W. Norton, 2003), 1. The term "politics of symbolism" is Robert Dallek's, *Ronald Reagan: The Politics of Symbolism* (Cambridge: Harvard University Press, 1984).

63. After World War II, the majority of Americans could be called "middle class." But a recent study by Pew Research showed that by early 2015, 120.8 million adults were living in middle-income households, compared with 121.3 million in lower- and upper-income households combined. Most of that change reflected an increase in upper-income households, while about a third of the change came from families moving down in income. As a result, the majority of Americans were either upper-income or lower-income—but not "middle class"—a demographic shift that, Pew said, "could signal a tipping point." Pew Research Center, "The American Middle Class is Losing Ground," December 9, 2015, http://www.

pewsocialtrends.org/2015/12/09/the-american-middle-class-is-losing-ground/, January 21, 2017.

64. See, for an illustration, Tschachler, *Political Fatherhood*, chapter 13.

65. In 1917, a year before Austria became a republic, Hugo von Hofmannsthal hailed Maria Theresa as the mythic mother who gives life to the entire empire. Modern research, however, sees her rather as a strict mother, not a nurturant parent, as for instance, Elisabeth Badinter in *Le Pouvoir au féminin. Marie-Thérèse d'Autriche, 1717–1780. L'impératrice reine* (Paris: Éditions Flammarion, 2016).

66. By 2012, the gap between the richest 1 percent of Americans and the remaining 99 percent was the widest since the 1920s, and getting worse. Incomes of the wealthiest 1 percent rose nearly 20 percent; incomes of the remaining 99 percent rose 1 percent in comparison. In January 2014, Melissa S. Kearney, director of the Hamilton Project at the Brookings Institute and professor of economics at the University of Maryland, testified to a congressional committee that between 1975 and 2010 the lower 20 percent saw a 3.7 percent growth of income; the growth of income for the upper 5 per cent was 57 percent. Wiseman, "Richest 1 percent earn biggest share since '20s," *AP News*, September 10, 2013, http://apnews.excite.com/article/20130910/DA8NN7U02.html, July 9, 2014; "Income Inequality in the United States," *Wikipedia*, n.d., http://en.wikipedia.org/wiki/Income_inequality_in_the_United_States, January 5, 2017; Melissa S. Kearney, "Income Inequality in the United States," *Brookings*, January 16, 2014, http://www.brookings.edu/research/testimony/2014/01/16-income-inequality-in-the-united-states-kearney, July 9, 2014, and Thomas Piketty, *Capital in the Twenty-First Century*, trans. Arthur Goldhammer (Cambridge, MA-London: Harvard University Press, 2014).

67. Werner Sombart, *Why Is There No Socialism in the United States?* Ed. with an Introductory Essay by C. T. Husbands, foreword by Michael Harrington (New York: M. E. Sharpe, 1976), 13–14, 18–20. What Sombart didn't see was that the differences between Americans and Europeans was not just the Americans' desire to get rich, but the opportunity to do so by enterprise instead muddling along with government work as in Europe. Sombart also erroneously believed that the "capitalist disposition" along with all other factors preventing socialism would soon disappear.

68. Figures are from Jeff Madrick's review article "America: The Forgotten Poor," *The New York Review of Books* LXIV (June 22, 2017), 49–50.

69. Ms Dillon was at the podium describing the Trump organization's plan to completely isolate the President-elect from his business interests. See "Live Video and Analysis: President-elect Donald Trump's Press Conference," *New York Times*, January 11, 2017, http://www.nytimes.com/interactive/2017/01/11/us/politics/live-video-analysis-donald-trumps-P-conference.html?_r=0, January 13, 2017. As for writings on Trump's personality, just to keep track has become virtually impossible. Here's a selection: Michael Kranish and Marc Fisher, *Trump Revealed: An American Journey of Ambition, Ego, Money, and Power* (New York: Scribner, 2016); David Frum, *Trumpocracy: The Corruption of the American Republic* (New York: Harper, 2018); David Cay Johnston, *It's Even Worse Than You Think: What the Trump Administration is Doing to America* (New York: Simon & Schuster, 2018); Michael Wolff, *Fire and Fury: Inside the Trump White House* (New York: Henry Holt, 2018), and *Siege: Trump Under Fire* (New York: Henry Holt, 2019); Bob Woodward, *Fear: Trump in the White House* (New York: Simon & Schuster, 2018), and, for good measure, Anonymous, "I Am Part of the Resistance Inside the Trump Administration," *New York Times*, September 5, 2018, https://www.nytimes.com/2018/09/05/opinion/trump-white-house-anonymous-resistance.html?action=click&module=Top Stories&pgtype=Homepage, September 6, 2018.

70. The six faith leaders Donald J. Trump invited to pray at his inauguration came from diverse backgrounds, but they all had in some way signaled their approval of his great wealth. Tom Gjelten, "With His Choice of Inauguration Prayer Leaders, Trump Shows His Values," *NPR* (National Public Radio), January 13, 2017, http://www.npr.org/2017/01/13/509558608/with-his-choice-of-inauguration-prayer-leaders-trump-shows-his-values, January 15, 2017. The group included Bishop Wayne T. Jackson, an African-American megachurch leader from Detroit; Paula White-Cain, a Florida woman known for her lavish lifestyle and preaching on "abundancy"; Marvin Hier, a rabbi from Los Angeles; the Reverend Samuel Rodriguez, a Hispanic evangelical from California; Franklin Graham, the son of Billy Graham; and Cardinal Timothy Dolan, the archbishop of New York.

71. Fran Lebowitz, qtd. in Wills, "Where Evangelicals Came From," *New York Review of Books* 54:7 (April 20—May 10, 2017), 26, 28–29, qtd. 29. On the question why poor people in America do not rise up to demand more from a system that is so obviously failing them, see Francesco Duina, *Broke and Patriotic*. On the cultural underpinnings of wealth in America, see also Winfried Fluck, "What is so bad about being rich? The representation of wealth in American culture," *Comparative American Studies* 1:1 (2003), 53–79; Matthew Warshauer, "Who Wants to Be a Millionaire: Changing Conceptions of the American Dream," *ARNet*, February 13, 2003, http://www.americansc.org.uk/Online/American_Dream.htm, March 8, 2012, and, on how the rich are weaponizing their pursuit of wealth with the help of "thought leaders" empowered by them, Daniel W. Drezner, *The Ideas Industry: How Pessimists, Partisans, and Plutocrats are Transforming the Marketplace of Ideas* (New York: Oxford University Press, 2017).

Epilogue

1. John Connally, qtd. in Robert L. Hetzel, *The Monetary Policy of the Federal Reserve: A History* (Cambridge, UK: Cambridge University Press, 2008), 106; a. Ralph J. Benko, "The Dollar is our currency,

but your problem," *The Gold Standard Now*, The Lehrman Institute, n.d., http://www.thegoldstandardnow.org/key-blogs/1635-the-reserve-currency-status-of-the-dollar, September 18, 2014, and Dodd, *The Social Life of Money*, 45–46, 98–99.

2. Figures are from World Gold Council, "Quarterly times series on World Official Gold Reserves since 2000," December 8, 2016, http://www.gold.org/research/quarterly-times-series-world-official-gold-reserves-2000, accessed February 24, 2017.

3. Belov, "The Dollar Bears the Blow," qtd. in Alaina Lemon, "'Your Eyes Are Green Like Dollars': Counterfeit Cash, National Substance, and Currency Apartheid in 1990s Russia," *Cultural Anthropology* 13:1 (1998), 22–55, qtd. 51*n*17.

4. Jeffrey Frankel, "The U.S. dollar's status has fallen—but not uniformly," *The Guardian*, November 22, 2013, https://www.theguardian.com/business/economics-blog/2013/nov/22/us-dollar-status-fallen, April 28, 2017.

5. In the 1850s, for instance, ten dollars were sufficient to cover a family's cost of living for a week. After the Civil War, two dollars were the basic bet in horse racing (it also was a good price for a bit of action). In 1919, a gallon of gas stood at 25 cents. The price remained under 40 cents until the oil shocks of the 1970s; it hit the one-dollar mark only in 1980. As of 2011, you may even be charged five dollars or more. On the relative values of dollars, see John J. McCusker, *How Much Is That in Real Money? A Historical Price Index for Use as a Deflator of Money Values in the Economy of the United States*, second revised edition (Worcester, MA: American Antiquarian Society/Newcastle, DE: Oak Knoll, 2001). Conversions from historic dollars (and pounds and shillings) to current American dollars can be made using Samuel H. Williamson's very helpful online device, "Seven Ways to Compute the Relative Value of a U.S. Dollar Amount, 1774 to present," MeasuringWorth, 2012, http://www.measuringworth.com/uscompare/, accessed February 24, 2017.

6. Miller and Schwartz, "The Icon of the American Republic," 521–23, and Thisthlethwaite, "The Face of the Nation," 37.

7. Presidential Coin Act, December 22, 2005 (Public Law 109–145). All references to the Presidential Coin Program in this and the following paragraph are to U.S. Mint, "Presidential $1 Coins," n.d. https://catalog.usmint.gov/coin-programs/presidential-1-coins/, May 2, 2017. The U.S. Mint offers free informational materials via www.usmint.gov/$1coin, accessed December 22, 2007.

8. Tschachler, *The Greenback*, 125 and, for the political controversies surrounding the national motto, 190–95.

9. United States Mint, "Presidential $1 Coins," web document and, on the visual appearance of the coins, Vermeule, *Numismatic Art in America*, 247–48. Here's an example: "Upon the release of the first presidential dollar, observers noted that the somewhat lumpy features of Washington suggested that he had been in a bare-knuckle boxing match with a prominent pugilist" (246). It remains a matter of debate, though, whether these observations targeted sculptor/engraver Joseph Menna or Gilbert Stuart's "Athenaeum" portrait, which served as Menna's model.

10. A smaller, 1 5/16-inch version can be purchased for $6.95. Visit the U.S. Mint's website, www.usmint.gov, for more information. For the Washington medal, view https://catalog.usmint.gov/george-washington-bronze-medal-3-inch-101.html?cgid=presidential#_ga=1.132283532.301505574.1481532670&start=1, accessed February 24, 2017.

11. See United States Mint, "First Spouse Gold Coin Program," April 11, 2017, https://www.usmint.gov/learn/coin-and-medal-programs/first-spouse-gold-coins, May 11, 2017. For Franklin's dream, see his letter to John Jay, qtd. in Q. David Bowers and David M. Sundman, *100 Greatest American Currency Notes* (Atlanta, GA: Whitman Publishing, 2005), 63; for Franklin's unpublished "A Thought Concerning Medals," see *The Papers of Benjamin Franklin*, Digital Edition (Los Altos, CA: Packard Humanities Institute), n.d., http://franklinpapers.org/franklin/framedVolumes.jsp?vol=38&page=486, May 11, 2017.

12. Hobsbawm, *The Invention of Tradition*, 13.

13. Commemorative coins used to be available only from collectors but beginning with the Jackie Robinson silver dollar of 1997 they have been available directly from the United States Mint. For an overview of "commems," see Yeoman, *Guide Book of United States Coins*, 264–322 and, specifically on the "return of commemorative coinage," Vermeule, *Numismatic Art in America*, 217–34.

14. Ginsberg, "American Change," 68 and, for a description and evaluation of the coin, Vermeule, *Numismatic Art in America*, 229–31; for Fraser's models for the 1932 quarter dollar, see *ibid.*. 168.

15. Vermeule, *Numismatic Art in America*, 92–93; MacNeil, *The President's Medal*, 40–45. For *The Angel of* Purity, visit the Philadelphia Museum of Art, http://www.philamuseum.org/collections/permanent/290521.html?mulR=2031152831|1, accessed April 18, 2017.

16. Vermeule, *Numismatic Art in America*, 96. The classic device of jugate busts reappeared on the Sequicentennial of American Independence half dollar of 1926, which paired Washington's bust with that of the living president, Calvin Coolodge. *Ibid.*, 160, 164.

17. Reference to "moderation and seriousness of purpose" is to art historian Chandler Post, qtd. in Vermeule, *Numismatic Art in America*, 102. For a detailed description and analysis of the "artistic revolution" set in motion by Theodore Roosevelt, see 102–30. On the "Renaissance in American money," see a. Doty, *America's Money*, 169–73.

18. Roosevelt, qtd. in Garrett and Guth, *100 Greatest U.S. Coins*, 20.

19. Barbara J. Gregory, "The Golden Age," *The Numismatist* 126:3 (March 2013), 12.

20. Doty, *America's Money*, 198.

21. On the properties of an icon, see Miller and Schwartz, "The Icon of the American Republic,"

521–23. Reference to "a certain depth, a certain verticality" is to Goux, "Cash, Check, or Charge?" 117.

22. See "Wheresgeorge," n.d., www.wheresgeorge.com/press, accessed January 23, 2017.

23. The German site address is www.wo-ist-mein-geld.de, accessed March 19, 2007; for other site addresses, see "Currency Bill Tracking," Wikipedia, http://en.wikipedia.org/wiki/Curren-cy_bill_tracking, accessed September 6, 2018.

24. See Christopher Null, "Review of *Twenty Bucks*," 1999, www.filmcritic.com, accessed March 21, 2007; no longer available as of 2017.

25. "The closer he seems," the historian Edward Lengel wrote (*Inventing George Washington*, 211), "the more easily he slips away."

26. See Duina, *Broke and Patriotic*.

27. The *Washington Examiner*, respectively for September 24, 2008, and December 14, 2011. From "*The Washington Examiner*," *Wikipedia*, April 21, 2017, https://en.wikipedia.org/wiki/The_Washington_Examiner#cite_note-:1-2, April 28, 2017.

28. Benjamin R. Freed, "Washington Examiner to Cease Daily Publication and Become Political Weekly," *DCist*, March 19, 2013, http://dcist.com/2013/03/washington_examiner_to_cease_daily.php, April 28, 2017.

29. Kglobal, "Americans for George," http://kglobal.com/results/americans-for-george, accessed April 18, 2017. COINS Act stands for "Currency Optimization, Innovation, and National Savings Act," H.R. 2977.

30. Stefan Hankin, "Americans for George," Lincoln Park Strategies, January 31, 2017, http://lpstrategies.com/case-studies/americans4george, accessed August 22, 2017, and "Leave the $1 Bill Alone," *The Numismatist* (May 2012), 33. During his decade-long career as a market researcher and analysts, Stefan Hankin was part of the polling team that helped Barack Obama became the 44th President of the United States.

31. "Americans for George," April 27, 2012 https://www.facebook.com/amerforgeorge, accessed April 18, 2017.

32. In *Achieving Our Country: Leftist Thought in Twentieth-Century America* (Cambridge-London: Harvard University Press, 1998), Richard Rorty in the final years of the twentieth century implored Americans to return to the patriotic politics of Roosevelt. For a similar plea, see Senator John McCain's farewell statement, *Politico*, August 27, 2018, https://www.politico.com/story/2018/08/27/full-text-john-mccains-farewell-statement-797487, September 6, 2018 and, most recently, Jill Lepore, for whom patriotism, in *This America*, is a natural and virtuous love of one's country and not to be confused with nationalism, which involves hatred of foreigners, immigrants, and minorities. President Roosevelt used the phrase "unity of purpose" in his Annual Message to Congress (State of the Union Address) on January 6, 1941. In the address, the President also outlined the basic rights of all people (freedom of speech and worship, and freedom from want and fear), hence the address has become known as the "Four Freedoms Speech." A year later, Roosevelt used his address on the occasion of the United Nations Flag Day, to say that these four freedoms "are the rights of men of every creed and every race, wherever they live." Franklin D. Roosevelt Presidential Liberary and Museum, File No. 1353-A, "Message to Congress," January 6, 1941, http://www.fdrlibrary.marist.edu/_resources/images/msf/msf01407, and File No. 1423, "United Nations Flag Day Address," June 14, 1942, http://www.fdrlibrary.marist.edu/_resources/images/msf/msfb0036, both retrieved January 6, 2019.

33. Lengel, *Inventing George Washington*, ix; for "adopted political heirs," see Brookhiser, *Founding Father*, 168.

34. Martha Nussbaum, *The Monarchy of Fear: A Philosopher Looks at Our Political Crisis* (New York: Simon & Schuster, 2018), 7.

35. The "America, I am your father" likeness of Washington (originally created for May Fourth or Star Wars Day in 2017) was posted on Mount Vernon's Instagram on June 15, 2018, https://www.instagram.com/p/BkDfo1Ojl6_/?hl=en&taken-by=mount_vernon, accessed June 24, 2018. For a picture of a George Washington meatloaf, go to Instagram, https://www.instagram.com/p/BeHfZv-JFXAy/; the meatloaf's creator is a Carol Falkowski from Minnesota, the author of *Meatloaf Outside the Pan*. The George Washington meatloaf is not in the book, but you can view it on Ms Falkowski's website, at http://outsidethepan.com, accessed February 6, 2018. For the story about the strands of Washington's hair, see the *New York Post* of February 18, 2018, https://nypost.com/2018/02/13/strands-of-george-washingtons-hair-found-in-book/, retrieved February 15, 2018. The "hair-raising" discovery was made at Union College's library in Schenectady in upstate New York. The strands of white hair had belonged to Elizabeth Schuyler, wife of Alexander Hamilton, who gave it to their third son, James A. Hamilton. Elizabeth Schuyler was the daughter of General Philip Schuyler, who served in the Revolutionary War. For the "Founding Fathers currency set," go to https://catalog.usmint.gov/2018-americas-founding-fathers-currency-set-B15037.html?cgid=premium-products—start=1, accessed April 8, 2019. The notes have matching serial numbers beginning "2019." The set is packaged in a 9.5 x 10-inches tri-fold folder featuring portraits of Presidents Washington and Jefferson, and an American flag and a bald eagle in flight. A clear, acid-free polymer sleeve protects each note.

36. The story of the faithful representative is retold in Schwartz, *American Symbol*, 200; for reenactments of the Delaware River crossing, see Marling, *Washington Slept Here*, 20. On the Society of the Cincinnati donation, see Kahler, *The Long Farewell*, 116.

37. "Dream Big," *The Numismatist*, July 2016, 27. For the Americana Totem Pole, see Juilee Decker, "Paintings and Sculptures," in *The American President in Popular Culture*, ed. John W. Matviko (Westport, CT–London: Greenwood Press, 2005.), 15–32, here 21–22.

38. "Every American considers it his sacred duty

to have a likeness of Washington in his home, just as we have images of God's saints." Pavil Svinin, *Picturesque United States of America 1811, 1812, 1813*, qtd. in Barbara J. Mitnick, "Parallel Vision: The Literary and Visual Image of George Washington," in *George Washington: American Symbol*, ed. the same (New York: Hudson Hills Press, 1999), 55–69, qtd. 59.

39. Mitnick, ed., *American Symbol*, 23, plate 29 and, on Wesselmann's as well as other modern and postmodern appropriations of the face of the nation, Thistlethwaite, "Hero, Celebrity, and Cliché," 141–52. On the functional parallels between Washington portraits and religious icons, see Miller and Schwartz, "The Icon of the American Republic," 516.

40. The expression possibly dates to military usage in World War II, when "the day the eagle sh*ts" meant payday, the eagle then standing for the U.S. government. Today, the expression reflects on decision making under poverty. As Bertrand et al. have shown, poor people are more likely to respond to real outcomes than to their description. See Marianne Bertrand et al., "Behavioral Economics and Marketing in Aid of Decision Making Among the Poor," *Journal of Public Policy and Marketing* 25 (2006), 8–23. For "cash ghetto," see Weatherford, *The History of Money*, 210.

41. Geoffrey Ingham, *The Nature of Money* (Malden, MA: Polity Press, 2004), 57. For a study of the stories told by the images on dollar coins, past and present, see Katsion, "'Symbols Are Important': Nation-States and the Images on Our Money."

42. Gerbner, "Society's Storyteller: How TV Creates the Myths by Which We Live," *Media & Values* 40–41 (Los Angeles: Center for Media and Values, Summer/Fall 1987), 8–9, qtd. 9.

43. Wini Breines, *Young, White, and Miserable: Growing Up Female in the Fifties* (1992; Chicago: University of Chicago Press, 2001), 40.

44. Eugenia Kaledin, *Daily Life in the United States, 1940–1959: Shifting Worlds* (Westport, CT: Greenwood Press, 2000), and Stephen E. Ambrose, *Eisenhower: The President* (New York: Simon & Schuster, 1984).

45. "[A]ll the eggheads are for Stevenson, but how many eggheads are there?" John Alsop, qtd. in Martin Halliwell, *American Culture in the 1950s* (Edinburgh: Edinburgh University Press, 2007), 21. On the election of 1952, see John Robert Greene, *I Like Ike: The Presidential Election of 1952* (Lawrence: UP of Kansas, 2017).

46. Daisy Bates, *The Long Shadow of Little Rock: A Memoir* (New York: David McKay, 1962), and Jean Edward Smith, *Eisenhower in War and Peace* (New York: Random House, 2012).

47. Visit the U.S. Mint's website, www.usmint.gov, for more information. For the law that only the portrait of a deceased individual may appear on U.S. currency and securities, see 31 USC 5114(b), revised from 31 USC 413, qtd. in Tschachler, *The Greenback*, 68.

48. See the third stanza of Friedrich Schiller's poem "To My Friends": "And the earth-god, Mammon, reigns supreme." *The Poems of Schiller*, 118, trans. Edgar A. Bowring, second edn., revised (London: George Bell and Sons, 1874), 118; German original, "*Und es herrscht der Erde Gott, das Geld*" ("An die Freunde," *Sämmtliche Werke*, 1:135).

49. David Blankenhorn, *Fatherless America: Confronting Our Most Urgent Social Problem* (New York: Basic Books, 1995), 95.

50. U.S. Department of the Treasury, Bureau of Engraving and Printing, "The Production Process: How Money Is Made Today," n.d., http://www.moneyfactory.gov/uscurrency/theproductionprocess.html, March 13, 2015. The 2017 "America's Founding Fathers Currency Set," priced at $21.95, features 2013 $1 and $2 notes from the Federal Reserve Bank of New York. For more information or to place an order, visit http://www.moneyfactorystore.gov/americasfoundingfathers2017currencyset.aspx, accessed April 18, 2017.

51. John McCain, qtd. in *The Numismatist*, October 2015, 27.

52. Coins, *pace* John McCain, do not last forever. On the other hand, the life span of $1 notes has increased dramatically over the years, from about 3.3 years in 2011 to 5.9 years by the end of 2013 and still rising, the result of improved technology and policy changes by the Federal Reserve. What also matters is how frequently the bills change hands. As more and more people make cashless transactions, paper dollars do not circulate as much as they used to. All this decreases the financial benefit of replacing the $1 note with a $1 coin. Instead of eliminating paper dollars, the Government Accountability Office therefore recommends that the Treasury be allowed to alter the metal composition of all coins. See U.S. GAO, "Annual Report on Duplication and Cost Savings," May 21, 2019, https://www.gao.gov/duplication/overview, retrieved May 25, 2019.

53. "Americans for George," *Facebook*, April 27, 2012, https://www.facebook.com/amerforgeorge, accessed April 18, 2017.

54. United States Bureau of Engraving and Printing, "Annual Production Reports," n.d., http://www.bep.gov/resources/productionannual.html, January 9, 2017; Governors of the Federal Reserve System, "Currency in Circulation: Volume," February 5, 2016, https://www.federalreserve.gov/paymentsystems/coin_currcircvolume.htm, January 9, 2017. Most dollar bills produced by the BEP serve to replace torn and worn bills, as the average life-span is a mere 18 to 22 months. Altogether in 2015, the BEP produced some 7.319 billion notes, about 12 per cent of notes produced worldwide.

55. Stuart Hall, "Cultural Studies: Two Paradigms," in *A Cultural Studies Reader: History, Theory, Practice*, ed. Jessica Munns and Gita Rajan (London-New York: Longman, 1995), 194–205, qtd. 199. Quite similarly, Terry Eagleton: "Culture can be loosely summarized as the complex of values, customs, beliefs and practices which constitute the way of life of a specific group." *The Idea of Culture* (Malden, MA: Blackwell, 2000), 34.

Bibliography

Adams, Charles Francis. "The State of the Currency II." *Hunt's Merchants' Magazine* (December 1839): 505–17.

Albanese, Catherine L. *Sons of the Fathers: The Civil Religion of the American Revolution.* Philadelphia: Temple University Press, 1976.

American Numismatic Society. "Introduction to Numismatic Terms and Methods." N.d. Web. April 17, 2017. http://numismatics.org/seminar/termsmethods/.

Aron, Paul. *Why the Turkey Didn't Fly: The Surprising Stories Behind the Eagle, the Flag, Uncle Sam, and Other Images of America.* Lebanon, NH: UP of New England, 2013.

Baker, William S. *Bibliotheca Washingtoniana: A Descriptive List of the Biographies and Biographical Sketches of George Washington.* Philadelphia: Robert M. Lindsay, 1889.

_____. *Medallic Portraits of Washington.* 1885. 2nd ed. Ed. Russell Rulau and George Fuld. Iola, WI: Krause, 1999.

Bancroft, George. *History of the United States of America: From the Discovery of the Continent.* Vol. I. 1834; New York: Appleton & Co., 1888.

Barber, John Warner. *Interesting Events in the History of the United States.* 2nd ed. New Haven, CT: J. W. Barber, 1830.

Bender, Klaus W. *Geldmacher. Das geheimste Gewerbe der Welt.* Weinheim, Germany: Wiley-VCH, 2004.

Benjamin, Walter. "Capitalism as Religion." *Walter Benjamin: Selected Writings.* Vol. 1. *1913–1926.* Ed. Marcus Bullock and Michael W. Jennings. Trans. Rodney Livingstone. Cambridge, MA: The Belknap P of Harvard University Press, 1996. 288–291.

Berger, John. *Ways of Seeing.* 1972; London: Penguin Classics, 2008.

Boehm, Gottfried, et al., eds. *Figur und Figuration. Studien zu Wahrnehmung und Wisssen.* München: Fink, 2007.

Bowers, Q. David. *The History of United States Coinage as Illustrated by the Garrett Collection.* Los Angeles: Bowers & Ruddy Galleries, 1979.

_____. *Obsolete Paper Money Issued by Banks in the United States, 1782–1866.* Atlanta, GA: Whitman Publishing, 2006.

_____. *Whitman Encyclopedia of Colonial and Early American Coins.* Atlanta, GA: Whitman Publishing, 2008.

_____. *Whitman Encyclopedia of Obsolete Paper Money.* 8 vols to date. Atlanta, GA: Whitman Publishing, 2014.

_____. *Whitman Encyclopedia of U.S. Paper Money.* Atlanta, GA: Whitman Publishing, 2009.

Brookhiser, Richard. *Founding Father: Rediscovering George Washington.* New York: Free Press, 1996.

Brumwell, Stephen. *George Washington: Gentleman Warrior.* New York-London: Quercus, 2012.

Bryan, William Alfred. *George Washington in American Literature 1775–1865.* New York: Columbia University Press, 1952; reprint, Westport, CT: Greenwood Press, 1970.

_____. "George Washington: Symbolic Guardian of the Republic, 1850–1861." *William and Mary Quarterly* 3rd ser. 7 (January 1950): 53–63.

Burrell, Brian. *The Words We Live By: The Creeds, Mottoes, and Pledges That Have Shaped America.* New York: Free Press, 1997.

Butter, Michael. *Der "Washington-Code": Zur Heroisierung amerikanischer Präsidenten, 1775–1865.* Figurationen des Heroischen, Vol. 3. Göttingen: Wallstein Verlag, 2016.

Chernow, Ron. *Washington: A Life.* New York: Penguin, 2010.

Clinton, Hillary Rodham. *What Happened.* New York: Simon & Schuster, 2017.

A Companion to George Washington. Ed. Edward G. Lengel. Malden, MA: Wiley-Blackwell, 2012.

Cunliffe, Marcus. *George Washington: Man and Monument.* New York: New American Library, 1958.

Cunningham, Noble E., Jr. *Popular Images of the Presidency: From Washington to Lincoln.* Columbia: University of Missouri Press, 1991.

Davies, Glyn. *A History of Money from Ancient Times to the Present Day.* 3rd ed. Cardiff, UK: University of Wales Press, 2002.

Dennis, Matthew. *Red, White, and Blue Letter Days: An American Calendar.* Ithaca, NY: Cornell University Press, 2002.

Documentary History of Banking and Currency in the United States. Ed. Herman E. Krooss. Introduction by Paul A. Samuelson. 4 vols. 1969; New York: Chelsea House Publishers, 1983.

Dodd, Nigel. *The Social Life of Money.* Princeton, NJ: Princeton University Press, 2014.

"Dollar Bill under Threat: Congress Considering Elimination of Dollar Bill." *The Examiner.* Washington, D.C., April 27–28, 2012, 1.

Doty, Richard. *America's Money—America's Story.* Second Edition. Atlanta, GA: Whitman, 2008.

_____. *The Macmillan Encyclopedic Dictionary of Numismatics.* London: Hale, 1982.

_____. *Pictures from a Distant Country: Images on 19th-Century U.S. Currency.* Raleigh, NC: Boson Books, 2004.

Duina, Francesco. *Broke and Patriotic: Why Poor Americans Love Their Country.* Stanford, CA: Stanford University Press, 2017.

Eagleton, Catherine, and Jonathan Williams. *Money: A History.* 2nd ed. London: The British Museum Press, 2007.

Eisen, Gustavus A. *Portraits of Washington.* 3 vols. New York: Robert Hamilton, 1932.

Eliassen, Meredith. "George Washington, Death, and Mourning." *A Companion to George Washington.* Ed. Edward G. Lengel. Malden, MA: Wiley-Blackwell, 2012, 576–91.

Ferguson, Robert A. *The American Enlightenment, 1750–1820.* Cambridge, MA: Harvard University Press, 1997.

Foucault, Michel. *The Order of Things: An Archaeology of the Human Sciences.* New York: Pantheon, 1970.

Friedberg, Arthur L., and Ira S. Friedberg. *Paper Money of the United States: From Colonial Times to the Present.* 17th ed. Clifton, NJ: Coin and Currency Institute, 2004.

Fuld, George. "Coinage Featuring George Washington." *Coinage of the American Confederation Period.* Ed. Philip L. Mossman. Coinage of the Americas Conference, Proceedings No.11. New York: American Numismatic Society, 1996. 165–259.

_____. "Early Washington Medals." *American Journal of Numismatics.* Second Series 14 (2002): 105–63.

Gabriel, Gottfried. "Aesthetics and Political Iconography of Money." *Pictorial Cultures and Political Iconographies: Approaches, Perspectives, Case Studies from Europe and America.* Ed. Udo J. Hebel and Christoph Wagner. Berlin-New York: de Gruyter, 2011. 418–428.

_____. *Ästhetik und Rhetorik des Geldes.* Stuttgart-Bad Canstatt: frommann-holzboog, 2002.

Galbraith, John Kenneth. *Money: Whence It Came, Where It Went.* Boston: Houghton Mifflin, 1975.

Garrett, Jeff, and Ron Guth, *100 Greatest U.S. Coins.* Atlanta, GA: Whitman Publishing, 2005.

Garson, Robert. "Counting Money: The United States Dollar and American Nationhood, 1781–1820." *Journal of American Studies* 35:1 (2001): 21–46.

Ginsberg, Allen. "American Change." *Reality Sandwiches: 1953–1960.* 1963; San Francisco: City Lights Books, 1976. 67–69.

Goodwin, Jason. *Greenback: The Almighty Dollar and the Invention of America.* New York: Henry Holt, 2003.

Goux, Jean-Joseph. "Cash, Check, or Charge?" *The New Economic Criticism: Studies at the Intersection of Literature and Economics.* Ed. Martha Woodmansee and Mark Osteen. New York-London: Routledge, 1999. 114–27.

_____. *The Coiners of Language.* Trans. Jennifer Curtiss Gage. Norman: University of Oklahoma Press, 1994.

_____. "Numismatics: An Essay in Theoretical Numismatics." *Symbolic Economics: After Marx and Freud.* Trans. Jennifer Curtiss Gage. Ithaca, NY: Cornell University Press, 1990. 9–63.

Grierson, Philip. *Numismatics.* Oxford: Oxford University Press, 1975.

Hamilton, Alexander. "Report on Establishing a Mint." *Reports of the Secretary of the Treasury of the United States.* Vol. 1. Washington, D.C.: Blair & Rives, 1837. 133–56.

Haxby, James A. *Standard Catalog of United States Obsolete Bank Notes, 1782–1866.* 4 CD-ROMS. Iola, WI: Krause Publications, 2009. (Abbrev. as Haxby.)

Heij, Hans A.M. de. *Designing Banknote Identity.* Amsterdam: De Nederlandsche Bank, 2012.

Helleiner, Eric. "National Currencies and National Identities." *American Behavioral Scientist* 41:10 (October 1998): 1409–36.

Hessler, Gene. *The Engraver's Line: An Encyclopedia of Paper Money and Postage Stamp Art.* Port Clinton, OH: BNR Press, 1993.

Higginbotham, Don, ed. *George Washington Reconsidered.* Charlottesville: University Press of Virginia, 2001.

Higham, James. *Strangers in the Land: Patterns of American Nativism, 1860–1925.* New Brunswick, NJ: Rutgers University Press, 1955; reprint. New York: Atheneum, 1981. 264–99.

History of the George Washington Bicentennial Celebration. 5 vols. Washington, D.C.: United States George Washington Bicentennial Commission, 1932.

Hobsbawm, Eric. "Mass-Producing Traditions: Europe, 1870–1914." *The Invention of Tradition.* Ed. the same and Terence Ranger. Cambridge, UK: Cambridge University Press, 1983. 263–307.

Hobsbawm, Eric, and Terence Ranger, eds. *The Invention of Tradition.* Cambridge, UK: Cambridge University Press, 1983.

Hörisch, Jochen. *Kopf oder Zahl. Die Poesie des Geldes.* Frankfurt am Main: Suhrkamp, 1996.

Hurle, Andrew. "Abstractions of Value." *The Numismatist* 127:9 (September 2014): 30–36.

Hurst, James Willard. *A Legal History of Money in the United States, 1794–1970.* 1973; Frederick, MD: Beard Books, 2001.

Hymans, Jacques E. C. "The Changing Color of Money: European Currency Iconography and Collective Identity." *European Journal of International Relations* 10:1 (March 2004): 5–31.

Irving, Washington. *George Washington: A Biography.* Abridged and ed. with an introduction by Charles Neider. New York: Da Capo Press, 1994.

_____. *A History of the Life and Voyages of Christopher Columbus.* 3 vols. New York: G. & C. Carvill, 1828.

_____. *Life of George Washington.* 5 vols. New York: Putnam, 1856–1859.

Jefferson, Thomas. "The Declaration of Independence as Adopted by Congress." *Concise Anthology of American Literature.* Fourth Edition. Ed. George McMichael. Upper Saddle River, NJ: Prentice Hall, 1998. 375–78.

_____. *Thomas Jefferson: Writings.* Ed. Merrill D. Peterson. New York: Library of America, 1984.

Kahler, Gerald E. *The Long Farewell: Americans Mourn the Death of George Washington.* Charlottesville: University of Virginia Press, 2008.

Katsion, John R. "'Symbols Are Important': Nation-States and the Images on Our Money." *Discourse: The Journal of the SCASD* 2 (Fall 2015): 35–51.

Krooss, Herman E., ed. *Documentary History of Banking and Currency in the United States.* Introduction by Paul A. Samuelson. 4 vols. 1969; New York: Chelsea House Publishers, 1983.

Lauer, Josh. "Money as Mass Communication: U. S. Paper Currency and the Iconography of Nationalism." *The Communication Review* 11 (2008): 109–32.

Leisering, Peter. "DDR-Banknoten als Spiegel der gesellschaftlichen Situation." *Der schöne Schein. Symbolik und Ästhetik von Banknoten.* Ed. Stefan Hartmann and Christian Thiel. Regenstauf: Gietl Verlag, 2016. 127–48.

Lengel, Edward G. *Inventing George Washington: America's Founder, in Myth and Memory.* New York: HarperCollins, 2011.

Lepore, Jill. *This America: The Case for the Nation.* New York: Liveright, 2019.

Lincoln, Abraham. *The Collected Works of Abraham Lincoln.* Ed. Roy P. Basler. New Brunswick, NJ: Rutgers University Press, 1953–1955.

Loock, Kathleen. "Goodbye Columbus, Hello Abe!—Changing Imagery on U.S. Paper Money and the Negotiation of American National Identity." *Almighty Dollar: Paper and Lectures from the Velden Conference.* Ed. Heinz Tschachler, Eugen Banauch, and Simone Puff. American Studies in Austria, Vol. 9. Wien-Münster: LIT Verlag, 2010. 81–101.

MacCannell, Dean. "Sights and Spectacles." *Iconicity: Essays on the Nature of Culture. Festschrift for Thomas A. Sebeok on his 65th Birthday.* Ed. Paul Bouissac, Michael Herzfeld, and Roland Posner. Tübingen: Stauffenberg Verlag, 1986. 421–35.

MacNeil, Neil. *The President's Medal, 1789–1977.* New York: Clarkson N. Potter in association with the National Portrait Gallery of the Smithsonian Institution, 1977.

Marling, Karal Ann. *George Washington Slept Here: Colonial Revivals and American Culture, 1876–1986.* Cambridge, MA: Harvard University Press, 1988.

Marshall, John. *The Life of George Washington.* Philadelphia: C. P. Wayne, 1804–1807.

Mihm, Stephen. *A Nation of Counterfeiters: Capitalists, Con Men, and the Making of the United States.* Cambridge, MA: Harvard University Press, 2007.

Miller, Eugene F., and Barry Schwartz. "The Icon of the American Republic: A Study in Political Symbolism." *The Review of Politics* 47:4 (October 1985): 516–43.

Mitchell, W. J. T. *Picture Theory: Essays on Verbal and Visual Representation.* Chicago: University of Chicago Press, 1994.

Mitnick, Barbara J., ed. *George Washington: American Symbol.* New York: Hudson Hills Press, 1999.

Money Talks: Explaining How Money Really Works. Ed. Nina Bandelj, Frederick F. Wherry, and Viviana A. Zelizer. Princeton, NJ: Princeton University Press, 2017.

Morison, Samuel Eliot. *Admiral of the Ocean Sea: A Life of Christopher Columbus.* 2 vols. Boston: Little Brown, 1942.

Morrison, Jeffry H. *The Political Philosophy of George Washington.* Baltimore, MD: Johns Hopkins University Press, 2009.

Mossman, Philip L. *Money of the American Colonies and Confederation. A Numismatic, Economic and Historical Correlation.* Numismatic Studies 20. New York: American Numismatic Society, 1992.

Mudd, Douglas A. "Image and Republican Sovereignty: Negotiating the Numismatic Iconography of the Early Republic." *ANA (American Numismatic Association) Journal* 1:1 (2006): 29–41.

Musante, Neil. *Medallic Washington.* 2 vols. London-Boston: Spink Books, 2016.

Muscalus, John A. *An Index of State Bank Notes That Illustrate Washington and Franklin*. Bridgeport, PA: Historical Paper Money Research Institute, 1938.

Musella, Francis. "Benjamin Franklin's Nature Printing on Bank Notes." in Alan M. Stahl, *Money on Paper: Bank Notes and Related Graphic Arts*. Princeton, NJ: Princeton University Press, 2010. 17–25.

Neal, John. *Observations on American Art: Selections from the Writings of John Neal*. Ed. Harold E. Dickson. State College, PA: Pennsylvania State College, 1943.

_____. *Randolph: A Novel*. 2 vols. Philadelphia: Charles I. Jack, 1823.

Newman, Eric P. *The Early Paper Money of America*. Fourth edition. Iola, WI: Krause Publications, 1997.

Nordham, George W. *George Washington and Money*. Washington, D.C.: UP of America, 1982.

_____. *George Washington: Vignettes and Memorabilia*. Philadelphia and Ardmore, PA: Dorrance, 1977.

Nussbaum, Arthur. *A History of the Dollar*. New York: Columbia University Press, 1957.

O'Donnell, Chuck. *The Standard Handbook of Modern United States Paper Money*. 7th ed. Iola, WI: Krause Publications, 1982.

Prescott, William Hickling. *History of the Reign of Ferdinand and Isabella the Catholic*. 2 vols. 1837; Philadelphia: Lippincott, 1872.

Rabinowitz, Howard N. "George Washington as Icon, 1865–1900." *Icons of America*. Ed. Ray B. Browne and Marshall W. Fishwick. Bowling Green, OH: Bowling Green State University Popular Press, 1978. 6–86.

Rizzo, Sergio. "'Show Me the Money!'" *M/C: A Journal of Media and Culture* 7:1 (January 2004). Web. June 22, 2006. http://www.media-culture.org.au/0401/09-rizzo.php.

Robertson, Frances. "The Aesthetics of Authenticity: Printed Banknotes as Industrial Currency." *Technology and Culture* 46 (2005): 31–50.

Sachs-Hombach, Klaus, ed. *Bildwissenschaft*. Frankfurt am Main: Suhrkamp, 2005.

Samuel, Lawrence R. *American Fatherhood: A Cultural History*. Lanham, MD et al.: Rowman & Littlefield, 2016.

Schiller, Friedrich von. *The Poems of Schiller*. Trans. Edgar A. Bowring. Second ed., revised. London: George Bell and Sons, 1874.

Schmölders, Günter. *The Psychology of Money and Public Finance*. Sel. and introd. Björn Frank and Erich Kirchler. Trans. Iain Grant and Karen Green. Basingstoke, UK: Palgrave Macmillan, 2006.

Schwartz, Barry. "George Washington: A New Man for a New Century." *George Washington: American Symbol*. Ed. Barbara L. Mitnick. New York: Hudson Hills Press, 1999. 123–39.

_____. *George Washington: The Making of an American Symbol*. New York: Free Press, 1987.

Shell, Marc. *Art and Money*. Chicago: University of Chicago Press, 1995.

Silverman, Kenneth. *A Cultural History of the American Revolution: Painting, Music, Literature, and the Theatre in the Colonies and the United States from the Treaty of Paris to the Inauguration of George Washington, 1763–1789*. New York: Thomas Y. Crowell, 1976.

Smith, Richard Norton. *Patriarch: George Washington and the New American Nation*. Boston-New York: Houghton Mifflin, 1993.

Smorag, Pascale. "From *Columbia* to the *United States of America*: The Creation and Spreading of a Name." *American Foundational Myths*. Ed. Martin Heusser and Gudrun Grabher. Tübingen: Gunter Narr Verlag, 2002. 67–82.

Snowden, James Ross. *A Description of the Medals of Washington*. Philadelphia: Lippincott, 1861.

Sparks, Jared. *The Life of George Washington*. Boston: Tapan & Dennett, 1839.

Stahl, Alan M. "Capping Liberty: The Invention of Numismatic Iconography for the New American Republic." Exhibition, Firestone Library, Princeton University, March 3, 2012—July 8, 2012. Web. September 2, 2014. http://rbsc.princeton.edu/capping-liberty/case/5.

_____. *Money on Paper: Bank Notes and Related Graphic Arts*. Princeton, NJ: Princeton University Press, 2010.

Standish, Miles. *The Art of Money: The History and Design of Paper Currency from Around the World*. San Francisco: Chronicle Books, 2000.

Taylor, Mark C. *Altarity*. Chicago: University of Chicago Press, 1987.

_____. *Confidence Games: Money and Markets in a World without Redemption*. Chicago: University of Chicago Press, 2004.

Thiel, Christian. "Banknoten im Blickpunkt der Wissenschaft: Fragen—Perspektiven—Desiderata." *Der schöne Schein. Symbolik und Ästhetik von Banknoten*. Ed. Stefan Hartmann and Christian Thiel. Regenstauf: Gietl Verlag, 2016. 45–76.

_____. "Der schöne Schein. Banknoten als Untersuchungsgegenstand einer visuellen Soziologie." *Soziale Welt* 64 (2013): 191–216.

Thistlethwaite, Mark E. "The Face of the Nation: George Washington's Image and American Identity." *Visual Cultures—Transatlantic Perspectives*. Ed. Volker Depkat and Meike Zwingenberger. Publications of the Bavarian American Academy, 14. Heidelberg: Universitätsverlag Winter, 2012. 35–52.

_____. "Hero, Celebrity, and Cliché: The Modern and Postmodern Image of George Washington." *George Washington: American Symbol*. Ed.

Barbara J. Mitnick. New York: Hudson Hills Press, 1999. 141–52.

Tomasko, Mark D. "Bank Note Engraving in the United States: A Short Primer." in Alan M. Stahl, *Money on Paper: Bank Notes and Related Graphic Arts*. Princeton, NJ: Princeton University Press, 2010. 3–16.

_____. *The Feel of Steel: The Art and History of Banknote Engraving in the United States*. 2nd ed., rev. and expanded. New York: American Numismatic Society, 2012.

_____. *Images of Value: The Artwork Behind US Security Engraving 1830–1980s*. New York: The Grolier Club, 2017.

Tschachler, Heinz. *All Others Pay Cash: Dollar Bills and Their Cultural Work*. Heidelberg: Universitätsverlag Winter, 2008.

_____. *Americans for George: Das Gesicht der Nation und der schöne Schein der Papierdollar*. Bochum, Germany: Verlag Dr. Dieter Winkler, 2015.

_____. "Dollar Bill." *American Icons: An Encyclopedia of the People, Places, and Things that Have Shaped Our Culture*. Ed. Dennis R. Hall and Susan Grove Hall. Westport, CT: Greenwood Press, 2006. 1:205–12.

_____. *George Washington and Political Fatherhood*. Jefferson, NC: McFarland, 2020.

_____. "George Washington: Gallant Revolutionary." *The Numismatist* 131:2 (February 2018): 39–44.

_____. *The Greenback: Paper Money and American Culture*. Jefferson, NC: McFarland, 2010.

_____. *The Monetary Imagination of Edgar Allan Poe: Banking, Currency and Politics in the Writings*. Jefferson, NC: McFarland, 2013.

_____. "The Wildman in the New World." *The Numismatist* 132:9 (September 2019): 39–47.

Tuckerman, Henry T. *The Character and Portraits of Washington*. New York: Putnam, 1859; facs. ed. New York: Adamant Media Corp., 2006.

United States George Washington Bicentennial Commission. *History of the George Washington Bicentennial Celebration*. 5 vols. Washington, D.C.: Bicentennial Commission, 1932.

Vermeule, Cornelius C. *Numismatic Art in America: Aesthetics of the United States Coinage*. 2nd ed. Atlanta, GA: Whitman, 2007.

Washington, George. *The Writings of George Washington from the Original Manuscript Sources, 1745–1799*. Ed. John C. Fitzpatrick. 37 vols. Washington, D.C.: U.S. Government Printing Office, 1931–1944.

_____. *Writings*. Ed. John Rhodehamel. New York: Library of America, 2011. Abbr. as *WWR*.

Weatherford, Jack. *The History of Money: From Sandstone to Cyberspace*. New York: Crown Publishers, 1997.

Weems, Mason L. *The Life of George Washington; Curious Anecdotes, Equally Honorable to Himself, and Exemplary to His Young Countrymen*. 27th ed. Philadelphia: Joseph Allen, 1837.

_____. *The Life of Washington*. Ed. Marcus Cunliffe. Cambridge, MA: Belknap P of Harvard University Press, 1962.

Wells, Jim. "Strokes of Genius: Gilbert Stuart's Brush with Numismatics." *The Numismatist* 124:12 (December 2011): 40–46.

Wick, Wendy C. *George Washington, an American Icon: The Eighteenth-Century Graphic Portraits*. Charlottesville: University of Virginia P for the Smithsonian Institution Traveling Exhibition and the National Portrait Gallery, 1982.

Wörterbuch der Münzkunde. Ed. Friedrich von Schrötter, N. Bauer, Kurt Regling, A. Suhle, R. Vasmer, and J. Wilcke. Berlin-Leipzig: Walter de Gruyter, 1930.

Yeoman, R. S. *A Guide Book of United States Coins*. Ed. Kenneth Bressett. 61st ed. Atlanta, GA: Whitman, 2007.

Index

Numbers in ***bold italics*** indicate pages with illustrations

www.ingramcontent.com/pod-product-compliance
Ingram Content Group UK Ltd.
Pitfield, Milton Keynes, MK11 3LW, UK
UKHW051930100926
8556IPUK00022B/1467